Creating Aging-Friendly Communities

Creating Aging-Friendly Communities

ANDREW E. SCHARLACH
AMANDA J. LEHNING

OXFORD
UNIVERSITY PRESS

OXFORD

UNIVERSITY PRESS

Oxford University Press is a department of the University of
Oxford. It furthers the University's objective of excellence in research,
scholarship, and education by publishing worldwide.

Oxford   New York
Auckland   Cape Town   Dar es Salaam   Hong Kong   Karachi
Kuala Lumpur   Madrid   Melbourne   Mexico City   Nairobi
New Delhi   Shanghai   Taipei   Toronto

With offices in
Argentina   Austria   Brazil   Chile   Czech Republic   France   Greece
Guatemala   Hungary   Italy   Japan   Poland   Portugal   Singapore
South Korea   Switzerland   Thailand   Turkey   Ukraine   Vietnam

Oxford is a registered trademark of Oxford University Press
in the UK and certain other countries.

Published in the United States of America by
Oxford University Press
198 Madison Avenue, New York, NY 10016

Library of Congress Cataloging-in-Publication Data
Scharlach, Andrew E., author.
Creating aging-friendly communities / Andrew E. Scharlach,
Amanda J. Lehning.
pages cm
Includes bibliographical references and index.
ISBN 978-0-19-937958-3
1. Population aging—United States.   2. Older people—Services for—United States.
3. Older people—United States—Social conditions.   4. Community development—United States.
5. City planning—United States.   I. Lehning, Amanda J., author.   II. Title.
HQ1064.U5S35 2016
305.260973—dc23
2015024580

CONTENTS

INTRODUCTION

Why America's Communities Must Become More Aging Friendly

How do you want to live as you grow older? Will you be integrated into the life-blood of your community, actively involved in meaningful relationships and activities, able to go where you want—whether to the grocery store, the doctor, a place of religious practice, a friend's house? Or, will you feel like a prisoner in your own home, isolated from the rest of the community, at the mercy of a world designed for automobiles that you cannot drive safely? Increasingly, the answers to these questions very much depend on the community in which you live.

This book is about creating communities that are "aging friendly"—places where older adults are actively involved, valued, and supported (Alley, Liebig, Pynoos, Banerjee, & Choi, 2007) in a manner that reflects their unique developmental needs and priorities. We use the term *aging friendly* rather than *age friendly* or *elder friendly* in recognition of the dynamic, transactional nature of the aging process as it unfolds in an ever-changing environmental context.

The Future Is Now

Less than 20 years from now, 78 million Americans—fully 20% of the population—will be over the age of 65. Twenty-three million—6% of the population—will be over the age of 80. More than a third will be over the age of 50. If you were born before 1995, you will be in the majority. And, if you were born before 1970, you will be one of those 78 million Americans ages 65 or older (U.S. Census, 2014).

Already, many of America's cities and towns have entered that future world. If you live in Pittsburgh, Buffalo, Miami, Cleveland, Hartford, or Tampa–St. Petersburg, more than 20% of residents are already over the age of 60. Eighty-nine

U.S. towns have at least 50% of their residents age 65 or older (City-data.com, 2015). In one third of U.S. counties, at least 40% of residents are ages 50 or older, and in 87 counties, at least 50% of residents are 50 or older (G. S. Thomas, 2012).

How are America's cities and towns responding to these changing demographic realities? Some are building more senior housing, adding paratransit buses, or even converting elementary schools into senior centers. But, is that enough? Think about your own community. Could you get around if you were unable to drive a car? Are there housing options if you needed to downsize, were unable to keep up with home maintenance, or wanted a more communal living situation? Are neighbors available for a friendly chat or to help when needed? How could you spend your time if you were no longer working?

Currently, the physical and social infrastructure of most cities and towns is best suited to young families and simply does not correspond to the needs and situations of an aging population. Developing a program focused on just social services, health care, or even transportation is insufficient to enable older adults to live full and meaningful lives. What we need are fundamental changes in the design and social structure of our communities, based on a more nuanced understanding of the aging process and the challenges and opportunities afforded by an aging population.

This Book—What You Can Expect

We have written this book to provide planners, policymakers, scholars, and community members of all ages with an evidence-based approach for making communities better places in which to age. Based on the need to redesign America's communities to respond to the realities of a rapidly aging populace, the book proposes an empirically based conceptual model of the characteristics of an "aging-friendly" community and examines the types of systems that need to change, the specific changes needed, and promising strategies for achieving those changes. Throughout this book, we call attention to the importance of considering the needs and preferences of all segments of the population in current and future efforts to understand and develop aging-friendly communities, and suggest ways to address gaps in current knowledge and practice.

The book addresses five basic questions:

1. What does it mean for a community to be "aging friendly"? (For example, what is the conceptual basis for developing aging-friendly communities, and what are the goals that aging-friendly communities can and should try to achieve?)
2. What specific modifications can increase a community's aging friendliness? (For example, what is the evidence base for developing aging-friendly communities, what changes have shown the most promise to enhance individual and community well-being, and what have not?)

3. How can change occur? (For example, what can be done to change community systems and infrastructures to help them become more aging friendly, what is being done, and how effective are current efforts?)

4. Do current efforts benefit all older adults and all types of communities? (For example, have the needs and preferences of older adults from different races, ethnicities, and cultures been considered, and are recommended changes feasible or even desirable for all types of communities, including advantaged as well as disadvantaged, urban as well as rural?)

5. Where do we go from here? (For example, what can and should be done at the local, state, and national levels? What roles can and should older adults play, and what additional knowledge and information are needed?)

Plan of the Book

Part I examines what it means for a community to be aging friendly in light of evidence regarding the interrelationships between individual well-being and the physical and social contexts within which individuals live. Chapter 1 describes the challenges facing America's cities and towns as a result of ongoing demographic and social changes, as well as the opportunities that are emerging therefrom. Chapter 2 examines the underlying purpose of creating communities that are more aging friendly, namely, to enable community members to live fully throughout their lives. Current conceptualizations of "healthy aging" are reviewed, and a new, integrative model is proposed. Chapter 3 explores ways in which physical and social environments can affect optimal functioning and well-being among older persons and community members of all ages. Chapter 4 then summarizes the characteristics that make a community aging friendly and the implications for cities and towns wishing to promote the ability of community members to experience optimal well-being throughout their lives.

Part II examines the specific characteristics of an aging-friendly community—with particular attention to the areas of mobility, social engagement, and physical and social well-being. Chapter 5 describes proven approaches for overcoming mobility barriers through aging-friendly physical environments and transportation systems. Chapter 6 explores the evidence regarding community approaches for promoting social engagement in later life. Chapter 7 examines the characteristics of aging-friendly health and social supports for promoting personal well-being in the face of age-related life changes.

Part III examines what communities can do to implement the aging-friendly improvements identified in Part II and the effectiveness and limitations of specific approaches. Chapter 8 introduces a typology of community change models, based on an analysis of existing community aging initiatives in the United States. Chapter 9 describes prominent national and international community planning models for fostering aging-friendly community change, including their accomplishments and limitations. Chapter 10 examines the strengths and potential limitations of cross-sector collaborations, where existing organizations work together in new ways to better meet the needs of community seniors. Chapter 11 explores community development initiatives, which strive to engage older adults and other community residents in grassroots efforts to make communities more aging friendly.

Part IV examines the challenges that await our communities and ourselves. Chapter 12 critically analyzes the strengths and limitations of existing efforts to foster aging-friendly communities, including underrepresentation of some communities and population groups in current programmatic and research models. In Chapter 13, the book's final chapter, we reprise the key themes of the book and address their implications for the future. Summarizing the current status of existing knowledge regarding aging-friendly communities, we examine where we are now, where we need to go, and how we might get there together. The book concludes with an Appendix that provides a list of key resources for creating aging-friendly communities.

Welcome to this journey into the future of America's communities. We look forward to taking it together—as aging individuals and as community members.

PART I

AGING AND COMMUNITY

1

Aging in America

Challenges and Opportunities for Communities

The Aging of America's Cities and Towns

The changing age composition of the United States, in terms of both the proportion of older adults and their social and demographic characteristics, presents challenges and opportunities for America's cities and towns, which are ill-equipped to meet the needs of an aging population. As has been noted repeatedly, the population of the United States is aging. At the turn of the twentieth century, approximately 3 million Americans were ages 65 or older, representing only 4% of the total population; by the turn of the twenty-first century, that number had risen to 35 million, around 12% of the population (Federal Interagency Forum on Aging-Related Statistics, 2012). The oldest members of the baby boom generation turned 65 in 2011, commencing a rapid increase in the number of older adults that will continue until at least 2030. By that time, 72 million Americans will be ages 65 or older, initiating a new era in which about one in five Americans will be 65 or older for the foreseeable future (Federal Interagency Forum on Aging-Related Statistics, 2012).

This increase in the proportion of older adults only presents part of the picture, as there are substantial cohort and age variations within the elderly population. First, while the term *older adults* is often used to describe anyone over the age of 65, this group includes two or even three generations who may have markedly different life histories and current situations. For example, individuals who were born after World War II have benefited from a time of dramatic economic and social expansion in the United States and throughout much of the world, while many of those born earlier suffered through the aftereffects of the Great Depression. An emerging literature is documenting the many ways that baby boomers differ from previous generations in terms of education levels, employment history, racial and ethnic composition, family life, gender roles, and perceptions about aging, among others (Pruchno, 2012).

Second, there are likely important differences in health and service needs between the young-old and the oldest old, typically defined as those ages 85 or older, a group expected to more than triple and reach 19 million by 2050 (U.S. Census Bureau, 2010). For example, while rates of disability among persons in their 60s are hardly greater than for younger adults, nearly half of persons 85 or older have limitations in basic activities of personal care (Federal Interagency Forum on Aging-Related Statistics, 2012). In addition, while about 1 in 8 people ages 65 or older have been diagnosed with Alzheimer's disease, almost 1 in 2 of the oldest old may have this disease (Alzheimer's Association, 2014).

Furthermore, the demographic composition of the older adult population is rapidly changing. First, the gender is changing somewhat. In 2010, women represented 57% of persons 65 or older and 67% of persons 85 or older. Due to projections of a faster rise in life expectancy among men, the sex ratio is projected to change, and by 2050 women will account for 55% of persons 65 or older and 61% of persons 85 or older (Vincent & Velkoff, 2010). Second, the older adult population, much like the rest of the U.S. population, is becoming more diverse racially and ethnically. In 2008, of the older adult population, 80% was non-Hispanic White, 9% was African American, 7% was Hispanic of any race, and 3% was Asian. By 2050, the percentage of non-Hispanic Whites is expected to drop to 58%, while the proportion of other racial groups will increase, with 20% of the population Hispanic, 12% African American, and 9% Asian (Federal Interagency Forum on Aging-Related Statistics, 2012). These changes are important for many reasons, including the income and health disparities that are related to race and ethnicity. For example, older African Americans and Hispanics are more likely to live in poverty than Whites or Asians (Federal Interagency Forum on Aging-Related Statistics, 2012). Cultural differences also likely exist, particularly among the 4.5 million older immigrants in the United States, the majority of whom moved from Latin American and Asian countries (Terrazas, 2009). At the same time, African American and non-Hispanic White older adults are more likely to live alone or in nontraditional relationships than are other racial and ethnic groups, in part as a result of declining marriage rates, increasing divorce rates among existing marriages, and changing family and societal norms regarding independence and autonomy.

Third, there are substantial variations in social and economic well-being among the older adult population. On average, older adults are less likely to live below the poverty line than are other age groups. For example, 10% of those 65 or older in 2007 were in poverty compared to 18% of those younger than 18 years (Federal Interagency Forum on Aging-Related Statistics, 2012). However, as noted, some groups of older adults are especially vulnerable, reflecting lifelong patterns of economic opportunity and deprivation as well as increasing social and economic disparities in the United States. Moreover, poverty increases with age, suggesting that the growth of the oldest old may be accompanied by growth in the number of older adults living in poverty.

In addition, because the federal poverty line fails to take into account all of older adults' basic living costs, including those for health care and transportation, this measure underestimates the extent of economic vulnerability among this segment of the population. This has led to the development of an age-specific measure of financial adequacy called the Elder Economic Security Standard Index. Research using this measure in California indicated that more than half of older adults living alone and more than one quarter of older couples lack adequate income to cover basic expenses (Wallace, Padilla-Frausto, & Smith, 2010). Furthermore, the impact of the recent "Great Recession" and potential future cuts to Social Security benefits, which in 2010 kept approximately 35% of older adults above the poverty line (Caldera, 2012), could lead to a higher percentage of poor or near-poor older adults. It remains to be seen whether existing policies, programs, and infrastructure targeted toward older adults can effectively serve a population that will look quite different sociodemographically than that for which they were originally intended.

A final notable change relates to where older adults are living, particularly in terms of an increasing focus on aging in place. We define *aging in place* as the ability to remain in one's own home or community as long as desired, even when experiencing potential age-related changes in health, social and financial resources. In surveys conducted by AARP and the AdvantAge Initiative, an overwhelming majority (at least 80%) of older adults indicated that they would like to remain in their own homes for as long as possible. Public policies reflect a growing emphasis on aging in place. For example, for older adults requiring a high level of assistance, state and federal government policies increasingly are encouraging the use of home- and community-based services and discouraging the use of nursing homes. Partly in response to this desire to age in place, new nonprofit models of community-based care, most notably those offered by Naturally Occurring Retirement Community Supportive Service Programs (NORC-SSPs) and Villages, are trying to help their members access the necessary supports and services to allow them to remain in their homes.

An increasing focus on aging in place may have important implications for the future composition of cities and towns. First, there is evidence that the vast majority of frail and disabled older adults are living in community settings rather than in long-term care institutions. For example, the number of older adults living in a nursing home has stayed about the same since the 1970s, at about 1.3 million (Hayutin, 2012). During this same period, the older adult population increased from about 28 million to nearly 36 million, so that the proportion of older adults living in a nursing home has actually declined by 20%, from 4.5% in the mid-1970s to 3.6% in the mid-2000s. This decline has been particularly precipitous among those 85 or older, 26% of whom lived in nursing homes in the mid-1970s and only 14% by the mid-2000s (Hayutin, 2012). In some areas, a decline in nursing home use may be due to restricted options. In Detroit, for instance, 16 nursing homes have closed since the year 2000 and there are no planned replacements (Detroit Area Agency on Aging, 2010). Second, geographic mobility among older adults has decreased in recent years, with 3.2% of those ages 65 or older moving in 2010–2011 (U.S. Census Bureau, 2012), compared to about 4.4% in 1999–2000 (U.S. Census Bureau, 2001).

While the reasons for this decline are not yet clear, it is possible that some of the older retirees who in the past may have relocated to another town or city because of amenities may now have greater desire and ability to age in place. Other older adults may be less able to move, such as those whom Torres-Gil and Hofland (2012) described as "stuck in place," rather than aging in place, meaning that they lack the financial or social resources to relocate. Older adults who move to distant locations to enjoy warmer weather, recreational activities, and a community of like-minded older adults tend to be younger, healthier, and wealthier than older adults who do not (Wilmoth, 2010). Older residents of America's cities and towns will therefore have a diverse range of assistance needs, with some requiring extensive formal and informal supports, some requiring none, and many others falling somewhere in between.

There is typically one of two reactions to the changing demographics of this country. The first, and most common, is one of doom and gloom, epitomized by the labeling of the aging of the U.S. population as a "silver tsunami," equating it to a huge wave leaving destruction in its wake. The second reaction embraces the possibilities and opportunities of an exciting new world on the horizon, which we have termed a "silver sunrise." It is our belief that neither scenario is entirely accurate, but that an aging population presents both challenges and opportunities for communities throughout the country, and indeed throughout the world, as indicated in the Active Aging Charter adopted by the G8 Ministers of Labor at their 2000 Conference in Turino, Italy:

- The aging of our societies will create new opportunities as well as challenges;
- There is nothing inevitable about the impact of aging on society;
- Older people represent a great reservoir of resources for our economies and societies.

Challenges of an Aging America

Although this book is focused on the ways in which America's cities and towns can respond more effectively to the aging of their residents, it is important to consider issues at the national level that are likely to have implications at the local level. These include federal policies that exacerbate older adults' social and economic vulnerability; inadequate long-term care policies; changes in the structure of families and other natural support systems; and insufficient or inappropriate local physical and social infrastructures.

Economic resources have an impact on older adults directly and indirectly, not only in terms of meeting basic needs of daily life but also in terms of accessing adequate housing, transportation, activities, and other amenities necessary for physical, social, and psychological well-being. As noted, not only does the official poverty level inadequately capture economic vulnerability among older adults because it fails to keep pace with the cost of housing, health, and long-term care (Wallace et al., 2010), but also the percentage of poor and near-poor elderly will likely increase in the coming years for a variety of reasons.

First, the type of pensions offered by employers has gradually shifted from defined-benefit plans, which pay a certain amount over the lifetime of a retiree, to defined-contribution plans, which are dependent on individual investment returns (Federal Interagency Forum on Aging-Related Statistics, 2012). Second, Social Security benefits may be reduced as soon as 2036, when the number of workers per benefit recipient will reach a low of 2.1 (Waid, 2012). Social Security is a substantial financial resource for many older adults, providing half of older Americans with the majority of their income (Caldera, 2012). Social Security is a particularly important source of income for African American and Latino older adults, with approximately one fourth depending on Social Security for at least 90% of their household income (Caldera, 2012). More immediately, the Great Recession of 2007–2009 negatively affected other sources of income for older adults. In a recent survey by the AARP Public Policy Institute (PPI; AARP PPI, 2012), more than two fifths of baby boomer respondents reported that their income had declined during the recession. The Great Recession was particularly devastating to those close to retirement, who may have needed to use some of their retirement savings to compensate for the loss of a job and who have less time to recover financially from a drop in the value of their homes or investments (AARP PPI, 2012).

Existing long-term care policies are inadequate to respond to the increasing numbers of persons with disabilities at all ages, especially among older adults. While there are a number of factors affecting elder health, well-being, and the ability to age in place, the availability and quality of long-term care plays a significant role for those needing formal assistance. In the United States, long-term care is fragmented, expensive, and insufficient to meet the needs of persons with disabilities. The United States lacks an overall system of long-term care, offering instead an uncoordinated patchwork of community-based programs with varying eligibility criteria, costs, and availability. This fragmentation contributes to the high levels of unmet need that characterize long-term care in this country, with one survey reporting that more than half of older adults with functional limitations do not receive needed assistance (Feldman, Oberlink, Simantov, & Gursen, 2004).

Long-term care is expensive—for elders, for their families, and for society. In the most recent estimates available, spending on long-term care totaled $207 billion in 2005 (Komisar & Thompson, 2007), and this may quadruple by 2050 (Burman & Johnson, 2007). While nursing home care is the most expensive, costing on average nearly $70,000 per year in 2008 (MetLife Mature Market Institute, 2008), home- and community-based service rates can also be high, with home care aides costing an average of nearly $20 per hour nationally in 2011 (Genworth Financial, 2011). The burden of covering these costs is shared by a variety of public and private sources, with Medicaid accounting for almost half of all long-term care spending, Medicare for 20%, individuals and families for 18%, and long-term care insurance about 10% (Komisar & Thompson, 2007). However, long-term care cost estimates do not include spending by older adults and their families on sources of care that are not monitored by the Centers for Medicare and Medicaid Services, such as home health aides who are not employed by an agency. An increase in long-term care spending may be spurred not only by an increase in the number of older adults, but also by an increase in health problems. There is some evidence, moreover, that the improvements in health observed in recent generations of older adults may be reversing among baby boomers and subsequent age cohorts (Martin, Freedman, Schoeni, & Andreski, 2009). Long-term care expenses often exceed the financial resources of older adults, who then must either "spend down" their assets to qualify for Medicaid coverage, forgo formal services altogether and depend on family and friends, or make do with substantial unmet needs. Furthermore, a number of state efforts to reduce the costs of Medicaid are targeting long-term care, potentially restricting even further public financing options for formal assistance for those living in poverty.

Family members and other informal caregivers are the largest source of support for older adults in the United States. The estimated economic value of informal caregiving rose from $375 billion in 2007 to $450 billion in 2009, driven by the combined impact of increases in the number of caregivers, hours of care provided, and equivalent costs (Feinberg, Reinhard, Houser, & Choula, 2011). However, while the number of elders in need of assistance are increasing, changes in family structure and social roles are having an impact on the ability of family members to meet those needs. Decreased fertility rates, greater numbers of women in the workforce, and the geographic dispersion of families have reduced the availability of younger family members to help older adults with their daily activities (Spillman & Pezzin, 2000). While there currently are more than 14 adults of prime caregiving age (i.e., age 45–64) for every person over the age of 85, by 2050 this ratio will drop to less than a 4:1 ratio (Redfoot, Feinberg, & Houser, 2013). If these trends continue, older adults may have fewer sources of instrumental assistance, social support, and family interaction in the future.

Older adults therefore face a variety of social and economic conditions that serve as potential barriers to their ability to age well. These barriers at the state and national levels are further compounded by the fact that the physical and social features of the majority of cities and towns in the United States are not conducive to meeting the needs and desires of a growing, increasingly diverse older adult population.

Historical developments throughout the twentieth century created a physical infrastructure often inhospitable to older adults, particularly those with limitations in health and functioning. In many cities and towns, especially in suburban and rural areas, older adults have few housing alternatives beyond the single-family home, in part because zoning regulations restrict the number of unrelated people who can live together (Daniels, 1994) and limit multifamily housing (Pollak, 1994). Many older adults therefore live in homes that exceed their current space needs and are unaffordable in terms of taxes, housekeeping, and other maintenance costs (Golant, 1992). The layout and design of many cities and towns also create barriers to older residents' ability to access community businesses, services, and activities. The dominance of single-family homes, as well as policies such as those regarding federal highway construction, facilitated the growth of suburban sprawl that now characterizes much of this country (Jackson, 2003). Suburban environments primarily are designed for automobiles, typically separating residential from commercial areas. While the majority of adults ages 65 or older drive as their primary mode of transportation, typical age-related declines in sensory and motor skills as well as more serious functional and cognitive impairments reduce the ability of some older adults to safely operate their own vehicles. Few older adults live in mixed-use neighborhoods where they can safely walk to a grocery store, pharmacy, or other services and gathering places. The lower population density of suburban areas also limits the availability of efficient public transportation. Indeed, about one third of older adults do not have any public transportation where they live (Rosenbloom & Herbel, 2009).

America's cities and towns also typically lack an adequate social infrastructure for promoting the health and well-being of their older residents. One important social feature is social capital, which reflects the ways social networks and interactions influence collective action for mutual benefit (Kawachi, Kennedy, Lochner, & Prothrow-Stith, 1997). Communities and neighborhoods with social capital are characterized by high levels of trust, exchange of information and assistance, and norms of reciprocity and cooperation (Cattell, 2001). Some observers (e.g., Phillipson, 2007; Putnam, 2000) have noted a decline in social capital over the second half of the twentieth century. This decline may be in both "bonding capital" that forms among homogeneous groups of people (e.g., older adults) and "bridging capital" that forms through social relationships among heterogeneous groups of people (e.g., older and younger adults) (Putnam, 2000, p. 22). A substantial proportion of older adults appear to be isolated from other residents in their town or city, without access to the social capital that could lead to positive community change, the social support that provides access to needed assistance, and the social interaction that can make life enjoyable. Furthermore, many cities and towns lack other social features that could help older adults remain connected to the larger community, such as adult learning programs, part-time employment positions, volunteer activities that utilize their skills and experience, and other opportunities to engage in enjoyable and meaningful activities.

Opportunities of an Aging Population for Communities

Today's older adults on average enjoy greater education, better overall health, and lower disability rates than previous generations. With an infrastructure that facilitates and supports their community involvement, an aging population can make important contributions to their cities and towns. Older adults can serve the community formally by engaging in volunteer activities, such as tutoring in an elementary school, maintaining a community garden, registering residents to vote, and working at a food bank, among others. Older adults also make valuable contributions through informal roles. For example, older adults can improve neighborhood safety by providing extra eyes on the street, particularly during the daytime when many younger adults and their children are at work and school. They can serve as potential role models to younger generations and transmit the historical meaning of the neighborhood to more recent arrivals. Many older adults provide care to family members; 13% of all of those who provide care to an adult with health or functional limitations are age 65 or older (National Alliance for Caregiving and AARP, 2009), and 2.4 million older adults are the primary caretakers of their grandchildren (U.S. Census Bureau, 2006). Without their older caregivers, these adults and children might otherwise require assistance from paid care providers or institutions.

Cities and towns therefore have the opportunity to benefit from a population with potentially more time, knowledge, skills, and wisdom than those at younger ages. Older adults also benefit from remaining in, and contributing to, the communities in which they have spent much of their lives. Over time, individuals develop feelings of attachment to place, including to their home, immediate neighborhood, and city or town (Burns, Lavoie, & Rose, 2012). This place attachment can result in three different processes (Rowles, 1983), each of which may positively affect health and well-being. First, place attachment may have psychological benefits because the memories embedded in physical environments help individuals to develop and maintain a personal identity and self-construct. Second, place attachment may have social benefits, in terms of both social connections with others and a sense of belonging to a social group. Third, place attachment may have physical benefits because it allows older adults to better navigate their environment even if they have a disability or chronic condition, promoting a sense of autonomy and independence (Sixsmith & Sixsmith, 2008). Furthermore, older adults may have stronger feelings of place attachment than younger people, given that they have likely resided in the same place for a longer period of time (Hodge, 2008) and may spend more time in their home and neighborhood on a day-to-day basis, especially if they are retired or experience mobility restrictions (Burns et al., 2012).

Recognizing that the relationship between older adults and their cities or towns can be mutually beneficial, W. H. Thomas and Blanchard (2009) have proposed the concept of "aging in community." As noted in the first section of this chapter, aging in place has been defined in terms of an elder's ability to remain in the same home or community even when experiencing potential age-related changes in health, social, and financial resources. Aging in community acknowledges that when older adults stay in their community, it can promote not only their own health and well-being but also the health and well-being of the entire community. While aging in community emphasizes the vital roles that older adults can play in improving the way of life for all residents, it also facilitates the inclusion of people of all ages, abilities, and racial and ethnic backgrounds. It proposes the ideal of relatively tight-knit communities in which older adults and other residents work together to enhance the lives of everyone. Ideally, communities also encourage sustainable lifestyles, support physical and mental health, are accessible to everyone regardless of ability, nurture mutual aid between residents, and foster opportunities to participate in community life (W. H. Thomas & Blanchard, 2009).

An Emerging Response: Communities Becoming More Aging Friendly

The concept of aging in community reflects an emerging approach to addressing the needs and desires of older adults, one that acknowledges the importance of focusing on individual characteristics (i.e., health, social, and economic resources); environmental characteristics (i.e., the physical and social infrastructure of cities and towns); and their interaction. This emerging approach aims to make cities and towns more "aging friendly," a concept that has been embraced by a growing number of organizations and governments. Making an existing community more aging friendly generally involves enhancing the extent to which the physical and social environments facilitate elder health, well-being, and the ability to age in place to achieve a better person-environment fit. An aging-friendly community has been defined as "a place where older adults are actively involved, valued and supported with infrastructure and services that effectively accommodate their needs" (Alley, Liebig, Pynoos, Banerjee, & Choi, 2007, p. 5). In Chapter 4, we expand this definition to reflect aging-related developmental needs and priorities, the fulfillment of which involves three related objectives: (a) minimizing mobility barriers, (b) enhancing social engagement, and (c) optimizing multidimensional well-being.

The aging-friendly community concept has achieved widespread acceptance among many community and aging services organizations, although sometimes under different labels, including "elder-friendly community," "livable community," "lifetime neighborhood," and "community for all ages." Some organizations, such as the National Association of Area Agencies on Aging (n4a), have conducted surveys of America's cities and towns to assess their "aging readiness." Other organizations, such as AARP and the Visiting Nurse Service of New York, have surveyed older adults themselves to obtain their perspectives and assess the extent to which their needs are being met by their local communities. As early as 2000, AARP published *Livable Communities: An Evaluation Guide* to enable community members to assess the aging friendliness of their own communities. A number of organizations and government agencies also have developed awards to recognize and inspire innovative community initiatives, including the Livable Communities Awards sponsored by AARP and the National Association of Home Builders, and the Building Healthy Communities for Active Aging National Recognition Program of the U.S. Environmental Protection Agency. Other initiatives are helping to promote aging-friendly community change by developing and distributing white papers and guides. Throughout the country, residents and nonprofit organizations are beginning to ask their elected officials to make aging-friendly changes in their local communities or provide funding for aging-friendly projects.

Internationally, the World Health Organization (WHO) has established a Global Network of Age-Friendly Cities and Communities, with more than 200 members in more than 20 countries, including the AARP Network of Age-Friendly Communities in the United States. The WHO Global Network serves as a framework for implementing the principles of aging friendliness that have been identified and developed as part of WHO's Global Age-Friendly Cities and Communities Project, which obtains input regarding community aging friendliness directly from local groups of older adults and constituents. The initial phase of the WHO project, begun in 2005, included older adults in 33 cities in 22 countries, including Portland, Oregon. Portland and New York City also were among the first members of the WHO Global Network.

Cities and towns have developed a variety of different strategies for bringing about aging-friendly community change, as we discuss in Part III. Some of these initiatives take a more top-down approach and focus on community-wide education, assessment, and planning. Although not always, these initiatives often work directly with local governments and hence tend to focus on the types of changes under local governments' purview, such as modifications to the built environment and mobility options. Examples of these types of initiatives include the Visiting Nurse Service of New York's AdvantAge Initiative, the WHO Global Age-Friendly

Cities and Communities Project, and AARP PPI's Livable Communities. Other initiatives attempt to develop collaborative partnerships among nonprofit organizations in an effort to improve existing services and enhance elders' access to them. An example of this type of initiative is the NORC-SSP model, which promotes formal partnerships among housing providers, health and social service organizations, and other community stakeholders to better meet the needs of relatively dense concentrations of older residents, such as in an apartment complex. A third type of initiative takes a more bottom-up, community development approach and is often developed by older residents rather than an existing nonprofit organization or governmental agency. An example of this type of initiative is the Village model, local membership-driven organizations that promote access to existing services as well as opportunities for social engagement. As we discuss in this book, each of these approaches has not only important strengths but also challenges.

Challenges to Creating Aging-Friendly Communities

While the kinds of community changes described here represent promising approaches to meeting the needs of an aging population, America's cities and towns face numerous challenges in their path to becoming more aging friendly. Questions arise with regard to how aging friendliness is conceptualized and defined, where and how changes are implemented, and for whom. To be most effective, community efforts need to respond to the unique challenges and opportunities of later life, consider the wide range of needs and capabilities of current older adults as well as future aging cohorts, reflect existing evidence regarding the kinds of physical and social environmental modifications that are most likely to promote the well-being of older adults and their communities, and incorporate proven community change processes. Efforts also must reflect the changing social and demographic realities associated with an aging population, while considering the needs and preferences of all segments of the community within the confines of current and likely future political and economic realities. Aging-friendly community change will require the involvement of governments, community organizations, businesses, and private citizens of all ages. And, older adults must be integrally involved as well—not only as service recipients but also as full community members and change partners.

Throughout this book, we examine challenges such as these and suggest promising responses based on the best available evidence—from theory, empirical research, and community best practices. In doing so, we hope to enhance the ability of planners, policymakers, researchers, and community members of all ages to help communities respond more effectively to the realities of our rapidly aging population.

2

Aging Well

Introduction

Before examining how communities can become more aging friendly, it is important to consider the ultimate purpose of those efforts—to enable community members to live full and meaningful lives as they age. As we will see, living fully in later life presents challenges as well as opportunities that differ somewhat from our earlier years. These differences reflect not only physical and cognitive changes but also relatively predictable psychological and social changes that affect how we relate to the world around us. Understanding these changes, and their implications for individual and communal well-being, is of central importance for improving the lives of older adults and making communities more aging friendly.

This chapter examines the challenges and opportunities of the later years and what it means to age well. In reviewing conceptual and empirical literature on the aging process, we describe three primary approaches to conceptualizing aging and aging well: (a) observable manifestations of physical, mental, and social functioning; (b) subjective perceptions of older adults themselves; and (c) processes of adaptation across the life span. We then introduce an integrated model that combines these various perspectives and serves as a framework for examining community efforts to promote aging friendliness.

Functional Perspectives on Aging Well

The aging process most often is described primarily in terms of physical, mental, and social functioning, using terms such as "successful aging," "healthy aging," or "active aging." The most widely cited conceptualization of successful aging is that of Jack Rowe and Robert Kahn, who posited three interrelated functional criteria: (a) avoidance of disease and disability; (b) maintenance of high levels of physical and cognitive functioning as one ages; and (c) active engagement in social and productive activities (Rowe & Kahn, 1998). Based on findings from the MacArthur Foundation Study of Successful Aging and other research, Rowe and

Kahn differentiated older adults into three groups: (a) usual agers, who exhibit typical nonpathologic age-related functional changes; (b) diseased agers, who experience illness-related declines in functioning that exceed the norm; and (c) successful agers, who exhibit little or no functional changes as they age—that is, they continue to function at levels typical of persons younger than themselves.

Similarly, healthy aging has been defined by the U.S. Centers for Disease Control and Prevention as "the development and maintenance of optimal physical, mental and social well-being and function in older adults" (Lang et al., 2006, p. 3). Recent European efforts have adopted a similar focus on functional ability, prioritizing "active ageing." The 2012 "European Year for Active Ageing and Solidarity Between Generations" promoted "growing old in good health and as a full member of society, feeling more fulfilled in our jobs, more independent in our daily lives and more involved as citizens" (Europa, 2012, p. 1).

Functional definitions of successful aging are consistent with the principles of activity theory, which proposed staying active and engaged as the key to physical and psychological well-being in later life (Neugarten, Havighurst, & Tobin, 1961). In doing so, functional perspectives fit well with the prototypically American emphasis on youth, materialism, and ultimately doing rather than being. Guided by what has been termed "the cult of busyness" (Cruikshank, 2003; Holstein & Minkler, 2003), we ask one another "what do you do?" as if productive activity was the most important way in which to define our lives. Those who are retired or unable to work, whether because of age, disability, or lack of opportunity, are left with little in the way of a response, and this is especially the case for persons who are older and less advantaged.

Some have questioned whether functional approaches essentially see successful aging as "not aging." From a functionalist perspective, aging seems inherently deleterious, and the only healthy response to aging is avoiding or delaying it to the extent possible. Carol Ryff and Burt Singer (2009), for example, defined healthy aging as "the maximal delay of illness, disease, disability, and hence mortality." From this perspective, older adults can be considered "successful" if they age as little as possible, experiencing few of the expectable functional impairments that are normal as individuals age (Rowe & Kahn, 1998). Yet, as Steve Zarit (2009) noted, "By the time people are 80, almost everyone has one or more chronic disease" (p. 681). Does this suggest that no one over the age of 80 is aging well?

Older adults are exhorted to resist or avoid the health problems, debilities, and other functional limitations that typically come with age. Success can be found in actively opposing one's inevitable decline: "Successful aging . . . can be attained through individual choice and effort" (Rowe & Kahn, 1998, p. 37). As Gitlin noted, "The basic developmental task in old age is the maintenance or restoration of loss" (Gitlin, 2003a, p. 629). On the one hand, this paints an inspiring, and in some ways quintessentially American, view of aging: Disease and disability, like other natural processes, can be vanquished, or at least forestalled, with sufficient ingenuity and hard work. This may be one reason why the American Academy of Anti-Aging Medicine has four times as many members as does the American Geriatrics Society. Of course, this is the same perspective that leads us to believe that death is a failure—whether of individuals who do not take proper care of themselves, medical professionals who do not catch diseases in time, or health care systems that do not provide the needed interventions.

A particularly pernicious corollary of this perspective is the assumption that those who experience age-related declines have only themselves to blame. If a good old age can be attained through individual choice and effort, then are we to conclude that those who are ill or impaired, or are not able to maintain high physical and cognitive functioning, do not care enough or have not tried hard enough to resist these developments? As noted by Holstein and Minkler (2003), the functional perspectives of Rowe and Kahn and others tend to ignore cumulative advantage and disadvantage processes. Early life care and other contextual experiences affected by structural inequality shape future experiences by altering the probability that forthcoming opportunities will be constructive or deleterious. It is clear that those who are advantaged earlier in life are more likely to avoid disease and disability, while adversity earlier in life can make one more vulnerable to functional limitations in one's later years, regardless of individual choice or effort. Moreover, disadvantages tend to accumulate across the life cycle, with early disadvantage limiting positive opportunities and thereby increasing vulnerability to life stressors that contribute to increased illness and functional limitations in later life.

Meeting the rather restrictive criteria imposed by many functional definitions of "successful aging" seems to be reserved primarily for the privileged few. McLaughlin and her colleagues, for example, analyzed data from the Health and Retirement Study to determine what percentage of older adults met Rowe and Kahn's (1998) criteria for successful aging, here operationalized as not having a major disease, not having limitations in basic personal care activities, having minimal difficulty with mobility or endurance, having cognitive functioning scores in the top half of the distribution, being engaged in productive activity, and being married or socially connected. Only 10.9% of Americans ages 65 or older were found to meet these basic criteria in 2004, down from 11.9% six years previously (McLaughlin, Connell, Heeringa, Li, & Roberts, 2010). Moreover, older adults who were older, less educated, less well-off financially, non-White, Hispanic, or male were found to be significantly less likely to be aging successfully, at least according to these functional criteria.

A similar study of 21,493 older adults in 14 European countries and Israel found that only 8.5% of older adults met the Rowe and Kahn (1998) criteria of aging successfully. And, as in the United States, successful aging was significantly less likely for individuals who were older, less educated, and less financially well-off, although in Europe men appear to be more likely to age successfully than women (Hank, 2011).

Finally, in a study examining successful aging among 867 Alameda County, California, residents ages 65 to 99, only 18.8% met Rowe and Kahn's (1998) three criteria for "successful aging" (i.e., absence of disease or disability, unimpaired physical and cognitive functioning, social and productive activities). However, fully one half of the older adults in this study considered themselves to be "aging successfully," including 35.5% of persons with disabilities. Moreover, consistent with concerns about structural inequality and cumulative disadvantage, the gap between self-assessment and objective criteria was greatest for African American elders and persons with less education.

Subjective Perceptions of Aging Well

Older adults' self-assessments of how well they are aging reflect considerations beyond objective physical health and functioning. This section examines criteria elders use to assess their own aging processes. As we will see, older adults' perceptions of what it means to age well generally include not only functional aspects of aging (e.g., good health and high levels of physical, cognitive, and social functioning) but also a number of interpersonal and attitudinal factors that are not captured by a functional perspective. Interpersonal factors identified by older adults include having close relationships, helping others, being respected by others, and having harmonious relationships. Attitudinal factors include maintaining a positive outlook, accepting age-related changes, enjoying life, being happy, having religious faith, and feeling a sense of purpose.

Tate and colleagues (Tate, Lah, & Cuddy, 2003), for example, conducted a survey of 1,821 men over the age of 65 regarding their personal definitions of successful aging. Consistent with the functional perspective, health was the most frequent response theme, with 30% of participants describing health-related issues. However, other important themes identified by these older men included, in order of importance, a satisfying lifestyle, keeping active physically and mentally, maintaining a positive attitude, having close relationships, maintaining independence, and accepting growing old.

Laditka and her colleagues (2009) examined perceptions of aging well among older adults in nine states participating in 42 ethnic-specific focus groups on brain health. Analysis of focus group themes identified six characteristics of aging well: living to advanced age, having good physical health, being cognitively alert, having a good memory, being socially involved, and having a positive mental outlook. While the first five themes are generally consistent with a functional model of successful aging, the final theme reflects respondents' emphasis on the importance of maintaining a positive attitude and a sense of acceptance even in the face of age-related life stressors.

Similarly, Knight and Ricciardelli's (2003) content analysis of interviews with 60 older adults ages 70 or over also found that, in addition to health and activity, respondents identified the following themes as associated with successful aging: personal growth, happiness, close relationships, independence, and an appreciation of life. A similar study by Von Faber and colleagues (2001) identified the following themes other than health and social involvement: contentment, personal relationships, adaptation to changes, and acceptance.

Older adults interviewed by Duay and Bryan (2006) also identified the importance of coping with changes, in addition to maintaining physical, mental, and financial health and social engagement. Coping strategies identified included proactively dealing with changes within one's control, positively accepting changes outside one's control, having a strong spiritual faith, maintaining a positive attitude, and learning new things. Older adults participating in focus groups organized for the 1995 White House Conference on Aging were asked, "What do you believe is the key to healthy aging?" Responses centered primarily on three themes: keeping active, having a positive outlook, and helping others (Keys to healthy aging, 1994).

While culture is apt to have a major influence on the experience of aging, reflecting the varied sociocultural contexts within which individuals live their lives, there has been relatively limited empirical attention to variations across ethnic and cultural groups with regard to conceptions of successful aging. Interestingly, large-scale surveys (e.g., Phelan, Anderson, Lacroix, & Larson, 2004) have found few differences between non-Hispanic Whites and other ethnic groups, although there is some evidence that Hispanic elders are more likely than other groups to rate themselves as aging successfully. Qualitative studies using focus groups, interviews, and other culturally sensitive research methods, however, have revealed important cross-cultural variations. To some extent, these variations reflect the tendency for Asian, African American, Latino, and Native American groups to highlight social goals rather than only individual concomitants of successful aging, and acceptance and faith rather than personal action (Torres, 2003).

For example, Japanese American focus group participants (predominantly Nisei) asked to describe "the characteristics of a Japanese American who is aging successfully" identified factors corresponding to the three functional domains identified by Rowe and Kahn (1998), as well as a number of characteristics more consistent with Japanese cultural values: having perseverance and acceptance in the face of adversity; promoting the well-being of family members and other persons; showing respect for elders; maintaining self-control; maintaining a positive public image so shame for one's self or one's family is not evoked; being optimistic; maintaining a sense of internal peace through traditional religious practices; and having financial security. Studies conducted among Thai and other Asian societies have likewise emphasized the importance of interpersonal well-being (e.g., harmony in one's interpersonal relationships, interdependence in giving and receiving assistance, and respect from others) as well as psychological well-being (e.g., acceptance of one's circumstances and enjoyment of simple pleasures) (Ingersoll-Dayton, Saengtienchai, Kespichayawattana, & Aungsuroch, 2004). The importance of economic self-sufficiency and harmonious relationships with elders and offspring among Asian and Pacific Island groups likely reflects Confucian traditions of independence and hierarchy as well as family-based social, economic, and political structures (Romo, Wallhagen, Yourman, Yeung, Eng, Micco, Perez-Stable, & Smith, 2013).

Research on African Americans' assessments of aging well has highlighted the importance of religiosity, service, and family, as well as actively working to maintain one's health and independence (Cernin, Lysack, & Lichtenberg, 2011; Romo et al., 2013; Troutman, Nies, Small, & Bates, 2011). While there is limited research on successful aging among Native Americans, Inuit villagers in Canada most often associate successful aging with willingness to transmit one's accumulated wisdom and knowledge to subsequent generations, reflecting the importance of older community members in preserving tradition and ensuring the future well-being of the community (Collings, 2001).

In addition to the functional domains proposed by Rowe and Kahn (1998) and others, subjective self-perceptions highlight a variety of prominent social and psychological factors. Harmonious interpersonal relationships are mentioned frequently, including positive family relationships, family support, interdependence, and meaningful social connections. Also valued is having an impact on one's social environment, including helping others, transmitting experience-based knowledge and wisdom, ensuring family and societal continuity by preserving traditions, and receiving recognition and respect. Autonomy, self-determination, and the ability to make choices about oneself and one's life are considered important, as is personal growth. Finally, life satisfaction, the ability to maintain a positive outlook and a general appreciation for life in the face of aging-related changes in one's self and one's environment, is considered by many theorists as well as by older adults themselves to be an essential component of a good old age (e.g., Neugarten, Havighurst, & Tobin, 1961; Ryff, 1989). Indeed, "getting a maximum of satisfaction out of life" is widely considered to be the first definition of successful aging, appearing more than 70 years ago in the inaugural edition of *The Gerontologist* (Neugarten, Havighurst, & Tobin, 1961, p. 8).

Despite the apparent importance of subjective well-being, the processes by which positive self-perceptions arise remain rather elusive. On the one hand, satisfaction with specific life domains, such as work, marriage, health, and social relationships, has been shown to contribute to overall life satisfaction. However, subjective well-being also is stable over time, deviating less than expected in response to disruptions in specific domains; such findings prompt questions regarding whether life satisfaction is a result of satisfaction with individual life domains or whether an underlying perspective on one's life simply generalizes to various activity domains, albeit in independent ways.

Support for this last hypothesis comes from evidence that underlying personality dispositions have a direct effect on subjective well-being in later life. Among the personality characteristics that have been shown to contribute to a sense of subjective well-being are neuroticism, extraversion, conscientiousness, and agreeableness, four of the "big five" traits considered to be the most salient aspects of personality. It also seems likely that subjective well-being would be affected by interactions between external conditions and a variety of psychological mediational processes that affect how we make sense of our life circumstances, including a positivity bias designed to reduce internal conflict and maintain a positive sense of self toward the end of one's life (Fredrickson & Carstensen, 1990). Moreover, subjective well-being may itself affect these mediational processes; for example, individuals who are basically unhappy are more sensitive to negative social inputs than are happy people. Finally, self-perceived well-being is by definition subjective, and efforts to study it are complicated by reliance on self-reports rather than objectively verifiable achievement of specific goals.

Taken together, existing research based on older adults' perceptions of successful aging suggests six primary domains: physical health, cognitive functioning, psychological well-being, social relationships, spirituality, and financial security (Scharlach & Hoshino, 2012).

Adaptation Across the Life Span

Finally, aging well can also be understood as a process of ongoing adaptation, rather than as a set of specific characteristics or goals achievable only by a subset of older persons. From this perspective, aging well reflects ongoing adaptation to the challenges and opportunities that arise in later life and throughout the life course (Marsiske, Lang, Baltes, & Baltes, 1995; Ryff, 1989). Adaptive processes in later life differ from earlier adulthood in two ways: (a) Physical, cognitive, social, and role changes of later life are likely to call forth adaptive processes that are less salient at other periods of life; and (2) adaptive processes themselves are apt to change in response to age-related changes in abilities and priorities. Accepting and adapting to age-related changes, whenever they occur, are therefore potentially important aspects of aging well. In some studies, elders' perceptions of how they handled age-related physical changes determined whether they viewed themselves as aging successfully.

The classic model of adaptation posited by Paul and Margret Baltes conceived successful aging as a process of selective optimization with compensation (SOC) (P. B. Baltes & Baltes, 1990). According to this model, age-related restrictions in functioning and opportunities require individuals and their environments to prioritize those domains of functioning that are most important to achieving valued personal goals, a process called selection. Optimization occurs as individuals adopt intentional strategies designed to enhance their capacity for achieving desirable outcomes within these selected domains. When internal or external resources are no longer sufficient to achieve the intended outcomes, it becomes necessary to compensate through the use of other physical, psychological, or technological aids or by learning new skills. For example, individuals who previously had been actively involved on a daily basis in a wide variety of paid and unpaid activities (e.g., paid employment, helping out at church, caring for grandchildren) might become more *selective* about the number of roles and extent of involvement in each so they can devote precious time and energy to the activities considered most important and meaningful (e.g., giving up paid employment and doing less for the church in order to spend more time with grandchildren). They might exercise more and get more rest to *optimize* their ability to keep up with energetic young grandchildren. Finally, they might *compensate* for declining strength and balance by using a cane, resting periodically on a park bench while the children play, and sometimes asking other family members or friends to assist in looking after the children when they are too tired to do so.

Utilization of selection, optimization, and compensation strategies has been associated with a variety of salutary outcomes, including life satisfaction, positive emotions, and psychological well-being, even after controlling for age, health, and personality characteristics (A. M. Freund & Baltes, 1999, 2002). While compensation and optimization generally show the greatest association with well-being, these strategies tend to decline in later life, most likely resulting from a decrease in available internal and external resources for responding to increasing life demands (Lang, Rieckmann, & Baltes, 2002; Ouwehand, de Ridder, & Bensing, 2007). Selection processes, on the other hand, are more likely to strengthen with age, whether because of an active process of focusing energies on high-priority goals or because of an inability to marshal the resources to focus on other goals (A. M. Freund & Baltes, 2002). Disentangling age-related changes in the use and impact of selection, optimization, and compensation strategies requires longitudinal research with a range of aging situations.

From a developmental perspective, "aging well" involves not only adaptive responses to age-related stressors once they have occurred but also proactive efforts to reduce the likelihood, intensity, or impact of future stressors (Ouwehand et al., 2007). According to the proactivity model of successful aging (Kahana & Kahana, 1996), age-related preparatory actions (e.g., health promotion, financial planning, skills acquisition, investing in long-term relationships) are an important component of adaptational processes. Evidence regarding the proactivity model indicates that proactive coping in preparation for future changes is associated with better quality of life years later (Kahana, Kelley-Moore, & Kahana, 2012; Prenda & Lachman, 2001). Advance planning is especially beneficial for persons age 60 to 75, although the actual use of such strategies appears to decline with age, most likely as a result of increasing health and economic demands that reduce the availability of discretionary psychological and material resources to invest in future planning (Ouwehand et al., 2007).

The proactivity model reminds us that aging is a lifelong process, and part of living well at any age is preparing for what is to come next. Aging well, therefore, requires living our lives not only to maximize fulfillment in the present but also to create the internal and external conditions for fulfillment in the future. Middle-age adults who attempt to avoid the reality of aging by focusing only on the present (or the past, trying to regain their younger selves) can hardly be considered to be preparing adequately for their later years. Yet, many Americans apparently do little planning for their later years, if the nation's overall negative savings rate, the low uptake of long-term care insurance products, and the premiums paid for houses with multiple floors and other potential aging impediments are any indication.

An Integrated Model

Building on the contributions of functional, phenomenological, and adaptational perspectives on successful aging, we now propose an integrated model of aging embodied in six interrelated constructs: continuity, compensation, control, connection, contribution, and challenge, as illustrated in Figure 2.1.

Continuity. Preserving a positive sense of self and subjective well-being typically involves maintaining lifelong interests and activities, even as individuals

Figure 2.1 Integrated model of aging well.

experience the challenges of normal aging. Maintenance concerns increase in later life not only as a result of age-related reductions in functional ability, but also because environments are not well designed to enhance the functioning of older community members, as discussed in greater detail in Chapter 3. While familiar life roles and activities become no less important, maintaining them often becomes more difficult. Maintenance activities that preserve one's sense of personal identity and continuity of self-construct may become especially important in later life, in the face of a variety of forces that threaten to undermine one's sense of self and disconnect a person from much that previously had given their life meaning: an ageist society that sees older adults as less valuable; social interactions that focus on physical attributes (e.g., appearance and functional ability) rather than enduring nonobservable characteristics; and physical and social changes that make it difficult to continue activities and relationships that previously reinforced self-concept and self-worth.

Consistent with subjective perspectives on successful aging, and as posited by continuity theory (Atchley, 1971), there is ample evidence that the goals and values that guided our lives when we were younger maintain their importance as we age (e.g., S. Kaufman, 1986). Major personality characteristics change remarkably little throughout the adult life cycle (R. R. McCrae & Costa, 1990), and if anything become more pronounced. To some extent, consistent with Rowe and Kahn's (1998) concept of "successful aging," aging well involves minimizing age-related impacts on who we are and what we do. Life satisfaction is associated with the extent to which we are able to maintain as much consistency as possible between our earlier self and our present self, between the activities that have been important to us in the past and our current activities. However, as discussed in Chapter 3, this requires physical and social environments that provide opportunities for older adults to enact the values and goals that have guided their life choices previously. So, an aging-friendly community is one in which individuals are able to continue personally and societally meaningful life patterns as they age, with no unnecessary barriers to doing so. Lacking adequate options, it is possible that elders' focus on continuity, on maintaining rather than seeking new experiences, may also reflect an adaptive response to a disabling environment in which physical, social, and attitudinal barriers to change may be insuperable.

Compensation. Functional impairments, at any age, are apt to disrupt our sense of continuity, prompting adaptations in one's self or one's environment. As noted by Schulz and Heckhausen (1996), nonnormative events also can undermine goal attainment, as can nonrandom failures experienced by individuals of all ages as they try to take on new challenges. In later life, the sheer number of physiological, social, and environmental dislocations make it likely that substantial age-related failures will occur. Inevitably, individuals must compensate for the inability to meet goals consistent with their needs, desires, or self-construct, whether due to personal or environmental limitations. Successful adaptation, therefore, requires adequate supports and accommodations to ensure that the basic health and social needs of individuals with age-related disabilities are met (P. B. Baltes & Baltes, 1990).

Consistent with an adaptation perspective, compensation processes are required to maintain a maximum amount of continuity or ability to attain other goals in the face of age-related personal or environmental barriers. Doing so requires new abilities, alternative means of achieving goals, modifications to the external environment, or assistance, whether from others or from nonhuman sources (e.g., obtaining practical assistance with meeting concrete needs that one can no longer meet independently). External compensation efforts involve becoming more selective about the range of activities pursued to achieve one's goals, as proposed by the concept of SOC (P. B. Baltes & Baltes, 1990).

Internal compensation efforts focus on modifications in psychological structures in an effort to manage frustration, limit blows to self-esteem, and enable maintenance of a relatively continuous sense of self. While overall values and goals may remain relatively consistent, aspirations may be adjusted to reflect changing circumstances, less demanding social reference standards may be adopted, or the reality of one's new situation may be minimized or redefined. As Romo and his colleagues found in their interviews with disabled older adults, a key theme of successful aging involves "living with a new reality," which requires the use of coping strategies to adapt one's norms to one's circumstances, whether by acknowledging or rejecting one's changing reality (Romo et al., 2013).

Control. Associated with compensation is the theme of control. Control is considered a primary human motivation and a central theme of human development across the life cycle (Heckhausen & Schulz, 1995). Rather than seeing individuals simply as passive respondents to the challenges of later life, control theory suggests that individuals will actively strive to modify their environments and themselves to maximize goal achievement and minimize distress. From this perspective, the ability to control the impact of internal and external changes is considered to be a primary indicator of successful aging (Schulz & Heckhausen, 1996), and "individuals who are able to engage and impact the environments around them for the longest period of time would be judged most successful" (p. 711). Moreover, consistent with functional and subjective perspectives, the actual ability to control one's self and one's environment, and the perception that one can do so, is considered a fundamental objective in and of itself, although it seems likely that the importance and potential salutary impact of individual personal control may vary across cultural contexts (e.g., Hayashi, Ostrom, Walker, & Yamagishi, 1999; Steptoe, Hamer, & Chida, 2007).

Two types of control are posited: primary control and secondary control, similar to earlier cognitive developmental processes of assimilation and accommodation (Brandtstädter & Rothermund, 2002). Primary control targets the external world and involves actively attempting to manipulate the physical or social environment to attain one's goals. Secondary control primarily involves internal psychological processes, whereby individuals modify cognitions and emotions to maintain positive self-esteem in the face of failures in primary control efforts. Consistent with our previous discussion of adaptational processes in later life, internal compensatory processes include adopting goals that are more attainable, strategic social comparisons, less-demanding comparisons with one's earlier self, and self-protective causal attributions (Schulz & Heckhausen, 1996).

There is some evidence that people shift the focus of their control strategies as they age, emphasizing secondary control to a greater extent than primary control. Schulz and Heckhausen (1996), for example, suggested that secondary control processes increase throughout life, whereas primary control peaks before the age of 60 and declines uniformly thereafter. This may well be adaptive, given the extent to which age-related losses and other changes may not lend themselves to easy solutions. However, there is ample empirical evidence that opportunities to employ primary coping strategies in response to even relatively minor challenges can yield substantial benefits for psychological and physical well-being, including better self-rated health and functional status (Schulz, Heckhausen, & O'Brien, 1994; M. Seeman & Lewis, 1995); reduced incidence of various diseases (Marmot et al., 1997); better cognitive functioning (T. E. Seeman, Berkman, Kohout, Lacroix, Glynn, & Blazer, 1993); and reduced mortality (M. Seeman & Lewis, 1995).

Opportunities to exert control over one's self and one's environment may be especially important in the context of physical and social environments that pervasively undermine autonomy and self-control in later life (e.g., M. M. Baltes, 1988; Schulz et al., 1994). In a classic study (Rodin & Langer, 1977), nursing home residents given greater responsibility were more active, more sociable, in better health, and less likely to die over an 18-month period. Even something as minor as giving nursing home residents the ability to determine the frequency and duration of contact with a friendly visitor has been associated with reduced use of prescription medications, more participation in activities, greater happiness, and decreased loneliness (Schulz, 1976).

Connection. Meaningful interpersonal relationships are repeatedly cited by older adults as particularly important as they age, contributing to health and well-being in a variety of ways. Elders generally strive to remain socially engaged, even in the face of substantial personal and contextual barriers. Health problems and disabling conditions, however, can restrict mobility and interpersonal communication, making contact more challenging. At the same time, there is apt to be a decrease in opportunities due to depletion of social networks because of death, illness, and retirement, coupled with ageist and disablist norms that contribute to social isolation by fostering feelings of inadequacy and invisibility.

Socioemotional selectivity theory suggests that the increased importance of existing relationships and contexts in later life may be due in part to recognition that there is limited time left to live, rather than to aging or disability per se (Carstensen, 1993). The perception that future time is limited increases the importance of emotionally meaningful interactions, especially ones that reinforce a positive sense of self. To the extent that older persons believe that their future time is limited, they are more likely to manage their time and energy to maximize positive interactions with familiar interpersonal contacts rather than seeking potentially stressful new contacts or information (Carstensen, Isaacowitz, & Charles, 1999). For example, the desire to meet new people with whom to socialize seems to decline with age and ability (Fredrickson & Carstensen, 1990).

Contribution. Prosocial activities, such as helping others and contributing to communal well-being, frequently are identified by older adults as characteristics of subjective well-being. A "contributory orientation" has been proposed as an important component of aging-related psychosocial development and adaptation (Kahana, Midlarsky, & Kahana, 1987). Meaning and purpose are apt to assume greater importance in late life, in part because of the nearness of death and in part because of the loss of valued roles (e.g., work, marriage, parenthood) that sustain a sense of purpose earlier in life. Long considered a "roleless role" (Rosow, 1974), retirement and the later years bring fewer opportunities to engage in activities that are recognized and valued by societal structures, putting greater onus on individuals to find meaning and a sense of self-efficacy through informal contributions. These informal contributions can take a variety of paths: formal volunteer activities through charitable organizations, religious or cultural institutions, and social or athletic clubs; engagement in civil society and formal civic governance structures; informal assistance to friends or neighbors; and care for spouses, partners, and other family members. Many of these activities are subsumed under the concept of civic engagement.

Approximately three fourths of older adults participate in unpaid contributory activities, including formal volunteer roles and providing care to family members (R. Johnson & Schaner, 2005), while 30% to 50% engage in formal volunteer activities (Zedlewski & Schaner, 2005). Family assistance comprises about 60% of the total time contributed, with about equal amounts of time spent on caring for spouses, grandchildren, and parents. The remaining 40% is devoted to a combination of formal and informal volunteer activities.

Contributing to others, whether through formal structures or informal roles, has been shown to have a variety of potentially salutary implications for health and well-being in later life. Volunteering is associated with better health, fewer functional limitations, lower utilization of health services, and decreased mortality risk (Gottlieb & Gillespie, 2008; Luoh & Herzog, 2002). Participants in the Changing Lives of Older Couples study who were actively engaged in helping others had lower mortality rates over a 5-year period, whereas receiving help was not associated with any mortality benefits (S. L. Brown, Nesse, Vinokur, & Smith, 2003). Similarly, among older adults participating in the Asset and Health

Dynamics Among the Oldest Old (AHEAD) study, those who volunteered at least 100 hours per year had significantly lower 2-year mortality rates than did those who did not do so (Luoh & Herzog, 2002). Older adults who participate in formal volunteer activities also are less likely to develop depression, experience less anxiety, and have higher levels of life satisfaction, compared with those who do not volunteer (Hao, 2008; Musick & Wilson, 2003).

Volunteer work and other contributory activities support physical and psychological well-being through a number of mechanisms that are especially salient in later life. At a time when declining personal capacity and dependency-inducing physical and social contexts foster subjective experiences of marginalization, purposelessness, and helplessness, meaningful and agentic activities can reinforce a greater sense of mastery, personal control, and self-efficacy, along with a renewed sense of meaning and purpose. At the same time, helping others can promote physical and cognitive stimulation, enhance social bonds, evoke social approval, and increase other social and psychological resources (Gottlieb & Gillespie, 2008; Kahana et al., 1987). In so doing, contributory activities can help to sustain a positive self-concept in the face of threats caused by changing capacity, lack of clearly defined role structures, and an ageist society that devalues individuals based on their age and ability. Notably, in one study in which older adults were interviewed about the quality of their current lives, participants said that volunteering "made them feel like true contributors to society" (p. 437).

Challenge. Adaptation and growth continue throughout life, although the process may change with age. Organisms, from the cellular level to social organizations, require ongoing stimulation to grow and flourish, even just to survive. Whereas high levels of environmental demands or other external threats can have potentially deleterious short-term consequences, smaller intensity demands can stimulate growth, resilience, and coping ability, a concept called *hormesis* (Cook & Calabrese, 2006). Through a process of stress conditioning, manageable challenges can foster positive compensatory responses that strengthen an organism's ability to adapt constructively when faced subsequently with more intense stressors.

Humans show a strong preference for tasks that extend or challenge their existing abilities, preferring tasks with intermediate levels of difficulty rather than those they can easily accomplish (Schulz & Heckhausen, 1996). However, as discussed in Chapter 3, physical and social environments seldom provide the optimum levels of stimulation and growth appropriate for aging bodies and minds. Rather, environments tend to be so challenging and unsupportive for older adults that constructive adaptation is impossible or so undemanding that they induce excess dependency and learned helplessness. Disuse, rather than actual disease, is the greater contributor to cardiovascular vulnerability, musculoskeletal fragility, and premature frailty in later life (W. Bortz, 2009; W. M. Bortz, 1982).

There is ample evidence regarding the potential benefits of repetitive exposure to appropriately challenging conditions in later life, whether the challenges are physical, intellectual, or social (Rattan, 2008). Physical exercise in later life is associated with salutary effects on physical and mental health as well as years of healthy life expectancy. Regular physical activity has been shown to reduce the risk of numerous chronic diseases, including congestive heart disease and cancer of the breast or colon (see Rolland, van Kan, & Vellas, 2010). Participating in structured exercise activities (e.g., walking for exercise, exercise classes, weight-lifting) contributes to strength and mobility and significantly reduces the likelihood of becoming frail (Peterson et al., 2009). Even among persons who already are frail, physical activity can improve physical functioning, increase muscle strength, reduce activity limitations, and enhance psychological well-being (see Etkin, Prohaska, Harris, Latham, & Jette, 2006). Strength training alone can reduce age-related bone loss and muscle mass loss while contributing to morale and self-efficacy.

Repeated physical activity may also improve brain health, potentially forestalling the development and rate of cognitive decline. Aerobic exercise, in particular, seems to enhance executive function, perhaps by contributing to greater cardio-respiratory fitness as well as greater neurological mass in critical sections of the brain (Rolland et al., 2010). Yet, more than one third of older adults are sedentary, engaging in no leisure-time physical activity (Etkin et al., 2006).

Mental stimulation also contributes to physical and cognitive gains. Everyday forms of learning apparently activate neuron receptors, helping keep brain cells functioning at optimum levels (L. Chen, Rex, Sanaiha, Lynch, & Gall, 2010). Engaging regularly in activities such as reading, socializing, playing bridge, and playing board games provides mental stimulation that contributes to improved working memory and delayed cognitive decline (Wilson, Segawa, Boyle, & Bennett, 2012). A Cochrane review of 15 clinical trials (Woods, Aguirre, Spector, & Orrell, 2012) found that cognitive stimulation even among people with dementia had a beneficial effect on memory and intellectual functioning, as well as improved social functioning and quality of life.

Conclusion

In this chapter, we have taken a close look at what it means to age well in order to clarify the goals of efforts to make communities more aging friendly. Unlike previous approaches, which frequently have described aging primarily in terms of functional deficits, we adopt a more comprehensive approach, which takes into account subjective, interactional, and symbolic aspects of aging in addition to functioning. From this perspective, aging can be understood as an adaptive developmental process rather than only as specific characteristics or indicators of "success."

We presented a new, integrated model of "aging well," drawing on functional, phenomenological, and adaptational perspectives as well as evidence from life span developmental psychology. Aging well involves an ongoing process of adaptation centered on six developmental tasks of later life: (a) self-construct preservation in the face of personal and environmental threats (continuity); (b) behavioral and psychological adaptation to age-related challenges (compensation); (c) preservation of perceived self-efficacy (control); (d) meaningful constructive interpersonal relationships (connection); (e) generativity in public and private spheres (contribution); and (f) stimulation and growth in multiple domains of functioning (challenge).

In the chapters that follow, this six-factor model provides a basis for examining community aging friendliness, strategies for creating more aging-friendly physical and social environments, and promising programmatic and policy interventions.

3

The Community Context for Aging Well

Introduction

This chapter continues to examine the ways in which aging well involves a combination of objective functioning, subjective perceptions, and ongoing adaptation. Chapter 2 proposed six developmental tasks of critical importance in a person's later years. In this chapter, we explore how the community context can potentially promote or inhibit these aging-related processes and thereby have an impact on the ability to age well. Further chapters then examine more fully the empirical evidence linking the community context to aging well, including the ways the community can minimize mobility barriers (Chapter 5), promote social engagement (Chapter 6), and optimize health and well-being (Chapter 7).

In the present chapter, we discuss major theories from environmental gerontology that have attempted to explicate the fit between the aging individual and the home and community context, including both the physical environment and the social environment. As we discuss, the community context may include perceived characteristics as well as objective characteristics.

We begin with a description of the ecological model of aging, which was the first major theory to emerge from environmental gerontology and had a major influence on subsequent theories and conceptual models. These include the following: the disablement process, which is concerned with individual and environmental features that affect physical functioning; theories of relocation in later life, focusing on the different push and pull factors that contribute to an elder's decision to move or age in place; residential normalcy, combining concepts from environmental gerontology with concepts from residential relocation; and the ecological framework of place, which provides a holistic approach to conceptualizing person–environment transactions over time. We conclude by considering the potential benefits of "aging in place" versus the potential risks of being "stuck in place" (Torres-Gil & Hofland, 2012). The idea of being stuck in place highlights many of the concepts introduced in the environmental gerontology literature, as well as some remaining questions that require further empirical and conceptual consideration. Before delving into the theory, however, we consider the relationship between individuals and the community context in general, as well as some of the potential reasons why the effects of community environments may differ for older adults compared to residents at younger ages.

The Increasing Importance of the Community Context

Until relatively recently, the theoretical and empirical literature on health and well-being primarily emphasized the importance of individual-level risk factors (e.g., race and ethnicity, gender, health behaviors) and largely neglected the potential influence of the community context. The end of the twentieth century, however, witnessed an increase in the number of publications exploring the ways that community contexts contribute to individual outcomes. Research in public health, social work, medicine, nursing, sociology, and urban planning, among other disciplines, has found that the community context matters for individuals of all ages. In public health, for example, evidence supporting the existence of social determinants of health (e.g., Marmot et al., 1991), also known as socioeconomic gradients in health (e.g., Krieger, Chen, Waterman, Rehkopf, & Subramanian, 2003), spurred scholarly interest in neighborhood effects research (Diez Roux, 2001) and policy and programmatic interest in interventions that aim to bring about community change. We have seen a similar uptick in social work scholarship on the influence of community contexts, as researchers have called for social workers to "move beyond a solely individual deficit model" (Holland, Burgess, Grogan-Kaylor, & Delva, 2011, p. 703) and recognize the interaction between individuals and their surrounding family and community systems.

Research indicates that the community context contributes to a variety of positive and negative outcomes, including high school graduation (Crowder & South, 2011), alcohol consumption in young adults (Cerda, Diez Roux, Tchetgen, Gordon-Larsen, & Kiefe, 2010), and depressive symptoms across the life span (Mair, Diez Roux, & Galea, 2008). Empirical research has also documented the differential effects of various aspects of community environments, including the built environment (e.g., access to parks and sidewalks; Singh, Siahpush, & Kogan, 2010), the social environment (e.g., social capital; Carpiano, 2007), and the composition of community members (e.g., percentage affluent; Browning, Cagney, & Wen, 2003).

There is reason to believe, however, that the community context becomes increasingly important in our later years. The spatial distribution of the places we regularly travel to and from typically becomes smaller as we age. Older adults' life space (also known as their "activity space"; Schonfelder & Axhausen, 2003) tends to constrict, particularly if they experience difficulties in physical or mental functioning (Sartori et al., 2011). Consequently, older adults tend to spend more hours of the day in the environment immediately surrounding their home (Forrest & Kearns, 2001), particularly if they no longer work or have physical limitations that restrict their ability to travel around their community (Burns et al., 2012).

In part because they are more geographically bound, older adults are often more dependent on neighborhood-based social ties. In contrast, younger adults' social networks are more geographically dispersed and often are based on work associations or common interests (Forrest & Kearns, 2001; Guest & Wierzbicki, 1999; Phillipson, 2007). This may be due to age differences, with research indicating that older adults are more emotionally invested in their community than are their younger counterparts (Phillipson, Scharf, Kingston, & Smith, 2001). This may also be due to cohort differences, as both scholars and older adults have recently noted a general loss of community compared to earlier time periods (Phillipson, 2007). Furthermore, some commentators believe that older adults today have stronger social attachment to place than previous cohorts because they are more likely to have lived in their neighborhoods for multiple decades (Scharf, Phillipson, & Kingston, 2003).

Place attachment may be one of the mechanisms through which community contexts affect elder health and well-being. According to Rowles (1983), place attachment stems from three sources. First, older adults develop a sense of "physical insideness" (p. 302) that allows them to navigate their environment, even if they are experiencing a disability, because they are so familiar with every physical detail. Second, social integration with both the community at large and their age peers creates a sense of "social insideness" (p. 302) that serves as a source of assistance as well as feelings of belonging. Finally, through a sense of "autobiographical insideness" (p. 303), older adults derive meaning for their own lives as well as their community's past, present, and future. For example, in their case study of a small town in Kansas, Norris-Baker and Scheidt (1990) reported that some older residents created a sense of identity by taking on the unofficial role of local historian, which afforded them respect from other community members. Others relied on existing physical structures, including those that were falling apart and neglected, to reminisce about the past (Norris-Baker & Scheidt, 1990). According to Butler (1963), reminiscence is a key component of the life review process, which in turn is crucial to maintaining a positive self-concept in later life.

Environmental Gerontology

Theoretical frameworks guiding community context research across age groups can be classified as either *structural* models or *ecological* models. Structural models assume that all residents are similarly affected by the physical and social environment (Aneshensel et al., 2007). For example, Bandura's (1969) social cognitive theory, which has often been used to guide research on environmental influences on health behaviors (Stahl et al., 2001), proposes that individuals engage in certain practices based on observations of and feedback from their social and physical environment. Structural models include the contagion model of community influence, whereby unsafe behaviors such as smoking, drinking, and drug abuse are transmitted to all of those living in an area characterized by poverty (Browning et al., 2003). Similarly, the community context has been described as providing either restrictions or incentives for healthy behaviors through access to recreational facilities or farmers' markets (Stahl et al., 2001), presumably offering these amenities to all residents.

Ecological models, on the other hand, recognize that the impact of the community context depends on the characteristics of the individual (Aneshensel et al., 2007). Individuals not only respond to but also interact with their environment. The field of environmental gerontology, which emerged in the early 1970s, is especially concerned with ecological models, in that it seeks to describe the relationship between an older adult and his or her environment (Wahl & Weisman, 2003) as well as the implications of this relationship for quality of life (Golant, 2003). Although, as discussed toward the end of this chapter, our understanding of the interactions between older adults and their environments remains somewhat limited.

Ecological Model of Aging

The most prominent scholar of environmental gerontology was M. Powell Lawton, and his ecological model of aging (also known as the press-competence model) is the work most cited in the field (Golant, 2012; Wahl & Weisman, 2003). Lawton and his coauthor Lucille Nahemow first presented this model in their 1973 chapter, "Ecology and the Aging Process," which to this day is cited in most of the literature examining person–environment interactions in later life (Cvitkovich & Wister, 2003; Wahl, 2001).

The ecological model of aging proposes that elders' behaviors and outcomes are a result of the interaction between the competence of the individual and the environmental press of the context (Lawton, 1982). Competence is defined as the individual's abilities in areas such as physical, cognitive, and psychological functioning (Lawton, 1982; Lawton & Nahemow, 1973). Environmental press is comprised of the environmental characteristics that place demands on the individual, and those demands can be objective (e.g., stairs in the home that must be climbed to access a bedroom) or subjective (e.g., perceived expectations of family members) (Lawton, 1982). The model portrays aging as a process that requires "continual adaptation" (Lawton & Nahemow, 1973, p. 619) because individual competence and environmental press are constantly changing. Individual competence changes not only because of internal physiological changes but also because of daily interactions with the environment. Similarly, environments can change for a number of reasons, including through aging-related processes as well as through interactions with individuals. That is, both individuals and their environments can influence or respond to one other (Lawton & Nahemow, 1973).

Outcomes such as health and well-being emerge from person–environment interactions, as individuals attempt to match the surrounding environment's demands with their capabilities (Newcomer & Griffin, 2000). Environmental press is not intrinsically positive or negative but, depending on the competence of the individual, can lead to positive or negative behaviors and outcomes (Lawton, 1982). When demand is too high or too low for an individual's level of competence, the older adult is likely to experience negative outcomes. For example, multistory housing with steps may demand too much from an older adult with mobility limitations, resulting in an increased risk of falls or restricted daily movements from one floor to another. Ideally, however, the environment presents the highest possible level of demand without creating negative experiences, which Lawton called the "zone of maximum performance potential" (Lawton, 1982). Individuals can also exhibit adaptive behavior and have positive experiences when the environment presents a slightly low amount of press, called the "zone of maximum comfort" (Lawton, 1982). Lawton and Nahemow (1973), for example, called for those planning and administering supportive services to tailor them to individuals' abilities so that support encourages the use of skills without creating undue stress or overstimulation. They also warned against providing too much assistance, which may cause older adults to lose the ability to perform self-care activities.

There is therefore a range of environmental press that can lead to positive outcomes. However, that range is much narrower for those with less competence. The *environmental docility hypothesis* (Lawton & Simon, 1968) proposes that there is an inverse relationship between individual competence and the influence of the environment, calling attention to the ways competence contributes to differences in vulnerability. Alternatively, the *environmental proactivity hypothesis* (Lawton, 1985) suggests that older adults with high competence have more influence over their environments and are better able to use the environment's resources to meet their needs. Taken together, these two hypotheses indicate that "the less competent are controlled by, and the more competent are in control of, the environment" (Lawton, 1998, p. 4).

Variations in sidewalks highlight these differences. The majority of older adults with or without mobility limitations can navigate wide sidewalks that are well maintained. If sidewalks are narrow, cracked, uneven, or blocked by debris, however, those who are using a walker or a wheelchair may not be able to safely use them, while those without mobility problems can still walk down the block to visit a neighbor or get to the grocery store. Furthermore, Lawton believed that limitations in both biological and social resources constrain an elder's ability to control not only the environment but also the ability to choose to move to a different environment (Lawton, 1982). As we discuss further in this chapter in the section on being stuck in place, some scholars have started exploring the ways limited financial resources can also restrict elders' control over and choice of environments.

In addition to the ecological model of aging and its associated hypotheses, Lawton contributed to environmental gerontology by hypothesizing that there are three basic functions of the environment: maintenance, stimulation, and support (Lawton, 1982); these are analogous to the functions of continuity, challenge, and compensation in our developmental model. First, the environment can serve a *maintenance* function because of its familiarity and predictability (Lawton, 1982). As discussed in the section on the increasing importance of the community context, familiarity with the home and neighborhood helps older adults maintain a sense of identity and experience the benefits of place attachment. Furthermore, when features of the home and neighborhood are constant and predictable, older adults can focus their energy on skills and activities other than navigating their environment (Lawton, 1982). Second, the environment can provide *stimulation* when it requires a response from the individual (Lawton, 1982). Older adults, particularly those who are ages 85 or older, may spend much of their time in their home (M. M. Baltes, Maas, Wilms, Borchelt, & Little, 1999) but can still experience novelty in this environment if, for example, friends or family come to visit. Finally, the environment can offer *support* to those with functional limitations. Connecting these concepts to those introduced in the ecological model of aging, stimulation occurs when environmental demand is increased, while support occurs when environmental demand is reduced (Lawton, 1982).

Other early environmental gerontology theorists also explored the interaction between aging individuals and their surrounding environment, most notably Eva Kahana (Kahana, 1982) and Frances Carp (Carp, 1976; Carp & Carp, 1984). Kahana's person–environment congruence model is similar to Lawton's in its focus on the interaction between individuals' needs and preferences and the surrounding environment (Kahana, 1982). Moreover, Kahana also recognized the need for modifying individuals, their environment, or both when the person–environment interaction results in a mismatch. Kahana added to this literature by proposing that person–environment fit contributes to, but is not the same as, well-being or optimal functioning (Kahana, 1982; Lawton, 1999). That is, health and well-being or functioning, rather than person–environment fit, should be the outcome of interest. She was particularly interested in understanding the process by which person–environment interactions affect the aging individual, and she hypothesized variations in the magnitude of positive or negative outcomes depending on the extent of mismatch between personal competence and environmental demands (Kahana, 1982). In contrast with Lawton, then,

Kahana's model does not conceptualize interactions between older adults and their environment as falling within a particular zone, but instead as falling along a continuum ranging from match to mismatch, which in turn influences outcomes that are also arrayed along a continuum ranging from positive (e.g., high emotional well-being) to negative (e.g., depression).

Carp's complementary/congruence model shares with Lawton's model a focus on the ways the environment affects aging individuals with low competence. This model contributes to environmental gerontology by separating *basic needs* from *higher order needs* (Lawton, Altman, & Wohlwill, 1984). When older adults experience limitations such as impaired physical or cognitive functioning, the optimal environment should complement or support these limitations to ensure older adults can continue to meet their basic needs (Lawton et al., 1984). Carp proposed that in the complementary part of the model, either high personal competence or an appropriately supportive environment has a direct impact on well-being. This complementary part of the model appears consistent with Lawton's environmental proactivity hypothesis and environmental docility hypothesis. In the congruence part of the model, person and environment characteristics are not positive or negative on their own, but rather the importance is the match or mismatch between the person and the person's environment (Carp & Carp, 1984). Even aging individuals with high competence may still experience poor outcomes if the environment does not provide for their higher order needs. For example, an older adult without cognitive and physical impairments may still feel socially isolated in a neighborhood with low levels of social cohesion where neighbors rarely interact with one another.

These models have generally produced more theoretical propositions than empirical research findings. While they are regularly cited in the environmental gerontology literature, particularly the ecological model of aging, the general consensus among scholars is that theories in this field have limited utility for research purposes (Scheidt & Norris-Baker, 2003). Indeed, Lawton (1998) noted that the concepts of these different models have not been fully articulated, making them difficult to measure. This explains why to date there has been little empirical work testing their propositions (Kendig, 2003; Scheidt & Windley, 2006).

Furthermore, these models focus primarily on physical and cognitive functioning, rather than on other potential changes that can occur in later life. In addition, while the ecological model of aging stresses the importance of person–environment interactions, Lawton and Nahemow's (1973) approach seems to depict a stimulus–response relationship between the environment and the older adult. For example, it proposes that if environmental press is too high, then an individual may engage in maladaptive behavior. In recent years, there has been growing interest in understanding a more transactional relationship between individual and environmental factors by incorporating concepts from theories that acknowledge that individuals are both reactive and proactive, such as

M. M. Baltes and Baltes' (1990) selective optimization with compensation model (Perry, Andersen, & Kaplan, 2013). In later years, Lawton (1998) described his model as a heuristic for guiding investigations of person–environment interactions in later life, rather than as a formal theory (Scheidt & Norris-Baker, 2003). Notwithstanding these critiques, these models have expanded the scope of gerontology by calling attention to the ways that home and community contexts play an important role in elder health and well-being.

The Disablement Process

One can see the influence of Lawton and Nahemow (1973) and their focus on adaptation in the disablement process, first articulated by Verbrugge and Jette in 1994. The disablement process conceptualizes disability as a product of personal capabilities and environmental demand (Verbrugge & Jette, 1994), or in Lawton's terminology, behavior is the product of competence and environmental press. The pathway to disablement begins with the presence of disease (e.g., arthritis), potentially followed by impairments (e.g., inflammation and pain in the knees) and functional limitations (e.g., difficulty bending the knees), which then may result in disability as a result of deleterious environmental conditions (e.g., inability to walk up stairs or stand from a sitting position) (Verbrugge & Jette, 1994).

Three types of personal and environmental factors can have an impact on the disablement process (Verbrugge & Jette, 1994). *Risk factors* are predisposing characteristics of the individual and the environment, such as genetics, lifestyle, and social support, which contribute to the onset of disablement. *Interventions* are personal and environmental changes, such as behavior alterations, medical care, and home modifications that slow, reverse, or even prevent disablement. Finally, *exacerbators,* such as architectural barriers and limited transportation options, speed up the disablement process. The disablement process suggests that changes in the physical and social environment can reduce the level of disability associated with chronic diseases. To date, however, the majority of studies examining disability focused on the characteristics of the individual rather than the surrounding environment or the interaction between the two (P. Clarke & George, 2005).

Residential Relocation

As noted in the section on environmental gerontology, the ecological model and other similar frameworks typically focus on health and well-being as the primary outcome of interest. Another group of gerontological scholars is interested in understanding the individual and environmental characteristics that determine whether older adults remain in their current environment or relocate to a new one. These scholars have attempted to explicate the push and pull factors that influence older adults' decisions to relocate, particularly after they retire. As noted in Chapter 1, only slightly more than 3% of adults ages 65 or older relocate each year, which means that a typology or model of residential relocation applies to a small proportion of the older adult population. However, these frameworks also point to the environmental characteristics that might enable an older adult to remain in his or her current community.

Litwak and Longino (1987) proposed that retirees make three types of moves. The first type of move occurs soon after retirement when older adults relocate to be closer to amenities, such as warmer weather, leisure activities, and a network of friends and age peers (Litwak & Longino, 1987). These movers are typically healthy, wealthy, and married and therefore rarely require assistance from informal or formal caregivers. The second type of move is thought to occur later and is often precipitated by the combination of functional decline and the death of a spouse. In this type of relocation, older adults move near to or in with adult children or other family members to receive emotional or instrumental assistance (Litwak & Longino, 1987). In the third type of possible move, older adults relocate to long-term care settings when their health needs exceed the abilities of their children or other community-based caregivers (Litwak & Longino, 1987). Like the ecological model of aging, this typology focuses on the ways older adults adapt to changes in themselves and their surrounding environment (Perry et al., 2013). The first move is driven by personal preferences to live in a particular social and physical environment and facilitated by personal health and financial and social resources. The second and third moves are driven by a mismatch between individuals and their home and community environments as a result of major life changes (e.g., widowhood) or decrements in health.

Unlike the ecological model of aging, this typology of late life migration has been tested empirically and has received some support in the research literature. Elders who are relatively younger, wealthier, and healthier tend to move to locations farther away because of amenities and comfortable surroundings (Smith Conway & Houtenville, 2003; Wilmoth, 2010). Moreover, research has found that elders with slightly poorer health are more likely to move close to family after a life crisis, and those who are older and experience a steep decline in health are at a higher risk for relocation to a long-term care facility (Wilmoth, 2010). Furthermore, this typology has served as a foundation for studies examining the community contexts that attract older retirees. For example, Smith Conway and Houtenville (2003) documented that environmental characteristics, including public spending on health and welfare, weather, and tax rates, can act as push and pull factors for older movers.

Wiseman's behavioral model of elderly migration also conceptualizes relocation in later life as driven primarily by a desire for amenities or a need for assistance (Wiseman & Roseman, 1979). This model provides more explanation for the process of residential relocation, viewing it as an interaction between triggering mechanisms and personal resources (Wiseman & Roseman, 1979).

Triggering mechanisms can be either internal or external and can be either push factors or pull factors (Wiseman, 1980). The death of a spouse, retirement, mismatch with the social and physical environment, or health declines, for example, can trigger older adults to leave their current home and community, serving as push factors. The availability of leisure activities or a community context congruent with changing lifestyle preferences can also act as pull factors for a new home and community (Perry et al., 2013; Wiseman, 1980).

One contribution of Wiseman is his discussion of the differences between local moves, which he proposed are most often triggered by housing and neighborhood problems, and nonlocal moves, which are frequently triggered by major life events (Wiseman & Roseman, 1979). In addition, he recognized that triggering mechanisms provide the initial motivation to consider a change in residence, but actual relocation depends on individual needs, preferences, and resources (Wiseman, 1980). The outcome of this decision-making process is not necessarily relocation, as older adults may decide to age in place instead. Resources play a key role, and another important contribution of Wiseman was his delineation between voluntary and involuntary movers and voluntary and involuntary stayers (Perry et al., 2013). Older adults without retirement savings, for example, have less ability to respond to either push or pull factors, similar to Lawton's hypothesis that individuals with fewer physical and mental resources are more impacted by the environment. Wiseman also acknowledged that his model has little utility for understanding the relocation process of older adults who are excluded from the decision-making process, such as those who defer to the wishes of family members or are forced to move against their will (Wiseman & Roseman, 1979).

Since the development of Longino's typology and Wiseman's behavioral model, other theorists and researchers have sought to clarify the myriad considerations involved in residential relocation in later life. Some scholars have called for an improved accounting of the heterogeneity of older movers, as well as the housing types currently available to older adults, such as continuing care retirement communities (CCRCs) and assisted living facilities (Oswald & Rowles, 2006; Smith Conway & Houtenville, 2003). Rather than precipitated by a triggering mechanism, for example, Oswald and Rowles (2006) proposed that relocation results from a confluence of factors emerging from basic and higher level needs, as described in the complementary/congruence model (Carp & Carp, 1984). Furthermore, characteristics of the current community context, such as strong place attachment and social ties, may discourage older adults from relocating (Longino, Perzynski, & Stoller, 2002). That is, the home and community may act as "pull" factors in the current environment, discouraging older adults from leaving.

Another aspect of relocation requiring more exploration is the role of other persons in relocation decisions. Building on Wiseman's ideas about involuntary movers and stayers, scholars have highlighted the role of family members and other informal sources of support in making decisions about relocation (Smith Conway & Houtenville, 2003). For example, moving in with adult children because of chronic illness or widowhood is much less likely if those children lack the willingness or capability to provide support and assistance. Finally, some older adults live in multiple locations, such as those who migrate seasonally by spending the winter months in a community with warm weather and the summer months in the community where they previously worked and raised their children. One qualitative study found that older adults in this group perceive varying levels of place attachment to their two communities (McHugh & Mings, 1996). To date, however, the residential relocation literature has only addressed the relocation process of cyclical movers in a limited way.

Residential Normalcy

A more recent theoretical development in the gerontological literature is that of Stephen Golant (2011), who has put forth a model that aims to holistically describe the adaptive strategies utilized by older adults to control their environments and maintain a sense of well-being. According to this model, older adults experience residential normalcy in environments where they feel both comfortable and in control (Golant, 2011). The model proposes that older adults are continuously appraising the fit of their environment using two different criteria. First, *residential comfort experiences* encompass the degree to which home and community contexts foster positive emotions and memories, while minimizing stress and hassles (Golant, 2012). Second, *residential mastery emotional experiences* reflect the extent to which contexts make older adults feel safe, secure, and in control of their lives (Golant, 2012). Both of these types of experiences in turn affect elders' self-concept and emotional well-being (Golant, 2003).

While the model suggests that residential normalcy is the ultimate goal, a number of factors influence whether an older adult will attain this state. First, older adults do not necessarily place equal weight on both types of emotional experiences. Because comfort and control can exist independently of one another, the model proposes that person–environment fit is often a matter of degree rather than "an all or nothing affair" (Golant, 2012, p. 32). For example, older adults may feel that their community makes them feel happy, content, and stimulated, which are emotions Golant (2012) characterized as residential comfort experiences. At the same time, the same community might make them feel submissive, uncertain, and fearful, which are emotions he characterized as reflecting the absence of residential mastery experiences. The decision to change or adapt the environment, however, depends on the relative importance the individual places on each type of emotional experience (Golant, 2011). If the ability to exercise personal choice in everyday activities is paramount, then residential mastery emotional experiences will be the most salient in appraisals of person–environment fit. Conversely, if participation in enjoyable activities and interactions is the most important, then consideration of residential comfort experiences will override feelings of powerlessness. Older adults may therefore settle for a less-than-optimal community context if it provides the experiences that are most important to them.

Second, older adults do not all have the same capacity to adapt to an environment that no longer meets their comfort or control needs (Golant, 2011). If older adults perceive their environment as lacking in residential comfort experiences, residential mastery emotional experiences, or both, there is no guarantee that they will make the changes necessary to achieve residential normalcy. Golant (2011) observed that older adults have different repertoires of coping. In assimilative coping, the individual tries to continue pursuing the same goals in spite of health declines or environmental limitations (Cappeliez & Robitaille, 2010). That is, the individual makes modifications to compensate for personal or environmental barriers in order to continue participating in lifelong interests and activities. For example, an older adult may install a stair lift to continue to live on both floors of a home, or learn how to navigate the public transportation system to continue to visit friends after giving up the car keys. In accommodative coping, the individual adjusts expectations and goals to reflect the realities of health problems and other limitations (Cappeliez & Robitaille, 2010). All of the change is within the individual and typically involves reframing his or her life situation. According to Golant (2011), older adults differ in terms of the financial and emotional resources necessary to engage in these coping strategies. Furthermore, older adults vary in terms of their willingness to pay the financial and emotional costs associated with adapting to their context (Golant, 2011).

Another potential coping strategy is for the older adult to move to a different home and community context. According to Golant (2011), voluntary residential relocation is only considered after the older adult has tried to adapt to his or her current situation through assimilative and accommodative changes. In addition, moving will not occur unless it is perceived as a feasible option based on physical, psychological, social, and, particularly, financial resources. Furthermore, the older adult must believe that relocation will result in improved outcomes, such as increased feelings of both comfort and mastery. This involves expectations that the act of moving will not exceed their threshold for stress or negative emotional experiences (Golant, 2011). Relocating may result in not only financial losses but also emotional ones. Downsizing to a one-bedroom apartment, for example, may be a better fit for an older adult who is no longer able to maintain a single-family home on a large lot. This move, however, also likely means that the older adult must give away many of his or her possessions and lose contact with longtime neighbors. However, although Golant's model of residential normalcy was first discussed approximately a decade before the writing of this book, we could not locate any studies that have attempted to test its major propositions.

Golant's residential normalcy model adds more complexity to our understanding of individuals' appraisals of their person–environment fit, as well as some of the internal and external modifications to potentially achieve a better fit, and hence better health, well-being, and quality of life. Through its emphasis on ongoing person–environment transactions, this model echoes some of the key propositions of the integrated developmental model presented in Chapter 2, which could provide a developmental context for comfort and mastery experiences.

Ecological Framework of Place

We noted when first discussing environmental gerontology that ecological models focus on the interaction between individual attributes and environmental conditions. As the different (and overlapping) theories from environmental gerontology suggest, one key attribute to consider is age. Indeed, the field of environmental gerontology is based on the premise that older adults interact differently with their environments than those who are younger. The ecological framework of place (EFP) (Diaz Moore, 2014) provides a model for understanding environmental influences on aging well from a life course perspective. This dynamic and nuanced approach gives particular attention to the subjective nature of person–environment fit, rooted in the ever-changing socially constructed meanings and experiences that shape human experience. From this perspective, individuals and places are seen as active partners in a dynamic process of ongoing negotiations designed to promote person–environment fit and enhance socially meaningful experiences.

The EFP defines *place* as "a milieu involving people ('place participants'), the physical setting, and the program of the place, all catalyzed by situated human activity and fully acknowledging that all four may change over time" (Diaz Moore, 2014, p. 184). Place reflects not only the objective characteristics of the physical setting but also the activities that are made possible by the physical setting and the socially shared expectations that affect how those activities are understood and evaluated. Individuals are considered "place participants," who bring a set of competencies, intentions, desires, and needs, all based on a lifetime of experiences. Furthermore, individuals and their environments both change with time.

Person–environment fit, then, reflects the fit between what participants need and want, on the one hand, and what is considered to be possible in a particular environment, on the other. From this perspective, disjunctions occur when settings change over time or when the needs and goals of their human inhabitants change over time. Individual settings, furthermore, exist within a system of other settings (e.g., buildings, neighborhoods, cities), which may reflect greater or lesser degrees of person–environment fit. It is possible, therefore, to adapt one's home environment to age well, yet live in a neighborhood where the physical and social environment make aging well virtually impossible. By combining key insights from environmental gerontology, architecture, and developmental psychology, EFP provides a comprehensive new framework that has substantial heuristic value. However, it remains to be seen whether its principles can be used to construct testable hypotheses or contribute to more aging-friendly environments.

Aging in Place Versus Being Stuck in Place

Aging in place has been defined as "the ability to live in one's own home and community safely, independently, and comfortably, regardless of age, income, or ability level" (Centers for Disease Control and Prevention [CDC], 2013). These various models from environmental gerontology suggest that the ability to age in place in the same home and community depends on the fit between the needs and preferences of aging individuals and their surrounding environment. Aging in place in one's home and community is assumed to contribute to positive outcomes for older adults, their families, and their communities. For older adults, the benefits of aging in place may come from the sense of familiarity, identity, and place attachment that accompanies living in the same home and community for many years of one's life, enabling easier fulfillment of the need for continuity, compensation, connection, and the like (Burns et al., 2012; Sixsmith & Sixsmith, 2008; Wiles, Leibing, Guberman, Reeve, & Allen, 2012). In addition, the overwhelming majority of older adults reported in surveys that they would like to remain in their current residence for as long as possible (Feldman et al., 2004). For older adults experiencing health problems, aging in place may also be less expensive than some of the alternatives to remaining in one's home and community, such as institutional long-term care (Sixsmith & Sixsmith, 2008). Furthermore, aging in place may benefit the larger community, as it allows older adults to continue to contribute as volunteers, caregivers, and neighbors.

Although an increasing number of public policies and community-based programs aim to help older adults age in place, our knowledge of this concept is limited in several ways. First, few research studies have examined the factors that can help older adults age in place. Instead, the majority of the relevant research has identified risk factors for nursing home placement (e.g., Andel, Hyer, & Slack, 2007; Banaszak-Holl et al., 2004; Bharucha, Pandav, Shen, Dodge, & Ganguli, 2004). Aging in place, however, is not simply the avoidance of institutional care. Moreover, these studies often examine the influence of individual factors, such as race, gender, functional limitations, and illnesses, rather than environmental factors. One exception is the inclusion of social support (e.g., Banaszak-Holl et al., 2004), although as we examine in Chapter 6, the social environment encompasses much more than social support. We therefore have little research evidence regarding the environmental factors that allow older adults to age in place. More important, empirical research documenting the effects of person–environment interactions on aging in place is extremely limited, perhaps because of the difficulty of operationalizing and statistically modeling this process.

Remaining in one's home and community is likely not the optimal situation for everyone. While remaining in the same neighborhood and dwelling *may* have beneficial effects for older adults, their families, and their communities, there is little rigorous research regarding the costs and benefits of doing so. Furthermore, some scholars (e.g., Golant, 2008b; Phillipson, 2007) have raised concerns about the different experiences of aging in place, noting that not everyone is able to live "safely, independently, and comfortably," as proposed by the CDC (2013) definition of aging in place. In recent years, there has been more attention to variations within the older adult population, particularly in terms of individual resources. This is exemplified by a growing recognition that aging in place is not always desired, and that being "stuck in place" (Torres-Gil & Hofland, 2012) may lead to negative outcomes in health and well-being.

Research studies report an increased likelihood for poor physical and mental health for older adults living in neighborhoods characterized by high residential stability of older residents (Aneshensel et al., 2007; Cagney, Browning, & Wen, 2005), suggesting that remaining in one's home and community does not always lead to aging well. For example, after years of neglect and disinvestment, an urban neighborhood's physical environment may be characterized by dilapidated or abandoned buildings, poorly maintained roads and sidewalks, limited public transportation, and few service providers or retailers. It may concomitantly experience residential turnover, eventually resulting in few opportunities for social interaction, a loss of trust, and an increase in crime. Alternatively, gentrification may lead to redevelopment, an influx of younger and higher income residents, and the replacement of existing businesses and services by those catering to younger residents (Lees, Slater, & Wyly, 2007). In either case, older adults without financial resources may be stuck in a community context that is a mismatch for their needs and preferences because they cannot afford to move to a different home or community. Older adults without money may also have less ability to adapt themselves or their environment to achieve residential normalcy. Replacing stairs with a ramp to the front door, for example, can be expensive and therefore not financially feasible for everyone.

Conclusion

As discussed in this chapter, conceptual models such as the ecological model of aging, disablement process, behavioral model of elderly migration, residential normalcy, and the EFP seek to understand how person–environment interactions influence outcomes in older adults, such as person–environment fit, relocation, and health and well-being. Despite refinement and efforts to take into account the complexity of person–environment interactions, scholars have acknowledged that there are "key theoretical gaps in environment-aging relations" (Scheidt & Windley, 2006, p. 109). These include inadequate understanding of the ways in which community contexts affect older individuals, as well as the ways older individuals change their communities. While most of the theoretical and empirical work focuses on the current community context, some environmental effects may accumulate over time (Rogowski, Freedman, & Schoeni, 2006). Another major gap is taking a life course perspective (Scheidt & Windley, 2006), not only at the individual level, but also at the community level. Individuals have different life course trajectories that result in different needs and wants later in life. Similarly, communities have different life course trajectories, as suggested by the EFP (Diaz Moore, 2014). For example, housing and infrastructure can be preserved or replaced, and different populations can migrate in and out.

Our understanding of the mechanisms by which community contexts contribute to aging well and other important personal and societal outcomes is still developing. It is clear, however, that place matters and very likely matters more for older adults. As we discuss further in this book, while empirical research on community contexts is challenging and still emerging, there is some evidence that aging-friendly community environments can minimize mobility barriers, enhance social engagement, and optimize health and well-being.

4

Toward Aging-Friendly Communities

Introduction

This chapter examines the conditions that determine whether community environments are "aging friendly." In doing so, we contextualize the person–environment transactions envisioned by environmental gerontology (as discussed in Chapter 3), in terms of the underlying purpose of those transactions, to enable community members to age well (as discussed in Chapter 2). As noted in these previous chapters, aging friendliness emerges in the interaction between individuals' characteristics (e.g., health, social, and economic resources) and the environmental context (e.g., the physical and social infrastructure of cities and towns), reflecting in part Lawton's ecological perspective on the potential enabling or disabling impact of environments. Paul and Margret Baltes, for example, asserted that "Optimal aging refers to ... aging under development-enhancing and age-friendly environmental conditions" (P. B. Baltes & Baltes, 1990, p. 8). While they considered this "a kind of utopia," their definition nevertheless points clearly to the dynamic interplay between individuals and their environments, a central focus of this chapter.

In this chapter, we examine the definition of aging friendliness, the compensatory and enabling goals of aging-friendly communities, the specific attributes that characterize aging-friendly approaches, and the indicators that have been developed for assessing the aging friendliness of individual communities. We conclude by proposing an integrative model that reflects three overarching objectives of aging-friendly communities: (a) minimizing mobility barriers; (b) promoting social engagement; and (c) optimizing multidimensional well-being.

Aging Friendliness

A community can be considered aging friendly if it enables community members to live full and meaningful lives as they age, consistent with residents' aging-related developmental needs and priorities. This definition embodies five related, but conceptually and empirically distinct, constructs: (a) livability (i.e., promoting the health and well-being of all inhabitants); (b) elder friendliness (i.e., promoting the well-being of elderly residents specifically); (c) life span development (i.e., supporting constructive developmental processes, especially but not exclusively in the last part of the life cycle); (d) communality (i.e., promoting constructive community bonds and systems); and (e) transactionality (i.e., promoting person–environment adaptation over time) (Scharlach, 2015).

Livability suggests that aging-friendly communities also are "healthy communities"; that is, they support the well-being of all residents, as envisioned by the World Health Organization's (WHO's) 2009 Zagreb Declaration for Healthy Cities: "A healthy city is a city for all its citizens: inclusive, supportive, sensitive and responsive to their diverse needs and expectations". By *elder friendliness*, we mean that aging-friendly communities are especially concerned about the interests and needs of older adults, which sometimes can differ from those of other age groups. *Life span development* implies that aging-friendly communities not only are beneficial for current older adults but also foster constructive adaptational processes throughout the life course, as envisioned by the six domains of our integrated model of healthy aging: continuity, compensation, control, connection, contribution, and, challenge.

Aging-friendly communities are *communal*, in that they focus not only on the well-being of individuals but also on the functioning and well-being of the entire community, strengthening formal and informal social structures, promoting social capital formation, and contributing to constructive changes in community infrastructure and systems. Finally, aging friendliness is *transactional*, in that it promotes mutual constructive adaptation between individuals and their environments as each continually changes over time. In aging-friendly communities, individuals and their environments adapt in constructive ways to support positive aging. Furthermore, aging friendliness is not some ideal end state, but rather an ongoing process of continual adaptation over time. The dynamic nature of this process is reflected in WHO's 1998 definition of a healthy city: "A healthy city is one that is continually creating and improving those physical and social environments and expanding those community resources which enable people to mutually support each other in performing all the functions of life and developing to their maximum potential" (Nutbeam, 1998, p. 359).

Aging-Friendly Communities

Goals of Aging-Friendly Communities

Aging friendliness implies that communities provide residents with adequate aging-related supports as well as opportunities, what might be called compensatory goals and enabling goals. Most early conceptualizations of aging friendliness highlighted the compensatory roles of communities, focusing primarily on whether physical and social environments met older residents' needs for safety and security in the face of declining abilities. This focus on responding to aging-related deficits is reflected, for example, in the Prevention Research Centers' Healthy Aging Research Network's description of the conditions necessary for healthy aging: "Physical environments and communities are safe, and support the adoption and maintenance by individuals of attitudes and behaviors known to promote health and well-being, and by the effective use of health services and community programs to prevent or minimize the impact of acute and chronic disease on function" (p. 3).

Enabling perspectives on aging friendliness, on the other hand, tend to focus primarily on optimizing physical and social functioning, including opportunities for older residents to participate more fully in valued social roles in areas such as employment, social participation, and independent living. Such goals are perhaps best captured in the term *active aging*, which has been a primary focus of European policy efforts in the 21st century, as noted in Chapter 2. The Madrid International Plan of Action on Ageing and the Political Declaration adopted at the Second World Assembly on Ageing in April 2002, for example, focused on three priority areas: older persons and development; advancing health and well-being into old age; and ensuring enabling and supportive environments. More recently, the 2012 European Year for Active Ageing and Solidarity between Generations promoted "growing old in good health and as a full member of society, feeling more fulfilled in our jobs, more independent in our daily lives and more involved as citizens". Similarly, AARP's Livable Communities initiative identified elder-friendly "livable communities" as "facilitat[ing] personal independence and the engagement of residents in civic and social life" (AARP Public Policy Institute, 2005a, p. 2).

Our focus in this book is on both compensatory and enabling goals, consistent with a number of other recent conceptualizations of aging friendliness. Alley and her colleagues, for example, defined an elder-friendly community as "a place where older people are actively involved, valued, and supported with infrastructure and services that effectively accommodate their needs" (Alley et al., 2007). Similarly, WHO's Age-Friendly Environments Programme (WHO, 2007, p. 1) defines an age-friendly city as one that "encourages active ageing by optimizing opportunities for health, participation and security in order to enhance quality of life as people age."

Combined with the principles of individual development and environmental contexts discussed in Chapters 2 and 3, these various conceptualizations suggest that aging-friendly communities enhance person–environment fit (e.g., mobility and environmental accessibility, residential normalcy and stability, and autonomy) to achieve age-related compensatory goals (e.g., promoting safety and security while protecting physical and mental well-being) and enabling goals (e.g., facilitating engagement in meaningful social roles and other opportunities for personal fulfillment).

Attributes of Aging-Friendly Communities

Achieving these goals requires that physical infrastructure and social systems are designed in such a way that they enable members to age well or at a minimum do not create unnecessary barriers to doing so. There have been numerous efforts to identify the specific environmental attributes that characterize an aging-friendly community, sometimes from the perspectives of older adults themselves, sometimes from the perspectives of planners and other experts, and sometimes empirically. Three overarching domains of community aging friendliness emerged from these various efforts: (a) mobility and environmental fit; (b) social engagement; and (c) multidimensional health and well-being.

Elders' perspectives. Some of the first efforts to identify aging-friendly community attributes involved focus groups with older adults and other stakeholders. The University of Calgary's Elder Friendly Communities Project, an early precursor of subsequent national and international initiatives, identified a set of elder-friendly characteristics based on focus groups with 176 seniors and caregivers, 27 service providers, and 22 community leaders and experts, along with in-home interviews with 54 older adults and 3 adult children in four Calgary neighborhoods. The four characteristics of community aging friendliness that emerged from these efforts were (a) personal safety, including assistance to age in place; (b) self-reliance, including access to information, transportation, and affordable services; (c) community participation, including staying active and involved in meaningful roles; and (d) being valued and respected for one's contributions.

AARP's Livable Communities initiative conducted 14 focus groups with a diverse sample of older adults and caregivers in 13 cities in five states (Arizona, Florida, Iowa, New York, and Washington) in an effort to identify the features of a livable community (AARP Public Policy Institute, 2005). Characteristics identified by focus group participants fell into three general areas: (a) adequate mobility options; (b) affordable and appropriate housing; and (c) supportive community features and services. Specific mobility features included a reliable public transportation system, elder-friendly roads, and a physical environment that fosters walking. Housing characteristics included a full range of housing options, accessibility, and affordability. Supportive community features included access to shopping; nearby quality health facilities; opportunities for recreation and culture; a safe and secure environment; and other supportive services, such as meals programs and homemaking services.

A similar methodology was utilized by the Visiting Nurse Service of New York's AdvantAge Initiative, which conducted focus groups with older adults in four cities, asking them to describe "the attributes that a community would need to have for it to be considered elder friendly" (Feldman et al., 2004, p. xi). Four overarching characteristics of an elder-friendly community emerged from an analysis of the descriptions provided by focus group participants: (a) addresses basic needs, including safety, assistance, food, and housing; (b) maximizes independence, including access to needed social services and transportation; (c) optimizes physical and mental health and well-being, including access to needed health services; and (4) promotes social and civic engagement, including social connections, volunteer work, and civic, cultural, religious, and recreational activities.

Finally, WHO's Ageing and Life Course Programme's Global Age-Friendly Cities project, which is described in greater detail in Chapter 9, created a framework for conducting focus groups designed to evaluate community age friendliness and stimulate local mobilization efforts in cities throughout the world. To date, focus groups with older adults, caregivers, and service providers have been conducted in at least 22 countries on six continents. Focus group participants are asked to consider potential improvements in eight specific domains, based on aging-friendly characteristics previously identified by AARP and the Visiting Nurse Service of New York.

The WHO project's eight domains comprise three overarching areas: (a) physical infrastructure, (b) social opportunities, and (c) supportive services. The three physical infrastructure domains are the ability to get to places when needed; the ability to age comfortably and safely within one's home and chosen community; and outdoor spaces and buildings that promote safety and accessibility. The three social domains are engagement in fulfilling social, cultural, and recreational activities; opportunities for civic engagement and other productive roles; and respectful and inclusive attitudes of the community as a whole toward older people. The two supportive service domains are access to a wide range of health and social services and access to information and technologies that enable elders to obtain needed information and stay connected.

Perspectives of experts. Similar characteristics of aging-friendly communities have been identified by leading experts and professional and governmental organizations. In one study, 15 national experts were polled regarding the characteristics they considered essential for an "elder-friendly community" (Alley et al., 2007). Consensus emerged around 15 characteristics in six domains: (a) supportive and accessible housing options; (b) accessible and affordable transportation; (c) community involvement opportunities; (d) positive social environment; (e) responsive health and long-term care services; and (f) personal safety.

The National Association of Area Agencies on Aging (n4a), in collaboration with the International City/County Management Association and Partners for Livable Communities, identified seven areas of "aging readiness" as part of its Aging in Place Initiative, which involved surveys of local governments in the United States: (a) housing; (b) transportation; (c) social, cultural, and educational enhancement; (d) community engagement; (e) recreational and health promotion opportunities; (f) health and social services; and (g) public safety services.

Similarly, the Canadian Association of Retired Persons (CARP)'s Age-Friendly Cities Initiative identified three composite domains of aging friendliness: (a) accessible and affordable living environments; (b) mobility (including affordable and accessible transportation as well as barrier-free access to public spaces); and (c) social cohesion, participation, and inclusion.

Consistent with the attributes identified by these various initiatives, the U.S. Environmental Protection Agency's (EPA's) Building Healthy Communities for Active Aging used the following four characteristics to assess community efforts to integrate the principles of smart growth with the concepts of active aging: (a) environmental safety (including safe and pleasant homes and neighborhood options); (b) adequate transportation and mobility; (c) social participation; and (d) physical well-being (including healthy food, physical activity, and health care services and supports).

Empirical approaches. In one of the few empirical efforts to identify age-friendly community attributes, Smith and colleagues conducted an exploratory factor analysis (EFA) of Detroit area data regarding the presence of characteristics suggested by the EPA's four domains of environmental safety, transportation and mobility, social participation, and physical well-being (Smith, Lehning, & Dunkie, 2013). The EFA yielded six factors with eigenvalues greater than 1, individual items having factor loadings greater than or equal to 0.4, and face validity. The six factors identified in this manner were (a) lack of neighborhood problems with personal or environmental safety; (b) easy access to stores and other amenities; (c) social interaction; (d) social support; (e) participation in community groups and volunteer activities; and (f) access to health and mental health care services.

Overarching Domains of Community Aging Friendliness

Some have suggested that the entire range of aging-friendly characteristics can be collapsed into two separate dimensions: physical and social. Lui and colleagues (Lui, Everingham, J., Warburton, Cuthill, & Bartlett, 2009), for example, developed a unidimensional model of aging-friendly community initiatives, reflecting a single continuum ranging from physical infrastructure (outdoor spaces, transportation, housing, information, services) to social infrastructure (community planning, employment, civic participation, social inclusion, safety). Such simplistic representations of aging friendliness tend to overlook the interpenetrating nature of physical and social environmental features, as well as the purposes that such features are intended to achieve.

Transportation and mobility are a case in point. While fixed-route and flexible-route public transportation are important components of any transportation system, the larger issue for older adults is one of mobility and accessibility, that is, how to get where they want and need to go when they want and need to get there. *Optimal mobility*, for example, has been defined as "relative ease and freedom of movement in all of its forms" (Satariano et al., 2012, p. 1508). From this perspective, meeting elders' mobility needs requires both an adequate physical infrastructure (e.g., buses, cars, roads) and the availability of social supports (e.g., drivers, companions, and personal assistance). Mobility needs can be met by public fixed-route or paratransit services, by a taxicab, by a companion who accompanies a senior in his or her own car and provides verbal cueing, by a volunteer who drives the senior, or by a companion who accompanies the senior on a public bus. Walkability becomes a key consideration, as does road design, vehicle design and customization, and technological assistance. Clearly, physical infrastructure is only part of the story, and efforts to differentiate aging-friendly components as either physical or social infrastructure are apt to be problematic.

Similarly, housing is important to the extent that it provides a safe, secure base for meeting one's physical and social needs while helping to preserve a relatively stable sense of personal identity, continuity, and meaning. From this perspective, adequate housing involves not only a physical structure but also considerations of location, affordability, customization, maintenance, ambient assistive technologies, supportive services, and a variety of alternative housing options within the community. Moreover, social factors such as the density of interpersonal social networks and the amount of social participation are highly dependent on housing factors and in turn contribute to residential stability (Chaskin, 1997).

With this in mind, Lui and colleagues (Lui et al., 2009) argued that the ideal aging-friendly community has an integrated physical and social environment, where older residents are actively involved in all aspects of community life and governance, within a climate of inclusiveness and respect. This suggests that aging friendliness involves minimizing environmental and social barriers while maximizing independence, choice, and connection.

Aging-friendly community environments, therefore, can be expected to include the following:

1. An adequate general physical and social infrastructure that promotes health and well-being for everyone;
2. Minimal age-related barriers faced by older community members in trying to access that infrastructure;
3. Compensatory and enabling features that respond to the particular age-related needs and sensibilities of older community members; and
4. Mechanisms for engaging older adults as valued contributors to community life.

Based on this analysis, we propose six aspects of community aging friendliness, in three overarching domains:

1. Environmental fit and accessibility
   a. Built environment (housing options, accessible design, affordability)
   b. Transportation/mobility (roads, sidewalks, conveyances, and supports)
2. Social engagement
   a. Social inclusion (social participation, social/recreational/cultural/educational activities, meaningful roles)
   b. Social environment (positive attitudes about aging, age-mindful public policymaking)
3. Multidimensional health and well-being
   a. Health/independence (accessible and affordable health and social services, health promotion, functional assistance, financial well-being, supportive services)
   b. Safety/security (protection from crime and abuse)

Intersecting with these domains are a number of cross-cutting considerations, including access (e.g., availability, affordability, accessibility, appropriateness, and acceptability of physical and social resources); equity (e.g., economic, geographic, linguistic, cultural, and ability-related disparities in accessibility and impact); and scope (e.g., whether the community of interest is a neighborhood or municipality, urban or rural, geographically defined or consensually defined, and physically manifest or virtual).

Assessing Aging Friendliness

Aging-Friendly Indicators

To assess the aging friendliness of a particular community, goals and attributes need to be operationalized in terms of specific measurable indicators. In this section, we review some of these indicators and the ways in which they have been implemented. We note a number of potential limitations, including a reliance on nonrepresentative samples of older adults or publicly available data sources that were not intended to measure aging-friendly community characteristics.

AdvantAge Initiative. The Visiting Nurse Service of New York's AdvantAge Initiative developed a needs assessment instrument that has been implemented in communities throughout the United States. Using surveys of representative samples of older community residents, the AdvantAge Initiative assesses older adults' perceptions of personal and community well-being in four broad domains (Feldman et al., 2004): (a) basic needs; (b) physical and mental health and well-being; (c) independence; and (d) social and civic engagement.

A community's ability to *address basic needs* is assessed with 10 measures asking whether affordable housing is available, housing is modified to accommodate mobility and safety, the neighborhood is safe and livable, people have enough to eat, and assistance services are available and residents know how to access them. Community ability to *optimize physical and mental health and well-being* is assessed with 11 measures asking whether residents are in good health, participate in regular physical exercise, receive vaccinations and other preventive health services, obtain needed medical care, obtain needed mental health services, can afford medical and dental care and medications, and know whether palliative care services are available in their community. Community ability to *maximize independence* is assessed with five measures asking whether respondents have access to public transportation, receive adequate assistance with personal care and household chores, provide help to persons who are frail or disabled, and obtain relief from their caregiving responsibilities. *Promoting social and civic engagement* is assessed with seven measures asking whether respondents are working for pay if so desired; participate in volunteer work; socialize with friends or neighbors; attend religious services; attend public events, movies, or clubs; participate in social, religious, or cultural activities; and say they live in a "helping community."

Active Ageing Index. Based in part on the AdvantAge Initiative, the European Commission's Active Ageing Index (AAI) was developed in an effort to provide a metric for assessing the "untapped potential" of the older population in EU countries. The AAI follows the conceptual framework of the 2012 European Year for Active Ageing and Solidarity Between Generations, which defined active aging as "the process of optimising opportunities for health, participation and security in order to enhance quality of life as people age" (WHO, 2002).

The index utilizes national administrative and survey data to measure active aging performance across four domains: (a) independent and autonomous living; (b) social activity and participation; (c) employment; and (d) enabling environment for active aging in the future. *Independent and autonomous living* is assessed with eight measures: percentage of persons age 55 or older living independently; their poverty rate compared with the country as a whole; their median income compared with younger persons; percentage who cannot afford to meet basic material needs; percentage exercising at least five times per week; percentage who are able to obtain health and dental care when needed; percentage living in an area with crime or violence; and percentage who participated in educational activities in the past week.

Social activity and participation is assessed with four measures: percentage of persons age 55 or older providing unpaid voluntary activity at least once a month; percentage providing care for children or grandchildren at least once a week; percentage providing care to elderly or disabled relatives at least once a week; and percentage participating in organized political activities or contacting a political representative in the past year. *Employment* is assessed with measures of labor force participation in the past week for persons age 55 or older, by age group.

Finally, *enabling environment for active aging in the future* is assessed with six measures: life expectancy at age 55; percentage of life expectancy at age 55 expected to be disability free; self-reported positive mood; percentage using the Internet at least once a week; percentage who meet socially with friends, relatives, or colleagues at least once a week; and percentage who have completed high school.

Best Cities for Successful Aging. The Best Cities for Successful Aging index, developed by the Milken Institute, attempts to take a comprehensive approach to assessing community aging friendliness. Using information from the U.S. Census and other publicly available sources, the Best Cities index examines 78 indicators reflecting eight factors thought to affect older adults' quality of life: community social environment and climate; health care; wellness; living arrangements; transportation and convenience; financial well-being; employment and education opportunities; and community engagement. Some indicators are relevant regardless of age (e.g., cost of living, crime and safety, overall economic prosperity, and weather), while others are thought to be of particular relevance to older persons (e.g., high-quality health care and wellness programs, the availability of specialized housing and living arrangements, financial factors, transportation and convenience, continuing education and job training programs, and community engagement).

A composite ranking of a city's potential for "successful aging" is calculated based on a weighted sum of indicator scores for the eight factors: general characteristics represent 15% of the total composite score, health care 15%, wellness 15%, living arrangements 10%, transportation/convenience 10%, financial well-being 20%, employment/education 10%, and community engagement 5%. Slightly different weights also are used for large and small municipalities and for persons 65–79 and 80+; for example, scores for persons 65–79 weight more heavily financial and educational characteristics, whereas scores for persons 80+ weight more heavily living arrangements, economic well-being, safety and security, and weather.

Numerous articles in the popular press use similar types of publicly available data to identify "best places for seniors" or "best places to retire." Examples include *Money* magazine's list of "best places for elders to live," *US News & World Report*'s list of "best affordable places to retire," *AARP* magazine's "best places to retire," *MoneyRates.com*'s "best states for retirement," and *Sperling's* "best cities for seniors." The criteria used to make these assessments generally are similar, focusing primarily on cost of living, tax rates, medical care, and leisure activities, criteria that only partially reflect the more comprehensive, conceptually driven characteristics others have identified. The focus on economic conditions likely reflects the target audiences of these publications, who are apt to be more advantaged than the average older person.

Livable Community Indicators for Sustainable Aging in Place. In 2013, the MetLife Mature Market Institute, in collaboration with the Stanford Center on Longevity, developed a report identifying a set of community characteristics that are postulated to facilitate aging in place (MetLife Mature Market Institute,

2013). Based on a review of the research literature and interviews with 19 aging experts, the authors proposed three community characteristics that can help older adults age in place: (a) accessible and affordable housing options; (b) features that promote access to the community (e.g., safe and walkable neighborhoods, transportation options); and (c) a wide range of services and opportunities for community engagement (e.g., healthy food, social integration, health and supportive services). This indicator system focused on using existing data sources easily accessed by local governments. While these indicators are an initial step toward assessing the community, the authors acknowledged the limitations of using existing data, particularly the limited data available on community social environments.

WHO Age-Friendly Cities Indicator Project. As described in the section on elders' perspective, WHO's Global Age-Friendly Cities project in 2007 identified eight key domains of urban life in which interventions could potentially improve opportunities for health, participation, and security, as described previously. In 2012, the WHO Centre for Health Development in Kobe, Japan, in consultation with the WHO Department of Ageing and Life Course, initiated a 3-year project to develop core indicators to operationalize these domains in order to measure city age friendliness more empirically (WHO Centre for Health Development, 2015).

Indicator development involved a comprehensive process, including all of the following components:

1. a review of existing literature on the determinants of health and active aging;
2. a review of indicators already in use in international and national initiatives related to ageing, health, and the urban environment;
3. consultations with teams of experts;
4. extensive peer review; and
5. a pilot study conducted with local government and community representatives from over 40 cities across 15 countries.

In developing the indicators, particular attention was given to data quality considerations such as the following: measurability; validity; replicability; sensitivity to change; disaggregation possibilities; alignment with local goals and targets; ability to be linked to action; responsiveness to local influence; ease of collection; and social acceptability. Each resulting indicator was operationalized so that it could be assessed in one of two ways: through the use of administrative data typically available from government agencies or through self-report surveys with older adults or other community members.

This extensive development process led to identification of 14 core indicators, 5 supplemental indicators, and 2 equity indicators. Core physical domain indicators were neighborhood walkability; accessibility of public spaces and buildings; accessibility of public transportation vehicles; accessibility of public transportation stops; and affordability of housing. Core social domain indicators were positive social attitude toward older people; engagement in volunteer activity; paid employment; engagement in sociocultural activity; participation in local decision-making; availability of information; availability of social and health services; economic security; and quality of life. Supplemental indicators were accessibility of priority vehicle parking; accessibility of housing; participation in leisure-time physical activity in a group; engagement in lifelong learning; and Internet access. Equity indicators were population-attributable risk (i.e., comparison of target group [e.g., 65+] against population at large) and inequality (i.e., comparison of one group [e.g., 65+] against another group [e.g., 18–64]).

AARP Livability Index. The AARP Livability Index is a Web-based tool for assessing the "livability" of more than 200,000 neighborhoods across the United States. An interactive website (https://livabilityindex.aarp.org/) enables individuals to find an overall livability score for a particular address, zip code, or community, as well as a score for each of seven major livability categories: housing, neighborhood, transportation, environment, health, engagement, and opportunity. Users also can customize the index to place higher or lower emphasis on the livability features of most importance to them. The Livability Index website also provides examples of local policy options for increasing livability in each domain of interest, as well as lists of publications from AARP, federal agencies, and other sources for further information about each domain.

Housing livability includes measures of accessibility (percentage of housing units in the metropolitan area that have extrawide doors or hallways, floors with no steps between rooms, and an entry-level bedroom and bathroom); housing options (percentage of housing units in the neighborhood that are not single-family, detached homes); and affordability (monthly housing costs in the neighborhood, percentage of median income devoted to monthly housing costs, and number of subsidized housing units per person in the county). Neighborhood livability includes proximity to destinations (grocery stores and farmers' markets, parks, libraries, access to jobs using transit, access to jobs by auto); diversity of destinations; activity density (jobs and people per square mile); personal safety (crime rate); and neighborhood quality (vacancy rate). Transportation livability includes convenience (number of buses and trains per hour in the neighborhood, number of walking trips per day in the neighborhood, and time spent in traffic); costs (annual transportation expenditures); safety (local speed limits, number of fatal crashes per year); and accessibility (percentage of transit stations and vehicles that are accessible per the ADA [Americans With Disabilities Act]).

Environmental livability includes water quality and air quality (unhealthy air quality days per year, near-roadway pollution, local industrial pollution). Health includes healthy behaviors (tobacco use, obesity prevalence, exercise opportunities), access to health care, and quality of health care (preventable hospitalization rate, patient satisfaction). Engagement includes Internet access; civic engagement (number of civic, social, religious, political, and business organizations per person in the county; percentage of county residents who voted in the last election); social involvement (extent to which residents in the metropolitan area eat dinner with household members, see or hear from friends and family, talk with neighbors, and do favors for neighbors); and cultural, arts, and entertainment institutions. Finally, opportunity includes income inequality, job availability, education levels, and age diversity.

Livability calculations are based on data from a wide variety of public and private sources. Transportation livability, for example, utilizes data from the U.S. Census Bureau, the Federal Transit Administration, the National Highway Traffic Safety Administration, Texas A&M University's Transportation Institute, as well as private proprietary data sources. While some of these data are available at the neighborhood level, others are based on estimates for the entire metropolitan area or county.

Strengths and Limitations of Existing Indicator Systems

Some aging-friendly indicator systems, such as the AdvantAge Initiative, rely primarily on community surveys. A strength of self-report data is its potential ability to provide a sense of older adults' own perspectives on their own well-being and that of their communities, laying a foundation for citizen engagement in community change processes. However, community surveys tend to underrepresent the perspectives of vulnerable groups, and participant self-reports may be inadequate for describing broader community conditions.

Publicly available administrative data, on the other hand, can be a particularly useful way to obtain information about broader community conditions. The major limitation of administrative data, however, is that they seldom reflect meaningful aging-friendly community characteristics, largely because they were not originally designed with community aging friendliness in mind. The Milken Institute's Best Cities for Successful Aging index, for example, assesses community support for elders' economic well-being using statistics regarding local cost of living, job growth, unemployment, and income inequality, apparently based on untested assumptions about the relationship between these conditions and elders' current or future economic well-being; no data are collected from elders themselves, which would more directly assess their real or perceived economic security. Elder community engagement is assessed by counting the number of museums, cultural and religious institutions, entertainment venues, public libraries, YMCAs, and senior activity programs and the proportion of community residents who are 65 or older. Similar concerns exist regarding the use of administrative data to assess other community conditions, such as safety and security, housing options, employment opportunities, and educational opportunities.

An additional concern about publicly available data sources is that they tend to be available only for relatively large and well-established political and geographical locations, such as major cities, states, and countries. Such data often underrepresent or omit entirely smaller, less populous, and frequently more diverse areas. The Milken Institute's index, for example, relies primarily on census data that are available for metropolitan statistical areas, geographical regions with relatively high population densities that are not necessarily legally defined administrative divisions such as counties or states or necessarily even legally incorporated as a city or town.

As noted, the recently developed AARP Livability Index and WHO Age-Friendly Cities indicator system try to address some of the limitations of self-report and administrative data by combining information from a wide range of sources, including census data, accessibility records, planning applications, labor statistics, voting records, law enforcement reports, geographic information system (GIS) mapping, and community surveys, among others. Similarly, the European Commission's AAI combines information from the EU Statistics on Income and Living Conditions, the European Health and Life Expectancy Information System, the EU Labour Force Survey, the European Social Survey, the European Quality of Life Survey, and a Special Eurobarometer Survey on Sport and Physical Activity. Combining data from a number of disparate sources, however, can pose a variety of challenges: Complete information is not always available; data often reflect nonequivalent sample frames; some population groups or locations tend to be underrepresented; and aggregating data from multiple sources requires relatively sophisticated statistical ability not usually available to community planners and other local initiative leaders.

Conclusion: An Integrative Model of Aging Friendliness

Based on the findings presented in this chapter, we propose an integrative model of aging friendliness, with overarching goals reflecting three essential dimensions of neighborhoods associated with aging well, including characteristics that transcend physical, social, and experiential domains (Chaskin, 1997):

1. *Minimal mobility barriers.* Age and disability should not be barriers to having one's needs met, including getting where one needs to go. Private spaces and relevant public spaces should promote healthy aging, and individuals should be able to move easily and safely from one to the other (e.g., not be dependent on automobiles, no unnecessary environmental barriers, etc.).

2. *Social engagement.* Age and disability should not be barriers to meaningful social inclusion and participation (e.g., social integration, informal networks,

meaningful social roles, etc.). As noted by Lui and his colleagues, "A supportive context with positive social relations, engagement and inclusion is a core prerequisite for ageing well" (Lui et al., 2009, p. 120). "One defining characteristic of a livable community is the high level of engagement of its residents with one another and with the life of the community itself" (AARP Public Policy Institute, 2005, p. 20).

3. *Multidimensional elder health and well-being.* Age and disability should not be barriers to personal well-being, including basic safety and security, personal control, and the ability to delay or avoid undesired relocation (e.g., health promotion, supportive services, etc.). As used here, health includes physical, psychosocial, cultural, and spiritual well-being (Scharlach & Hoshino, 2012). Psychosocial well-being includes opportunities for continuity, compensation, control, connection, contribution, and challenge.

This integrative model serves as the framework for our examination of aging-friendly community components in the next three chapters.

PART II

CHARACTERISTICS OF AGING-FRIENDLY COMMUNITIES

5

Overcoming Physical Barriers
to Aging Well

Mobility and the Built Environment

Introduction

Aging well requires that home and community infrastructures promote access and mobility. As described in Chapter 3, the ecological model of aging calls attention to the interactions between individual competence and the press of the surrounding environment (Lawton & Nahemow, 1973). As we age and experience increasing physical, cognitive, and sensory limitations, we may also experience reduced mobility due to the demands of our housing and community environments. Houses with stairs can make it difficult to move around in or leave one's home. Many neighborhoods are entirely residential, without any stores, restaurants, or services within walking distance. Roadways are designed primarily for vehicle traffic and can be challenging for pedestrians to navigate safely. If an older adult can no longer safely drive a car, often there are few alternative mobility options available that are affordable and convenient. In this chapter, we examine approaches for overcoming the barriers that can constrain older adults' ability to live safely in their homes and get around their community through the development of aging-friendly built environments and transportation systems.

We begin by providing an overview of the current status of housing and community environments in the United States, including their limited ability to facilitate adequate access and mobility for older adults. We then describe the characteristics of aging-friendly housing, community design, and transportation infrastructures. While highlighting some promising approaches to modifying the physical environment, we also note some of the questions that remain regarding environmental modifications. The empirical literature, for example, includes few rigorous evaluation studies of communitywide changes to enhance mobility among older adults. We conclude with some examples of promising efforts to promote elder mobility, which can contribute to the evidence base on aging-friendly communities.

Environmental Barriers to Mobility in Later Life

The ways many communities have been designed and developed pose a significant barrier to our ability to age well. Many Americans today live in communities characterized by low-density development that separates residential areas from those allowing other land uses. In the United States, a combination of federal and state policies, local ordinances, private business decisions, and individual preferences led to our present situation, in which many communities create numerous barriers to elder mobility.

Zoning decisions in the United States are primarily under the purview of local governments. At the end of the 19th century, the growth of industry and mass migration to cities created unsanitary and overcrowded living conditions that fostered the spread of deadly communicable diseases such as tuberculosis and cholera (Schilling & Linton, 2005). Many communities responded by adopting zoning ordinances requiring the separation of commercial and industrial areas from residential areas and implementing local laws mandating adequate living conditions, such as New York City's Tenement House Act of 1901 (Schilling & Linton, 2005). These public health and quality-of-life rationales for zoning were upheld in the Supreme Court's decision in *Ambler Realty v. Village of Euclid* in 1926 (Schilling & Linton, 2005).

Since that time, however, what is called Euclidean zoning has been viewed by housing scholars as primarily protecting property interests and designating areas for single-family housing (Pollak, 1994; Schilling & Linton, 2005). Single-family homes typically provide higher tax revenues and place less demand on local services than multifamily and subsidized housing, thereby creating fiscal incentives for municipal governments to favor this form of development (Schill, 2005). Beginning in the 1970s, many suburban municipalities adopted growth control measures, such as large minimum lot mandates, adequate public facility requirements, and caps on home-building permits (Byun, Waldorf, & Esparza, 2005). Ordinances that restrict legal occupancy to a single family and limit the construction of additional structures on a property have also contributed to making single-family homes the dominant form of housing in this country (Daniels, 1994; Pollak, 1994). Historically, the federal government has generally stayed out of local zoning decisions, and only a few states (e.g., California, New Jersey) call for zoning practices that promote the development of affordable or multifamily housing (Schill, 2005). There are therefore few constraints placed on municipalities in their zoning decisions and little incentive to coordinate regionally. Indeed, as noted by Fischel (1978), "The 'general welfare' of the community, which zoning is supposed to promote, refers exclusively to existing residents, not to potential residents or people in nearby communities" (p. 67).

The rise of the personal automobile as the primary mode of transportation further spurred the development of single-family homes separated from commercial and industrial areas. The automobile has been identified as the major catalyst behind suburban sprawl, supplemented by federal policies after the Second World War, such as the Interstate Highway Act, low gasoline costs, and tax breaks for mortgages (Dagger, 2003; Frank, 2000). As noted by Handy (2005), there is a reciprocal relationship between transportation and land use patterns. For example, the construction of highways encourages the creation of new housing developments, shopping malls, and office parks. In turn, these low-density suburban communities necessitate travel by car and offer few alternative mobility options.

In addition to public policies, individual choice has played a large role (Handy, 2005). That is, many people now live in the suburbs because they want to be there—they want more space, a yard, or highly rated public schools. Low-density residential development has actually accelerated in recent decades. For example, in the 1990s low-density communities grew at two times the rate of metropolitan areas (Berube, Singer, Wilson, & Frey, 2006). In a study of counties near Washington, D.C., exurban development grew more than 6% annually between 1986 and 2009 (Suarez-Rubio, Lookingbill, & Elmore, 2012). Furthermore, driving is the most common mode of transportation primarily because people want to drive; even in some high-density urban neighborhoods, many people use their car to meet most of their travel needs (Handy, 2005).

Housing Environments: Barriers to Accessibility and Affordability

Over 90% of older adults say they would like to remain in their own homes for as long as possible (AARP Public Policy Institute [PPI], 2005a; Feldman et al., 2004). Older adults also perceive a number of benefits associated with living independently rather than moving in with relatives or to congregate settings, including privacy, personal control over their lives, and proximity to neighbors and friends (Means, 1997). Older adults also derive symbolic meanings from their home and possessions (Gitlin, 2003a). Two major characteristics common to a large amount of existing housing in the United States, however, create barriers to older adults being able to remain in their current dwelling.

The first relates to housing affordability. Many older adults express doubt that they will have enough money to age in place in their current home (Mack, Salmoni, Viverais-Dressler, Porter, & Garg, 1997). In a 2003 national survey of older adults, the majority reported they spent more than a third of their income for housing (Feldman et al., 2004), which is typically viewed as the threshold for affordability. In the same survey, 34% of the respondents reported not feeling confident they would be able to afford their current residence as they age (Feldman et al., 2004). Given high rates of home ownership among those age 65 and older, one might assume that they have relatively low housing costs. For example, approximately 80% of older homeowners no longer have to make mortgage payments (Golant, 1992). However, the costs of maintaining a home present a significant barrier to aging in place. First, older homeowners still have significant housing costs in terms of insurance, property taxes, and utility bills (Golant, 1992). Second, in part because older adults remain in the same dwelling for many years (Golant, 1992), they tend to live in older homes that may require more repairs and maintenance (Daniels, 1994). Finally, as their household sizes shrink, many elders live in dwellings that exceed their current needs, resulting in excessive costs for housekeeping, heating and cooling, and yard care at the same time their financial resources are likely declining (Golant, 2006). The zoning practices favoring large single-family homes over multifamily or other forms of housing (e.g., shared housing, accessory dwelling units [ADUs]) restrict elders' options if they wish to relocate to a smaller residence in the same community.

The second barrier relates to the absence of adequate accessibility features in most existing housing (Maisel, Smith, & Steinfeld, 2008). Federal laws, such as the Fair Housing Amendments of 1988 and the Fair Housing Act, mandate the inclusion of accessible features, such as wide entrances and doorways, accessible light switches, and bathroom walls reinforced to accommodate grab bars, in new multifamily housing (Kochera, 2002). These provisions, however, do not apply to single-family dwellings or multifamily buildings with fewer than four units (American Planning Association, 2006). Environmental hazards and inaccessible features are frequently observed in the homes of older adults, particularly in bedrooms, kitchens, and bathrooms (Gill, Williams, Robison, & Tinetti, 1999; Gitlin, Mann, Tomit, & Marcus, 2001).

Home modifications are becoming increasingly common; for example, between 1978 and 1995 the prevalence of home modifications increased, particularly for ramps, wide doors and hallways, and accessible bathroom features, while unmet need for modifications decreased (Newman, 2003). Older adults experiencing physical health problems, such as limitations in activities of daily living, are more likely to have home modifications (Mathieson, Kronenfeld, & Keith, 2002; Tabbarah, Silverstein, & Seeman, 2000). Almost one quarter of older adults, however, report an unmet need for home modifications (Newman, 2003). In part, this unmet need may be due to the costs of home modifications, which can range from less than $1,000 for adding grab bars, handrails, and lever-style doorknobs, to around $3,000 for wheelchair ramps and more than $10,000 for a stair lift (MetLife Mature Market Institute, 2010). In addition, some disability-related modifications, such as wide, barrier-free hallways, may be beneficial for individuals in wheelchairs but less helpful or even detrimental for older adults with normal age-related balance problems. Older adults who are female, non-White, low income, and live in older homes in neighborhoods characterized by crime and other signs of disorder are at a greater risk for unmet needs for modifications (Newman, 2003; Tabbarah et al., 2000).

Some developers have incorporated universal design features such as wide doorways, large bathrooms, and sloped entry paths (Connell & Sanford, 2001). However, features aimed specifically at individuals with a disability, such as grab bars and wheelchair lifts, are much less common (Connell & Sanford, 2001). Prior research has demonstrated benefits of home modifications and environmental adaptations, including a lower risk of experiencing health problems (Liu & Lapane, 2009); slower decline in instrumental activities of daily living (IADL) independence; improved self-efficacy for informal caregivers (Gitlin, Corcoran, Winter, Boyce, & Hauck, 2001); and a reduction in health care expenses (Stearns et al., 2000). Furthermore, modifying the home environment is viewed as a promising intervention to improve the quality of life of individuals with dementia and their caregivers (van Hoof, Kort, van Waarde, & Blom, 2010). More than 90% of housing in the United States, however, is estimated to be inaccessible to individuals with disabilities (Steinfeld, Levine, & Shea, 1998).

Community Design: Barriers to Walking

Community design in many neighborhoods, particularly those in suburban, exurban, and rural areas, severely restricts community access for those residents who no longer operate their own vehicle. Many roadways in the United States appear to be designed for "the safety, convenience and comfort of motor vehicles" (U.S. Department of Transportation, 2007, p. 3), rather than ensuring that those who are walking or using other forms of transportation, whether because of health limitations, financial restrictions, or personal preference, are able to reach their destinations.

In terms of the disablement process, community design presents barriers that act as exacerbaters, limiting the ability of individuals with functional impairments to engage in everyday activities (Clarke & George, 2005). In low-density areas, walking to the grocery store, pharmacy, post office, or hairdresser, among other destinations, may not be possible even for older adults without functional limitations. Housing developments may be located miles away from shopping centers, sidewalks may not be present along the route, and pedestrian crosswalks across main thoroughfares may be few and far between. Older adults with even normal aging-associated decrements face additional barriers, including an absence of benches, poorly maintained sidewalks with cracks and debris that increase the risk of falls, and crosswalk signal timing that

it to cross the street. In a survey conducted by AARP, 40% of respon-
)orted that the sidewalks in their neighborhoods were inadequate, and
orted being unable to safely cross main roads (Lynott et al., 2009).

The physical layout of communities may also have an impact on future disability by limiting opportunities for walking and other physical activities.
Walking is the preferred form of exercise for older adults (D. O. Clark, 1999),
and previous studies have documented the positive impact of walking on health
and well-being. Regular walking is associated with a decreased risk of physical
limitations and mortality (Simonsick et al., 1993), cognitive impairment (Yaffe,
Barnes, Nevitt, Lui, & Covinsky, 2001), and loss of mobility (LaCroix, Guralnick,
Berkman, Wallace, & Satterfield, 1993). While individual-level factors, such as
physical health and knowledge of the benefits of physical activity, affect elders'
propensity for walking and engaging in other forms of exercise, so do community
characteristics such as the presence of sidewalks and parks (Schutzer & Graves,
2004; Wilcox, Bopp, Oberrecht, Kammermann, & McElmurray, 2003).

Transportation Environments: Barriers to Life-Sustaining and Life-Enhancing Trips

As with Americans of all ages, the overwhelming majority of older adults get
around their communities in a car (Feldman et al., 2004). In their analysis of
urban trip data from the 2001 National Household Travel Study, Pucher and
Renne (2003) reported that older adults take almost 90% of their trips in a car
and on average make more than half of these trips as the driver, a higher percentage than most younger age groups. Research suggests that almost all older adults
who are currently driving plan to do so for as long as possible (Kostyniuk &
Shope, 2003). Indeed, a growing proportion of older adults are able to continue
operating their own vehicle into their later years. For example, among adults ages
70–85 years, the percentage of those who do not drive declined from approximately 28% in 1993 to 16% in 2008 (M. Choi & Mezuk, 2013).

Older adults consistently indicate that driving is their preferred mode of transportation (Burkhardt, McGavock, Nelson, & Mitchell, 2002; Rudman, Friedland,
Chipman, & Sciortino, 2006). Compared to other forms of transportation, such
as public transit or getting rides from family and friends, driving is viewed as having several advantages, such as faster travel times, door-to-door travel, and control over when and where an elder wants to go (Burkhardt et al., 2002). In focus
groups, older adults describe driving as not only the most convenient and flexible mode of mobility but also part of their self-identity (Burkhardt et al., 2002;
Glasgow & Blakely, 2000). This suggests that giving up the car keys not only has
consequences in terms of restricted mobility but also can negatively affect elders'
feelings of independence and self-worth.

Both individual and environmental factors can create barriers to elders' ability to continue driving. A number of potential functional and cognitive impairments can make it difficult for older adults to safely drive their own car. These include vision problems, which can make it difficult to read road signs and see pavement markings, curbs, pedestrians, and other cars (Lynott et al., 2009). Indeed, many former drivers have cited declining vision as the cause of their driving cessation (Dellinger, Sehgal, Sleet, & Barrett-Connor, 2001). Impaired cognitive functioning can decrease information-processing speed, attention, and reaction time (Brenner, Homaifer, & Schultheis, 2008). Many older drivers self-regulate their driving habits to try to remain on the road for as long as possible (Adler & Rottunda, 2006), using such strategies as avoiding highways, only driving during the day, avoiding rush hour, and traveling only along familiar routes. Despite these efforts to avoid dangerous situations, older adults have more accidents per trip made than any other age group and account for 18% of all motor vehicle deaths (Rosenbloom, 2004). Certain types of roads and intersections may be particularly dangerous for older drivers. For example, older adults are involved in a high number of traffic accidents while turning left (National Highway Traffic Safety Administration, 2014), which can be difficult to navigate if one is experiencing aging-related reductions in visual acuity, peripheral vision, concentration, or reaction speed (Lynott et al., 2009).

Data from both the 2001 and 2009 National Household Travel Surveys indicated mobility rates decline after the age of 65 (Pucher & Renne, 2003; Pucher, Buehler, Merom, & Bauman, 2011), and it seems likely that this decreased mobility is due at least in part to reductions in driving. Compared to older drivers, those who do not drive make 15% fewer trips to life-sustaining destinations (e.g., pharmacies, doctor's offices) and 65% fewer trips to life-enhancing destinations (e.g., movie theaters, religious institutions, friends' houses) (U.S. Government Accountability Office [GAO], 2004). Driving cessation can result in a number of negative consequences, such as decreased physical functioning (J. D. Edwards, Lunsman, Perkins, Rebok, & Roth, 2009), increased depressive symptoms (Marottoli, Mendes de Leon, Glass, & Williams, 1997), and a greater risk of institutionalization (Freeman, Gange, Munoz, & West, 2006), any of which could further reduce mobility. In addition, a study using nationally representative data found that even when controlling for physical and mental health, former drivers decreased their participation in social engagement activities, including employment and volunteering (Curl, Stowe, Cooney, & Proulx, 2014), suggesting that older adults are not typically able to simply replace driving with other forms of mobility.

Few older adults use public transportation as their primary mode of travel; for example, one study reported only 5% of adults age 50 and older regularly use public transportation (Ritter, Straight, & Evans, 2002). According to Rosenbloom and Herbel (2009), only about two thirds of older adults have public transit in their communities, and less than one quarter of rural residents of any age have access to public transportation (Kerschner & Hardin, 2006; Kochera, Straight, & Guterbock, 2005). Even when public transit exists, it is often inadequate for older adults, offering frequent service to office parks and other destinations targeted at commuters, rather than medical complexes, senior centers, and other destinations more relevant to older adults. In focus groups, older adults described public transit as unsafe, unresponsive, and inconvenient (Adler & Rottunda, 2006). This may be particularly true in communities characterized by low-density development, where it may not be feasible to provide fixed-route bus and rail systems because of low ridership and greater travel distances.

Because of these limitations in fixed-route transit systems, some older adults have expressed a preference for alternative transportation services, including door-to-door services such as senior vans and paratransit. While the Americans With Disabilities Act mandates that all public transit agencies provide complementary paratransit services for those who are unable to use fixed-route services due to a disability (Koffman, Raphael, & Weiner, 2004), these services are accompanied by a number of restrictions. For example, they are typically only available in areas already served by public transportation, often require reservations at least 24 hours in advance, frequently involve long and unpredictable wait times, and may involve multiple transfers when individuals need to cross into other service areas (Nelson\Nygaard Consulting Associates, 2002). For older adults who require more assistance, paratransit may not always offer door-through-door (as opposed to door-to-door) service. Paratransit travel is also considerably more expensive than fixed-route services, costing public transit agencies on average $29.28 per one-way trip in 2007 (Rosenbloom & Herbel, 2009). In response to these high costs, transit providers have been following ADA eligibility criteria more strictly in recent years (U.S. GAO, 2004), which an estimated 42% of older adults with a disability do not meet (Rosenbloom, 2009). Senior vans share many of the limitations of paratransit, including requiring advance reservations and transportation provided only within a specific city or county. This has led to the development of private senior transportation services such as SilverRide, as well as traditional taxi services, although high per ride costs make such services unaffordable for many older persons.

Many older adults who do not drive therefore depend on friends, family, and neighbors to meet their mobility needs. Riding as a passenger in an automobile has some advantages over public transit and alternative transportation, including door-to-door service to a wide range of destinations (Burkhardt et al., 2002). Older adults who rely on their social network for rides, however, travel less than any other group (Burkhardt, 2000). Older adults in this mobility group likely have to travel at the convenience of the driver (Burkhardt et al., 2002). While getting rides may offer the opportunity for social contact, older adults may experience feelings of obligation, imposition, and dependency (Ritter et al., 2002). The lack of viable transportation alternatives also can have negative consequences for those providing the rides. For example, in a recent study, 42% of caregivers reported missing work occasionally, and another 13% decided to give up work entirely to provide transportation to an older care recipient (Taylor & Tripodes, 2001).

Characteristics of an Aging-Friendly Housing and Community Environment

As should be clear from the preceding section, many communities in the United States do not have aging-friendly housing and community environments. In this section, based on a synthesis of findings and propositions from the existing literature, we outline aging-friendly characteristics in the areas of housing, community design, and transportation.

Affordable and Accessible Housing Options

A community with aging-friendly housing has multiple residential options that can meet the needs and preferences of older adults with a variety of financial, social, and health resources. This in turn may allow older adults to age well and remain in their existing community if this is what they choose.

Cities and towns that offer primarily single-family homes on large lots are likely only meeting the needs of a segment of their aging population. Even older adults who lived much of their adulthood in a single-family home may downsize for a multitude of reasons, including reduced income postretirement, decreased need for space after children have moved away, or limitations in home maintenance and housekeeping activities due to a disability or aging-related decreases in energy or ability. Constructing more multifamily apartments and condos is one strategy for increasing housing options. Other strategies require little in the way of new construction. For example, cities and towns could allow some single-family homes to be converted into shared housing for several unrelated individuals. Pollak (1994), for example, recommended that cities and towns consider altering zoning laws to make an exception for shared housing for situations when at least one resident is an older adult. A related option is known as share-a-home, in which several older adults live in the same house (or adjacent houses) and hire someone to help with cooking, cleaning, shopping, and potentially personal care (Folts & Muir, 2002).

A final example is an ADU, also called a second unit, elder cottage, or mother-in-law apartment, which is an attached or detached unit located on the same lot as an existing home (Pynoos, Nishita, Cicero, & Caraviello, 2008). An ADU can be in a garage, basement, or other part of the house but must have a private kitchen and bathroom to allow the resident some privacy (Liebig, Koenig, & Pynoos, 2006). Granny flats, for example, which first emerged in Australia, are small, temporary structures that can be placed on a relative's or other person's property (Folts & Muir, 2002). A growing number of cities and towns have adopted an ADU ordinance since the 1980s as they address sprawl and the need for affordable housing (Chapman & Howe, 2001). More recently, cities and towns have recognized that ADUs can help older adults remain in their community; for example, the city of Philadelphia changed its zoning code to allow for ADUs (with some restrictions) following the efforts of Philadelphia Corporation for Aging's (PCA's) Age-Friendly Philadelphia initiative, among others (PCA, 2011b). Older adults who can no longer remain in their own home can relocate to an ADU in their community (Pynoos et al., 2008). Older adults who want to remain in their own home can create an ADU on their own property for supplemental income or to provide housing for a caregiver (Pynoos et al., 2008).

Aging-friendly housing also includes features that allow older adults with a disability to move freely within their own home and access other people's homes. The term *visitability* refers to home features that allow an individual with a disability to safely and comfortably enter and visit a home (Pynoos, Caraviello, & Cicero, 2009). Specifically, visitability involves having an entrance without steps, wide interior doorways, and a bathroom on the first floor (Pynoos et al., 2009). *Universal design* includes features that create a home environment that can be used by people of all abilities (Center for Universal Design, 1997). Universal design goes beyond visitability to include features such as wide hallways that allow wheelchairs to pass through; a kitchen, bathroom, and bedroom on one level; nonslip surfaces on floors and bathtubs; handrails on steps and grab bars in the shower; smooth thresholds between rooms; adequate lighting; and lever door handles, among others (National Association of Home Builders, 2014b). While universal design features make home environments accessible and usable for those with a disability or sensory impairment, they also have positive effects for those of any age, physical stature, or ability. For example, creating smooth thresholds between rooms not only improves accessibility for those using a wheelchair or walker but also reduces a trip hazard for everyone.

As noted, the majority of housing in the United States lacks visitability or universal design features. Improving the accessibility of housing involves incorporating these design features into new housing as well as modifying existing housing. In terms of policy, the American Planning Association (2006) called for improved enforcement of federal accessibility laws (e.g., the Architectural Barriers Act of 1968, Section 504 of the Rehabilitation Act of 1973, the Americans With Disabilities Act of 1990, and the Americans With Disabilities Act Amendments of 2008), as well as the adoption of local codes encouraging or requiring visitability and universal design in new construction. In addition, because older adults report that high costs are a major barrier to making modifications to improve their home's accessibility (Bayer & Harper, 2000), the federal government could increase funding for home modification assistance currently available through various programs from the U.S. Department of Housing and Urban Development, the Department of Energy, the Administration on Aging, the Department of Veterans Affairs, and the Social Security Administration (Smith, Rayer, & Smith, 2008), and local governments could supplement this support using money from the Community Development Block Grant Program (Pynoos et al., 2009).

Achieving greater availability of accessible housing, however, will require the participation and support of constituents outside federal, state, and local governments. Those involved in constructing or remodeling housing need to develop the skills to make homes accessible, as well as incorporate these features even when not required by law. Some contractors, architects, remodelers, and interior designers, for example, are participating in the Certified Aging-in-Place Specialist (CAPS) program, developed by AARP, the National Association of Home Builders and their 50+ Housing Council, and Home Innovation Research Labs. Professionals who have earned a CAPS designation complete required coursework, pass an exam, and are expected to adhere to a code of ethics (National Association of Home Builders, 2014a). The private sector has also been instrumental in the development of ambient-assisted living aids, such as smart homes, wearable and other home sensors, and assistive robotics. These may be helpful for everyone, and particularly important to help older adults with a higher level of physical disability, cognitive impairment, or risk of injury, to live on their own.

Still, the majority of housing in the United States could be considered "Peter Pan" housing, designed only for those who will never grow old (Pynoos et al., 2008). For example, older adults participating in focus groups have expressed a desire for new housing to include a driveway or parking space immediately outside the home, a full bathroom on the main level, a bedroom on the main level, an attached garage or covered parking, wide doorways, entrances without steps, and bathroom aids (AARP PPI, 2005b). Furthermore, most existing housing lacks critical features such as accessible bathrooms, ramps, handrails, and grab bars (Joint Center for Housing Studies of Harvard University, 2014). Only 1% of homes in the United States provide the five universal design features that have been recommended for older adults, specifically a no-step entry, extrawide doorways, lever-style faucets and handles, accessible switches and controls, and single-floor living (Joint Center for Housing Studies of Harvard University, 2014). As noted previously in Chapter Three of this book, the overwhelming majority of older adults want to age in place in their current home (Feldman et al., 2004), and the ability to do so is thought to improve quality of life because of the symbolic meaning derived from one's home and possessions (Gitlin, 2003a). If the market demand for universal design or visitability only includes those who currently have a disability, however, then the percentage of housing with such features will continue to be small, creating barriers to aging in place.

Walkable Neighborhoods With Close Proximity to Goods and Services

An aging-friendly community facilitates walking for both transportation and physical activity. Walkable neighborhoods are typically characterized by roadway infrastructure and design that allow pedestrians to safely navigate the neighborhood, as well as higher density and mixed-use development so that destinations are within reasonable walking distance.

Infrastructure that creates a walkable neighborhood includes sidewalk repair, widening existing sidewalks to improve accessibility for those who use wheelchairs, new pedestrian pathways or sidewalks, improved street lighting (Heath, 2006), and traffic-calming measures such as narrow lanes, raised crosswalks, and speed humps (Retting, Ferguson, & McCartt, 2003). Walkability increases when neighborhoods also have a gridlike street pattern with few cul-de-sacs or dead-end streets (Saelens, Sallis, Black, & Chen, 2003) and are esthetically pleasing to pedestrians (Heath, 2006). For example, recommendations to ensure street connectivity include frequent spacing of intersections (i.e., every 200 to 500 feet), a maximum distance of one-quarter mile to walk the perimeter of a block, a high number of intersections per square mile (i.e., 120 to 240), and a high ratio of four-way to three-way intersections (Plater-Zyberk & Ball, 2012). While sidewalks usually belong to the municipal government, property owners are often charged with daily maintenance, including removing weeds, snow, and ice. Some cities and towns also place responsibility for repairing cracked or uneven sidewalks on homeowners. Typically, other maintenance and construction that contributes to walkability falls under the purview of the local government.

One way municipalities can improve the walkability of their jurisdiction is to follow Complete Streets guidelines, which call for the design of streets not only for automobiles but also for all users (Lynott et al., 2009). Complete Streets advocates have proposed three principles to guide street design: (a) reducing vehicle travel speeds, particularly in areas used by both automobiles and pedestrians; (b) improving the physical layout of streets to make them easier for drivers and pedestrians to navigate; and (c) enhancing visual cues and information for drivers and pedestrians (Lynott et al., 2009). These could include some combination of wide sidewalks, bike lanes, bus lanes, median islands, frequent crosswalks, crossing signal timers for walking at a pace of 1 meter per second (Retting et al., 2003), roundabouts, and narrower car lanes, among others (Smart Growth America, 2014).

Walkability also involves higher density development and the proximity of residential areas to commercial areas, such as grocery stores, pharmacies, and other shops, as well as parks and recreation areas. As noted in this chapter when providing an overview of environmental barriers to mobility, at the end of the 19th century cities developed zoning restrictions to address the spread of infectious diseases that posed significant public health risks (Satariano, 1997). In recent decades, in response to the increasing prevalence of preventable conditions such as obesity, diabetes, and heart disease, public health advocates have called for local governments to alter their zoning practices and offer incentives for mixed-use development to create more physically active environments (Satariano, 1997; Schilling & Linton, 2005). This involves allowing mixed-use neighborhoods with both residential and commercial uses, higher-than-usual densities, a variety of housing types, transit-oriented or pedestrian design, and easy access to destinations (Inam, Levine, & Werbel, 2002). Local governments can offer developers a number of incentives to incorporate mixed-use and alternative development into projects, such as offering local tax subsidies, subsidizing or providing needed infrastructure improvements, allowing higher densities, reducing parking requirements, waiving permit fees, or fast-tracking permit processes.

Walkable neighborhoods can at times pose safety risks, however, because areas with retail establishments and restaurants also tend to attract more vehicle traffic. In Boston, for example, research with baby boomers in late middle age indicated areas characterized by access to goods and services also had more traffic accidents, particularly those involving pedestrians (Lee, Zegras, & Ben-Joseph, 2013). Furthermore, research is inconclusive regarding whether traffic-calming measures reduce pedestrian crashes, and indeed some features, such as crosswalks with markings, may actually lead to more pedestrian-vehicle accidents (Retting et al., 2003) because pedestrians gain a false sense of security that cars will obey traffic laws.

In general, however, while research on walkable or "activity-friendly" (Ramirez et al., 2006) neighborhoods is typically cross sectional and correlational rather than causal (Satariano & McAuley, 2003), empirical work to date suggests multiple benefits of this type of community design. Walkable neighborhoods appear to have positive effects for residents of all ages in terms of physical activity (Aytur, 2007; Heath, 2006; Sallis & Kerr, 2006); obesity (Frank, Andersen, & Schmid, 2004); and walking for transportation or leisure (King et al., 2005; McCormack, Giles-Corti, & Bulsara, 2008). For example, those living in neighborhoods with direct pathways (e.g., continuous sidewalks) to a variety of destinations are more likely to be physically active for at least 30 minutes a day compared to those living in less walkable neighborhoods (Frank, Schmid, Sallis, Chapman, & Saelens, 2005). For older adults specifically, walkable neighborhoods are associated with an increase in physical activity (Berke, Koepsell, Moudon, Hoskins, & Larson, 2007; Sallis & Kerr, 2006) and daily walking to get places (Van Cauwenberg et al., 2013). In addition, neighborhood walkability appears to decrease limitations in IADLs (Freedman, Grafova, Schoeni, & Rogowski, 2008) and depressive symptoms, potentially because walkable neighborhoods facilitate greater access to social networks and community programs and services (Berke, Gottlieb, Moudon, & Larson, 2007).

Transportation Choices

...endly cities and towns provide residents with a variety of ways to travel ...ound their community. They offer supports and infrastructure to help older drivers safely operate their own vehicle for as long as they choose, as well as provide alternative transportation options for those who do not drive.

Similar to other age groups, in recent decades older adults have become more reliant on the automobile to meet their travel needs (Rosenbloom, 2004). While driving rates decline as people age, and drop substantially after the age of 85 (Ritter et al., 2002), older adults on average take 90% of their trips by car, the majority of the time as the driver (Pucher & Renne, 2003). Many older adults could safely continue to drive if federal, state, and local governments changed roadway design and infrastructure to better meet their needs. The Federal Highway Administration's *Highway Design Handbook for Older Drivers and Pedestrians* (2001) provides recommendations for intersections, highway interchanges, passing zones, road curvature, construction zones, and railroad crossings. Specific changes that have been recommended include improving the visibility of road markings (e.g., using reflectorized paint), increasing the size of letters on street signs, and simplifying intersections (Herbel, Rosenbloom, Stutts, & Welch, 2006; Rudinger, Donaghy, & Poppelreuter, 2004; Wachs, 2001). Making left-hand turns when having to yield to oncoming traffic, for example, is particularly difficult for older adults, who may not be able to accurately assess the position and speed of oncoming traffic (Jovanis, 2003; Staplin, Harkey, Lococo, & Tarawneh, 1997). Infrastructure improvements that would enhance older driver safety at such intersections include providing unrestricted sight distance for oncoming traffic, adding a protected left-hand turn phase with a green arrow, and constructing an offset turn lane (Federal Highway Administration, 2001; Jovanis, 2003; Lynott et al., 2009).

While older adults often change or give up their driving habits when they experience health impairments, some continue to drive in spite of risks to the safety of themselves or others. For example, cognitive limitations can negatively affect the ability to drive, yet research suggests that more than one third of older adults with cognitive impairments still drive their own vehicle (B. Freund & Szinovacz, 2002). Through focus groups with older adults, Adler and Rottunda (2006) identified three types of older adults with differing approaches typically taken when their health and functioning affect their ability to drive: (a) proactives, who make the decision on their own; (b) reluctant accepters, who slowly realize they need to give up their car keys at the urging of their family; and (c) resisters, who are unrealistic about their driving skills and only stop driving when forced to by others.

Increasing older driver education and assessment programs is one way to increase the safety of older drivers as well as other people on the road. Driver education could include the classroom training provided through AARP's 55

Alive Mature Driver Program and the National Safety Council's Coaching the Mature Driver (Stutts, 2003), as well as road training. To date, however, to our knowledge the effectiveness of these programs has not been demonstrated. Older adults themselves have recommended driver assessment with mandated road tests after a certain age, vision exams, a written exam on traffic laws, and an evaluation of flexibility, cognitive functioning, and reflexes (Adler & Rottunda, 2006). For example, in British Columbia, Canada, drivers age 80 and older are required to complete a medical assessment of their driving abilities and may have their licenses revoked or driving restricted (e.g., to specific areas, speed zones, times of day) (Nasvadi & Wister, 2009). This program has resulted in a reduction in vehicle crashes in general as well as at-fault crashes by older drivers (Nasvadi & Wister, 2009).

Another change local governments might consider is allowing individuals to operate slower-moving vehicles (i.e., vehicles that typically can reach a maximum speed of 20–25 miles per hour), such as electric wheelchairs or golf carts, on roads. Some cities have passed ordinances that would permit these slower-moving vehicles on roadways, albeit with restrictions (e.g., only on streets with speed limits at or below 30 miles per hour) (Bryce, 2006). Blooming Prairie, Minnesota, for example, passed an ordinance allowing motorized golf carts on streets if they have a permit, proof of insurance, and a slow-moving vehicle sign (Stewart, 2014). This strategy may be particularly beneficial in areas with retirement communities.

Focusing solely on personal vehicle travel, however, neglects the transportation needs of a significant portion of the older adult population. Even with older driving rates increasing, an estimated half million individuals over the age of 70 stop driving each year, with men and women living an average of 6 and 10 years, respectively, beyond their ability to drive (Foley, Heimovitz, Guralnik, & Brock, 2002). In light of research indicating that those who receive rides from family and friends travel less than those who use any other form of transportation (Burkhardt, 2000), relying on elders' informal support networks is an inadequate solution to ensuring community mobility in later life.

Communities that are aging friendly should also provide alternatives to vehicle travel. One option is fixed-route public transit, which may not only improve community mobility for older adults who are unable to drive because of a disability or limited finances but also has potential benefits for health and functioning across the life course. One study reported that a switch from driving to public transit can increase physical activity, reduce obesity, and decrease medical expenses for persons of all ages (R. D. Edwards, 2008). Communities with public transit also are required by the ADA to offer access to paratransit for persons unable to use public transit because of a disability. Cities and towns without public transit, however, including many exurban and rural areas, do not have to offer paratransit (Baily, 2004).

Supplemental transportation systems include community- or volunteer-based services for those whose mobility needs are not being met by existing public transportation and paratransit services (Nelson\Nygaard Consulting Associates, 2002). Senior vans or shuttles provided by local governments or nonprofit organizations, for example, offer an alternative to personal auto travel. Taxis (and now ride-share programs such as Uber and Lyft) can also improve community access for older adults. While older adults report limitations using taxis, including high costs, difficulty getting in and out of the vehicle, and not feeling safe (Kendig & Stacey, 1997), research suggested that 90% of the trips taken by individuals who are unable to use fixed-route buses could be made by taxis. Volunteer transportation programs also can play an important role. The Independent Transportation Network, for example, provides local affiliates with software to help them more efficiently match volunteer drivers with older adults and individuals with disabilities who need help with transportation. Finally, mobility management programs familiar with the entire range of fixed-route, paratransit, demand-responsive, and volunteer transportation services available in the area could help older adults to access the optimal service for their mobility needs (Sterns, Antenucci, Nelson, & Glasgow, 2003).

Transportation options vary widely among communities (Eby, Molnar, & Kartje, 2008), and the optimal mix of different forms of transportation likely also varies. The Beverly Foundation's (2010) 5 A's of Senior-Friendly Transportation offers a framework to evaluate whether a community's transportation options, including public transit, paratransit, supplemental transportation services, and other public and private services, meet the needs of older residents. First, transportation should be *available* in convenient locations with 24-hour service to a variety of destinations. Existing transportation, however, is often insufficient, and even older adults living in urban areas with public transit often view their options, especially buses, as too distant to walk to and with inconsistent schedules (Hensher & Reyes, 2000). Second, transportation options should be *acceptable* to older adults so that they feel safe and comfortable. This may include adding bus and train stop amenities, such as benches and protective covering from the weather or training drivers to be sensitive to and aware of the needs of older adults (Burkhardt et al., 2002; U.S. GAO, 2004). Third, transit services should be *accessible*. Some fixed-route systems, for example, offer training programs to help older adults develop the knowledge necessary to navigate the system, as well as low-floor buses and other vehicle modifications to promote ridership by older adults and persons with a disability. There is some evidence that accessibility features can increase ridership, as the introduction of low-floor buses in Britain led to a 10% increase in the number of people taking public transit (Suen & Sen, 2004). Fourth, the system should be *adaptable* to the needs of older adults, soliciting their feedback in the design and provision of services and offering alternative transportation options, such as door-through-door service and multiple-stop trips, for those unable to use fixed-route transit. Finally, public transit should be *afford* offering discounted or free fixed-route transportation to older adults (e.g., ϲ the 50% discount during off-peak hours required by federal law (Koffmar. ᴄ. ᴀ.., 2004) and finding other resources, including volunteers, to provide supplemental transportation services. As Kerschner and Hardin (2006) noted, "providing good transportation for the public does not necessarily result in good transportation for seniors, but improving transportation for seniors will improve transportation for everyone" (p. 5), suggesting that following these recommendations likely will also help meet the mobility needs of residents of all ages.

Benefits and Challenges of Aging-Friendly Housing and Community Environments

Throughout this chapter, we have cited research indicating that aging-friendly housing and community environments likely result in positive outcomes for older adults. Indeed, reviews of published studies in the areas of housing, community design, and transportation have concluded that in general the empirical evidence supports such environmental modifications. For example, authors conducting a systematic review found support for a link between accessible home environments and improved disability-related outcomes, such as independence in activities of daily living (Wahl, Fange, Oswald, Gitlin, & Iwarsson, 2009). A review of articles published between 1990 and 2010 concluded that neighborhoods with pedestrian-friendly streets and traffic conditions, close access to stores and recreational areas, and frequent intersections promoted walking in older adults (Rosso, Auchincloss, & Michael, 2011). Furthermore, a systematic review of peer-reviewed articles from 1985 to 2013 found evidence of physical health, mental health, and physical activity benefits associated with a number of the characteristics described in this chapter, including walkable neighborhoods with a variety of nearby destinations, accessible housing, and transportation options (Annear et al., 2014).

Aging-friendly characteristics in the areas of housing, community design, and transportation also are thought to have numerous other benefits. For example, many aspects of aging-friendly physical environments reflect principles promoted of the New Urbanism movement within urban planning. Building on the ideas Jane Jacobs put forth in *The Death and Life of Great American Cities* (1961), New Urbanism calls for the replacement of restrictive zoning practices and community design decisions that isolate community residents from one another. New Urbanism is essentially a reaction to many of the barriers to aging-friendly communities we described in this chapter, including neighborhoods that permit only single-family homes and community design and infrastructure that promote automobile travel (Ellis, 2002). Elements of New Urbanism of particular relevance to aging-friendly communities include pedestrian- and transit-oriented design, a diverse mix of housing types, street connectivity, neighborhood goods and services, public spaces that encourage social interaction, and respect for existing residents (Plater-Zyberk & Ball, 2012).

Communitywide changes such as these also can potentially address other concerns about the environment (e.g., climate change, overdevelopment of green space), finances (e.g., rising gasoline costs), and health (e.g., consequences of a lack of physical activity) (Dunham-Jones & Williamson, 2012). For example, reviews by the Transportation Research Board and the Task Force for Community Preventive Services both reported a consistent relationship between land use patterns (e.g., mixed-use development, residential density, and street connectivity) and physical activity for persons of all ages (Sallis & Kerr, 2006). Furthermore, as noted in the section on affordable and accessible housing options, the increasing number of local governments permitting ADUs since the 1980s is not only in response to the growing aging population but also an effort to increase the supply of affordable housing and reduce sprawl (Chapman & Howe, 2001).

Despite the apparent benefits of aging-friendly housing and community environments, efforts to promote aging-friendly changes face a number of challenges. The first challenge relates to the adequacy of existing evidence regarding the actual impacts on elder health, well-being, and the ability to age in place. Currently, we cannot confidently attribute health and well-being outcomes to a community's physical infrastructure. That is, because few existing studies employ longitudinal or randomized control designs, it is difficult to make causal inferences about these environmental modifications. Instead, it may be that certain community environments attract those who are already healthier or more socially engaged. For example, those who live in walkable neighborhoods that allow residents to get to shops and restaurants by foot may be predisposed to be more physically active than those who do not. Furthermore, the pathway from the built environment to health outcomes likely involves reciprocal causation and feedback loops (Diez Roux, 2004). As discussed in Chapter 3, ecological models of aging call attention to the interaction between older persons and their environment. Older adults not only react to their environments but also can change their environments. Developments in measurement and analytical methods will advance our understanding of the complex processes and outcomes of these person–environment interactions, but research to date is limited by methodological shortcomings.

A second challenge emerges from questions about people's actual desire to live in homes and neighborhoods that are aging friendly. For example, a common criticism of New Urbanism is that it ignores the reality of many people's preferences for the privacy and spatial separation afforded by suburban and rural neighborhoods (Ellis, 2002). We noted previously the small market for certain accessible housing features. A survey of housing developers revealed there is a growing market for neighborhoods with mixed-use development, pedestrian-oriented design, alternative transportation options, and high-density housing; however, such features still appeal to only a minority of people, at least in the United States (Inam et al., 2002). Some residents continue to resist aging-friendly changes to their neighborhood, expressing NIMBY ("not in my backyard") and BANANA ("build absolutely nothing anywhere near anything") views (Plater-Zyberk & Ball, 2012). Across the country there are numerous examples of community residents and neighborhood associations delaying, preventing, or dramatically shrinking the size of mixed-use and multifamily developments because of concerns about traffic congestion and noise. Furthermore, some residents may fight against allowing these different forms of housing, as well as the construction of senior housing, because of ageism and prejudice against those from different racial, ethnic, and socioeconomic backgrounds than themselves. It seems likely that regardless of whether proposed environmental modifications are labeled "aging friendly" or "New Urbanist," they will be opposed by a segment of the population.

A third challenge is the need to tailor housing and community environment changes to the unique needs of each community. The goal of these aging-friendly housing and community environment characteristics is to minimize the barriers to mobility and access in private and public spaces that can occur with age and disability. However, there are multiple pathways to aging friendliness, and the feasibility and desirability of each characteristic will vary. As Ellis (2002) noted, "Community planning processes must balance respect for the past with realistic assessments of what is possible in the future" (p. 267).

Any strategies to improve a community's aging friendliness must therefore consider both the existing infrastructure and new development. For example, because many existing suburban developments were designed with car travel in mind, they often do not include sidewalks. Adding wide sidewalks with benches, trees, and adequate lighting may encourage residents of all ages to walk around their neighborhood. Rather than building high-rise apartment or condo buildings, allowing ADUs in neighborhoods currently zoned only for single-family use could increase neighborhood density (Plater-Zyberk & Ball, 2012). In addition, spot zoning (i.e., allowing for an exemption from current zoning law) could allow for a corner store or restaurant to provide closer proximity to goods and amenities. According to Ellis (2002), 95% of all new building in the United States is currently taking place in suburban areas, which offers many opportunities for more dramatic changes to housing and community environments. To facilitate neighborhood social interaction, new developments could place garages in the back of houses and bring houses with front porches closer to the street. Higher density housing could also be constructed near light rail stops. Without such high-density development, it is not financially feasible for communities to invest in public transportation.

Promising Initiatives

In Part III of this book, we provide in-depth descriptions of a variety of aging-friendly community change initiatives, many of which address changes in the physical environment. In this chapter, we want to highlight a few promising examples of local efforts to make physical environments and transportation systems more aging friendly.

One example is the Community Aging in Place: Advancing Better Living for Elders (CAPABLE) program by Johns Hopkins University, which focuses on addressing environmental contributors to disability for low-income African American elders living in Baltimore, Maryland. This intervention includes home visits by an occupational therapist, registered nurse, and handyman team for older adults with limitations in personal activities or IADLs. The handyman team is paid by a local AmeriCorps site called Civic Works. CAPABLE reflects the propositions of the disablement process by recognizing that disability can be caused or exacerbated by conditions of the built environment. In a recent randomized control trial, older adults in the intervention group received an average of $1,300 in home repairs and modifications (e.g., fixing shaky stair banisters, lowering appliances to a reachable height) and assistive devices (e.g., installing safety equipment in the bathroom) (Szanton et al., 2011). Over the 6-month study period, those receiving the intervention showed reductions in their perceived fall risk and improvements in their activities of daily living and IADL functioning and quality of life (Szanton et al., 2011).

Another promising example is the work to make parks more aging-friendly by PCA's Age-Friendly Philadelphia initiative (described further in Chapter 9). The impetus for this effort came from a 2011 survey of the city of Philadelphia, which indicated that while the overwhelming majority of older adults lived near a park or recreation area, nearly three quarters had not used these facilities in the past year (K. Clark, 2014). After partnering with the Fairmount Park Conservancy, PCA created a workgroup with members of the city's parks department and nonprofit aging services providers to develop an Age-Friendly Parks Checklist to identify features that would increase park use by older residents (Glicksman, Clark, Kleban, Ring, & Hoffman, 2014). Such features include firm wheelchair-accessible paths, railings for stairways, and shaded areas (K. Clark & Glicksman, 2012). The checklist was then evaluated with focus groups of older adults selected from local senior centers and senior housing facilities (K. Clark & Glicksman, 2012). Moving forward, the checklist will help PCA identify Signature Age-Friendly Parks that already include many aging-friendly features, as well as inform future park improvement projects (K. Clark & Glicksman, 2012). PCA is optimistic that many parks will become more aging friendly because the Parks Department is already considering some of the suggested changes and others benefit younger parks users as well by, for example, increasing park safety (Glicksman et al., 2014).

A third example is that of the Atlanta Regional Commission's (ARC's) Lifelong Communities initiative (described in more detail in Chapter 9), which hosted a charrette in 2009 to guide their efforts to make the region's housing, transportation, and community design align with the needs of the older adult population. A *charrette* is a collaborative, intense planning-and-design process. In this case, ARC partnered with Duany Plater-Zyberk & Company, an architectural and urban-planning firm, to hold a 9-day charrette with local and national experts in areas such as accessibility, planning, design, transportation, health care, and aging. The charrette was guided by the three policy goals of Lifelong Communities: (a) promote housing and transportation options; (b) encourage healthy lifestyles; and (c) expand information and access. Furthermore, their work followed the principles of New Urbanism. At the end of the charrette, the group had developed master plans for five community sites in the region, prepared model standards and zoning codes, and detailed development principles for the entire region as the aging population increases. For example, they identified street connectivity as a high priority and devised plans to reconnect streets that have been cut off from each other by suburban development and cul-de-sacs. They recommended the inclusion of more mixed-use zoning areas and the provision of more special use permits for congregate forms of housing (e.g., shared housing). They also called for an end to setback requirements for housing so that houses can be located closer to the sidewalk and street. Transportation was also viewed as a critical need for the region, and charrette participants proposed extending the mobility network to include a shuttle system to provide greater access to public transit. Finally, they called for the development and maintenance of parks and green spaces to provide social gathering areas in communities throughout the region. As the ARC's Lifelong Communities initiative continues its work, it prioritizes incremental changes whenever possible to help existing communities become more aging friendly.

Conclusion

Historical developments in many communities across the United States, planned and unplanned, intentional as well as unintentional, have created a physical infrastructure that can prevent older adults from easily getting around their neighborhoods. In addition, it appears that many communities' physical environments have negative implications for residents of all ages. Neighborhoods dominated by single-family homes on large lots may stifle the development of social capital that can promote the health and well-being of residents. Streets designed primarily for cars without well-maintained (or sometimes any) sidewalks may discourage residents from walking, thereby precipitating the onset of disease and disability. Aging-friendly communities, in contrast, provide housing options that can meet the needs of a variety of residents, not only those who are young, healthy, and wealthy. They encourage residents of all generations to be active in their community and provide alternative forms of transportation that are comfortable, convenient, and safe. While there are challenges to developing, implementing, and evaluating these changes to the physical infrastructure, both empirical and anecdotal evidence suggest they can help older adults overcome physical barriers to aging well.

6

Promoting Social Engagement

Introduction

In this chapter, we examine the potential benefits of social engagement, which include two interrelated components: (a) supportive interactions with family members and friends and (b) participation in meaningful social activities. Social engagement is important for individual well-being at any age but assumes increased importance in later life, as familiar social roles are lost, activity spaces contract, and future horizons become more limited. As we shall see, older adults who remain socially active are generally happier and healthier than those who do not. Indeed, as Rosow observed nearly 50 years ago, "The most significant problems of older people . . . are intrinsically social. The basic issue is that of their social integration" (Rosow, 1974, p. 8).

The chapter begins with a review of the importance of social contact and the ways in which it is affected by aging, before turning to social participation and the factors affecting older adults' participation in meaningful social roles. We then examine the ways in which social engagement is affected by the environments within which older adults live, concluding with an analysis of innovative programs and policies that have been developed to overcome environmental barriers and foster social engagement in later life.

Types of Social Engagement

Social engagement combines social contact (e.g., informal social networks, personal relationships, social support) and social participation (e.g., formal roles and activities, activity participation, volunteer roles, religious participation). Each of these has both objective and subjective components. Objective components include the actual amounts and types of social involvement, including the frequency of social interaction and types of social activities. Subjective components include the reflective meanings attached to social involvement, including sense of belonging, identification, emotional connections to persons or places, and sense of purpose.

Social Contact

Impact of Aging on Social Contact

As discussed in Chapter 2, emotionally meaningful social interactions assume increasing importance with age (Carstensen et al., 1999). Older adults consider "staying connected with friends and family" to be the most important factor contributing to a high quality of life, even more important than financial well-being, at least according to 4,000 U.S. seniors who responded to the United States of Aging Survey in 2013, conducted by the National Council on Aging (NCOA), United Healthcare, and *USA Today* (2013).

Social contact, however, generally tends to decrease with age. Older people have smaller social networks than do younger people (Marcum, 2013), and they tend to spend more time alone (Cornwell, 2011). Discretionary social contacts are especially likely to decrease with age, with social networks becoming less varied and increasingly focusing on family contacts (Ertel, Glymour, & Berkman, 2009; Shaw, Krause, Liang, & Bennett, 2007). Reduced contact with friends and acquaintances is mostly due to the combined impact of personal physical and cognitive limitations, the loss of friends through illness or death, and the loss of employment-based social relationships due to retirement (Hess & Ennis, 2012).

Social and environmental factors play a part as well, including access barriers such as inadequate transportation systems and supports, inaccessible buildings, and mobility systems that privilege medical visits over social activities. Social marginalization of older adults also is a result of ageist attitudes that decrease informal intergenerational contact, reinforce social segregation of older community members, and interfere with development of a shared sense of community (Harewood, Pound, & Ebrahim, 2000). The physical and social separation among age groups results from a combination of geographic mobility, locating work away from residences, and the tendency of retirees to feel unwelcome in a "work world" populated by persons of "working age."

As a result of these forces, social networks in later life can shrink to the point that older adults become socially isolated. Social isolation can reflect an objective separation from a social network (e.g., living in a rural area, living alone) or more subjective feelings of loneliness (Golden et al., 2009). The likelihood of living alone, for example, increases dramatically with age, especially among older women. About 28% (12 million) of all noninstitutionalized older persons live alone, up from 10% in 1945 and 20% in 1960 (U.S. Census Bureau, 2014). Older women are nearly twice as likely to live alone as are older men. The proportion living alone increases with advanced age; among women aged 75 and over, for example, almost half live alone. The Census Bureau projects dramatic increases in the numbers of older adults living alone in the coming decades, especially women, racial minorities, unmarried older adults, and those with no living children.

Already, in three states (North Dakota, South Dakota, Nebraska), nearly one of three older persons lives alone (U.S. Census Bureau, 2014).

Social isolation can contribute to depressive symptoms and feelings of hopelessness (Golden et al., 2009), as well as increased vulnerability to illness and death (Patterson & Veenstra, 2010; Tomaka, Thompson, & Palacios, 2006). Between 15% and 45% of older adults report at least occasional feelings of loneliness (Golden et al., 2009; Lauder, Sharkey, & Mummery, 2004). These percentages increase among the oldest old, with approximately 50% of those ages 80 and over reporting they often felt lonely (Pinquart & Sorensen, 2001). One notable exception to these general trends is research suggesting that the oldest old experience an increase in the amount of contact with their social network (Cornwell, Laumann, & Schumm, 2008) and the number of family members in their network (van Tilburg, 1998), perhaps reflecting an increase in assistance from relatives.

The Benefits of Social Contact

Age-related declines in social contact are of particular concern in light of the benefits of strong social relationships, especially in later life. Social relationships promote personal well-being in a variety of ways. As we age, social relationships provide a sense of belonging and connection and support a positive sense of self (N. L. Stevens & van Tilburg, 2000). As Bassuk and colleagues noted, "Commitment to family and friends may be an elderly person's raison d'etre, providing a sense of purpose and meaning to life" (Bassuk, Glass, & Berkman, 1999, p. 171). Social relationships also provide a basis for social and emotional support to help cope with the challenges of later life. Social support can help to buffer the threat to psychological well-being posed by major role-identity losses in later life (e.g., partner, employment, or parental). Among older widows and widowers, for example, peer support can play a particularly important role in helping cope with the potentially negative psychological repercussions of major life disruption (Greenfield & Marks, 2004).

Contact with friends is especially beneficial in later life and tends to become more important and more rewarding with age. The same cannot necessarily be said about relationships with family members. While family relationships are determined by factors over which one has relatively little control, friendship relations are basically voluntary associations with persons who share relatively similar characteristics, experiences, and lifestyles (Birditt, Jackey, & Antonucci, 2009; S. Y. Chen & Fu, 2008). Although family members and friends both provide emotional support, family relationships are more likely to focus on instrumental support, while friendships provide companionship, social integration, and reassurance of one's self-worth (Messeri, Silverstein, & Litwak, 1993).

Probably because of this voluntary nature, relationships with friends are more based on reciprocity than family relations (Dupertuis, Aldwin, & Bosse, 2001), but they also require more maintenance effort (Roberts & Dunbar, 2011). This might help to explain the finding that the perceived quality of family relations tends to be lower than friendship relations. For example, in one German study that included a nationally representative survey of more than 2,000 older adults, contact with friends was associated with increases in positive affect and life satisfaction and decreases in negative affect, while contact with family members was associated with not only increased positive affect but also increased negative affect (Huxhold, Miche, & Schüz, 2014). Even more striking, contact with friends was associated with reduced mortality, while contact with family members was not (Maier & Klumb, 2005).

Social contact also has significant health implications. Social integration has been linked to higher overall levels of well-being (Fiori, Smith, & Antonucci, 2007), including better self-rated health, fewer depressive symptoms, a decreased risk of mortality (Antonucci, Fuhrer, & Dartigues, 1997; Uchino, 2004), and increased expectations of being able to remain in one's home or community (Tang & Lee, 2011). There is growing evidence that positive social relationships stimulate the immune system, helping to combat infections, attack tumors, and protect against autoimmune diseases, ultimately contributing to substantial reductions in mortality (Uchino, Holt-Lunstad, Uno, Campo, & Reblin, 2007). In a recent meta-analysis that examined data from 308,849 individuals followed for an average of 7.5 years, people with stronger social relationships had a 50% increased likelihood of survival than those with weaker social relationships. This level of influence is comparable to well-established risk factors for mortality, such as smoking and alcohol consumption, and is greater than the risk associated with physical inactivity or obesity. Furthermore, this finding remained consistent across age, sex, initial health status, length of follow-up, and cause of death, underscoring its generalizability (Holt-Lunstad, Smith, & Layton, 2010).

Social isolation, on the other hand, is a proven risk factor for a variety of deleterious health, social, and psychological outcomes (House, 2001). Socially isolated individuals are more likely to experience heightened cortisol levels, elevated blood pressure, and decreased resistance to disease in later life (Glass, Mendes de Leon, Marottoli, & Berkman, 1999), making them more susceptible to developing heart problems, infections, and other life-threatening illnesses (Steptoe, Shankar, Demakakos, & Wardle, 2013). Moreover, older people without social ties have twice the odds of experiencing cognitive decline compared to those with five to six social ties (Bassuk et al., 1999), experience greater suicidal ideation, and are more likely to end up in a nursing home (Giles, Glonek, Luszcz, & Andrews, 2007). For these reasons, older adults with fewer social contacts are significantly more likely to decline or to die than those with more extensive ties, even after adjusting for potentially relevant sociodemographic and health characteristics such as age, occupational status, and preexisting illness (Bassuk et al., 1999; Lyyra & Heikkinen, 2006).

Interventions designed to enhance natural social support networks have met with mixed success. Many studies have involved professional efforts to activate support for persons dealing with specific health-related problems, such as heart conditions, stroke, or eating disorders. While some of these interventions have produced a modest increase in perceived social support, they typically have not resulted in measurable improvements in health or well-being (Ertel et al., 2009). Support groups and other group-oriented programs, on the other hand, have shown greater success than interventions aimed specifically at increasing contact within individuals' social networks. Most successful are programs that engage older adults in productive activity rather than just in establishing social relationships for their own sake (Ertel et al., 2009).

Social Participation

Impact of Aging on Social Participation

Social participation generally follows a curvilinear path, increasing until age 65 or 70, and then decreasing thereafter (Cornwell et al., 2008; Verbrugge, Gruber-Baldini, & Fozard, 1996). Volunteer participation, for example, generally seems to decline after the age of 75, although some older adults remain involved in socially productive activities until a very old age (van Groenou & van Tilburg, 2012). While some of this decline can be attributed to declines in health and functioning, the lack of available opportunities, shrinking social networks, family care responsibilities, access barriers, and deleterious public attitudes can each undermine opportunities for participation in meaningful social roles (van Groenou & van Tilburg, 2012; J. Wilson, 2000). Because volunteering and other social activities typically take place away from one's home, participants may need to expend substantial energy to participate, especially given the presence of unsupportive or inaccessible built environments. Not surprisingly, social participation is greatest when opportunities are more accessible and more widely available (Valdemarsson, Jernryd, & Iwarsson, 2005).

In the United States, social exclusion of older persons results not only from decreased access to valued roles and opportunities but also from the ageist norms that define those roles as valuable. Norms regarding what is desirable, worth doing, and worth having reflect the values and priorities of young and middle-aged adults (e.g., employment), rather than those in a later stage of the life course (Scharf, Phillipson, Kingston, & Smith, 2001). In the face of potential obstacles, psychological resources, such as confidence, optimism, and resiliency, are strong predictors of social engagement (Matz-Costa, 2011; Xanthopoulou, Bakker, Demerouti, & Schaufeli et al., 2007).

A number of studies suggest that participation in productive social roles has increased in recent years among older adults (Maier & Klumb, 2005), apparently due in part to increased education, better overall health, an upward trend in network size among the young-old, and possibly the increased need for low-cost human resources in the face of declining public support for community social services (van Groenou & van Tilburg, 2012). For example, after declining dramatically during the last half of the 20th century, labor force participation rates increased 25% for older men and 45% for older women during the first decade of the 21st century. By contrast, labor force participation rates declined for younger men and women during this same period. Labor force participation rates are highest among individuals with higher education levels and among women who are divorced or separated, two groups that have been expanding dramatically in recent years (U.S. Census Bureau, 2014).

The Benefits of Social Participation

Participation in meaningful social roles that benefit oneself or one's community, including paid or unpaid work as well as leisure activities, is especially beneficial for older adults (Glass, Mendes de Leon, Bassuk, & Berkman, 2006). The meanings given to social activities are generally considered to be more important for personal well-being than is the actual amount or type of activity (e.g., Gallimore, Goldenberg, & Weisner, 1993), although some studies have found strong evidence of direct effects of the activities themselves regardless of their subjective characteristics (e.g., House, Robbins, & Metzner, 1982; Lubben, 1988).

Social activities can help to promote social connections by providing a context for establishing and strengthening meaningful interpersonal bonds (G. D. Cohen et al., 2006) in spite of the potential deleterious social and psychological impacts of functional impairment, widowhood, and shrinking social support networks. Social participation also enhances access to positive social norms, tangible and intangible resources, and social support. There may be a reciprocal relationship between social participation, social contact, and social support, with each enhancing the likelihood and potential benefit of the other. Older adults who have friends who participate regularly in physical activity, for example, are more likely to participate in physical activity themselves (Booth, Owen, Bauman, Clavisi, & Leslie, 2000).

There is extensive evidence regarding the benefits of social participation for elders' health and well-being. Older adults who participate in paid employment, volunteering, informal social assistance, or community clubs and organizations consistently report better health than do those who do not participate in such activities (Hinterlong, 2006; Van Willigen, 2000; F. W. Young & Glasgow, 1998). Membership in church groups seems to be particularly beneficial and has consistently been found to contribute to lower mortality in a variety of populations, even after controlling for age, sex, race, and health status (e.g., House et al., 1982: T. E. Seeman, Kaplan, Knudsen, Cohen, & Guralnik, 1987). Even participating in a choral group can result in better overall health, fewer falls, fewer doctor visits, better morale, less loneliness, and greater activity levels than experienced by non-participants, largely because of the opportunities afforded for meaningful social engagement and mastery experiences (G. D. Cohen et al., 2006).

Active involvement seems to be key. Activities that require some degree of physical activity (e.g., social gatherings, church attendance, sporting events) are associated with reduced mortality, whereas more passive activities (e.g., watching television) are associated with increased risk of death (House et al., 1982). Physical stimulation appears to affect health and well-being primarily through physiological pathways, whereas social engagement affects well-being primarily through psychological pathways. Moreover, the health benefits of physical and social stimulation are approximately equivalent, suggesting the importance of social activities in later life, even among individuals with restricted physical capacity (Glass et al., 1999). Interestingly, persons who otherwise are the least physically active appear to enjoy the greatest mortality benefits of social and productive activity (Glass et al., 1999).

Social participation also can contribute to longer life. Older adults who participate in social or productive activities, including community groups, paid employment, or unpaid community work, tend to experience reduced mortality rates, and most of these associations continue to hold even after controlling for the effects of age, gender, disease, and physical and sensory impairment. Participation in social activities (e.g., visiting friends, group leisure-time pursuits) contributes to reduced mortality, likely through a combination of social involvement, personal fulfillment, physical and cognitive stimulation, and perceived mastery (Maier & Klumb, 2005). Mortality benefits seem to be greatest when activities explicitly involve other people (Walter-Ginzburg, Blumstein, Chetrit, & Modan, 2002).

The health benefits of social participation seem universal and generally persist even after controlling for potential mitigating factors such as socioeconomic and demographic characteristics, years of retirement, level of medical care use, and religious participation (Everard, Lach, Fisher, & Baum, 2000; Morrow-Howell, Hinterlong, Rozario, & Tang, 2003; F. W. Young & Glasgow, 1998). Furthermore, the health benefits of social participation seem to increase with age, with one study finding that the effect of volunteering on perceived health was more than 2.5 times greater for elderly persons than for young adults (Oman, Thoresen, & McMahon, 1999). Studies of social engagement across the life cycle have found that, after adjusting for a variety of risk factors, social participation affects mortality primarily for people ages 70 or older rather than for younger age groups (e.g., T. E. Seeman et al., 1987). Participation in structured community-based social activities may have particular benefits for some of the most socially isolated individuals. For example, elderly women who live alone participate in and benefit from senior centers more than do those who live with a spouse or partner (Aday, Kehoe, & Farney, 2006).

Social participation also has benefits for elders' cognitive functioning. We know that mental stimulation can help to prevent or delay dementia (Woods et al., 2012), but a 10-year study of persons 75 and older in Sweden also found that frequent participation in social activity (e.g., attending theater, concerts, art exhibitions; traveling; playing card games; participating in social groups or pensioner organizations) or productive activity (e.g., gardening, housekeeping, cooking, working for pay after retirement, doing volunteer work, sewing, knitting, crocheting, weaving) apparently reduces the risk of dementia. Furthermore, the cognitive benefits of social participation were independent of the influences of a variety of potential mitigating factors, including age, sex, education, prior cognitive functioning, presence of other chronic disease and depressive symptoms, or physical functioning (Wang, Karp, Winbald, & Fratiglioni, 2002).

Participation in meaningful social activities also is associated with better mental health, including fewer depressive symptoms (Glass et al., 2006; Mendes de Leon, Glass, & Berkman, 2003). In addition to promoting a greater sense of purpose and self-efficacy, social participation also can increase the availability of social and emotional support for dealing with challenging health-related conditions and other threats to psychological well-being associated with aging (Mendes de Leon et al., 2003).

Participation in formal volunteer activities and other societally valued roles seems to be especially beneficial. Older adults who occupy volunteer roles report significantly greater life satisfaction and psychological well-being than do their nonvolunteering counterparts, including increased life satisfaction and reduced depression symptoms (Kahana, Bhatta, Lovegreen, Kahana, & Midlarsky, 2013; Van Willigen, 2000). Such activities support psychological well-being by providing a structure through which older adults can maintain a sense of competence and self-efficacy, helping to protect against the threat to psychological well-being and sense of purpose that can accompany major role-identity losses (G. D. Cohen et al., 2006; Greenfield & Marks, 2004). Volunteering also has numerous benefits for older adults' physical health and well-being, including better self-rated health, increased physical activity, and improved functional ability (Barron et al., 2009; Kumar, Calvo, Avendano, Sivaramakrishnan, & Berkman, 2012). One study reported that volunteering resulted in a 24% reduction in mortality rates among older adults (Okun, Yeung, & Brown, 2013). The positive effects of volunteering are nearly as great as those associated with not smoking and larger than those associated with exercising four times weekly or attending religious services (Oman et al., 1999). Church-based volunteerism, the most common type of volunteering among older adults, is especially beneficial psychologically; volunteering for a senior citizens group, the second most common type of voluntarism among older adults, appears to be the most beneficial physically (Van Willigen, 2000).

In addition to the social and psychological benefits of social participation, volunteering and other productive forms of social participation also have potential community benefits, providing a mechanism for older community members to contribute to the social capital of their communities through the generative transmission of lifelong experience and wisdom (Morrow-Howell, Hinterlong, & Sherraden, 2001). Taken together, the value of unpaid contributions of older community members has been estimated at $2,698 per person, for a total value of more than $160 billion per year in the United States (R. Johnson & Schaner, 2005). Moreover, having older community members has been shown to have potential evolutionary benefits, enhancing the survival of young children by sharing food and providing child care, termed the *grandmother hypothesis*. In this way, the time and energy contributed by older adults might well be considered a community resource, a "public good," that enhances a community's social capital (Gray, 2009).

Social service organizations benefit substantially from using older volunteers, including cost savings to the organization through reduced workload demands on paid staff, increased service quality, greater variety of services provided, improved community relations, and greater public support for organizational programs. Furthermore, older volunteers also may be more knowledgeable about local community resources, social networks, cultural sensibilities, and other factors about which younger paid staff members may be less aware. Some studies have found evidence of improved quality of care associated with using volunteers, and individuals visited by friendly volunteer visitors have been found to experience reduced symptoms of depression compared with controls. In addition, one study by the NCOA found that engaging older adults in professional- and leadership-level volunteer roles resulted in a return on investment (ROI) of nearly 800% (NCOA, 2010b). As Putnam has noted, volunteering for a community organization holds the potential to enhance social capital and in so doing enhance the performance of social institutions and the quality of public life (Romo et al., 2013).

Factors Affecting Social Participation

Level of engagement is an important mediator of the potential impact of social participation. While any amount of social activity is generally associated with better well-being, greater involvement is generally associated with greater benefits for health and life satisfaction, at least up to a point (Adams, Leibbrandt, & Moon, 2011; Morrow-Howell et al., 2003). Health effects are particularly strong for individuals who tend to participate in a greater number of productive activities and spend more time doing those activities (Hinterlong, 2006). Volunteering in two or more organizations, for example, is associated with a 63% increase in perceived health and a 26% increase in life satisfaction, compared with volunteering for only one organization, and a 44% reduction in mortality compared to not volunteering at all (Oman et al., 1999).

Level of participation reflects not only the number of hours but also the extent of psychological investment. The benefits of social participation tend to be greatest when participants have a strong sense of engagement, where the activity is experienced as positive, fulfilling, meaningful, and interesting (Antonucci, 1990), and where it provides a sense of mastery or accomplishment (Herzog, Franks, Markus, & Holmberg, 1998). This may be why volunteerism and other activities considered socially productive have been found to be especially beneficial.

Of course, social participation is not always positive and depends on the nature of the activity and how it is perceived by oneself and others. Too much involvement, particularly in activities that are personally demanding, can be detrimental. There appears to be a curvilinear effect, whereby moderate amounts of involvement are more beneficial than low or overly high levels of activity (Van Willigen, 2000). One extensive study, for example, found that the positive impact of volunteering seems to peak at about 100 hours a year (or approximately 2–3 hours a week), with higher levels of involvement not associated with additional gains (Morrow-Howell et al., 2003). Moreover, particularly demanding activities, such as caring for a seriously disabled or demented family member, can be associated with substantial amounts of physical and psychological distress (Pinquart & Sörensen, 2003). Lack of recognition for one's efforts also can undermine the potential benefits of involvement in social activities (Matz-Costa, Besen, James, & Pitt-Catsouphes, 2014). Finally, it should be noted that people who are in poor health may lack the physical or mental stamina for active participation in available social activities, thereby potentially reinforcing their social isolation and yielding fewer opportunities to obtain the positive effects of social participation. Furthermore, a greater proportion of their social contacts may be illness or care related, providing social support but not necessarily the stimulation and fulfillment of more active and agentic forms of social participation.

Social participation in later life, and the multiple benefits accruing therefrom, therefore requires a supportive social and political environment, where individuals have the opportunity to devote discretionary time to community activities, without the demands being so great that potential salutary effects are wiped out. In societies that support voluntary community organizations and activities, volunteering and other productive social participation tend to flourish (van Groenou & van Tilburg, 2012).

The Community Context of Social Engagement

As noted in Chapter 3, the immediate physical and social environment assumes greater importance as we age, as a result of mobility limitations resulting from physical decrements, reductions in places to go or people to go with as a result of social losses, and environmental barriers that make mobility more challenging.

As a result, one's activity space tends to constrict with age, so that elders may spend more time in their immediate neighborhood, interact more with neighbors and less with more distant social contacts, and rely more on their immediate environments for resources such as grocery shopping, recreation, health care, and social contact (Cornwell et al., 2008). Older persons may be especially dependent on community social networks, in part because of physical and social barriers that limit options for movement and interaction across community boundaries. This is apt to be especially the case for individuals with relatively low physical, social, or economic resources.

Community connections may be somewhat less essential for individuals with high personal capital; indeed, highly resourced individuals may prefer the freedom and individual choice available in communities without firmly established norms and tight social networks. Although the evidence is somewhat mixed, it appears that groups who are more likely to be socially excluded, including older adults and those not participating in the labor force, continue to value neighborhood-based social ties, while those who are younger and employed place more value on social interactions outside their immediate environment (Guest & Wierzbicki, 1999). This suggests that the current cohort of older adults is likely to experience a decline in neighborhood social capital just as they have reached the life stage at which they depend on neighborhood ties the most.

Strong ties to neighbors may be especially important in preventing social isolation and promoting well-being in later life (Cornwell et al., 2008). Having more of a sense of belonging to a neighborhood is associated with better physical and mental health, lower stress, better social support, and greater physical activity (A. F. Young, Russell, & Powers, 2004), as well as increased longevity (Anme et al., 2007). Living in a community with greater social cohesion is associated with better physical and mental health. Environmental conditions can alleviate stress and promote physical and emotional well-being by providing a sense of safety and security, fostering behaviors that protect and promote good health, and enabling meaningful and supportive social opportunities (Stokols, 1992). In his classic study of the 1995 Chicago heat wave, Klinenberg (2002) found that heat-related deaths among older adults were more likely to occur in those neighborhoods with low levels of social interaction, and that even socially isolated elders were able to survive if their immediate social environment was characterized by strong social ties and frequent interactions among neighbors.

Neighborhood connectedness seems to be higher when there is greater stability and similarity among residents. For example, women who live longer at their current address have a greater sense of belonging to their neighborhood (A. F. Young et al., 2004), and older adults living in a neighborhood with a greater number of persons their own age seem to have fewer depressive symptoms (Kubzansky et al., 2005). It seems likely that there is a reciprocal effect of social contact and sense of community. While a positive social environment fosters social interaction and meaningful interpersonal bonds, the resulting sense of social solidarity and availability of social support is likely to foster a stronger sense of trust and security with the community as a whole (De Souza Briggs, Mueller, & Sullivan, 1997).

Environmental conditions can have an impact on health and well-being directly as well as indirectly, including the deleterious effects of environmental stressors such as noise, crime, economic distress, and interpersonal conflict. Older persons are apt to be more affected by such conditions than are younger community residents, in part because of age-related physical vulnerability and in part because of a greater amount of exposure, having lived in the community for a longer period of time (Robert & Li, 2001). Furthermore, safety concerns in physically and economically distressed communities can indirectly affect older residents of all socio-economic status levels by preventing them from traveling outside their homes to obtain needed medical care, get exercise, interact with neighbors or friends, or even buy healthy food (Minkler, 1992; Thompson & Krause, 1998). The deleterious effects of living in neighborhoods that are more economically vulnerable appear to be especially pronounced for older adults who live alone (Thompson & Krause, 1998). Not surprisingly, older women with poorer health who live in lower-income urban neighborhoods are especially likely to report a reduced sense of community connection. However, findings such as these need to be interpreted with caution. Neighborhoods are to varying degrees the product of self-selection, making cause and effect difficult to distinguish. It is not clear, therefore, whether neighborhood factors contribute to health and well-being or whether people in better health move to neighborhoods with more salutary characteristics.

Given the importance of community environments in later life, W. H. Thomas and Blanchard (2009), among others, have advocated that "aging in place" be replaced by "aging in community" as a goal, reflecting a belief that independence and self-reliance are insufficient if not accompanied by opportunities to maintain important interpersonal bonds and participate in meaningful social roles, within the context of a supportive community of reciprocal roles and responsibilities (Bassuk et al., 1999; Scharlach & Lehning, 2013).

Variations in Community Environments

As we saw in Chapter 5, the built environment can facilitate social interaction or can make it more difficult. Environments that are ill designed for normal aging-related changes may create mobility barriers that contribute to reduced intergenerational social contact and social participation. When the physical environments that individuals encounter in their daily activities, their "activity spaces" (Schonfelder & Axhausen 2003), are more physically separate, individuals tend to be more socially isolated, with reduced access to a community's social as well as material resources (Schonfelder & Axhausen 2003).

Individuals who live in close proximity, or are easily able to overcome geographical distance, are able to interact more frequently and develop stronger interpersonal bonds. Neighborhoods that are more densely populated contribute to increased neighborly activities and a stronger sense of community, as does living in apartment buildings with more green spaces where individuals can gather informally. Pedestrian-oriented, mixed-use neighborhoods where important destinations are within walking distance and daily activities can be performed without using a car tend to promote social interaction. Residents are twice as likely to know their neighbors, trust one another, and get together with friends, compared with those who live in less walkable neighborhoods (Leyden, 2003).

The concept of social capital provides a useful framework for understanding the potential ways in which social environments can foster social engagement. Social capital refers to the overall quantity and quality of community social relationships (Rostila, 2011), with a particular focus on mutually beneficial social interactions based on norms of mutual trust and reciprocity, as well as the benefits derived therefrom (Putnam, 2000). The three types of social capital are bonding, bridging, and linking capital: bonding capital refers to connections among similar individuals or groups (e.g., within age groups); bridging capital refers to connections across disparate community groups (e.g., intergenerational ties); linking capital refers to connections between community members and organizations or institutions (e.g., access to formal services) (Szreter & Woolcock, 2004).

Other important neighborhood social climate characteristics that have been identified include the following: social involvement (i.e., the extent of informal social contacts among community residents); social support (i.e., the extent to which community members help one another); social cohesion (i.e., the extent to which community members trust one another, like one another, and get along with one another); social identification (i.e., perceived similarity or sense of commonality, feeling that one belongs); collective efficacy (i.e., shared belief in the ability to work together to solve common problems); as well as residents' overall sense of "community" (i.e., feeling of solidarity, shared history and future) (A. F. Young et al., 2004).

Bridging the physical and social distance between individuals and community activity sites (e.g., through urban redesign or co-located residential and service functions) can enhance older adults' ability to participate in, and benefit from, meaningful social activity. Environments that are challenging, yet provide ample supports and resources, enhance social engagement through opportunities for autonomy, meaningful tasks, social support, and continued growth and learning. Information and communication technologies also can help older adults to overcome age-related barriers, enabling them to participate virtually in community activities from home.

Programs and Policies

Structured Social Programs

Senior centers. Senior centers and similar organizations have traditionally provided a supportive environment offering opportunities for social interaction, as well as participation in meaningful and rewarding social activities. Participation in senior center activities also can promote the development of meaningful social relationships, increased availability of social and emotional support, as well as increased opportunities to provide support to others. Indeed, in one study, 84% of female senior center participants provided transportation or other assistance to other center members at least occasionally (Aday et al., 2006). Senior center participation is associated with improvements in personal and social well-being, including reduced social isolation, increased life satisfaction, and increased confidence in one's ability to live independently (Aday et al., 2006; Pardasani & Thompson, 2012).

Structured social programs such as those provided by senior centers are apt to be especially beneficial for older adults with limited natural support networks, including those who live alone. For example, an examination of female senior center participants in seven states found that women who lived alone spent more time at the center, participated in a greater number of programs, were more likely to get together informally with other center members, were more likely to receive assistance from other center members, and were more likely to report psychological benefits of program participation compared to those living with a spouse (Aday et al., 2006).

Participants in senior centers and similar programs are more likely to be lower-income older adults with minimal disabilities (Pardasani & Thompson, 2012). Participation can become more challenging as individuals develop health problems that limit mobility or evoke negative responses from others. Health problems and transportation limitations are the most frequently cited reasons for reducing or ending senior center participation (Calsyn & Winter, 1999b; Pardasani & Thompson, 2012).

Existing programs have not done a good job of attracting or serving men or younger elderly individuals in their 60s and early 70s. To overcome access barriers and respond more effectively to the changing needs and values of older adults, a number of innovative models are emerging (Pardasani & Thompson, 2012). Some senior centers and other senior activity organizations are incorporating wellness programs, using existing physical and social contexts to promote and reinforce exercise, good nutrition, and other beneficial health behaviors (Aday et al., 2006; Pardasani & Thompson, 2012). Other programs are focusing on fostering productive activities, including skill development, volunteer training, and job placement. Such models tend to be more successful than traditional senior centers at attracting men and individuals under the age of 75.

Mather Café Plus. The Mather "Café Plus" concept, developed in Chicago by Mather LifeWays, a senior living provider, aims to appeal to a wide variety of age groups and interests in a more natural environment than a senior center. Looking from the outside like a typical coffee shop or café, the Café Plus concept provides not only meals and informal social interaction, but also a variety of structured activities, such as lectures, art classes, and fitness programs. In addition, seniors can obtain assistance with retirement planning and individualized information and referral to needed community services (Windhorst, Hollinger-Smith, & Sassen, 2010).

Variations on the Mather Café Plus concept are being developed in a variety of locations, often through collaborations among existing community-based organizations or establishments; by offering services in convenient settings close to where seniors live, such programs may overcome access barriers and make more efficient use of existing resources. In partnership with other community service providers, senior centers are able to offer programs and services at various neighborhood locations, thereby increasing the range of participation opportunities available, reducing duplication and enhancing resource efficiencies, and promoting a more integrated system of community-based care (Pardasani & Thompson, 2012).

Virtual social networks. Communication technologies provide a means for promoting structured social interaction among homebound elders and others who find it difficult to get to a community program like a senior center. The Senior Center Without Walls (http://www.seniorcenterwithoutwalls.org/), created by Episcopal Senior Communities in Oakland, California, uses telephone conference calls to enable older adults to access a variety of social activities, classes, support groups, and peer interaction; no special equipment is needed, and the calls are completely free. For older adults with Internet access, a growing number of websites and mobile apps provide a medium for maintaining existing social connections and developing new ones. Sites designed specifically for older adults, such as AARP's online community (http://community.aarp.org/) and My Boomer Place (www.MyBoomerPlace.com), provide a way to connect with people similar to oneself.

Volunteer Roles

As we have seen, contributory social roles such as volunteering can be especially beneficial to older adults and their communities, enabling older community members to make use of a lifetime of experience-based knowledge and skills to benefit their communities as well as themselves. In 2011, four of five cities and towns in the United States reported offering some kind of volunteer opportunity for older adults, up from 66% five years previously (National Association of Area Agencies on Aging [n4a], 2011), an increase that likely reflects growing appreciation for the potential value of older adult contributions as well as more systematic efforts to facilitate their active participation. In two thirds of these cases, the volunteer program is provided directly by the local government, with about one third of volunteer programs provided by other entities with public financial support. Common volunteer roles include counseling residents at a homeless shelter, driving older patients to medical appointments, tutoring elementary school students, providing literacy training to non-English-speaking neighbors, as well as serving on the board of a local social service agency or on a municipal planning commission (n4a, 2011).

To maximize their effectiveness, volunteer programs need to alleviate potential physical and social barriers that can constrain active participation by older persons. To offset the secondary costs of volunteering, programs frequently offer a small stipend or other financial or social incentives, as well as adequate training, support, and recognition (Fried, Freedman, Endres, & Wasik, 1997). Working together in self-directed teams has been shown to produce the greatest productivity and effectiveness while fostering the development of positive social networks and support (NCOA, 2010b). Other practices that have been found to contribute to high ROI in senior volunteer programs include seeking volunteer input in program development, using current volunteers to train and coach new volunteers, enabling volunteers to develop their own plans for completing work, and training volunteers to be advocates in the community (NCOA, 2010b).

Corporation for National and Community Service. Within the federal government, the Corporation for National and Community Service (CNCS) sponsors a Senior Corps that engages older adults as volunteers in service to their communities through three programs: Foster Grandparents, RSVP, and Senior Companions. These programs use a "Programming for Impact (PFI)" approach for designing volunteer assignments to ensure that priority community needs are addressed while the lives of the volunteers are enriched (CNCS, 2008). CNCS also sponsors a searchable database of local volunteer opportunities throughout the country (www.nationalservice.gov).

The Foster Grandparents program trains older adults to serve as tutors and mentors to young people with special needs. Foster Grandparents work in schools, hospitals, drug treatment centers, juvenile offender facilities, Head Start centers, child care centers, and other community and home-based sites. The RSVP program links the skills of retired volunteers with identified community needs. RSVP volunteers, working through sponsoring nonprofit organizations and public agencies, do whatever their talents and interests enable them to do to meet the needs of their community, such as organizing neighborhood watch programs, tutoring children, teaching English to immigrants, renovating homes, or helping communities recover from natural disasters. Senior Companions links program volunteers with homebound elderly and disabled adults, providing assistance designed to help them maximize their ability to maintain themselves in their own homes.

Senior volunteers typically help with chores such as light housekeeping, paying bills, buying groceries, and finding transportation to medical appointments.

Experience Corps. Volunteering in schools has been found to be a particularly beneficial contributory role for older adults. The Experience Corps program, for example, places older adults in public elementary schools for at least 15 hours a week. In addition to improvements in children's academic achievement, the program has had positive impacts on older volunteers' physical, social, and cognitive functioning (Fried et al., 2004). After 4 to 8 months of volunteering, 63% of Experience Corps participants reported being more physically active, 44% reported feeling stronger, and participants experienced fewer falls than a control group, with gains in intellectual functioning proving to be especially persistent (Parisi et al., 2014). Experience Corps volunteers also reported a significant increase in the number of people they could turn to for help, compared to a decline for those in the control group (Fried et al., 2004). Programs that link older volunteers with younger community members, such as Experience Corps, may be particularly effective at promoting a more positive image of the value that older persons bring to their communities (Fried et al., 1997). In addition, older volunteers who interact with younger people exhibit greater contentment than do those who interact solely with other older adults (Jirovec & Hyduk, 1998).

Intergenerational Programs

Intergenerational programs foster ongoing contact among different age groups through shared activities and tasks, promoting a sense of familiarity and mutual understanding that can help to overcome the effects of age-segregated physical and social environments. In so doing, such efforts also can help to develop meaningful social bonds among individuals of diverse ages and ethnicities, enhancing community social capital and intergroup solidarity (Manheimer, 1998). Intergenerational programs also provide a mechanism for older community members to experience a sense of contribution through the generative transmission of lifelong experience and wisdom. Intergenerational programs were available in fewer than one half of America's cities and towns in 2011 (n4a, 2011), offered by local governments as well as schools, community centers, and other local organizations.

Multigenerational community centers. Community centers have a long tradition in the United States, typically developed and sponsored by local municipalities or by organizations and interest groups as a place where their members can congregate (e.g., YMCA/YWCA, Jewish Community Centers, country clubs). Over time, many of these organizations have developed substantial social and recreational programs for older adults while maintaining programs for other age groups. Some of these organizations have developed structured intergenerational programs intentionally designed to promote contact among age groups, while others foster intergenerational contact informally. In so doing, it seems likely that such programs can help to reduce age segregation, overcome ageist stereotypes, and enable older adults to maintain meaningful interactions with younger generations. In one Japanese study (Anme et al., 2007), older adults who participated actively in their town's intergenerational community center were found to live longer than those who did not.

Communities for All Ages. Communities for All Ages (CFAA) is one of a variety of innovative intergenerational initiatives being developed around the country. CFAA, developed by the Intergenerational Center at Temple University, is an intergenerational community-building model that involves residents of all ages, local organizations, policymakers, funders, and media to foster positive community change around areas of common concern (C. Brown & Henkin, 2014). A key focus is on creating places and programs that promote positive interaction across the life cycle. Examples of specific projects implemented in the 23 community initiatives of CFAA include building multigenerational learning centers; developing leadership academies for residents of all ages; organizing farmers' markets and arts festivals to promote cross-cultural and cross-age understanding; and utilizing schools as centers for lifelong learning. Older adults have served as literacy tutors, youth and family mentors, parent outreach workers, and oral historians. Young people have provided respite services to frail elderly and their families, helped older immigrants and refugees learn English and prepare to become U.S. citizens, and provided chore services to older adults living at home. CFAA initiatives have yielded a variety of salutary outcomes, including increased food security for older adults; increased community engagement of older adults; expanded leadership and educational opportunities for older adults; stronger connections among people of different ages, races, and ethnicities; increased social capital across generations; and increased involvement of the aging network in community change efforts (C. Brown & Henkin, 2014).

Intentional intergenerational communities. One of the most interesting and comprehensive approaches for enhancing meaningful intergenerational involvement involves the creation of planned intergenerational communities, combining many of the aging-friendly physical and social environmental characteristics that we have described previously. These communities not only strive to promote meaningful intergenerational bonds by reducing age-segregated housing and other physical barriers to cross-generational contact, but also provide incentives to facilitate formal involvement of older adults and younger persons in each other's lives.

The Generations of Hope model, for example, involves intentionally designing communities in a manner that promotes intergenerational relationships and social inclusion of all ages, including an Intergenerational Center that supports group-specific as well as age-integrated programming. Older community members assume active volunteer roles, typically providing guidance and support to help other community residents deal with a common challenge (e.g., troubled youth, substance abuse, homelessness). In Hope Meadows, Illinois, for example, elders serve as tutors, mentors, companions, and "honorary grandparents" for children who have behavioral and emotional problems, promoting "family" connections, which in turn will help support the seniors as they age. In exchange for their contributions, older community members receive subsidized housing offering reduced rent, with the entire effort supported by foster care stipends plus government subsidies.

Policy Implications

Finally, it should be noted that social engagement exists within a societal context. Social participation in later life, and the multiple benefits accruing therefrom, requires a supportive social and political environment where individuals have the opportunity to devote discretionary time to community activities, receiving adequate accommodations and compensation to overcome age-related health and social network limitations. When economic pressures and lack of adequate governmental support require that community members give primary attention to informal care and other private roles, community involvement is apt to suffer (Hank & Erlinghagen, 2010). For example, participation in productive social activities such as volunteering tends to be especially high when public policies support community voluntary organizations and provide incentives for a mix of public and private responsibilities (van Groenou & van Tilburg, 2012).

Governmental and nongovernmental support is needed for senior volunteer programs and other civic engagement initiatives. Support also is needed for intentional intergenerational programs and social structures that promote meaningful roles for older adults and provide opportunities for frequent substantive interactions among persons of all ages. There also is a need for federal and state policy and financing incentives for the development of new programs that engage older adults in meaningful social roles and activities, subsidies and technical assistance for programs targeting underserved communities and populations, as well as greater collaboration and information sharing among existing programs (Manheimer, 1998). Finally, government can take the lead in helping to change public attitudes about aging and community involvement by promoting positive altruistic norms, recognizing the unique contributions that older community members make to the well-being of their communities, and demonstrating the potential value to individuals and society of a more socially engaged older population. For example, many local governments that are members of the European Healthy Cities Network have implemented initiatives to enhance older adults' contributions to the social and economic life of these cities, whether by raising public awareness of older people as a resource to society, promoting personal and community empowerment, improving access to the full range of community services, or making physical and social environments more supportive (Green, 2013).

Conclusion

Despite the importance of social engagement in later life, barriers to social contact and social participation increase with age. Age-related social and role changes, coupled with deleterious physical and attitudinal environments, can interfere with social involvement, making it more difficult to meet basic health and psychosocial needs as we become older and undermining the ability to age well.

Social engagement can be promoted through formal and informal social structures that offer meaningful social roles for older adults, promote reciprocal social exchanges that foster interdependence rather than inequity and disempowerment, and provide access to resources that promote personal well-being and fulfillment. Appropriate social participation opportunities can ameliorate the potential impact of age-related social and role changes, contributing to a stronger sense of community connection and involvement. Some local and state initiatives provide innovative models, which may point the way toward greater social engagement of older community members.

Communication technologies appear to hold substantial promise for overcoming barriers to social engagement by enabling interpersonal contact and social participation in the absence of physical proximity. How such technologies will mediate and transform human relationships, and even the meaning of "community," remains to be seen. Is face-to-face contact a necessary prerequisite for meaningful social bonds (what Calhoun called "dense, multiplex networks"), or will virtual communities afford new sources of meaning and connection? And, will older persons find fulfillment in these changing community structures, or will those who already are most vulnerable find themselves cast even further adrift in a world that is even less aging friendly?

7

Optimizing Personal Well-Being

Health and Social Supports

Introduction

This chapter examines existing approaches for promoting well-being in the face of age-related physical changes and social challenges through adequate aging-friendly health and social supports. The concept of aging-friendly communities expands the discussion of policies, programs, and infrastructure that can optimize quality of life in later years beyond traditional health and long-term services and supports (LTSS) to include the built environment (discussed in Chapter 5) and opportunities for social engagement (discussed in Chapter 6). As we describe in this chapter, however, community-based programs that prevent or delay chronic conditions and disabilities, as well as services and supports that meet the needs of disabled elders and their caregivers, are critical components of aging-friendly communities. We begin with an overview of the changes in physical health, cognitive functioning, and access to social supports that can occur as we grow older. We then describe health and social supports currently available in many communities and some of their limitations. As we shall see, health and LTSS in the United States are often characterized by a lack of communication and coordination, significant barriers to access, and substantial variations among states and communities. We discuss some federal and state initiatives that have developed innovative strategies to provide home- and community-based supports for older adults. The chapter concludes with recommendations not only to expand these fairly small programs but also to address other limitations of health and social supports that currently make it difficult for older adults to optimize their well-being.

Changes in Health and Social Supports

Health and Well-Being

Aging is accompanied by a variety of physical and cognitive changes that can threaten personal safety, security, quality of life, and the ability to age well. According to the Federal Interagency Forum on Aging-Related Statistics (2012), slightly more than three quarters of older adults report that their health is good, very good, or excellent, even though a significant proportion have chronic conditions or experience functional limitations. The Centers for Disease Control and Prevention (CDC, 2011) reports that 80% of older adults have at least one chronic condition, and half have at least two chronic conditions. The most common chronic illnesses include hypertension, arthritis, heart disease, cancer, diabetes, chronic bronchitis or emphysema, asthma, and stroke (Federal Interagency Forum on Aging-Related Statistics, 2012). In addition, 16% of older women and 11% of older men have clinically relevant depressive symptoms, as measured by the Center for Epidemiological Studies Depression Scale (CES-D) (Federal Interagency Forum on Aging-Related Statistics, 2012). Functional limitations are often measured by an older adult's ability to perform two different types of tasks. Activities of daily living (ADLs) are essential personal care tasks, including bathing, eating, dressing, toileting, getting in and out of bed, and walking across the room. Instrumental activities of daily living (IADLs) refer to more complex tasks, typically shopping, preparing meals, household chores, managing money, and administering medications. In 2009, of Medicare recipients living in the community, 37% had a functional limitation, including 12% with a limitation in IADLs only, 18% in one or two ADLs, 5% in three or four ADLs, and 3% with a limitation in five or six ADLs (Federal Interagency Forum on Aging-Related Statistics, 2012). We should note, however, that while ADLs and IADLs are often used as indicators of disability by health and long-term care providers, they do not fully capture the range of physical changes and difficulties that may occur in later life.

Limitations in health and physical functioning can lead to a number of negative outcomes for older adults. Chronic illnesses and disabling conditions contribute to negative quality of life, increased health and long-term care spending, and mortality. Depression has been linked with poor nutrition, acute and chronic physical health conditions, and unmet care needs (Alexopoulos, Bruce, Hull, Sirey, & Kakuma, 1999; N. G. Choi & Kimbell, 2009; Lillyman & Land 2007; Locher et al., 2005; McCrea, Shyy, Western, & Stimson, 2005; Paul, Ayis, & Ebrahim, 2006; Victor, Scambler, Bowling, & Bond, 2005). Alzheimer's disease and other forms of dementia contribute to a variety of negative outcomes, including illness and disability. In 2009, Alzheimer's disease was the fifth leading cause of mortality among those ages 65 and older (Federal Interagency Forum on Aging-Related Statistics, 2012). An estimated 15 million Americans provide care for someone with Alzheimer's disease or another form of dementia (Alzheimer's Association, 2014). Because of the long duration of dementia, this group of diseases can place a significant burden on informal and formal sources of care. Furthermore, as we described in Chapter 3, the effects of chronic conditions and limitations in physical functioning also reflect poor person–environment fit. The disablement process, for example, highlights how an inadequate physical infrastructure can exacerbate physical health and cognitive declines and thereby lead to disability.

Declining health and functioning also increases an older adult's risk for falls. An estimated one third of older adults age 65 or older and one half of those ages 80 or older experience a fall each year (Campbell, Borrie, & Spears, 1989). In addition to demographic risk factors (e.g., age, gender, race, and ethnicity), health problems such as physical impairment, cognitive decline, and chronic health conditions increase falls risk among older adults (Kelsey, Procter-Gray, Hannan, & Li, 2012; Kosma, 2014). A number of studies have also found that medications and their associated side effects, as well as cluttered home environments, contribute to falls (Kosma, 2014). According to Campbell (2013), approximately 80% of falls among older adults can be attributed to health and home environment problems. Falls can lead to serious injuries, which in turn can negatively affect elders' physical functioning and independence, and contribute to high health care costs for hospitalizations and other medical services (Halloran, 2013). For example, an estimated 360,000–480,000 older adults are treated for falls-related fractures each year (J. A. Stevens, Corso, Finkelstein, & Miller, 2006). Older adults who suffer a fall may also develop a fear of falling or, in more serious cases, experience postfall anxiety syndrome (CDC, 2010).

A number of studies have examined the ways health and functioning can lead to nursing home placement. For example, diabetes and incontinence have been identified as risk factors for institutionalization (Andel et al., 2007), as has depression (Gaugler, Yu, Krichbaum, & Wyman, 2009). A number of studies have demonstrated that limitations in ADLs increase one's risk for nursing home placement (Banaszak-Holl et al. 2004, Bharucha et al., 2004; S. Chen et al., 2008; Gaugler, Duval, Anderson, & Kane, 2007; McCallum, Simons, Simons, & Friedlander, 2005; Yaffe et al., 2002). Those with dementia have a particularly high risk of being admitted to a nursing facility (Andel et al., 2007; Banaszak-Holl et al. 2004, Bharucha et al., 2004, Yaffe et al., 2002; Gaugler et al., 2007), particularly when their caregivers are experiencing a sense of burden (McCallum et al., 2005).

While estimates of the percentage of older adults with a disability vary depending on the data source, there is general agreement among researchers that this number has decreased in recent years (Manton, Corder, & Stallard, 1997; Schoeni, Freedman, & Wallace, 2001). However, there is concern that future cohorts will need more assistance than today's elderly population. First, data indicate that improvements in disability rates at the end of the twentieth century were due primarily to a drop in limitations in IADLs and not in the basic ADLs that are a more severe indicator of disability (Schoeni et al., 2001). Second, the incidence of functional and cognitive impairment increases with age, and the 85 and older population is expected to more than triple over the next 40 years (U.S. Census Bureau, 2010). Forty-six percent of individuals ages 85 or older have difficulty walking, compared to 18% of those ages 65 to 74 (Schoenborn, Vickerie, & Powell-Griner, 2006). Third, the baby boomers appear to be in poorer health than the current cohort of older adults was at a similar stage of life. Between 1984 and 1996, for example, while disability rates were declining for older adults, they grew by 40% among those in their 40s (Lakdawalla, Bhattacharya, & Goldman, 2004). Between 1997 and 2006, adults ages 40 to 59 reported an increase in lung disease, diabetes, obesity, and cardiovascular disease compared to adults in this age group in the 1980s and early 1990s (Martin et al., 2009), suggesting that improvements in morbidity and disability rates among older adults will reverse in the near future.

Projections of increasing rates of dementia highlight a potential growth in disability and morbidity. Currently, the prevalence of Alzheimer's disease is 11% among all older adults ages 65 or older and 32% among those ages 85 or older (Hebert, Weuve, Scherr, & Evans, 2013). Because Alzheimer's disease is underdiagnosed, the Alzheimer's Association estimates that approximately half of the 5 million older adults with Alzheimer's are unaware that they have it. Furthermore, African Americans are estimated to have twice the risk of dementia compared to Whites (Potter et al., 2009), while Latinos have one and a half times the risk (Gurland et al., 1999). Over the next 10 years, the percentage of Americans with Alzheimer's disease will potentially increase by double digits (Alzheimer's Association, 2014). The annual number of individuals diagnosed with Alzheimer's disease will reach almost 1 million by 2050, and 60% of these new cases will be at least 85 years old (Hebert, Beckett, Scherr, & Evans, 2001).

Social Supports

Older adults also often experience changes in their access to social supports, as the number of individuals in one's social network generally decreases with age (Barnes, Mendes de Leon, Bienias, & Evans, 2005; McPherson, Smith-Lovin, & Brashears, 2006; Schnittker, 2007; Shaw et al., 2007), particularly in terms of network members who are not relatives (Shaw et al., 2007; van Tilburg, 1998). In Chapter 6, we discussed in detail the potential for aging-friendly communities to promote the social inclusion of older adults. We examine social supports here because many long-term services and supports potentially complement or substitute for the instrumental and emotional assistance offered through informal support networks. Indeed, older adults without access to social support are also likely to depend on formal LTSS, including institutional care, to meet their assistance needs (Robison, Shugrue, Fortinsky, & Gruman, 2014).

Social integration has been linked to a decreased risk of mortality, better self-rated health, fewer depressive symptoms (Antonucci et al., 1997; Uchino, 2004), higher levels of well-being (Fiori et al., 2007), and expectations of remaining in one's home or community (Tang & Lee, 2011). Social networks may play a particularly important role in terms of life satisfaction for individuals with disease and disability (Jang, Mortimer, Haley, & Borenstein Graves, 2004). Large, diverse social networks may be beneficial because they offer access to a variety of resources and sources of social support (Antonucci & Akiyama, 1995). Older adults who have friends and family members living nearby are more likely to receive tangible assistance with errands and other activities of daily living (Fiori, Antonucci, & Cortina, 2006), while those without social support are at an increased risk for institutionalization (Gaugler et al., 2007; Litwak & Longino, 1987; McCann et al., 2005). Other positive effects of support include improved mental health, better quality of life, and reduced mortality risk (Andrew, 2005; Borglin, Jakobsson, Edberg, & Hallberg, 2006; Krause, 1997). Even social support that does not involve direct assistance has a positive impact on older adults. Emotional support, for example, is related to a lower risk of mortality (Lyrra & Heikkinen, 2006). As another example, perceived support, reflecting confidence that others are available to offer assistance if needed, may decrease stress, while actually receiving assistance may reduce feelings of self-efficacy, self-reliance, and self-esteem (Krause, 2001).

Existing Community-Based Health and Social Supports

To compensate for inadequate person–environment fit associated with increasing health demands at a time of decreasing social resources, older adults are likely to benefit from a variety of community programs that aim to enhance their ability to address the changes in health and social supports that can emerge in later life. In this section, we briefly summarize the health and social supports typically available to older Americans and their limitations in helping older adults age well in their community.

Health and Wellness

The number and type of health care providers in a community, as well as hospitals and preventive services, can indicate how well a community is able to meet the medical needs of its residents. Communities where there are not enough primary medical, dental, or mental health care providers are called Health Professional Shortage Areas (HPSAs) by the U.S. Department of Health and Human Services. However, cities or towns that are not HPSAs can still lack adequate health care providers to meet the needs of all the people who live there. Hospitals provide the resources necessary to diagnose and treat chronic illnesses. Having more health conditions often requires the care of specialists, including geriatricians. Currently, however, the health care workforce is inadequately prepared to provide health care to the growing number of older adults. According to the Institute of Medicine's report *Retooling for an Aging America: Building the Health Care Workforce* (2008), there are only approximately 7,000 geriatricians practicing in the United States, while according to the U.S. Department of Labor's Bureau of Labor Statistics (2014), there are more than 31,000 pediatricians. In addition, less than 1% of pharmacists and nurses and 4% of social workers specialize in geriatrics (Institute of Medicine, 2008).

In addition to acute and chronic health care in the community, preventive health programs offer the promise of improving elder health, well-being, and the ability to age well in the community. Health promotion is an umbrella term for a variety of services and supports that encourage older adults to proactively improve their health (WHO, n.d.b), including screenings, vaccinations, physical activity programs, and social engagement (McMahon & Fleury, 2012). The CDC, for example, recommends that older adults receive vaccinations for pneumococcal disease, influenza, pertussis, shingles, and tetanus. Other key health promotion services, as recommended by the U.S. Preventive Services Task Force, include screening for a variety of chronic physical conditions (particularly breast cancer, diabetes, blood pressure, osteoporosis, sexually transmitted diseases, and obesity) and behavioral health monitoring and counseling (particularly for alcohol, tobacco, and depression) (Ogden, Richards, & Shenson, 2012).

Research, however, indicates many older adults do not receive preventive services, particularly if they are poor (Pham, Schrag, Hargraves, & Bach, 2005). For example, 90% of flu-related deaths occur among those ages 65 or older (Halloran, 2013), and influenza and pneumonia are among the leading causes of death for individuals in this age group (Heron et al., 2009). Yet, almost one third in this age group never receive an annual influenza immunization (Sambamoorthi & Findley, 2005), and many do not get a vaccination against pneumonia (Pham et al., 2005). Even among older Medicare recipients who report having a primary care physician and adequate resources to pay for preventive health services, less than 40% of women and 45% of men are up to date with all recommended screenings and vaccinations (Shenson, Adams, Bolen, & Anderson, 2011). In addition to increasing the availability of these health promotion services, some promising strategies to improve screening and vaccination rates include improved coordination of services, extended hours, offering services at nonmedical community locations (e.g., Vote and Vax, which offers vaccinations at polling places; churches and synagogues; beauty salons; grocery stores), and offering education and resources at community centers and the YMCA (Hoffman & Schwartz, 2008; Ogden et al., 2012; Thorpe, Ogden, & Galactionova, 2010). Furthermore, communities should offer a range of culturally appropriate strategies to encourage preventive health care utilization, including providing lay health advisors (also referred to as community health workers, peer health educators, or *promotores*) (Zonderman, Ejiogu, Norbeck, & Evans, 2014).

Physical activity is another critical aspect of health promotion that can optimize health and well-being (Carey et al., 2008; Villareal, Banks, Sinacore, Siener, & Klein, 2006; Wieckowski & Simmons, 2006). Regularly engaging in moderate or vigorous activities, including walking, gardening, and heavy housework, has been linked to a reduced risk of mortality, less decline in physical functioning (Simonsick et al., 1993), and improved mobility (LaCroix et al., 1993). In one study, physical activity had a stronger relationship with maintaining mobility than a variety of other health behaviors, including minimizing alcohol consumption, avoiding tobacco, and maintaining moderate body weight (LaCroix et al., 1993). The American College of Sports Medicine recommends that older adults exercise for 20 minutes per day for 3 days per week at a high intensity or 30 minutes per day for 5 days per week at a moderate intensity (Kosma, 2014).

Fitness programs for older adults result in increased physical activity (Hughes et al., 2006) and slower decline in cognitive and physical functioning (Dechamps et al., 2010). The Be Well intervention, for example, which provides both physical activity and nutrition education in biweekly classes over 16 weeks, is associated with positive effects not only in terms of weight loss but also in mental health and opportunities for social interaction (Kogan et al., 2013). According to a systematic review of the literature, however, there remains little evidence that physical activity interventions can definitively produce long-term lifestyle or health changes (Neidrick, Fick, & Loeb, 2012). This same review suggested that more time-intensive programs hold greater promise for increasing physical activity over a longer period of time (Neidrick et al., 2012). In a randomized trial, Fit and Strong!, which combines strength training, balance and flexibility exercises, walking, and health education, demonstrated benefits in physical activity levels, physical fitness measures, and mental health over an 18-month period when former participants received telephone reinforcement (Hughes et al., 2010).

Addressing the physical and social infrastructure of the community may also increase the likelihood that older adults will stick with an exercise routine. Offering social support for physical activity, for example, may increase elder's enjoyment and interest in certain activities and thereby lead to long-term lifestyle changes (Task Force on Community Preventive Services, 2002). As we described in Chapter 5, another strategy is creating neighborhoods that are more walkable through sidewalk repair, building new pathways, improving street lighting, making routes aesthetically pleasing (Heath, 2006), and adopting traffic-calming measures (Retting et al., 2003). Research on older adults indicates that walkable neighborhoods contribute to an increase in physical activity (Berke, Koepsell, et al., 2007; Sallis & Kerr, 2006) and daily walking as a means of transportation (Van Cauwenberg et al., 2013).

Some physical activity programs specifically aim to prevent falls among older adults. Fall prevention programs have received a great deal of attention in the research literature, and a number of systematic reviews and meta-analyses have reported on their effectiveness (El-Khoury, Cassou, Charles, & Dargent-Molina, 2013; Gillespie et al., 2012; McMahon & Fleury, 2012). Analyses by the Cochrane Collaboration, for example, found that tai chi, group exercise classes, and home-based exercise programs reduced falls by 28%, 29%, and 32%, respectively (Gillespie et al., 2012). A meta-analysis of 17 randomized controlled trials reported that fall prevention programs that include physical activity targeting a number of functions (e.g., balance, strength, flexibility, and endurance) improved muscle strength, coordination, reaction time, gait, and overall physical and cognitive functioning (El-Khoury et al., 2013). Furthermore, according to the same meta-analysis, these exercise programs can reduce falls that result in injuries by more than one third. Because older adults who walk fast are at an elevated risk for outdoor falls, it has been recommended that falls prevention programs not only encourage physical activity but also educate older adults about walking more slowly and carefully, particularly in unfamiliar environments (Kelsey et al., 2012).

One prominent example of a falls prevention program that includes a physical activity component is A Matter of Balance, which was originally developed by the Roybal Center for Enhancement of Late-Life Function at Boston University and the New England Research Institute. A Matter of Balance combines strength and balance activities, individualized plans for continued physical activity, environmental modifications to reduce falls risk, and cognitive-behavioral activities to increase personal feelings of control over falling (Tennstedt et al., 1998). Research indicated participants in A Matter of Balance increased their physical activity levels and self-efficacy for avoiding falls and experienced a decline in reported falls; furthermore, these findings occurred whether the intervention was implemented by professionals (Tennstedt et al., 1998) or volunteers (Healy et al., 2008).

Social Services and Supports

LTSS are defined by the Institute of Medicine (1986) as "a variety of ongoing health and social services provided for individuals who need assistance on a continuing basis because of physical or mental disability." These services include (a) in-home care (e.g., homemaking services, personal care); (b) physical supports (e.g., assistive technology, home modifications); (c) community-based services (e.g., meals programs, adult day care); and (d) facility-based care (e.g., nursing home care, assisted living care). An estimated 6 million adults ages 65 or older receive some form of LTSS (Kaye, Harrington, & LaPlante, 2010), of whom approximately 5.2 million receive community-based LTSS (Kassner, 2011). About 70% of older adults are expected to need LTSS at some point in their lives (Kemper, Komisar, & Alecxih, 2005). Yet, even with LTSS supports, older individuals in the United States have substantial unmet needs.

Many older adults may not be aware that Medicare plays a relatively limited role in public long-term services and supports compared to Medicaid. In a recent survey, 45% of older adults reported that they anticipated using Medicare for community-based services, yet Medicare home health care is limited primarily to short-term assistance while recuperating from an acute health care crisis requiring hospitalization (Robison et al., 2014). In 2000, for example, Medicare funded less than 13% of publicly funded community-based LTSS, compared to more than 71% funded through Medicaid (Miller, 2006).

In fact, the majority of public LTSS are provided through the Medicaid program, which is funded jointly by federal and state governments and is available only for persons meeting income criteria. States are required to offer home health care to Medicaid recipients and have the option to provide other services, such as physical therapy, personal care, and transportation (Milne, 2012). The majority of Medicaid spending for community-based LTSS is through the home- and community-based waiver program created through Section 1915(c) of the Social Security Act authorization of 1981, referred to as 1915(c) waivers (Harrington, Carrillo, Wellin, Miller, & LeBlanc, 2000; Summer, 2007). Waiver services, such as for personal care, medical equipment, home-delivered meals, and home adaptations, are targeted to those who would qualify for institutional care (Sands et al., 2008). Federal law prohibits states from spending more on waivers than nursing home care (Sands et al., 2008); therefore, Medicaid continues to have an institutional bias. While spending on Medicaid community-based LTSS increased from $17 billion to $42 billion between 1999 and 2007 (Ng & Harrington, 2011), only about one third of all Medicaid spending on LTSS for older adults and others with a disability is for supports in the community. States also can limit the numbers of elders served by waivers, often leading to waiting lists for services (Milne, 2012). In a recent evaluation of 39 states, for example, 395,000 people were on waiting lists for 1915(c) waiver services (Ng & Harrington, 2011).

Some LTSS are offered through programs mandated and supported by the Older Americans Act (OAA), first enacted by Congress in 1965. The OAA created what is referred to as the "aging network," comprising 56 state units on aging (SUAs), 655 area agencies on aging (AAAs), 243 indian tribal and native Hawaiian organizations, and thousands of service providers and volunteers (U.S. Department of Health and Human Services, 2004). Using a formula based on the state's proportion of the U.S. older adult population, approximately 70% of OAA funding is distributed to the states through Title III, Grants for State and Community Programs on Aging (Fox-Grage & Ujvari, 2014). States then use these funds to provide a variety of community-based services, such as home-delivered and congregate meals, family caregiver services (described in more detail in the next section), transportation, adult day health, preventive care, in-home assistance, and case management (K. S. Thomas & Mor, 2013). While anyone age 60 or older is eligible to receive Title III programs, the law also requires states to prioritize services to "older individuals with greatest economic need and older individuals with greatest social need, with particular attention to low-income minority individuals, older individuals residing in rural areas, low-income individuals, and frail individuals" (Fox-Grage & Ujvari, 2014, p. 1). In addition, states must target Title III-B in-home services to older adults who are frail, socially isolated, or homebound and those who are economically or socially vulnerable (K. S. Thomas, 2014).

While service recipients reported that OAA services are an effective strategy to help them age in place (Altshuler & Schimmel, 2010), funding remains low compared to LTSS funding from Medicaid. In fiscal year (FY) 2014, the federal appropriation for OAA was $1.88 billion, which when adjusted for inflation was significantly less than a decade before (Fox-Grage & Ujvari, 2014). Furthermore, the aging network is designed to be flexible to local needs; therefore, there is a great deal of variation in the SUAs and AAAs across the country in terms of their administration, infrastructure, and resources (Browdie, 2008). For example, some states provide an overmatch of funding above the 25% and 15% mandated for caregiver services and supportive services, respectively (Fox-Grage & Ujvari, 2014).

Home- and community-based support services are associated with improved physical functioning (Hadley, Rabin, Epstein, Stein, & Rimes, 2000), reduced depressive symptoms, increased life satisfaction, and a greater sense of mastery (Shapiro & Taylor, 2002). Formal community supports may also reduce the risk of nursing home placement. An evaluation of Medicaid waivers in the state of Indiana, for example, found that for each additional 5 hours per month of personal care, the risk of nursing home placement dropped by 5% (Sands et al., 2012). In the same study, homemaker services decreased the risk of nursing home admission by 13%.

Community-based LTSS may be particularly effective at delaying or preventing institutionalization for those with low-care needs. Recent analyses of administrative data, for example, found as states spend more on Older Americans Act programs and Medicaid home- and community-based services (HCBS), the number of nursing home residents with low-care needs, defined in terms of their ADL limitations, decreased (K. S. Thomas & Mor, 2013). Specifically, every 1% increase in state spending on in-home personal assistance was accompanied by an average statewide decrease of 177 low-care nursing home residents (K. S. Thomas, 2014). Home-delivered meals seem to be particularly effective, perhaps because meal drivers can detect emerging issues among isolated and homebound older adults (K. S. Thomas & Mor, 2013).

While these findings are promising, empirical evidence of the effects of various home- and community-based services remains sparse. In their review of

61 studies on adult day health programs, for example, Fields, Anderson, and Dabelko-Schoeny (2014) found that these programs are potentially beneficial for older adults and their caregivers, but many questions remain given the lack of rigorous evaluation studies. In addition, LTSS typically address individual functioning and limitations rather than the community physical or social environment. These services often do little to improve person–environment fit and therefore may have limited efficacy.

In addition to questions regarding the effects of community-based LTSS, there are a number of barriers to accessing these services. According to one survey, more than half of older adults with functional limitations did not receive the assistance needed (Feldman et al., 2004). One possible explanation for this high level of unmet need is that approximately 20% of older adults do not know where to find information about the health and supportive services available in their community (Feldman et al., 2004). Another explanation is that the supply of home- and community-based services, such as adult day health and home health assistance, is not meeting the demand. In focus groups, for example, Robison, Shugrue, Porter, Fortinsky, and Curry (2012) learned about significant gaps in home- and community-based care, including limited services available on nights and weekends, the absence of transportation assistance, and an inadequate supply of respite and adult day health programs. It appears that both the private market and public programs are not addressing need. Workforce issues are also a concern, as the low pay and physically demanding tasks that characterize in-home care contribute to high rates of turnover and uneven quality of care (Robison et al., 2012). The finding that hospitalizations often precipitate long-term nursing home placement also suggests the absence of transitional supports and appropriate coordination of discharge care to keep older adults living in the community (Robison et al., 2012).

There is clearly a need for more funding, particularly at the federal level, to promote more aging-friendly environments by increasing the availability and accessibility of health, wellness, and social support services. At a time when such funding appears to be effectively shrinking, however, as evidenced by annual appropriations for Older Americans Act programs, it seems unlikely that a bump in funding will happen any time soon. Perhaps a more feasible recommendation is increased federal guidance in expanding home- and community-based services at the state level through the provision of technical assistance and criteria for measuring progress toward rebalancing (Browdie, 2008).

Currently, there is little communication and coordination between and among health and social support providers (Keefe, Geron, & Enguidanos, 2009). At a federal policy level, one way to promote better coordination of care is for Medicare to reimburse physicians and other providers for their efforts to communicate and coordinate medical and nonmedical services (Archer, 2012). Coordination also depends on the efforts of those working in health and long-term care systems.

For example, both physicians and LTSS providers express frustration about their ability to communicate with each other (Fairchild, Hogan, Smith, Portnow, & Bates, 2002; Ruggiano et al., 2012). Given that they often serve as the main point of entry to health care services for older adults, it is particularly important for primary care physicians to become more knowledgeable about available community supports (Riggs, 2003/2004) or else include social workers and other community health workers in their practices.

Supports for Informal Caregivers

While formal services offered by public and private providers give community-based support to a significant number of older adults, informal sources, including family, friends, and neighbors, provide the majority of care in the United States. According to a report by the National Alliance for Caregiving (NAC) and AARP (2009), almost 80% of community-dwelling older adults who require assistance rely solely on informal caregivers. Estimates of the economic value of caregiving vary from approximately $100 billion to $450 billion (Arno, Levine, & Memmott, 1999; Feinberg et al., 2011; R. W. Johnson, 2008), figures that dwarf the value of formal care. Furthermore, informal care plays a role in preventing institutionalization in a nursing home (Charles & Sevak, 2005). Indeed, the long-term care system in the United States depends on the contributions of informal sources and will likely become even more reliant on caregivers in the future (Montgomery, 1999).

As noted, a significant proportion of older adults report unmet needs for home- and community-based services, and stagnant or reduced federal and state funding for public LTSS suggests this number will increase. In addition, because of changes in Medicare hospital reimbursement, older adults are often discharged with significant assistance needs. Concomitant with fewer formal supports are demographic trends that will likely affect the ability of family members to provide assistance to disabled elders (Montgomery, 1999; Spillman & Pezzin, 2000). More than 60% of informal caregivers are women, and the "typical" caregiver has been described as a woman in her mid-40s providing assistance to her mother (NAC and AARP, 2004). Increased female participation in the workforce, however, has reduced the time women are available to provide unpaid care. Lower birth rates combined with a rise in longevity means there are fewer younger family members to care for multiple older generations. Furthermore, as older adults live longer and potentially spend more years with a disability, husbands and wives may be less able to care for their spouse because they are coping with their own functional limitations.

Providing assistance to an older relative, friend, or neighbor can be a beneficial experience, contributing to a sense of purpose, feeling of usefulness, reciprocation for care provided earlier in life, and a strengthened relationship with the care recipient (Koerner, Kenyon, & Shirai, 2009). Caregiving also, however, can have negative consequences for a caregiver's social, physical, mental, and financial health. According to a national survey (NAC/AARP, 2004), more than half of caregivers provide more than 8 hours of care per week and on average offer such assistance for more than 4 years. This major time commitment means caregivers often neglect their own needs, and there is evidence of significant inequities in both health care and preventive health activities between caregivers and those not providing informal assistance (Talley & Crews, 2007).

Caregiving may also influence health and well-being by reducing opportunities for social interactions and leisure activities, cutting sleep (particularly for those living with their care recipient), and increasing physical strain when performing certain care activities. A meta-analysis of studies published over three decades reported that physical health problems among caregivers are due to such risk factors as caregiver age, caregiver depression, coresidence, low socioeconomic status, longer duration of care, care recipient cognitive impairment, and few sources of support (Pinquart & Sörensen, 2007). Decades of research has also documented that informal caregivers are at a higher risk for stress and depression than their noncaregiving counterparts (Pinquart & Sörensen, 2003). Further exacerbating stress are the financial implications of caregiving, as it has been estimated that caregivers lose nearly $660,000 in wages, pensions, and Social Security benefits to meet their caregiving responsibilities (Family Caregiver Alliance, 2012).

As demonstrated in a number of studies, caregivers who experience their own physical health problems, feel burden related to care, or are ill equipped to manage their care recipient's problems (including behavior changes associated with dementia) are more likely to place their care recipient into a long-term care facility (Buhr, Kuchibhatla, & Clipp, 2006; Gaugler, Kane, Kane, Clay, & Newcomer, 2003; Jette, Tennstedt, & Crawford, 1995). It seems clear that policies and programs are needed to optimize the health and well-being of caregivers and their older care recipients.

Despite the U.S. long-term care system's dependency on informal caregivers as the major source of care for older adults who need assistance with daily activities, to date there is only limited support for caregivers. The federal Family and Medical Leave Act (FMLA), which has been in effect since 1993, requires all public and private employers with at least 50 employees to offer up to 12 weeks of unpaid leave for family or medical issues, including informal caregiving for an older relative (U.S. Department of Labor, 2012). Since almost 60% of caregivers are employed at the same time they are providing assistance (NAC/AARP, 2004), job-protected leave may facilitate their ability to balance work and caregiving responsibilities. The FMLA, however, has a number of limitations to creating work environments that are more supportive and address the financial needs of caregivers (Rozario & Palley, 2008). Not all caregivers have the financial means to give up their wages for 12 weeks, so many who are eligible do not take advantage of this policy. Furthermore, many caregivers are ineligible, including the 40% of the workforce employed by smaller companies and those who are providing care to someone who is not a spouse, child, or parent, as these are the only permissible relations specified in the law.

More recently, the federal government has attempted to increase caregivers' access to supportive community-based services through the National Family Caregiver Support Program (NFCSP), created by the Older Americans Act Amendments of 2000. The NFCSP provides funding for five categories of services that aim to improve the quality of life of caregivers and facilitate their ability to provide assistance to an older adult. The service categories are (a) information (e.g., education about existing services in the community); (b) assistance (e.g., case management and service coordination); (c) individual counseling, support groups, and training (e.g., education about addressing problematic behaviors for those with dementia); (d) respite care (e.g., in-home respite during the day, overnight respite in a long-term care facility); and (e) supplemental services (e.g., home modification, financial planning, assistive devices) (U.S. Department of Health and Human Services, 2004). The NFCSP recognizes that the needs of the caregiver are intertwined with the needs of the care recipient. Respite care, for example, is a key support for caregivers, particularly the more than one third of caregivers who report they have no other sources of unpaid support (NAC/AARP, 2004). Research in California, however, indicated that respite care, which involves direct care to an older adult, is much more available than training and counseling, which involves direct service provision to the caregiver (Whittier, Scharlach, & Dal Santo, 2005). This may reflect the challenges AAAs are experiencing as they shift to a new population for service delivery (Whittier et al., 2005). The NFCSP also provides little funding given the large number of caregivers and their potential need for services (Riggs, 2003/2004). In FY2014, for example, the NFCSP was allocated $146 million to serve an estimated 42 million caregivers (Feinberg et al., 2011; Fox-Grage & Ujvari, 2014).

As with the larger long-term care system, community-based support for caregivers such as those funded by the NFCSP are often fragmented from each other and disconnected from the health care system (Riggs, 2003). Furthermore, other LTSS typically ignore the needs of family caregivers. This is in contrast to other countries, such as the United Kingdom, where the Carers (Recognition and Services) Act encourages health providers to conduct an in-depth assessment of the needs of those providing care on a regular basis (Seddon & Robinson, 2001). While evaluations of the Carers Act suggest some barriers to its implementation, it offers a promising strategy to increase the recognition of caregivers as an integral part of the care team with needs that both overlap with and are distinct from the needs of their care recipients (Seddon & Robinson, 2001).

Promising Initiatives to Create More Aging-Friendly Health and Social Supports

Since the 1980s, federal and state governments have developed a number of innovative programs aimed at improving access to and quality of community-based LTSS and ultimately reducing use of institutional settings. While progress toward rebalancing long-term care dollars toward home- and community-based services is somewhat uneven across states (Miller, 2012), there is evidence that various programs are leading to a more equitable division of funding between HCBS and institutional care (R. A. Kane, 2012). Given the complexity of public funding for LTSS, it is difficult to provide accurate estimates of shifting funding. However, the decline in recent decades in the percentage of older adults living in a nursing home (Hayutin, 2012) suggests these programs have achieved some success. Many of these programs, funded through Medicare, Medicaid, or the Older Americans Act, began as demonstrations and later expanded or became permanent programs (R. A. Kane, 2012). Generally, these programs employ two different strategies: moving older adults currently in nursing homes back into the community and preventing institutionalization in the first place (R. A. Kane, 2012).

The increasing availability of and public funding for community-based LTSS is due to a combination of factors. First, the Supreme Court's Olmstead decision in 1999 held that the state of Georgia had violated Title II of the Americans With Disabilities Act, which mandates that "no qualified individual with a disability shall, by reason of such disability, be excluded from participation, or denied benefits of, services, programs, or activities of a public entity, or be subjected to discrimination by any such entity" (Zendell, 2007, p. 98). While the Olmstead case focused on psychiatric patients (Palley & Rozario, 2007), this decision requires states to prevent unnecessary institutionalization for all populations. Specifically, the court held that unjustified institutionalization reinforces stereotypes that those with a disability are unable to contribute to their community and restricts individuals' ability to participate in family, economic, social, and civic life (Milne, 2012; Rosenbaum, Teitelbaum, & Stewart, 2002). States now have the responsibility to ensure that individuals with a disability have a reasonable opportunity to live and receive care in the most integrated setting possible (Milne, 2012; Rosenbaum et al., 2002). Between 5% and 12% of long-term nursing home residents and new admissions appear to have low care needs and could be served in the community if adequate supports were available (Mor et al., 2007).

A second factor motivating federal and state governments to "rebalance" public expenditures on LTSS toward community-based supports is the high cost of institutional care. A 2011 analysis by the MetLife Mature Market Institute found that annual nursing home care costs an average of $78,110 for a semiprivate room and $83,585 for a private room, compared to $27,664–$30,576 for daily in-home support and $18,200 for community-based support through adult day health services. We should note, however, that the estimated costs for community-based care fail to take into account the basic living expenses that are covered in a facility, such as room and board.

Next, we describe some of the more prominent efforts of federal and state governments to increase older adults' access to community-based LTSS and decrease the long-term care systems' reliance on institutional care. While not an exhaustive list, these programs highlight a variety of strategies currently being employed.

Money Follows the Person

In an effort to reduce unnecessary nursing home use, the Centers for Medicare and Medicaid Services (CMS) has been working with states for more than two decades to develop programs that transition individuals out of nursing homes and back into the community (Stone & Reinhard, 2007). One example of such a program is the Money Follows the Person (MFP) Rebalancing Demonstration Grant, which provides grants to states to move Medicaid-eligible nursing home residents back into their community. According to CMS, between the program's implementation in 2005 through 2013, MFP helped 40,500 people move out of a nursing home. Forty-four states and the District of Columbia currently participate. States receive grants and federal matching funds to (a) move nursing home residents to a home, apartment, or small group home and (b) offer more extensive and intensive home- and community-based services than those provided through Medicaid waivers. The program also allows states to test innovative services prior to seeking approval for their inclusion in state plans or waivers. The state of Washington, for example, developed a community bed-holding service to save an individual's place in an assisted living facility or adult family home if they needed a short-term hospitalization or nursing home stay (Peebles & Kehn, 2014). Wisconsin offers a housing counseling service for those transitioning back into the community to provide resources on home maintenance, energy assistance and weatherization, credit counseling, and education about renting and preventing evictions, among other services (Peebles & Kehn, 2014). Many states have also had success with programs beyond MFP to relocate nursing home residents back into the community. An evaluation of Ohio's nursing home diversion program, for example, which aims to prevent institutionalization as well as move residents out of nursing homes, reported that 80% of program participants were still living in the community after 6 months (Bardo, Applebaum, Kunkel, & Carpio, 2014).

Program for All-Inclusive Care for the Elderly

The Program for All-Inclusive Care for the Elderly (PACE) was originally developed by On Lok Senior Health Services in San Francisco, California, and became a permanent Medicare program in the Balanced Budget Act of 1997 after a successful demonstration (D. L. Gross, Temkin-Greener, Kunitz, & Mukamel, 2004). PACE is a Medicare Advantage program (R. L. Kane, Homyak, Bershadsky, & Flood, 2006) in which a provider receives a fixed capitated payment to deliver a wide range of acute and long-term care services. A multidisciplinary team, including physicians and nurses, coordinates and provides care at an adult day health center (Hansen & Hewitt, 2012), and PACE sites assume financial responsibility for providing those services, even if the cost exceeds the payment rate (Hansen & Hewitt, 2012).

Older adults can enroll in PACE if they meet the health and functioning requirements for nursing home placement and are either dually eligible for Medicare and Medicaid or can self-pay the portion of the capitation rate covered by Medicaid (Mui, 2002). PACE programs are often aimed at older adults experiencing frailty, a geriatric syndrome that increases an elder's risk for disability, disease, falls, hospitalization, and death (Cramm, Twisk, & Nieboer, 2014). PACE has expanded across the country but remains a relatively limited program, with currently 106 PACE programs located in 31 states. Relatively few older adults have enrolled in a PACE program because there are a small number of organizations that offer PACE and few older adults without Medicaid coverage are able to afford the Medicaid portion of the expenses (Gross et al., 2004).

Participant-Directed Services

Offering consumers greater control and autonomy is another strategy that can improve services for older adults and individuals with disabilities. The Cash and Counseling Program, for example, provides disabled Medicaid enrollees with a cash allowance that they can use to pay for individually negotiated goods and services designed to meet their needs, including in-home care (including care provided by a family member or friend), assistive devices, and home modifications (Carlson, Foster, Dale, & Brown, 2007). In the demonstration phase, funded jointly by the Office of the Assistant Secretary for Planning and Evaluation (ASPE) in the U.S Department of Health and Human Services and the Robert Wood Johnson Foundation, the program was implemented and evaluated in 3 states (Arkansas, New Jersey, and Florida), with an additional 12 states participating in the replication phase. In a randomized controlled trial, Cash and Counseling participants had a number of beneficial outcomes compared to those in traditional agency-based care, including higher satisfaction with services, fewer unmet needs, and better quality of life (Carlson et al., 2007). Telephone surveys also found that while younger adults with disabilities were more interested in receiving cash and having more control over their care compared to older adults, more than half of those ages 65 and older expressed a desire to participate in this model of service delivery (Desmond, Mahoney, Simon-Rusinowitz, & Shoop, 2001). Older adults seemed particularly interested in using the allowance to pay family members to provide care (Doty et al., 2012).

While the demonstration ended in 2009, the Robert Wood Johnson Foundation (2013) attributed the adoption and implementation of additional federal policies that facilitate states' provision of more participant-directed services to the success of Cash and Counseling. According to Doty and colleagues (2012), participant-directed services expanded to all 50 states over the course of the first decade of the 21st century, and the number of programs more than doubled between 2001 and 2011, when there were 298 programs in the United States. There remain concerns about the financial viability of participant-directed services, as Cash and Counseling enrollees incur higher Medicaid costs because they are able to access more services (Robert Wood Johnson Foundation, 2013), and these programs can potentially lead to a "woodwork" effect as those who would opt not to receive agency-based services come out of the woodwork for a cash allowance (Doty et al., 2012). There have also been concerns expressed about an increased risk of elder mistreatment if older adults have the primary responsibility for supervising their own care, but data collected from program counselors indicated few instances of abuse (Schore, Foster, & Phillips, 2007).

Another example of participant-directed care is California's In-Home Supportive Services Program (IHSS), which was developed before the Cash and Counseling demonstration. In 1979, California combined two existing programs to create what would later be known as IHSS: the Attendant Care program, which distributed cash payments to individuals with disabilities so that they could hire an attendant care provider, and the Homemaker-Chore program, in which county-employed caregivers provided services to individuals who were unable to hire or supervise their own service providers (County Welfare Directors Association of California [CWDA], 2003). IHSS is an entitlement program supported by federal, state, and local funding, and therefore anyone who is Medicaid eligible and disabled can enroll in the program (CWDA, 2003). Depending on their level of functional impairment, older and younger adults with disabilities receive such services as personal care, chore assistance, paramedical services, transportation, and protective supervision. Individuals who meet the low-income eligibility requirements receive free IHSS services, while higher-income participants pay part of the costs (CWDA, 2003). A large majority of IHSS recipients hire and supervise their own caregiver, but some receive services from an individual employed by a county or agency provider. By 2009, IHSS cost $5.5 billion a year to provide services to approximately 430,000 recipients (Legislative Analyst's Office, 2009), making it the largest personal assistance program in the

United States. To rein in costs, California has employed measures such as eliminating services for those above a certain functioning threshold and ending state subsidies for higher-income individuals who pay for a portion of their services (California Budget Project, 2009).

The Affordable Care Act

When Congress passed the Affordable Care Act (ACA) in 2010 (through two separate pieces of legislation—the Patient Protection and Affordable Care Act, and the Health Care and Education Reconciliation Act)—the provision receiving the most attention in terms of benefitting older adults was the Community Living Assistance Services and Supports (CLASS) Act. The CLASS Act called for the creation of a voluntary long-term care insurance program administered by the federal government (Miller, 2012). The program would have provided an average benefit of $75 per day to pay for long-term care services, including those provided by family members (National Council on Aging, 2010a), to older adults with ADL limitations or cognitive impairment (Archer, 2012) who had contributed to the program through payroll deductions during their employment (Lindberg & MacInnes, 2010). The law mandated that the CLASS Act could only be implemented if it was financially solvent for at least 75 years, a requirement that a subsequent analysis by the Department of Health and Human Services determined had not been met (Archer, 2012). Rather than making the adjustments necessary to ensure the program's solvency, Congress in 2013 repealed the CLASS program.

The ACA, however, includes a number of other provisions that offer the promise of expanding older adults' access to health and supportive services in their communities. In terms of health care, the ACA aims to reduce prescription drug costs when older adults experience what is known as the donut hole problem of Medicare Part D through a combination of federal rebates and subsidies and manufacturer discounts (Archer, 2012). In an effort to reduce hospital readmissions, the law cuts Medicare payments to hospitals with high rates of preventable hospital readmissions or hospital-acquired illnesses and increases reimbursement for hospitals meeting quality criteria (Archer, 2012). The ACA also facilitates the provision of community-based preventive and wellness services through community health teams comprised of a variety of professions, including nurses, social workers, nutritionists, and behavioral health practitioners (Ogden et al., 2012). Accountable Care Organizations that include community health teams, physicians, and hospitals, for example, can receive Medicare reimbursement if they meet cost-reduction and quality-of-care benchmarks (Archer, 2012).

In terms of supportive services, the ACA increases funding for Aging Disability and Resource Centers to expand older adults' access to a single point of entry for LTSS, makes it easier for older adults to qualify for the Money Follows the Person Demonstration, and extends protections against impoverishment for older adults when their spouse is receiving home- and community-based services (Miller, 2012). Furthermore, the State Balancing Incentive Program expands financial incentives for states making progress in shifting the proportion of Medicaid dollars spent from institutional-based care to community-based LTSS (Miller, 2012). Finally, the law will encourage greater coordination between Medicare and Medicaid and the future dissemination of promising models of care through the newly established Federal Coordinated Health Care Office and the Center for Medicare and Medicaid Innovation, respectively (Miller, 2012).

Emerging Technologies

While most of this chapter has focused on the role of public policies in the provision of health care and social supports, we also want to highlight some innovative interventions coming from the private market. Technological advances, for example, have substantial implications for improvements in health and wellness services. The range of technologies that can address health and social support needs includes mobile devices, sensors that can monitor the indoor and outdoor environment, and health information technology (Satariano, Scharlach, & Lindeman, 2014). While the impact of these nascent technologies is not fully understood, there is reason to believe that they can contribute to aging well. A review of the literature, for example, found strong emerging evidence that Internet-based chronic disease management programs can increase elders' knowledge, skills, and perceived self-efficacy to control their conditions, particularly when they include a Web 2.0 component that promotes interactions with health care providers and other sources of support (Stellefson et al., 2013). Similarly, research on home-based consumer health technologies, while having many limitations, suggests they have the potential to increase elders' ability to age in place by monitoring for falls and other safety risks (Reeder et al., 2013).

Conclusion

Few older adults live in communities that offer the wide range of affordable and quality health care and social supports that can enable them to live safely in their community and optimize their well-being. Many older adults do not receive recommended immunizations, screenings, and other wellness services, even when they are provided in the community. The majority of health care providers, including physicians, nurses, pharmacists, and physical therapists, receive little to no training about the potentially unique needs of their older patients. Federal and state LTSS focus primarily on meeting the social support and assistance needs of older adults living near or below the poverty line, leaving other older adults with responsibility for arranging and paying for care if they need to access formal sources. Public funding for existing programs, including support for caregivers, in-home care, and community-based programs, lags significantly behind the need. Some states have prioritized offering a continuum of community-based options for older adults, while others have done little to rebalance their systems away from primarily institutional-based care. Innovative programs that provide community-based LTSS serve small numbers of older adults and are available only in selected areas. Finally, health care and social supports focus primarily on the perceived deficits of the individual rather than poor fit between individual capabilities and environmental demands.

PART III

CREATING AGING-FRIENDLY COMMUNITIES

8

Approaches to Aging-Friendly Community Change

Introduction

This chapter introduces change models that can be utilized to help communities implement the aging-friendly improvements identified in Part II. We begin by considering the reasons why enhancing aging friendliness frequently requires communitywide system change. We then describe five core issues to consider in designing aging-friendly community change efforts and identify seven basic stages of community change. We conclude by positing an organizing framework of four types of aging-friendly initiatives, identified through an examination of community aging initiatives in the United States. We describe three of these four types of initiatives in greater detail in Chapters 9, 10, and 11.

The Need for Community Change

As we saw in Chapters 5, 6, and 7, maladaptive person–environment relationships with regard to housing, mobility, social engagement, and health and social services can interfere with elders' ability to meet their needs and limit physical, psychological, and social well-being. While substantial community infrastructure improvements are needed in each of these areas, the personal and environmental challenges associated with the aging process do not operate in isolation. Housing, mobility, and land use, for example, are integrally related to one another and directly affect social engagement and service use; at the same time, the availability of social support affects where we live as well as our ability to continue living there. Making communities more aging friendly therefore requires coordinated efforts that transcend individual programs or domains.

Current policies, resource channels, and program silos, however, serve as potential barriers to coordinated infrastructure improvements. Housing, transportation, health care, and social services each are administered by different government agencies, have different funding sources, and operate under different sets of regulations. Furthermore, city planners, transportation providers, public health departments, and aging services providers and advocates seldom work collaboratively to enhance the overall aging friendliness of the communities they serve. As a result of these separate silos, community programs tend to be highly fragmented and poorly coordinated.

A Community Focus

Recognizing the limitations of existing programs and services for meeting the changing needs of the increasing population of older adults, a growing number of communities across the country have developed initiatives designed to foster comprehensive changes in community physical and social environments (Hodge, 2008). These initiatives include efforts by the World Health Organization (WHO), U.S. Administration on Aging, Robert Wood Johnson Foundation, AARP, Visiting Nurse Service of New York, Grantmakers in Aging, and others, as we discuss in the following chapters.

What differentiates these types of community aging initiatives from traditional aging programs and services is their focus on the community itself as both a target for change and an essential component of the change process. Rather than solving problems one at a time, these initiatives focus on strengthening individuals as well as their environments and increasing the effectiveness of community systems. This reflects a shift from a residual approach concerned about ways to ameliorate problems that already exist to a preventive approach concerned about creating the kinds of physical and social environments that foster individual and societal well-being.

A Comprehensive Approach

A systemic approach to community change requires consideration of all aspects of the community, including the needs of individual community members and their relationships with one another, existing social organizations and institutions, the built environment, the political environment, and the local economy, among other factors. Initiatives to promote aging-friendly community change therefore might focus on any or all of the following: improving the functioning and participation of individual older adults, strengthening social networks, redesigning physical environments, improving service delivery systems, enhancing community functioning, or advocating for more responsive social and economic policies (Scharlach, 2009). In so doing, community change initiatives strive to build social capital, promote health and wellness, enhance social connectedness, improve individual self-sufficiency, and foster general community well-being.

Characteristics of an Aging-Friendly Community Approach

Achieving aging-friendly community change involves five interrelated issues: commitment, capacity, collaboration, consumer involvement, and comprehensiveness. Each of these issues presents critical options for initiative developers, with implications for the type of aging-friendly initiative that is developed, the approach that is employed, the initiative's ultimate effectiveness at achieving intended goals, and its sustainability over time.

Commitment

Efforts to help communities become more aging friendly require substantial ongoing commitment from community leaders and other key stakeholders. To begin with, aging-friendly initiatives must overcome ageist attitudes that see aging only as debility and older persons as having little to contribute to their communities. Developing and implementing an aging-friendly initiative also requires that an individual or group assume responsibility for critical activities such as initiation, operation, regulation, and governance. Furthermore, aging-friendly initiatives typically require that community sectors and systems are sanctioned to work together in new ways, often outside of traditional funding and programmatic silos. Given these attitudinal and structural barriers, strong commitment from community institutions and their leaders often is required to develop, and sustain, aging-friendly initiatives. Generally, community stakeholders need to believe that enhancing community aging-friendliness is inherently important, that a particular initiative has the potential to enhance the well-being of older residents and the entire community, and that the added value to the community justifies the cost. Without strong and sustained leadership, initiatives that exist outside of established programmatic and funding silos are apt to face substantial difficulty.

Capacity

The ability to access sufficient resources to devote to community change efforts is a second prerequisite. Given the need to overcome existing programmatic silos and other barriers, developing and implementing aging-friendly community change processes requires enhanced organizational capacity, including financial inputs as well as other resources such as in-kind contributions and volunteers. Potential resource sources include public funding, grants, donations, user fees, and community organizations. Generally, initiatives with funding from a variety of sources (e.g., dues, donations, fees, grants, public funding) are likely to be more financially secure than initiatives dependent on a single source (Carroll & Stater,

2009; Crittenden, 2000). Initiatives able to secure greater and more sustainable resources can generally employ more staff, develop a wider array of activities, reach a greater number of people, and ultimately have a greater overall impact. In our national survey of aging initiatives, described later in this chapter, obtaining adequate funding was the challenge cited most frequently by participating communities.

Collaboration

Given the complexity of issues involved in aging friendliness and the need for changes that transcend the abilities of any single agency or organization, initiative success requires the active involvement of multiple community systems and sectors. Among the sectors that should be involved in aging-friendly community change efforts are area agencies on aging (AAA) and local government agencies, community organizations, the private sector, younger community members, and consumers.

Area Agencies on Aging and Local Government

Local AAAs in 629 communities and 243 tribal organizations are charged by the U.S. Older Americans Act (OAA) with responsibility for planning and coordinating efforts to meet the needs of local older adults and serving as "the advocate and focal point for older individuals within the community by (in cooperation with agencies, organizations, and individuals participating in activities under the [area] plan) monitoring, evaluating and commenting upon all policies, programs, hearings, levies, and community actions which will affect older individuals" [The Older Americans Act of 1965, Section 306(a) (6)(B)]. A 2014 survey by the National Association of Area Agencies on Aging (n4a) found that more than 70% of AAAs had worked with other local government agencies or other entities to develop some kind of aging-friendly project or plan.

Community Organizations

Nonprofit organizations are another key partner. The involvement of established community organizations can contribute to greater initiative stability through access to in-kind supports and expertise, credibility, and a variety of funding sources and other outside resources (Carroll & Stater, 2009). Faith-based institutions and communities are often overlooked, despite their potential for enhancing broader community participation in community change efforts. Two thirds of older African Americans, for example, are connected with a church, suggesting that churches may play a critical role in promoting the inclusion of this segment of the older adult population.

Housing providers can be especially important contributors to community aging friendliness. Eskaton, a senior living provider in California, for example, also sponsors Live Well at Home, which provides care advisors, telephone reassurance, transportation, home care, and adult day care for individuals living in their own homes. Eskaton also developed a Livable Design national demonstration home and sponsors a Livable Design Seal of Approval certification program for homes that meet Livable Design standards. Episcopal Communities and Services, which operates continuing care retirement communities in Southern California, also is a sponsor of Pasadena Village, one of the approximately 150 such member-driven community initiatives in the United States, as we describe in Chapter 11. Finally, another senior living provider, Navigage, has launched SherpaLife, an online virtual community that offers dedicated personal concierge services, financial and legal consultation, and social activities.

Private Sector

The private sector includes for-profit commercial businesses that create and sell products and services. For most older adults and their families, the private marketplace is the primary source of products and services designed to help them live more safely and easily, get to where they want to go, and have better quality of life. Technological innovations, for example, have been developed almost entirely within the private sector. Businesses also contribute indirectly to aging-friendly initiatives by contributing to community economic well-being, providing public and private resources that can be committed to aging-friendly infrastructure improvements.

Younger Community Members

Younger community members also have an important role to play in helping communities become more aging friendly, for current cohorts of older adults as well as for future cohorts such as themselves. GenPhilly, for example, is a network of more than 400 "emerging leaders" in the city of Philadelphia who "are working to change stereotypes and establish Philadelphia as a lifelong community for all of us" (http://www.genphilly.org/). GenPhilly includes members working in the aging network as well as those working in other disciplines, and part of the hope is encouraging other disciplines to consider the needs of older adults in their work (K. Clark, 2014). The organization is supported and organized by the Philadelphia Corporation for Aging, the local AAA, and has a volunteer leadership committee composed of professionals from various Philadelphia organizations. Activities include regular network meetings, a LISTSERV and other communications through social media, and public events that aim to bring together individuals from different disciplines and different ages (K. Clark, 2014). While there has not yet been a formal evaluation of GenPhilly's effects on its members or older residents in Philadelphia, K. Clark (2014) credited the members' connections and resources as playing a major role in Age-Friendly Philadelphia projects, such as the development of an Age-Friendly Parks Checklist.

Consumer Involvement

Community residents can be involved in aging-friendly initiatives in a variety of ways: as consumers or service users; by providing input regarding the needs and priorities of community residents; by participating in planning and development efforts; as leadership, such as by serving on governance bodies; by serving in operational or service provision roles; and by providing or securing financial support.

Engaging older adults more fully in aging-friendly initiatives has a number of potential benefits, including greater responsiveness to community needs, increased buy-in from those most likely to be affected by initiative efforts, more appropriate and effective interventions, enhanced use of existing and new programs and services, and greater ultimate benefit for communities and their older residents (Parker & Betz, 2000). Participation in community change efforts can also foster capacity-building and empowerment, promoting new relationships and resources that can contribute to future community improvements (Goodman, Yoo, & Jack, 2006; Kubisch et al., 2002; Wallerstein & Bernstein, 1994).

Comprehensiveness/Specificity

Comprehensiveness and specificity refer to the scope of the initiative, including the range of functional and programmatic systems targeted by efforts to enhance person–environment transactions. As noted, the approaches taken by aging-friendly community initiatives vary dramatically. Some initiatives are focused primarily on changing the physical environment in an effort to make public and private spaces more accessible; other initiatives focus more on the social environment in an effort to increase social engagement, participation, and support (Lui et al., 2009). Communities participating in the WHO Global Network of Age-Friendly Cities and Communities, for example, target age-friendly features and barriers with regard to eight particular nonexclusive domains.

Comprehensiveness also refers to the population groups or geographic locations that are targeted. While some initiatives focus narrowly on segments of the population with particular social or demographic characteristics, others include virtually all community residents. Among the groups that might be targeted are the following: residents who are considered older (e.g., over the age of 60 or 65); individuals who are considered potentially vulnerable because of age (e.g., over the age of 80 or 85); those with deleterious health or social conditions (e.g., functional impairment, cognitive impairment, mental illness); those with potential risk factors (e.g., social isolation); those who are experiencing particular life transitions (e.g., retirement, widowhood); or those who are experiencing particular environmental transitions (e.g., relocation from one care setting to another) (Greenfield, 2012).

Similarly, some initiatives focus narrowly on specific geographic boundaries, while others encompass entire cities, counties, or regions. An aging-friendly initiative might target residents of particular buildings or groups of buildings; particular neighborhoods; communities with conditions that are considered potentially deleterious (e.g., crime, economic deprivation); communities experiencing environmental transitions (e.g., neighborhood redevelopment); or any other environments where aging-friendly improvements are needed.

Concerned primarily about issues of empowerment and inclusion, Gonyea and Hudson (2015) postulated three dimensions of inclusiveness in community aging initiatives: sector, environment, and population. The sector dimension assesses whether the public sector or the private sector is more involved in the change effort, including their respective types of involvement (e.g., funding, human resources, physical space) and levels of involvement (e.g., key actor, minor actor, no role). The environment dimension assesses whether the initiative is more concerned with changing the community's physical infrastructure (e.g., buildings, outdoor spaces, transportation, walkability) or social infrastructure (e.g., community and health services, civic participation and employment, cultural and recreational opportunities). The population dimension assesses whether the initiative is focused more on targeting advantaged or disadvantaged groups of older adults, considering factors such as economic condition, gender, race, ethnicity, functional capacity, and housing.

Stages of the Community Change Process

Aging-friendly community initiatives represent a specific application of general community change approaches, as applied to the challenges of enhancing aging-friendliness. The ultimate goal of community change efforts is to enhance a community's overall "competence" (Cottrell, 1976), in which relevant components (e.g., individuals, groups, organizations, institutions) can collaboratively identify community problems and needs, agree on goals and priorities, agree on how to achieve those goals, and collaborate effectively to take necessary action to enhance community well-being. Aging-friendly community change therefore requires attention to seven prototypic stages of the general community change process, as shown in Figure 8.1: (a) identification of a common concern; (b) promotion of community ownership; (c) collaboration; (d) intervention planning; (e) implementation; (f) outcome monitoring; and (g) sustainability.

Identifying a common concern that community members consider both important and achievable is a critical first step in any community change process

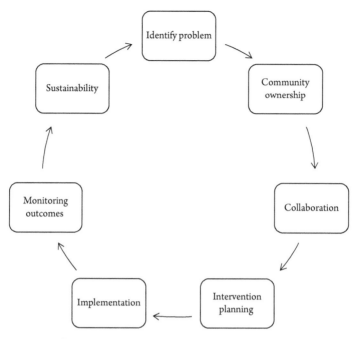

Figure 8.1 Stages of the community change process.

(Green & Haines, 2015; Kubisch et al, 2002). For example, cities participating in the WHO Global Network of Age-Friendly Cities and Communities typically conduct focus groups and key informant interviews with older adults, family members, and service providers to identify a city's age-friendly features in each of eight domains, as well as potential improvements that could enhance elderly residents' health, social participation, and security (WHO, 2007). Similarly, the AdvantAge Initiative of the Visiting Nurse Service of New York conducts community surveys to assess elderly residents' perceptions of community "elder friendliness."

After identifying a common concern, initiatives need to *promote community ownership* by fostering widespread community interest and promoting community involvement. Resident involvement in problem identification and intervention planning can help to ensure that issues, goals, and plans are both important and achievable (Green & Haines, 2015; Kubisch et al., 2002). Involving consumers in decision-making roles (e.g., providing oversight as a board member) also can foster innovative thinking, improve outcomes, and ensure that initiatives are responsive to local needs (Parker & Betz, 2000). Consumer involvement may not only lead to improved outcomes for change efforts, but also can have a positive impact on participants. Community involvement has been found to enhance self-efficacy (i.e., an individual's belief in his or her ability to achieve goals and make desired changes) (Bandura, 1982; Ohmer, 2008); skills (Foster-Fishman et al., 2006); personal feelings of empowerment; and collective efficacy (i.e., community members' shared beliefs that they can bring about desired community change) (Price & Behrens, 2003). Involvement also enhances community social capital by promoting trust among community members and institutions as well as fostering social norms that encourage participating in social change efforts (Sampson, 2003).

Change requires *collaboration* among stakeholders around common concerns. Collaboration typically involves coalitions among community organizations, service providers, government agencies, funding organizations, or community leaders (Kramer et al., 2005). Effective collaboration is based on a sense of mutual concern and respect among the various stakeholders, as well as a shared commitment to the well-being of the entire community. While developed in response to a specific initiative, coalitions link stakeholders in bonds that can endure and provide the basis for future collaborative activity (Stoecker, 2005). The Robert Wood Johnson Foundation's Community Partnerships for Older Adults (CPFOA) initiative, which we describe in Chapter 10, for example, represents an approach for encouraging the formation of partnerships among a variety of community stakeholders (e.g., policymakers, older adults, social service providers, local governments) (RWJF, 2011).

Intervention planning involves the specific steps required to produce desired changes, as specified in a theory of change (Anderson, 2004; Auspos & Kubisch, 2004). Intervention planning involves an organized effort, frequently initiated and convened by local government agencies or similar entities and including representatives from various community organizations. The Calgary Elder-Friendly Communities Project (CEFCP), for example, utilized a comprehensive theory of change to guide a community development process to enhance the well-being of seniors in underresourced neighborhoods (Austin, des Camp, Flux, McClelland, & Sieppert, 2005). As we describe in Chapter 11, the carefully conceived process engaged older neighborhood residents in selecting priority issues, developing a work plan, accessing resources, organizing workshops, hosting social activities, and implementing community development projects to address community-identified needs, with support from professional community development workers. In so doing, CEFCP aimed to foster enhanced community capacity and social capital that could continue to benefit these neighborhoods long after the project ended.

Implementation involves specific activities designed to make a community more aging friendly, including changes in the physical environment, social engagement, public policies, social programs, and other community domains. It is important to involve key stakeholders, those individuals and groups who are personally affected by a situation, care about the situation, and have the power to do something about it. Depending on the issue and context, this might include policymakers, funders, for-profit and not-for-profit service providers, community leaders, and community residents. Effective action is based in a common sense of empowerment—the belief that actions have a reasonable likelihood of producing desired outcomes. This is in contrast to a sense of disempowerment or helplessness, which reflects the experience-based belief that one's actions are unlikely to result in desired outcomes, thereby undermining the willingness and motivation to commit time, energy, and other resources to efforts to create desired changes.

It is necessary to *monitor outcomes* to assess whether the initiative is achieving its intended objectives (Green & Haines, 2007). Ideally, this involves a process of continuous quality improvement (CQI), through ongoing analysis of system performance to identify and correct processes that undermine goal achievement. CQI is differentiated from other quality approaches by its focus on determining and meeting the needs of end users/customers, its effort to identify root causes of poor performance, its data-based approach to management, and the shift of power and responsibility to practitioners in a position to improve quality on a daily basis (Shortell, Bennett, & Byck, 1998). One model for doing so is the Plan, Do, Study, Act (PDSA) paradigm developed by Edward Demings, an American engineer widely credited with helping Japan develop the manufacturing and business practices that paved the way for its post–World War II economic development. PDSA emphasizes that interventions are incomplete unless they include a process of CQI involving ongoing monitoring and adjustment.

Joining the WHO Global Network of Age-Friendly Cities and Communities, for example, requires that cities implement a four-step process of plan development, implementation, and modification somewhat similar to Demings's PDSA model: (a) establish mechanisms for involving older people and partnering with government and community organizations on aging-friendly community change efforts; (b) develop a 3-year citywide action plan based on the findings of a baseline assessment of community aging friendliness; (c) identify indicators to monitor plan implementation and assess progress against those indicators; and (d) revise the plan as needed to ensure broad responsibility for community aging friendliness (WHO, n.d.-a.).

Sustainability of change activities and outcomes is a critical and often-overlooked aspect of community change processes. Without modifications in existing structures and resources, there is little to sustain change over time. Structural changes might include informal interorganizational relationships and coalitions or institutionalization of a new community entity. Also needed is ongoing funding and other resources, preferably from a combination of public funding, donations, and nonprofit organizations. Diversified funding, incorporating support from a variety of private and public sources, could provide greater financial security and flexibility when compared to dependence on a single funding source (Carroll & Stater, 2009; Crittenden, 2000).

Aging-Friendly Community Change Approaches

As we have noted in this chapter, a variety of approaches exist that communities can take for pursuing aging-friendly community change, including the following: increasing public awareness; engaging in community planning; improving existing services or developing new services; having building coalitions among key stakeholders and organizations; providing advocacy; using community organizing; taking political action; and engaging in social and economic development.

In an effort to create an organizing framework of the various approaches for helping communities become more aging friendly, we have identified four principal conceptually distinct types of aging-friendly community initiatives based on their primary intervention modality: communitywide planning; cross-sector systems change; consumer-driven support networks; and single-sector services. Informed by Jack Rothman's classic community practice framework (Rothman, 1995, 2007), these four types of community aging initiatives vary with regard to their focus, scope, auspices, level and type of elder involvement, sources of funding, and primary methods for achieving their goals.

This typology is based on findings from our 2009 national survey of community aging initiatives, which examined the characteristics of 124 such initiatives in the United States identified through a Google search using "aging friendly," "elder friendly," and other relevant terms. The study was conducted at the request of leaders of major community aging initiatives from throughout the United States, and with support from the MetLife Foundation, in an effort to fill gaps in existing knowledge regarding the range of aging-friendly community initiatives in the United States and creating a foundation from which to develop future evaluations of the effectiveness and sustainability of such initiatives. In addition to documenting the range of initiatives, our study utilized survey data to develop a conceptually and empirically based classification system, based on observed variations with regard to initiative goals (i.e., focus and scope), auspices, participant roles, funding sources, and methods for achieving their goals.

Communitywide planning efforts typically focus primarily on communitywide needs assessment and strategic planning. The methods they employ include planning, assessment, community education, and promoting community awareness of the needs of older adults, typically relying on experts to solicit input from key stakeholders, based on preexisting frameworks or guidelines on aging friendliness. These mostly are "top-down" efforts involving representatives from local governments, social service providers, universities, and other professionals. Funding for these initiatives frequently comes from a combination of public funds, grants, and in-kind support. Prominent examples include WHO's Global Age-Friendly Cities Program and the AdvantAge Initiative, a national program of the Visiting Nurse Service of New York.

Cross-sector systems change efforts involve interorganizational collaborations across existing service delivery sectors to enhance existing programs and services for older adults. In our study, we identified two separate types of cross-sector initiatives: residence-based support services and other cross-sector systems change initiatives. Among the collaborating sectors are health care organizations, social service providers, housing providers, and transportation services, with external grant funding or public demonstration funds frequently serving as an incentive for organizations from disparate sectors to collaborate. The focus typically is on developing new programs or services, or enhancing the scope or reach of existing programs, rather than wide-scale community change. Collaborations between service providers and geographically defined housing settings are one prominent example. The Naturally Occurring Retirement Community Supportive Services Program (NORC-SSP) model described in Chapter 10, for example, involves collaborations among housing providers, health and social service organizations, to promote more aging-friendly living environments. Other cross-sector systems change initiatives focus more generally on some combination of community education and enhancing existing programs, services, and infrastructure for older adults. One prominent example is the Robert Wood Johnson Foundation's CPFOA, also described in Chapter 10.

Consumer-driven support networks involve mutual assistance and advocacy efforts among community residents. A key feature of these consumer-driven associations is a focus on peer support and other activities designed to increase community social capital. Because of their inclusive nature, these initiatives tend to involve older community residents in virtually all aspects of their activities, including developing the initiative, providing oversight and governance, and offering support and services to other members. These mostly are "bottom-up" efforts developed by residents of specific neighborhoods or towns. Funding comes primarily from fees (e.g., annual membership dues), gifts (e.g., contributions from members or others), and in-kind donations. Most of these initiatives consider themselves to be "villages," organizations based on Beacon Hill Village, a membership-based association created by a group of seniors living in the Beacon Hill neighborhood of Boston.

A fourth type, *single-sector services*, focuses primarily on improvements in a specific type of service or sector, such as transportation, housing, or recreation. Because these initiatives are typically more narrowly focused and are not working toward overall system change, we view them as different from aging-friendly community initiatives. While these initiatives are doing valuable work, we do not discuss them further in this book.

Conclusion

In this chapter, we saw how aging-friendly community change requires a systemic approach that transcends individual programs or sectors to respond to the interactional and dynamic nature of aging-related personal and environmental challenges. Effective aging-friendly community change requires adequate commitment, capacity, collaboration of major sectors and stakeholders, consumer involvement, and a comprehensive approach that is fully inclusive. Reflecting classic community practice methods, and based on findings from our national survey of aging initiatives, we identified four types of aging-friendly initiatives. In Chapters 9, 10, and 11, we examine communitywide planning models, cross-sector collaborations, and consumer initiatives, respectively, in greater detail, providing examples of each and reviewing the available evidence regarding their accomplishments and challenges.

9

Community Planning Models

Introduction

Community planning models include some of the most visible aging-friendly community initiatives across the United States and throughout the world. As described briefly in Chapter 8, our 2009 survey included a number of initiatives that employ a community planning model, the most prominent of which include participants in the World Health Organization's (WHO's) Global Network of Age-Friendly Cities and Communities (with AARP's Network of Age-Friendly Communities the U.S. affiliate) and in the AdvantAge Initiative, which is sponsored by the Visiting Nurse Service of New York.

The community planning model for making communities more aging-friendly aligns closely with what Weil, Gamble, and Ohmer (2013) classified as *social planning*, in which a variety of community stakeholders, including governments, neighborhood associations, social service providers, and residents, develop comprehensive proposals for action. Planning typically involves the participation of professionals or representatives from public agencies and therefore may tend toward more bureaucratic structures than other approaches to community change (Chaskin, 2005). According to Rothman (2007), the distinguishing feature of planning is its emphasis on data to guide the development and implementation of initiative efforts. At its most rationalistic extreme, planning may be entirely top down, with experts utilizing statistical modeling procedures to develop a comprehensive step-by-step plan that they impose on the community. This approach to planning, however, has been criticized as too technical for the complex problems confronting many communities and alienating to community stakeholders (Rothman, 2007). Participatory planning, in which the views of community groups are incorporated into plans and goals, is viewed by some scholars as a preferable approach (Checkoway, 1995; Minkler & Wallerstein, 2005; Rothman, 2007). Such an approach, while potentially adding time and effort, likely contributes to the sustainability and effectiveness of the community planning initiative as it may lead to a more comprehensive communitywide assessment and ensure the buy-in of many stakeholders (Rothman, 2007). As we shall see, aging-friendly community initiatives that use a community planning model have, to varying degrees, taken this more participatory approach.

In this chapter, we examine a variety of aging-friendly community change efforts utilizing a community planning approach. We also critically assess the progress and achievements of community planning models to date, with particular attention to emerging best practices for needs assessment, inclusive community plan development, and implementing plans at the local level. Like other community change models, these initiatives typically include a range of stakeholders, but what distinguishes them is the role that local (and sometimes state) government often plays. As we describe subsequently, governmental involvement is often necessary given the broad scope and range of activities undertaken by these initiatives. For example, community planning model initiatives often target the physical infrastructure for change, which requires support and actions by local government. While older adults are described as highly involved, their contributions are typically through providing input and information, developing the initiative, and receiving some services and support. These initiatives tend to take a top-down governance approach, and at the time of our survey in 2009 had engaged primarily in communitywide needs assessment and strategic planning. In the intervening years, many of these initiatives have moved forward with implementing at least some aspects of their strategic plans.

WHO Global Age-Friendly Cities and Communities Project

The WHO launched its Global Age-Friendly Cities initiative in 2006 when 158 focus groups with older adults, caregivers, and service providers for the aging it coordinated in 33 cities around the world (WHO, 2007). WHO's program takes a top-down governance approach to community change (Barusch, 2013). Prior to these focus groups, for example, WHO defined an aging-friendly city as one that "encourages active ageing by optimizing opportunities for health, participation, and security in order to enhance quality of life as people age" (WHO, 2007, p. 1). Based on earlier work by organizations for the aging (e.g., AARP) as well as the scholarly literature, WHO also identified eight features that could contribute to promoting this definition of age friendliness: outdoor spaces and buildings, transportation, housing, respect and social inclusion, social participation, civic participation and employment, communication and information, and community support and health (WHO, 2007). The focus groups then informed the identification of 88 features described as a "universal standard for an age-friendly city" (WHO, 2007, p. 11). Many of these features are viewed by WHO as making the city better not only for older adults but also for residents of all ages and capabilities (Buffel et al., 2012). All of these features are described in detail in WHO's 2007 report *Global Age-Friendly Cities: A Guide*. In Table 9.1, we offer some examples in each of the eight topics.

Table 9.1 **Selected Checklist Items From WHO Global Age-Friendly Cities**

Outdoor spaces and buildings	There are well-maintained and safe green spaces, with adequate shelter, toilet facilities, and seating that can be easily accessed.
	Roads have well-designed and appropriately placed physical structures, such as traffic islands, overpasses or underpasses, to assist pedestrians to cross busy roads.
	Services are clustered, are located in close proximity to where older people live, and can be easily accessed.
Transportation	Public transportation is affordable for all older people.
	Sufficient specialized transport services are available for people with disabilities.
	Information is provided to older people on how to use public transport and about the range of transport options available.
Housing	Housing is modified for older people as needed.
	There are appropriately qualified and reliable service providers to undertake maintenance work.
	A range of appropriate and affordable housing options is available for older people, including frail and disabled older people, in the local area.
Social participation	Community activities encourage the participation of people of different ages and cultural backgrounds.
	Facilities are accessible and equipped to enable participation by people with disabilities or by those who require care.
	Local gathering places and activities promote familiarity and exchange among neighborhood residents.
Respect and social inclusion	Older people are consulted by public, voluntary, and commercial services on ways to serve them better.
	Older people are provided opportunities to share their knowledge, history, and expertise with other generations.
	Economically disadvantaged older people enjoy access to public, voluntary, and private services and events.

(continued)

Table 9.1 **Continued**

Civic participation and employment	There is a range of options for older volunteer participation.
	There are flexible opportunities, with options for part-time or seasonal employment for older people.
	Advisory council, boards of organizations, and the like include older people.
Communication and information	Regular and reliable distribution of information is ensured by government or voluntary organizations.
	Individuals in public offices and businesses provide friendly, person-to-person service on request.
	There is wide public access to computers and the Internet, at no or minimal charge, in public places such as government offices, community centers, and libraries.
Community and health services	Health and social services are well distributed throughout the city, are conveniently co-located, and can be reached readily by all means of transportation.
	Home care services are offered that include health services, personal care, and housekeeping.
	Emergency planning includes older people, taking into account their needs and capacities in preparing for and responding to emergencies.

In 2010, WHO created the Global Network of Age-Friendly Cities, now referred to as the Global Network of Age-Friendly Cities and Communities to reflect the variety of localities participating in the initiative. In the United States, AARP recommends involving a variety of stakeholders in local efforts, including neighborhood associations, institutions of higher education, nonprofit organizations, community foundations, and older community residents. WHO and its national and regional affiliates require that a local government official with authority, such as a mayor, provide a written pledge a commitment toward age-friendly community change. Members are expected to share best practices and lessons learned with others in the network, but WHO and its network affiliates also provide technical assistance. AARP, for example, offers resources for conducting a survey of older community residents, recommendations for evaluating progress, and a monthly newsletter, among other resources. Many of these resources appear to be targeted toward policymakers and other professionals contributing to the initiative. According to the initiative's website (http://age-friendlyworld.org/en/), to become a member a local government must send a letter indicating commitment to engaging in community change efforts to create the physical and social infrastructure detailed in the checklist. Members are also expected to (a) develop strategies to ensure older residents' participation throughout the process, (b) conduct a communitywide assessment addressing the eight WHO domains, (c) produce a 3-year plan for action, and (d) construct indicators for evaluating progress in the action plan. The WHO Network included 210 cities and communities in 26 countries as of spring 2015.

Canada, for example, has played a large role in the Global Age-Friendly Cities and Communities project since early in the project's development, with the Public Health Agency of Canada (PHAC) giving funds to WHO to produce the 2007 guide, and four cities (i.e., Saanich, British Columbia; Portage la Prairie, Manitoba; Sherbrooke, Quebec; and Halifax, Nova Scotia) participating in the original round of focus groups (Plouffe & Kalache, 2011). By 2011, there were 560 communities in Canada that had initiated efforts to be more age friendly.

In the Canadian model, PHAC supports the work of provincial and local governments by facilitating communication and disseminating best practices. For example, PHAC, in collaboration with those working at the local level, has made a number of recommendations, such as including older residents in all stages of the age-friendly initiative; incorporating the needs of diverse older adults; forming cross-sector collaborations with traditional (e.g., aging services) and nontraditional (e.g., architects) partners; and, evaluating efforts to document successes (Plouffe & Kalache, 2011). Local communities must also demonstrate progress in meeting specific criteria to be officially part of Canada's larger age-friendly effort.

At the national level, PHAC has organized an Age Friendly Community Forum and webinar series to provide guidance for initiative participants, and provincial governments have used similar strategies to share resources. Experts at the national and regional levels also published a guide on developing an age-friendly initiative in rural communities. Branding and marketing are key components of age-friendly community initiatives in Canada, with provinces such as Quebec creating a formal recognition program and communities developing logos, holding public events, and putting up signs indicating they are an age-friendly community to publicize their efforts. Age-friendly changes to date include guidelines to increase the accessibility of walkways, bus stops, and housing in British Columbia; incorporating accessible design features in a recreation center in Manitoba; and providing a mobile library and more benches in Quebec.

In the United States, AARP reports that 44 towns, cities, and counties, representing localities inhabited by 28 million people, had enrolled in the age-friendly network as of the writing of this book (AARP, 2015). Members include major cities (e.g., San Francisco; Washington, DC; Denver; Boston); counties (e.g., St. Louis County and Westchester County in New York); and smaller cities and towns (e.g., Berea, KY; Ellsworth, ME; Carlsbad, NM). To provide more in-depth examples of the WHO and AARP network, we now turn to two prominent initiatives in the United States: Portland, Oregon, and New York City.

Age-Friendly Portland

Portland, Oregon, was the first U.S. city to participate in the WHO's initial Global Age-Friendly Cities project, conducting focus groups in 2006, being accepted for membership as one of the nine original members in the WHO's Global Network of Age-Friendly Cities in 2010, and becoming an inaugural member of the AARP network in 2012 (AARP, 2013). The Age-Friendly Portland initiative was launched and is coordinated by the Institute on Aging (IOA) at Portland State University, with guidance from an advisory council. The Age-Friendly Portland Advisory Council presently includes representatives from AARP Oregon, the nonprofit advocacy organization Elders in Action; Multnomah County Aging, Disability and Veterans Services Division; the City of Portland Bureau of Planning and Sustainability; Portland Metro (a regional government); Venture Portland; Terwilliger Plaza continuing care retirement community; Oregon Health and Science University; Ride Connection (a nonprofit organization providing accessible transportation options); Asian Health and Service Center; El Programa Hispano; the Oregon office of the Corporation for National and Community Service; and older community residents.

Portland takes a somewhat unique approach by using a city-university-community model, in which researchers and students from IOA emphasize translational research and community collaboration (Neal, DeLaTorre, & Carder, 2014). In addition, while addressing all 8 domains outlined by WHO (divided into 10 for the Portland effort), the Age-Friendly Portland effort initially focused on the role of city planning. For example, when the city solicited community input to update the city's comprehensive plan, the Age-Friendly Portland Advisory Council drew from data collected in the baseline assessment to provide concrete recommendations, such as offering incentives to developers to design and build more accessible housing and constructing more pedestrian-friendly neighborhoods. The coordinators of the Age-Friendly Portland Advisory Council were then invited to join the Mayor's Portland Plan Advisory Group to ensure that the needs of aging residents were taken into account in the new comprehensive plan.

Age-Friendly Portland is also working to improve the city's public transportation system for older adults and individuals with disabilities. Older adults who participated in focus groups for the project noted that Portland's public transit is generally accessible and affordable. Suggestions to increase elder ridership included improving availability by increasing service, particularly on nights and weekends; increasing acceptability through additional safety measures, such as security officers on light-rail trains; and promoting adaptability through pro-grams to teach older adults how to use public transportation.

Neal and colleagues (2014) noted that the Age-Friendly Portland initiative has been able to take advantage of prior relationships between IOA and local commu-nity and government agencies. Challenges have included turnover among elected officials and political appointees, ageism, and limited resources for implementing the Age-Friendly Portland Action Plan.

Age-Friendly NYC

The New York Academy of Medicine (the Academy) initiated the Age-Friendly NYC effort in 2007 through a partnership with the mayor's office and the New York City Council, making Age-Friendly NYC the second U.S. participant in the WHO Global Age-Friendly Cities project. As with other WHO participants, the initiative began with an assessment of the city's aging friendliness through focus groups and town hall meetings with a variety of stakeholders (including older adults); expert round tables on particularly salient issues (e.g., tenant rights, transportation, civic engagement), and feedback from academics and nonprofit leaders (Bloomberg & Quinn, 2009). According to the Academy (New York Academy of Medicine, 2012), Age-Friendly NYC solicited the participation of over 2,000 older residents through conversations conducted in six different languages. The mayor's office (at the time led by Mayor Michael Bloomberg) also examined the aging friendliness of city government services, with a focus on health and social services, social and civic engagement, and infrastructure (Bloomberg & Quinn, 2009).

Based on these data-gathering activities, in 2009 the city proposed 59 recom-mendations for aging-friendly changes, with an emphasis on projects that could be led by the public sector (New York Academy of Medicine, 2012). To ensure the feasibility and cost-effectiveness of the initiative, many of the recommendations target modifying existing city projects. Age-Friendly NYC also received $4 mil-lion in funding from private foundations, the Academy, and the city (Bruno, 2015). John Beard, the director of the WHO Aging and Life Course program, has called Age-Friendly NYC "one of the global leaders" of the age-friendly initiatives.

As described by Bloomberg and Quinn (2009), Age-Friendly NYC's efforts fall under four broader goals, which all relate to WHO's eight topics. First, the program aims to "improve social inclusion, civic participation, and employment opportuni-ties for older adults" (Bloomberg & Quinn, 2009, p. 10). Specific initiatives target-ing this goal include ongoing assessments of neighborhood aging friendliness to promote the inclusion of older adults in community decision-making, creating a time bank system to offer volunteer opportunities for older adults and residents of all ages, and developing job search and training services for older workers. Second, Age-Friendly NYC is working to "increase availability and affordability of safe, appropriate housing" (Bloomberg & Quinn, 2009, p. 10). The city is addressing housing through such changes as streamlining the application process to increase access to the Senior Citizen Rent Increase Exemption Program and improving marketing and outreach for the Senior Citizen Homeowner Assistance Program to provide loans for home modifications. The third goal is to "provide age-friendly public spaces and a safe means for reaching them" (Bloomberg & Quinn, 2009, p. 10). This involves such changes as making public transit more accessible through improved escalator and elevator service in subway stations, piloting a program to provide wheelchair-accessible taxicabs to riders with a disability, and making pedestrian-friendly improvements (e.g., longer signal times, crosswalk islands, curb ramps) at high-risk intersections. The final goal is to "ensure access to health and social services to support independent living" (Bloomberg & Quinn, 2009, p. 10). Meeting this goal includes enhancing services and activities at senior centers to better respond to the preferences and needs of a diverse population of older adults and redesigning the city's case management program to better facilitate older residents' access to benefits and supportive services.

One unique strategy of Age-Friendly NYC is the development of Aging Improvement Districts, which create cross-sector collaborations to implement needed changes identified by older residents in specific neighborhoods (New York Academy of Medicine, 2012). In 2010 and 2011, Age-Friendly NYC began three pilot improvement districts in East Harlem, Bedford-Stuyvesant, and the Upper West Side. Each improvement district is allocated $50,000 per year and requires the active participation of elected officials, community organizations, volunteers, and older residents. The effort begins with community consultations that address the goals identified by Age-Friendly NYC as well as concerns that are more local. As an example, since starting the initiative the East Harlem Aging Improvement District has implemented a variety of relatively low-cost efforts to address needs identified by older neighborhood residents (New York Academy of Medicine, 2012). East Harlem distributed "Age-Friendly New York City" stickers and folding chairs to stores and made specific recommendations for them to become more aging-friendly. Following conversations with the local councilwoman, the city's Department of Transportation installed benches in East Harlem in areas identified as lacking adequate seating. A group of community organizations produced a calendar (available online or in print) of aging-friendly events in the neighborhood. The local library and a museum also developed outreach efforts for older adults and shared best practices for serving older residents.

The AdvantAge Initiative

The AdvantAge Initiative, developed and administered by the Center for Home Care Policy and Research of the Visiting Nurse Service of New York, is a needs assessment and planning process that has been utilized in numerous cities throughout the United States. Based on focus groups with older adults in four cities (Allentown, PA; Asheville, NC; Chicago, IL; and Long Beach, CA), the AdvantAge Initiative developed 33 indicators organized within four "essential elements" of an "elder-friendly" community (Feldman et al., 2004). As shown in Figure 9.1, this framework, which now uses the term *age-friendly* rather than *elder-friendly*, proposes that an age-friendly community includes social and physical infrastructure that (a) addresses older adults' basic needs; (b) promotes and protects older adults' mental and physical health; (c) facilitates independence; and (d) encourages civic and social participation (Hanson & Emlet, 2006). The AdvantAge Initiative piloted a survey designed to test this framework and assess these 33 indicators in 10 communities across the United States that represented a variety of sizes and population demographics, including northwest Chicago, Illinois; Indianapolis, Indiana; Jacksonville, Florida; Lincoln Square neighborhood in New York City; Maricopa County, Arizona; Orange County, Florida; Puyallup, Washington; Santa Clarita, California; Upper West Side in New York City; and Yonkers, New York (Feldman et al., 2004). The AdvantAge Initiative's approach is to collect information to offer a "snapshot" of older adults living in a community, which can then be utilized by community stakeholders to make age-friendly improvements (Feldman et al., 2004). This information is

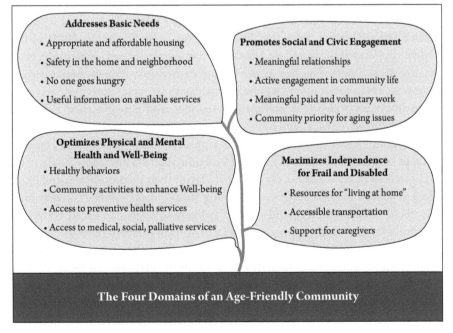

Figure 9.1 AdvantAge Initiative's four domains of an age-friendly community.

designed to capture community barriers to age friendliness and identify targets for intervention.

Hanson and Emlet (2006) provided an example of the AdvantAge Initiative at work in 1 of the 10 pilot communities, Puyallup, Washington. The AdvantAge Initiative conducted a telephone survey with 514 older adults randomly selected from the community to learn about older residents' experiences and perceptions of the community. Based on this assessment, the task force made a number of recommendations, many of which involved collaboration between public and private entities. For example, after learning that a considerable number of respondents did not know about the area agency on aging (AAA), the local AAA conducted an outreach campaign to promote its assistance services to older residents and professionals who regularly interact with older adults. This effort led to a 250% increase in senior information and assistance calls over a 1-year period. Local government allocated funding for pedestrian-friendly design improvements, including larger street signs and lighting that was more adequate. As a final example, a partnership between a variety of community stakeholders (i.e., the county health department, city parks and recreation department, nonprofit health research organization, and a local hospital) produced a local guide to low-cost or free exercise programs available in the community. A similar collaboration led to a walking group for older adults.

A unique feature of the AdvantAge Initiative is its attention to economic disparities. In the 2004 report disseminating the results from the AdvantAge Initiative national survey, Feldman and colleagues (2004) distinguished what they called the "Fortunate Majority," who enjoy relatively optimal levels of health and well-being, from the "Frail Fraction," who live below 200% of the federal poverty line, have low educational attainment, and experience poor health. Most elders classified as the Fortunate Majority express high satisfaction with their community, regularly participate in social activities, are confident they can access information and services, and perceive their health as good, very good, or excellent. For example, about three quarters of older adults in this group agree that they have had a positive influence on their community. In contrast, members of the Frail Fraction, who are also more likely to be African American or Latino, are dissatisfied with their community, spend more than one third of their income on housing (thus going over the conventional threshold of affordability), and are half as likely to engage in social activities. According to this study, approximately two thirds of elders in the Frail Fraction believe that elected officials are not concerned about their needs, indicating a significant proportion feel socially excluded. While Hanson and Emlet (2006) noted that using 200% of the federal poverty line does not provide a complete picture of the experiences of those who are economically vulnerable, by describing the two segments of the older adult population the AdvantAge Initiative highlights the need for the development and implementation of different types of interventions to address the wants and needs of both groups (Feldman et al., 2004).

Aging-Friendly Community Planning Initiatives Developed by Other Cities

Age-Friendly Philadelphia

Age-Friendly Philadelphia is an initiative of the Philadelphia Corporation for Aging (PCA), a nonprofit organization that serves as the city's AAA (K. Clark & Glicksman, 2012). PCA's Age-Friendly Philadelphia builds on the U.S. Environmental Protection Agency's (EPA's) Aging Initiative, which developed four principles of aging friendliness: (a) social connections and engagement (i.e., social integration, access to social support, and civic engagement opportunities); (b) neighborhoods and housing (i.e., appropriate housing conditions, variety of housing options, neighborhood access to services and shopping, neighborhood safety); (c) transportation and mobility (i.e., freedom to move around using one's own preferred mode of transport, accessible and convenient public transit); and (d) access to healthy activities (i.e., access to food, access to recreational activities) (U.S. EPA Aging Initiative, 2011). Based on extensive research using existing data collected from older Philadelphians, with a particular focus on using geographic information systems (GISs) to examine neighborhood factors, PCA's Age-Friendly Philadelphia modified the EPA principles to reflect Philadelphia's needs and policy priorities: (a) social capital; (b) flexible and accessible housing; (c) mobility; and (d) eating healthy (K. Clark & Glicksman, 2012).

The PCA's Age-Friendly Philadelphia has a number of unique features that distinguish its approach from other aging-friendly initiatives using a community planning model. PCA is one of the few AAAs that has its own research program; therefore, PCA's Age-Friendly Philadelphia has integrated research with policy and planning from the beginning. Research staff developed indicators of an age-friendly community and documented that the four principles contribute to optimal health among older adults, including those from diverse populations and varying financial resources (K. Clark & Glicksman, 2012). Rather than creating a new program that might require extensive financial and human resources, PCA's Age-Friendly Philadelphia works to bring together a variety of community organizations, including those that have not historically focused on older adults, and facilitates innovative ways to make Philadelphia more aging friendly. As part of PCA's technical assistance to other stakeholders, research staff have disseminated information about older city residents and evidence supporting different interventions. For example, PCA has created maps using GIS to identify neighborhoods with a high need for home repairs and the distance between bus stops and senior centers (PCA, 2011a). PCA's Age-Friendly Philadelphia decided to pursue this strategy after meetings with over 150 organizations in the city indicated a great deal of interest in serving older residents but little knowledge about how to do so (K. Clark & Glicksman, 2012).

A second distinguishing feature of PCA's Age-Friendly Philadelphia is the role of GenPhilly, a network of young professionals who focus on aging, to provide leadership in its efforts and contribute to the initiative's sustainability. As we discuss in Chapter 13, PCA created GenPhilly to enlist the participation of emerging leaders throughout the city in the Age-Friendly Philadelphia efforts. According to Kate Clark (personal communication, April 13, 2015), a staff member of PCA who devotes part of her time to coordinating GenPhilly, this network of aging ambassadors across the city has been key to the initiative's survival, given that PCA's Age-Friendly Philadelphia has almost no funding.

Since the initiative began in 2009, PCA has engaged in a number of efforts to promote Philadelphia's aging friendliness. For example, PCA collaborated with the largest city park's conservancy to produce an Age-Friendly Parks Checklist, which enumerates features that would promote elder's use of and enjoyment in parks (K. Clark & Glicksman, 2012). PCA has also worked with governmental and nongovernmental organizations, including a university planning department and the city's zoning code commission, to incorporate PCA's Age-Friendly Philadelphia principles into the city's zoning code. Specifically, they negotiated the inclusion of accessory dwelling units and requirements for visitability features in new home construction (K. Clark & Glicksman, 2012). Through a partnership with an existing coalition, PCA advocated for the city to make bus stops more amenable to older adults by providing shelter from the weather, benches, and adequate lighting. As a final example, PCA is encouraging senior centers and senior housing buildings to develop community gardens to provide activities for older adults and promote community engagement.

The Atlanta Regional Commission's Lifelong Communities Initiative

The Atlanta Regional Commission (ARC) is the planning agency and AAA for 10 counties in the Atlanta, Georgia, metropolitan area (ARC, 2007). As with many other initiatives using a community planning model, ARC's aging-friendly initiative began with a survey of older adults (in this case, adults ages 55 or over) living in its jurisdiction. Specifically, the survey assessed older residents' views on transportation, housing, health, preventive health, employment, physical activity, nutrition, civic engagement, long-term care, and the community. In addition, ARC gathered additional evidence of the region's need for an aging-friendly initiative by analyzing existing data from the U.S. Census Bureau, the Centers for Disease Control and Prevention, and travel surveys, among others. ARC then incorporated this information into its approach and activities for its Lifelong Communities Initiative (originally called Aging Atlanta). Lifelong Communities targets three areas to improve aging friendliness: (a) promote housing and transportation options, (b) encourage healthy lifestyles, and (c) expand access to services. Table 9.2 provides more detail about the specific goals within each of these areas.

Lifelong Communities has received funding for its initiative from a variety of sources, including the EPA, the U.S. Department of Housing and Urban Development (HUD), the Administration for Community Living (ACL), and the Robert Wood Johnson Foundation, and other private foundations. Its strategy

Table 9.2 **Goals of the Lifelong Communities Initiative**

Promote Housing and Transportation Options	*Encourage Healthy Lifestyles*	*Expand Access to Services*
Integrate older adults into local land use and community planning processes	Improve access to preventive health care and basic services	Educate older adults and caregivers about services early and often
Develop policy to promote housing options for older adults	Keep older adults active and engaged	Improve linkages among community-based service providers
Develop housing and housing programs for older adults	Educate older adults on critical health issues	
Include older adults in planning for and construction of new transportation projects	Improve capacity of the local health system to serve a growing older adult population	
Improve capacity of older drivers		
Improve public transit to serve the needs of older drivers		
Improve existing social service transportation systems		
Eliminate the need for older adults to drive		

for community change has been to bring together a variety of stakeholders, provide technical assistance, and contribute to policy change. The process undertaken by the initiative's leaders has involved: meeting with key stakeholders, including representatives from local and regional governments and older residents; hosting a large stakeholder meeting to review survey and other research data; forming local workgroups that target each of the three overarching goals; identifying local community goals and soliciting official support from local elected officials; and finally, developing a larger regional plan based on the local efforts. As reported by its former director Kathryn Lawler, similar to Age-Friendly Philadelphia, Lifelong Communities has facilitated the inclusion of many organizations and government agencies that have little previous experience working together or focusing on the needs of older adults.

Since it first formed in 2007, the ARC has catalyzed a number of changes throughout the Atlanta region. According to Kathryn Lawler, Lifelong Communities improved mobility options for older residents by training older residents how to use public transportation; creating a transportation voucher program that can be used for a variety of services, including rides from friends and family; and increasing the availability of countdown crosswalks in intersections throughout the area. One of the more innovative approaches of Lifelong Communities emerged from the goal of ensuring that both new and existing housing is accessible, affordable, and close to goods and services. To meet that goal, Lifelong Communities organized a charrette (i.e., an intense period of design activity) that brought together experts from the areas of community development, engineering, design, health, and aging to improve housing, transportation, and community planning in selected sites across the region. In addition, community residents, including older adults, were invited to participate in the presentation and review process. Participants strategized ways to provide a continuum of housing, including apartments, accessory dwelling units, and supportive housing, to meet the needs of residents of all ages. For example, charrette participants proposed changing zoning codes in specific neighborhoods to transform them from segregated use (i.e., single-family lots separated from commercial zones) to integrated use (i.e., a mix of residential and commercial building types) (Atlanta Regional Commission, 2009).

Strengths and Limitations of Community Planning Models

While it is beyond the scope of this chapter to describe every initiative in the United States using a community planning model to bring about aging-friendly community change, the examples provided highlight some of the common methods of this approach. First, reflecting a more top-down path to community change, these initiatives typically develop a model, checklist, or guide that specifies aging-friendly physical and social environmental features. Often, this checklist or guide is informed by some combination of a review of the empirical literature, conversations with recognized experts (both within and outside the field of aging), and surveys or focus groups with older adults. Second, more so than other approaches to aging-friendly community change, these initiatives recognize the ways the built environment can create barriers to elder health, well-being, and social inclusion. Common targets for change include transportation systems, zoning codes, and housing options. Third, and in part related, these initiatives require the active participation of local, regional, or state governments. The impetus for an aging-friendly initiative may come from a variety of sources, such as a university, aging services provider, community foundation, or mutual aid organization, but achieving many of the initiative's goals is not possible without government as an official partner. Fourth, given the broad scope of these initiatives and their tendency to target an entire city or metropolitan area, getting to the implementation stage can be a lengthy process. Indeed, these initiatives may take years to conduct a comprehensive community assessment and develop a strategic plan for aging-friendly changes. Finally, these initiatives place a high value on research and evaluation to document their effects on older adults and other community residents. While many of these initiatives may not yet have implemented changes they can evaluate, they often have future plans to do so.

The community planning model, however, is not without its challenges and limitations. Providing a checklist to participating communities may guide stakeholders who would otherwise feel overwhelmed, but it also raises questions regarding whether there are universal features of an aging-friendly community (Buffel et al., 2012). Communities vary in terms of their resources and assets, the needs and desires of their residents (both older and younger), and their population density, among other characteristics. The aging-friendly features of a rural community, for example, may look quite different from the aging-friendly features of an urban one. Based on their review of the aging-friendly community literature, however, Lui and colleagues (2009) discovered that the potentially unique needs of older adults living in rural communities frequently go unmentioned. One exception is the WHO-affiliated programs in Canada, which created an Age-Friendly Rural/Remote Communities project that found, for example, that promoting elder mobility in rural areas may depend more on facilitating the support of family and friends rather than providing public transportation (Menec, Means, Keating, Parkhurst, & Eales, 2011).

While some aging-friendly initiatives, notably the AdvantAge Initiative, call attention to the ways income can create significant disparities in later life, it is unclear the extent to which these programs are developing specific action items related to this segment of the older adult population. Cultural influences on expectations and preferences as we age can similarly affect the methods and targets for aging-friendly community change, yet this is also rarely discussed among community planning models, at least in published articles and reports. Indeed, as noted by Kathryn Lawler from the ARC (personal communication, June 28, 2012), a cookie-cutter approach will likely encounter resistance at the local level because communities do not want to be identical to their neighbors. While many of these community planning models encourage stakeholders to adapt recommendations to the local context, it is not always clear how this can be accomplished.

Some observers have also expressed concern about the extent to which the interests and perspectives of all older community residents are represented in community planning models. As noted by Lui and colleagues (2009) and described in publications by initiative participants (e.g., Bloomberg & Quinn, 2009; Neal et al., 2014), collecting information from older adults is often the first step in developing this type of aging-friendly community initiative. The extent to which older adults are involved beyond the initial surveys and focus groups for data-gathering purposes, however, remains in question and likely varies a great deal by community. Mobilizing and maintaining older residents' engagement in and support of an aging-friendly initiative is likely a critical component of its success (Menec et al., 2011), and best practices to facilitate elders' participation over time should be disseminated. Furthermore, the older adults who participate in the community assessment and strategic planning processes may not represent the wants and needs of all segments of the aging population, particularly those who are less civically engaged (Neal et al., 2014). As Buffel et al. (2012) pointed out, the meaningful participation of older residents with diverse financial, social, and health needs, as well as those from different racial and ethnic backgrounds, can lead to differences regarding community change priorities. Strategies for including disparate views and encouraging bottom-up participation in such top-down approaches should be shared widely.

Similar to cross-sector collaboration initiatives (described in detail in Chapter 10), community planning models face significant challenges forming and maintaining partnerships with a variety of stakeholders representing different sectors (e.g., public, private, nonprofit, voluntary, residents themselves) and different professions (e.g., social work, planning, public health, medicine, architecture, interior design). Kathryn Lawler (personal communication, June 28, 2012) recalled that during the charrette organized by the Lifelong Communities Initiative, it took 3 days for the participants to start understanding each other. Given that local government is typically viewed as a necessary partner, some observers have called for municipal or regional governments to take the lead in coordinating these efforts (Lui et al., 2009), a strategy employed by Canada. Given the often-limited resources available for these aging-friendly community initiatives, however, local governments may not have the ability to devote staff and other resources.

Whether it is from a public or private organization, someone needs to dedicate both human and financial resources to the collaboration. For Age-Friendly Philadelphia, for example, PCA, the nonprofit organization that acts as the AAA, serves the function of maintaining the momentum of aging-friendly efforts (K. Clark & Glicksman, 2012). Staff from PCA have devoted extensive time to cultivating relationships with a variety of organizations across the city and have negotiated conflicts that arise when potential partners perceive aging-friendly efforts as clashing with other organizational goals. As K. Clark and Glicksman (2012) noted, there are a number of additional barriers to sustaining relationships with all stakeholders, including staff turnover, funding cuts, and shifts in organizational priorities.

A final concern is whether the changes outlined by these community planning models actually lead to positive outcomes among older adults and residents of all ages. In 2009, Lui and colleagues observed that much of the literature on aging-friendly community initiatives offers detailed description of the processes undertaken by the initiative but provides little to no empirical evidence of the initiative's effects. Our own review more recently suggested increasing discussion about evaluations (e.g., Plouffe and Kalache's [2011] overview of research being conducted in British Columbia and Quebec). There are a number of reasons why few empirical studies have been published, including local variations to the models, the relatively recent development of many of these initiatives, and the complexity of documenting and evaluating communitywide change. Green (2012), for example, described the difficulties experienced by cities participating in WHO's initiative in trying to document the effects of large-scale changes to the environment. As noted, there is a general recognition among initiatives taking a community planning approach that they need to conduct methodologically rigorous evaluations of both the processes and the outcomes of their efforts. For example, as described in Chapter 4, WHO recently completed a 3-year process to develop a set of indicators and an assessment tool for participating communities to measure their aging friendliness. To date, however, there remain significant gaps in our knowledge of the effects of these models, including how their effects may vary depending on the local context.

Conclusion

Community planning models take a more top-down approach to helping communities become more aging friendly, typically engaging in communitywide needs assessment and strategic planning before attempting to bring about changes in the physical and social infrastructure. While they solicit the participation of older adults, these initiatives typically draw extensively from the expert knowledge of academics and researchers, local government employees, and other professionals, such as planners and architects. These initiatives have experienced a number of challenges, including gaining widespread buy-in from stakeholders and finding sources for funding; however, the initiatives highlighted in this chapter have also achieved successes that hold promise for making their communities more aging friendly.

10

Cross-Sector Collaborations

Introduction

In Chapter 9, we considered ways in which communities, frequently at the instigation of governmental or quasi-governmental bodies, can initiate community planning processes designed to foster aging-friendly community change. As we saw, creating actual community change requires the combined efforts of multiple entities and sectors. In this chapter, we examine ways in which various sectors can develop new ways of working together and sometimes even create new structures that transcend the confines of existing community agencies and organizations.

As we have seen, the problems experienced by older adults tend to reflect inadequate person–environment fit in a variety of intersecting domains. Such multidimensional problems necessitate the involvement of multiple sectors because no single entity is likely to have the resources or scope to meet the needs of any group of seniors or to respond comprehensively to the problems they experience. For example, improving mobility involves not only increasing the availability of fixed-route public bus lines but also enhancing older adults' ability to get where they need and want to go in a safe and efficient manner. For most older persons, getting places outside of walking distance involves automobiles, so improving mobility means looking at the vehicles that older people ride in, the roads on which those vehicles travel, and the individuals who drive those vehicles. If we think about mobility as getting where we want to go, rather than just transportation per se, then we also need to think about the overall physical and social environment, including urban planning decisions and zoning laws that affect the location of residential and commercial property, among other considerations.

Similarly, physical health and well-being involve not only adequate health care but also how we take care of ourselves and one another, including having places to walk and to exercise, being able to get out of one's home or apartment to the outside, feeling safe in one's neighborhood, having sidewalks to walk on, and having somebody to walk with. All of these factors are interrelated, and no single silo, whether in health care, housing, or parks and recreation, can work independently if we are going to achieve more aging-friendly communities.

Benefits of Cross-Sector Collaborations

Collaborations across existing service delivery sectors represent an effort to over-come the fragmentation, lack of coordination, and service gaps that are typical of community aging and long-term care service systems. For the most part, these systems exist as separate silos (e.g., transportation, housing, health care, social services) supported by separate financing sources, federal policies, state and local programs, and authorization and regulation systems. What results is a plethora of narrowly targeted programs that are highly fragmented and poorly coordi-nated (Kaye, 2014), but with substantial gaps in service delivery, financing, and information availability (R. A. Kane, 2012; Robert Wood Johnson Foundation [RWJF], 2011).

Improving community-based systems of services and supports for older adults requires communities to reach across institutional and generational boundar-ies to foster new relationships among the wide variety of community agencies and organizations that affect the lives of older adults (RWJF, 2011). A range of options is possible, along a continuum from competition to full integration: com-petition; coexistence; communication (e.g., information sharing); cooperation (e.g., working together on discrete projects on an ad hoc basis); coordination (e.g., systematic mutual adaptations for mutual gain); collaboration (e.g., longer-term coordinated actions involving shared goals, resources, and actions); and integra-tion (fully integrated programs and resources) (Cabaj, 2012).

Cross-sector collaborations may involve expansion of existing programs, development of new programs, or services to groups that previously have been overlooked or underserved. In so doing, collaborations can help to increase pro-gram efficiency, expand market penetration, improve program responsiveness, and often attract new resources. Better coordination of supportive services, for example, has been shown to enhance service efficacy, increase service satis-faction, reduce caregiver strain, shorten lengths of inpatient hospitalization, and decrease inappropriate use of emergency rooms (Rizzo & Rowe, 2006). Partnerships between age-friendly city initiatives and local health departments can enhance emergency preparedness, as is being done in Washington, D.C., through a collaboration between Age-Friendly DC, Resilient DC, Serve DC, and the District Health Department's Health Emergency Preparedness and Response Administration (for more information, see http://doh.dc.gov/resilience). In other communities, cross-sector collaborations are helping to improve service access, enhance service coordination, make physical environments more accessible, or promote public policies that support well-being in later life.

The collective impact approach (Kania & Kramer, 2011) provides a useful framework for understanding the value of cross-sector collaborations. As origi-nally proposed, the collective impact approach involves "the commitment of a group of important actors from different sectors to a common agenda for solving a specific social problem" (Kania & Kramer, 2011, p.37). This approach is posited to be especially effective with "adaptive problems," complex issues for which the problem is not well defined, there is no simple solution, and no single entity has the resources or authority to bring about the necessary changes, as is typically the case with efforts to help communities become more aging friendly. The collective impact approach reflects an understanding that social problems are complex and multidetermined, and that addressing such problems requires the active participation of stakeholders from many different sectors to avoid the duplication and fragmentation that typically occurs when organizations work in isolation. As Richardson and Allegrante (2002) noted, "Most of the problems we will face in the 21st century will require multi-sectoral, multi-disciplinary, and multi-component efforts" (p. 375).

Five key conditions distinguish collective impact from other types of collaboration: a common agenda, mutually reinforcing activities, shared measurement systems, continuous communication, and the presence of a backbone organization (Hanleybrown, Kania, & Kramer, 2012). A *common agenda* implies that participants have a shared vision for change, including a common understanding of the problem, shared goals and objectives, and agreement regarding how best to proceed. *Mutually reinforcing activities* involve coordinated efforts that contribute to common goals and can be adjusted as needed based on lessons learned. *Shared measurement systems* enable accountability and continuous quality improvement through the use of similar metrics for achieving agreed objectives. *Continuous communication* involves consistent and open information sharing among participants to build trust, ensure mutual objectives, and create common motivation. Finally, adequate *backbone support* is needed to guide vision and strategy, facilitate effective dialogue, manage data collection and analysis, support community engagement, and develop effective communications.

Interorganizational collaborations have advantages as well as potential challenges. As posited by resource dependence theory (Pfeffer & Salancik, 1978), organizations require external resources to accomplish their aims. An aging services provider, for example, might rely on other community organizations for referrals, technical assistance, other forms of in-kind support, endorsements, or collaborative advocacy efforts. By collaborating, organizations can support one another to achieve their individual and shared goals while avoiding competing for scarce resources. However, in doing so, organizations create interorganizational dependencies that can affect organizational autonomy and the distribution of power and resource allocation, potentially serving as disincentives to collaboration (Drees & Heugens, 2013). This is one reason why external incentives (e.g., financial support from government sources, philanthropic foundations, or private donors) typically are needed to promote new collaborative efforts. As Hanleybrown et al. (2012) noted, collaboration for collective impact is unlikely to succeed in the absence of three critical preconditions: a sense of urgency created by mutually experienced threats or opportunities; an influential leader or champion who can galvanize motivation and sustain participation; and adequate resources to invest in planning and development activities, incentivize sustained participant involvement, and support new institutional structures.

For all of these reasons, the process of collaborative development varies from community to community and tends to reflect local politics and interpersonal relationships. In this chapter, we examine three examples of prominent community initiatives designed to promote community aging friendliness by creating new ways of working together across silos to help communities respond more effectively to the needs of their elderly residents.

Examples of Cross-Sector Collaborations
Community Partnerships for Older Adults

Community Partnerships for Older Adults (CPFOA) was an 8-year national initiative designed to strengthen local long-term care and supportive services systems by fostering local collaborations among health and social service providers, government agencies, business leaders, local funders, and older community residents (Bolda, Saucier, Maddox, Wetle, & Lowe, 2006). Funded by the RWJF, the initiative provided at least $900,000 each to 16 communities to assist them to develop local collaborative partnerships, enhance community capacity, and improve service systems to better meet the needs of vulnerable older adults (RWJF, 2011).

The CPFOA was based on the rationale that "there is a patchwork in long-term-care services in communities—one of the goals was to make that patchwork behave more like a coordinated system" (RWJF, 2011, p. 3). With this in mind, the initiative had three overarching goals: (a) foster collaborative partnerships at the community level; (b) build community capacity to meet the needs of an aging society; and (c) improve long-term care and systems of support to better meet the needs of vulnerable older adults (RWJF, 2011).

Each of the 16 local partnerships was expected to (a) engage nontraditional partners, including elders themselves as well as local businesses, public health and safety officials, transportation providers, community developers, school districts, or policymakers; (b) develop a strategic plan supported by the community; (c) mobilize community resources to implement the strategic plan; (d) share leadership among the organizations and workgroups involved in the partnership; and (e) share resources, decision-making, and responsibility for sustaining the partnership. Program support was provided by the CPFOA National Program Office at the University of Southern Maine, Muskie School of Public Service, and included a strategic planning and partnership development model, technical assistance with implementation, and a variety of online resources.

Project examples. Partnerships carried out projects in areas such as the following: service provider training (e.g., elder abuse training for police officers); program development (e.g., transportation voucher programs); policy development (e.g., convincing policymakers to pass a senior housing ordinance); civic engagement (e.g., training elders as policy advocates); and public awareness (e.g., health promotion campaigns).

In San Francisco, for example, a Partnership for Community-Based Care and Support developed neighborhood coalitions designed to help home and community-based services providers work together to jointly identify problems and create shared solutions. The partnership was focused particularly on improving services for elders from underserved groups, including African Americans, Latinos, Asian Pacific Islanders, lesbians, gays, bisexuals, and transgender individuals (RWJF, 2011). The Boston Partnership for Older Adults, a coalition of more than 200 organizations and individuals, provided elder abuse training to the city's police officers and developed the first elder-friendly business district in the city's Mission Hill Main Streets district, including infrastructure improvements and other resources designed to help the district become a vibrant center of neighborhood civic life for older community residents (City of Boston, 2014). Pathways to Positive Aging, a partnership between the city of Fremont Human Services Department and more than 60 local senior service providers, cultural and faith groups, hospitals, long-term care facilities, and businesses, developed intergenerational programs between teenagers and frail seniors, trained postal workers to identify vulnerable seniors, developed culture-specific senior programs, and engaged older adults from minority ethnic groups as community ambassadors (RWJF, 2011).

Outcomes. A primary objective of CPFOA was to improve services for older adults, with a particular focus on the needs of underserved populations. An independent evaluation of the program by Mathematica Policy Research (B. Stevens, Lavin, & Cheh, 2006) found an overall increase in awareness and use of community-based services in the communities where partnerships were located, although the proportion of vulnerable adults who tried but could not access services also increased, possibly a result of increased public awareness of the need for assistance in the absence of increased availability of needed services (Kim & Cheh, 2010).

Leadership teams were an essential factor in the success of the collaborations. Leadership teams with greater participation by individuals and organizations whose priorities were aligned were more likely to generate new ideas and generally perceived greater organizational and community benefits. However, the evaluation found that partnerships were not always the most effective or efficient strategy for developing and implementing new programs. While the planning phase of the project did require a coalition, more than one third of the actions taken by the partnerships could have been implemented equally well by individual organizations. Examples of individually oriented programs and services that primarily involved a single organization included Atlanta's home repair program and Boston's program to train law enforcement officers about elder abuse (B. Stevens et al., 2006).

Interorganizational interaction and collaboration helped to generate new approaches to meeting the needs of older adults in these communities. Partnerships helped to enhance community social capital by encouraging broad civic participation in decisions about meeting community needs and engaging partners in community-level evaluation efforts (Giunta & Thomas, 2015). The partnerships with better representation and support from the community tended to have better outcomes. Furthermore, partnerships that were actively engaged in advocacy efforts to promote aging-friendly community policies were able to have an impact on local policymakers, although advocacy at the state level was less effective, most likely because of the many competing factors and players that influence the development of state policy (B. Stevens et al., 2006).

At the end of the grant period, 13 of the initial 16 partnerships were able to continue their work in some form, either through continued financial and in-kind investments by partner organizations or through program adoption by local government agencies (B. Stevens et al., 2006). The three that did not continue, including one that was discontinued before the project ended, experienced one or more of the following challenges: lack of sustainable funding, conflict with the host agency's mission or goals, staff turnover, or a major leadership transition (RWJF, 2011). Nearly 10 years later, partnerships remain active in at least seven of the original communities, which continue to share information and collaborate through a "Staying Connected" group that convenes at least annually and communicates via blog (http://cpfoastayingconnected.typepad.com/).

Healthy Aging Initiative of Contra Costa County

The Healthy Aging Initiative was a 5-year countywide initiative designed to help nonprofit organizations collaborate more effectively to better serve older adults living in Contra Costa County, a northern California county covering more than 700 square miles and containing more than a million residents, of whom 46% are White, 25% Hispanic, 16% Asian or Pacific Islander, and 10% African American; one third of residents do not speak English as their primary language (Holmes Research, 2007). The local Community Health Fund, with assistance from other local funding partners, convened an advisory group to identify gaps in existing services and assess the potential for organizations to respond. Among the issues identified were a lack of community awareness of the needs of older adults and services to meet those needs, organizations poorly suited to serving a diverse population of seniors, and turf wars for available funds.

Based on this initial analysis, the Healthy Aging Initiative identified five principal goals: (a) increase communitywide access to aging services for all seniors, regardless of circumstance; (b) increase opportunities for seniors to contribute to and participate in community life as valued participants; (c) increase understanding of diverse circumstances, lifestyles, and cultural backgrounds of seniors; (d) increase the number of nonprofit organizations and seniors collaborating to influence attitudes toward aging and older adults; and (e) increase opportunities for residents countywide to come together and act as advocates for actions and policies designed to make the county more aging friendly.

Central to achieving these goals was development of a Partnership for Healthy Aging, a collaborative effort designed to promote greater community awareness of the needs of older adults and a more efficient system of aging services throughout the county. The partnership held quarterly meetings among participating organizations to discuss ways to encourage coordination and efficiency among the nonprofit organizations serving seniors in Contra Costa County. These meetings provided opportunities for information sharing, cross learning, and development of professional relationships, as well as discussions of ways to promote greater community awareness of the needs of older community members and a more efficient system of services. In addition to convening these meetings and encouraging collaboration, the Community Health Fund administered a competitive grants program that provided support for initiatives that either developed new programs to serve area seniors or expanded existing programs to better meet the needs of underserved individuals or communities. Priority was given to collaborative efforts that required the active involvement of multiple organizations, including organizations that were not already providing services to seniors.

The Healthy Aging Initiative resulted in numerous important accomplishments during its 6 years of existence. Many new services were developed, and others were expanded, enabling participating organizations to provide assistance to more than 5,000 older adults who would not otherwise have received help. Services created or expanded included transportation to medical appointments, friends for homebound seniors, health navigators, access to health screening, respite programs, social adult day care centers, bill payment assistance, and case management. In response to gaps in culturally appropriate services for seniors with limited English and aging refugees and immigrants, the participating organizations created a number of new programs, such as peer companions for Vietnamese seniors and *promotores* (Spanish-speaking health educators and service coordinators) in the Latino community. In addition, new programs created hundreds of new volunteer opportunities for seniors, enabling them to do everything from providing rides for their peers to teaching classes, mentoring at-risk youth, and helping homebound seniors pay their bills on time.

The East County Healthy Aging Collaborative represented a targeted effort to develop a seamless system of services to seniors in one of the county's most underserved areas. Working together with pooled resources, local community organizations collaborated on efforts to increase community awareness of aging issues, identify unmet service needs, reach underserved seniors, and facilitate referrals among the organizations. In addition to providing services to numerous seniors who had not previously received assistance, the collaborative effort raised awareness of existing community resources, developed important new programs, enhanced transportation options and socialization opportunities, and engaged community members as volunteer outreach workers for local seniors.

The initiative also provided support for organizational capacity building to assist agencies to expand appropriately to meet the changing needs of community seniors in an evolving policy and financing context. Participating organizations were provided with training in strategic planning, fundraising, accounting systems, and cultural and linguistic competence. The initiative also facilitated cross learning regarding best practices, cross-referrals, and sharing of resources, such as volunteers, meeting space, and sometimes staff.

An independent evaluation of the Healthy Aging Initiative (Holmes Research, 2007) concluded that it resulted in the following outcomes: (a) greater community awareness of the needs of older community members; (b) creation of an array of new programs to address seniors' physical and mental health needs, many of which persisted after external funding expired; (c) increased numbers of seniors being served, especially those who were traditionally underserved due to economic, transportation, cultural, or linguistic barriers; (d) improved collaboration among senior-serving organizations, enabling a more effective and efficient service delivery system; (e) increased organizational capacity and board involvement; and (f) enhanced opportunities to promote aging friendliness throughout the entire county through the involvement of nonprofit organizations, government, business, and individuals from all walks of life.

Integrated Housing and Services

One of the most common types of cross-sector collaborations is between housing providers and health and social service organizations. These types of collaborations are a response to the large numbers of individuals who are growing older in environments not well designed for the needs of aging residents. The focus might be a traditional multifamily neighborhood or a more restricted area that is relatively homogeneous (e.g., a mobile home park, a cluster of multiunit buildings, or a single stand-alone multiunit building). The targeted area might therefore be considered an aging-friendly community in a restricted geographic location.

Such collaborations typically are an effort to overcome the fragmentation and lack of coordination often faced by individual older adults attempting to arrange for assistance independently from multiple providers. They also have the potential to be more responsive to the particular needs of older adults living in particular settings, thereby enabling service providers to refine their service offerings and modes of delivery to be more responsive to the needs of their elderly clients

(Golant, 2008a). The service-providing organizations have more of an opportunity to obtain information about the common needs of the older adults living in that environment and to modify their processes to better meet those needs. Assigning a dedicated service coordinator, social worker, or similar individual to a particular residential setting also provides visibility and facilitates informal contact, which can build trust and familiarity, thereby helping to overcome some of the traditional barriers to seeking help (Sheehan & Guzzardo, 2008).

Service access also is likely to be enhanced by offering services near people's residences, and often on site, rather than requiring potential service users to locate needed services themselves, initiate contact, and secure transportation when needed. In addition to the potential for enhancing accessibility and responsiveness, it is likely that services can be offered at lower cost because of the efficiency of being able to serve multiple individuals who live in close proximity (Golant, 2008a). Finally, especially relevant to the issues discussed regarding aging-friendly communities, collaboration between housing, health, and social services may enable more attention to person–environment fit and the ways in which various sectors can work together to overcome physical and social environmental barriers experienced by older adults. For example, overcoming mobility difficulties might require the combined efforts of physical therapy, social support, personal assistance, and environmental modifications (e.g., a handrail).

Supportive housing options that combine shelter (i.e., room and board) and assistance (e.g., long-term services and supports [LTSS]) under the same roof have been termed *clustered housing-care* (Golant, 2008a). Some of these consolidated settings are purpose built (or redesigned) for older residents. Common examples include senior communities, assisted living facilities, senior supportive housing, and service-coordinated senior housing such as that provided under the U.S. Department of Housing and Urban Development's (HUD) service coordinator program. The HUD program provides funding for owners of HUD-supported senior housing to hire on-site case managers responsible for identifying residents in need of support, linking residents with available community services, coordinating and monitoring service provision, developing volunteer programs, and promoting informal support networks among residents (HUD, n.d.).

Most of these initiatives are relatively self-contained, with little exchange or impact on the surrounding community. Some of these initiatives allow nonresidents to participate in social activities and use various services on site, utilize excess capacity (e.g., meals, personnel) to assist nonresidents living in their own homes, or work independently or collaboratively with other stakeholders to advocate for environmental modifications that would be beneficial for residents as well as other community members (e.g., crosswalks, sidewalk benches, etc.).

In Sweden, for example, nearly every community has one or more "service houses," with apartments that are purpose built for older residents, personal care assistants available 24/7, on-site health care clinics and social services, and common areas where meals and social programs are provided for residents as well as community members. Interestingly, recent Swedish legislation has begun to "unbundle" these various services, putting more responsibility on individual residents and other community members to arrange the particular mix of services they require from the particular providers they prefer (Sundström, Johansson, & Hassing, 2002).

Integrated service areas (ISAs) also provide housing, social support, and various levels of physical care through cross-sector collaborations among housing providers, social workers, care providers, architects, and local officials (Singelenberg, Stolarz, & McCall, 2014). As characterized by an interdisciplinary group of architects, city planners, service providers, and researchers from Germany, the Netherlands, Switzerland, Denmark, Sweden, Japan, and the United States (http://www.isa-platform.eu/news.html), ISAs involve the active participation of local citizens and local governments, including full participation of local stakeholders in deciding the types of housing and services. In addition, some ISAs include universal design in living spaces and public areas, assistance with personal care from specialists as well as other residents, a variety of care options, and space for community meetings and social activities (Singelenberg et al., 2014). Preliminary evidence from ISAs in the Netherlands indicated that ISA residents had more confidence that assistance would be available when needed (de Kam et al., 2012) and were more satisfied with their current living situation and less likely to perceive the need to move than were nonresidents with similar levels of disability (Singelenberg et al., 2014).

Cross-sector collaborations among housing and service providers can vary on a variety of dimensions, including the following (based on Golant, 2008a):

1. Auspices (e.g., which sector is principally responsible for the development and operation of the housing and support services and whether the entity is a public, for-profit, or not-for-profit organization);
2. Resident characteristics (e.g., levels of physical and cognitive functioning and the proportion of residents who are seniors);
3. Housing characteristics (e.g., whether the setting is a stand-alone building, a cluster of buildings, a small, homogeneous setting, or a multifamily neighborhood; whether the location is primarily urban or suburban or rural);
4. Environmental attributes (e.g., the design of individual dwelling units, common areas, and service provision spaces; overall accessibility, including whether the setting was purpose built for older residents);
5. Programs (e.g., the specific supportive services that are available, the involvement of residents in the design and implementation of the program, and whether some or all of the services are available to nonresidents);
6. Service delivery modes (e.g., which services are provided and by whom; whether services are provided on site or off site; whether services are accessed

at will or through a service coordinator or other gatekeeper; whether services are offered à la carte or as a bundled package; the cost of specific services, including whether some or all services are available at no cost);

7. Oversight (e.g., whether service quality and outcomes are monitored in any way, whether on a voluntary basis or through licensure or other external oversight);

8. Housing financing (e.g., how housing is paid for and whether housing is subsidized to increase access for some or all residents); and

9. Program financing (e.g., how services are paid for and whether services are subsidized to increase access for some or all residents).

Naturally occurring retirement community. The term *naturally occurring retirement community* (NORC) has been used since the 1980s to refer to settings (e.g., housing developments, apartment buildings, neighborhoods, or entire communities) that were not originally designed for seniors but that now contain relatively high concentrations of older residents (Hunt & Gunter-Hunt, 1986), typically through a combination of individuals having lived in the same places for many years, coupled with selective in-migration of new older residents and in some cases selective out-migration of younger residents. Golant has called such settings "deliberately occupied but unplanned elder residences" (2002, p. 67).

Nationally, it is estimated that about one sixth of households that include persons ages 55 or older are in communities where the majority of their neighbors also are 55 or older, and this does not even include retirement communities and other age-restricted settings (U.S. Census Bureau, 2004). Some of these settings are multifamily apartment buildings or a cluster of buildings, sometimes called *vertical NORCs*; others are relatively small, geographically defined neighborhoods known as *horizontal NORCs*.

NORC-Supportive Services Programs. The NORC Supportive Services Program (NORC-SSP) model involves cross-sector collaborations among housing providers, health and social service organizations, and a variety of other governmental and nongovernmental service provision and funding entities, who collaborate to enhance services and supports for older adults living in geographically defined areas with relatively high densities of older adults but were not specifically designed to serve aging persons. The NORC-SSP model has been described as a "community-level intervention in which older adults, building owners and managers, service providers, and other community partners create a network of services and volunteer opportunities to promote aging in place" (Bedney, Goldberg, & Josephson, 2010, p. 304).

NORC-SSPs receive financial support from a combination of government agencies, housing partners, philanthropies, corporations, and residents (Greenfield, Scharlach, Graham, Davitt, & Lehning, 2012). Through Title IV of the federal Older Americans Act (OAA), Congress supported 45 NORC-SSP demonstration projects in 26 states from 2002 to 2010, at the behest of and with technical assistance provided by the Jewish Federations of North America. Four of the 14 projects funded under the OAA's 2009 three-year Community Innovations for Aging in Place initiative also were NORC-SSPs. New York State provides ongoing funding for NORC programs in 54 housing developments and neighborhoods across the state, including 28 in New York City (NORC Blueprint, 2011). In addition, housing providers typically provide in-kind support by con-tributing office and program space, and some programs charge modest user fees to participating residents.

First developed within large apartment complexes in New York City to help older residents age in place with greater comfort and security (Vladeck, 2006), the model has since expanded to include buildings and entire neighborhoods in other parts of the United States (Greenfield, 2013). Working together, collaborat-ing service providers offer a coordinated set of services and programs, typically including the following: case management and social work services; health care management and prevention programs; education, socialization, and recreational activities; and volunteer opportunities for program participants and other com-munity members (Greenfield et al., 2012; Guo & Castillo, 2012; Pynoos, Liebig, Alley, & Nishita, 2005). Services range from information to personal assistance services. A service coordinator typically provides service referrals and counseling, as well as a variety of related functions: raising awareness about the NORC-SSP; collaborating with building managers, local service providers, businesses, and civic organizations; recruiting volunteers; engaging residents in leadership roles; and generally spearheading efforts to meet residents' needs (Bedney, Goldberg, & Josephson, 2010). Lincoln Guild Housing on the Upper West Side of New York City, for example, has an outreach program that provides social services and links residents with outside assistance, a nurse who visits weekly to check blood pres-sure and review medications, and discounts on personal emergency response sys-tems. There also are lectures on topics such as nutrition and estate planning and classes in ballroom dancing, t'ai chi, and exercise (J. Kaufman, 2014).

In addition to providing easy access to a range of services, the NORC-SSP model is based on the principles of senior empowerment and community building (Enguidanos, Pynoos, Denton, Alexman, & Diepenbrock, 2010). NORC-SSPs promote activity among older adults through recreation and socialization pro-grams and by encouraging participation in various community events and activities. In addition, NORC residents often are considered an essential part of program development, governance, and volunteer service provision and in some cases are actively involved in assisting one another (Greenfield, 2015). However, some NORC-SSPs have met with limited success in their efforts to engage residents in meaningful roles and promote a sense of program "ownership" (J. Kaufman, 2014).

NORC-SSPs have a variety of potential benefits for residents, for housing providers, for other participating organizations, and for communities. For residents, easy access to a variety of health and social services can make it easier for them to obtain the help they need when they need it (Golant, 2008a). Because service coordinators typically are available on site or nearby, they have opportunities to develop ongoing relationships with residents through informal individual and group activities, as well as committees and the like, helping the coordinators to become more aware of residents' unmet needs (Vladeck, 2004). In addition, service coordinators are more likely to notice changes in residents' physical, cognitive, and social functioning, enabling them to intervene before problems build into a crisis (Evashwick & Holt, 2000).

Participants in NORC-SSPs report improvements in social connections, service access, community participation, and perceived ability to age in place (Bedney, Schimmel, Goldberg, Kotler-Berkowitz, & Bursztyn, 2007). In a study of 461 participants in NORC-SSPs that were part of the OAA Title IV demonstration project, 88% said they knew more people as a result of their participation in a NORC-SSP, 95% said that they knew more about community services, 88% said they were more likely to continue to live in their current community, 84% said that they participated in activities or events more often, 81% said that they used community services more, 72% said that they left their homes more often, 70% said that they felt healthier than before, and almost half (48%) said that they volunteered more (Bedney et al., 2007). In a smaller study comparing 58 NORC-SSP participants with 70 building residents who did not participate, program participants were more satisfied with social life in the community and less depressed than before, whereas the opposite trends were found for nonparticipants (Cohen-Mansfield, Dakheel-Ali, & Frank, 2010).

There is some preliminary evidence suggesting that vertical NORCs may be more successful than horizontal NORCs, and that their residents may be more involved in the NORC-SSP, may receive a greater number of services, and may report greater satisfaction with the program (Enguidanos et al., 2010). It seems possible that NORC-SSPs may be more visible and clearly identifiable in vertical NORCs due to their contained, centralized settings, and that such settings may also promote greater collaboration and cross promotion between housing providers and outside health and social service providers.

Integrated housing services programs such as NORC-SSPs are apt to increase service efficiency through economies of scale, enabling service providers to offer a more comprehensive array of services less expensively to a large and relatively stable geographically clustered concentration of consumers, primarily by avoiding the substantial transportation time and expenses that typically are associated with individual providers traveling to see geographically dispersed seniors living in their own homes and apartments (Ormond, Black, Tilly, & Thomas, 2004). Furthermore, providers can more easily adjust their service time allotments to fit their clients' unique needs and are less likely to offer duplicated services, as would be the case if individual tenants were all making their own care arrangements (Ormond et al., 2004). NORC-SSPs also can enhance efficiency by facilitating coordination among the multiple community organizations that assist older adults, thereby helping to ameliorate barriers associated with different eligibility and scheduling requirements (Evashwick & Holt, 2000; Golant, 2008a). Housing providers are apt to benefit, as well, through increased resident stability and fewer health and residential crises, which are challenging for management and other residents.

There also are a number of ways in which NORC-SSPs can contribute to the general aging friendliness of their communities. Unlike traditional aging services, which are focused on serving older adults individually in response to their individual problems, the NORC-SSP approach includes all older adults who live in a designated community (where *community* in this case refers to a building or neighborhood with a relatively high density of older adults). Furthermore, older residents are viewed as active participants with multiple possible ways to be engaged, including participation on community advisory councils, awareness-raising campaigns, outreach efforts, and myriad other efforts on behalf of their local NORC community (Bedney & Goldberg, 2009). Hotel Oakland Village in Oakland, California, for example, displays a large banner on entering the building, proclaiming "participation = health" in English and Chinese. Such efforts reflect an attempt to engage residents as partners in fostering a sense of community that transcends traditional roles of "landlord" and "tenant."

Numerous NORC-SSP sites use their facilities as a base for serving other community members as well as their residents, such as by having a community nutrition site or adult day care center co-located in or near the NORC site. In so doing, they have the potential to increase interaction between residents and non-residents and enhance integration with the general community. Furthermore, community coalitions, composed of representatives from the housing provider, partnering organizations, and the residents themselves, help determine which services will be offered in response to the needs of a particular NORC population (Bookman, 2008; Ivery, Akstein-Kahan, & Murphy, 2010).

It should be noted that, despite their apparent benefits, enthusiasm for NORC-SSPs is not consistent universally. While dedicated programs and services may be beneficial for older residents, some younger residents may actually prefer that problematic older neighbors move elsewhere rather than obtaining the support they need to age in place (J. Kaufman, 2014), although intergenerational volunteer programs sponsored by some NORC-SSPs may help to attenuate such concerns. Because buildings are not necessarily designed for older adults, concern also has been expressed about the potential liability they might incur if an older resident became injured, or if a staff member or neighbor became injured trying to help an older person who has fallen or otherwise needs assistance. For this reason, some condominiums, co-ops, and tenant associations have developed protocols designed to exclude older adults who raise health or safety concerns or otherwise become too troublesome (J. Kaufman, 2014). In such cases, finding the appropriate balance between individual and shared responsibility, and between privacy and community, can be a challenge.

Finally, long-term sustainability has been a continuing challenge for NORC-SSPs. Many NORC-SSPs began with external funding from an OAA demonstration initiative, but then shifted to a combination of service fees, contributions, government contracts, and foundation grants when the OAA support ended. Resident membership fees have generally been modest, typically around $25/year, most activities are offered for free or at minimal cost, and reliance on fees from housing providers and tenant or homeowner associations are not sufficient to support the programs in most cases. Some NORC-SSPs, at least in New York, have been able to generate sufficient political capital to successfully advocate for ongoing funding from state and local governments, as well as other aging-friendly public policies. However, with the exception of New York, NORC-SSPs have had difficulty securing ongoing organizational commitment among the various program partners to sustain the programs, with many of these collaborations fading following the termination of federal OAA demonstration funding.

Challenges and Opportunities

Cross-sector collaborations represent a promising strategy for transcending existing funding and program silos to respond more effectively to the complex needs of an aging society and improve services to underserved seniors. As we have seen, many of these collaborations have focused on increasing service effectiveness, efficiency, and access, sometimes by developing new types of programs or services. While many of these efforts have had positive impacts for specific groups of community seniors, there is considerably less evidence of larger-scale improvements in community aging friendliness, whether by changes in physical or social environments, public policies, or even changes in overall service delivery systems.

Furthermore, while some cross-sector collaborations have been highly successful in achieving their goals, partnerships among disparate organizations and interests generally are notoriously difficult to sustain over long periods of time. The challenges they face include programmatic and funding silos, limited staffing resources, threats to organizational autonomy, and creation of sustainable structures that can continue independently over time. Pervasive resource shortages and funding silos can exacerbate turf issues, making collaboration of any kind potentially risky. For example, a number of CPFOA participants described conflicts with their local area agency on aging, which did not always support partnerships that included representatives from outside the traditional aging network (RWJF, 2011).

Keeping a partnership focused, organized, and productive requires adequate staffing. CPFOA participants, for example, uniformly reported the importance of having dedicated personnel to handle project management, communications, and other administrative tasks. However, it can be difficult for collaborating organizations to balance time committed to the collaborative with staff's usual responsibilities within their home organization. It also can be difficult for staff to know when they are acting on behalf of the collaborative and when on behalf of their own organization. Leadership capacity and leadership development pathways also are critical, especially given the dynamic nature of collaborations and their organizational fields. Nearly every CPFOA partnership site experienced disruptive changes in staff and leadership as a result of turnover, serious illness, or other personal or organizational factors. In some cases, the lead organization changed entirely.

Interorganizational partnerships among unequal partners can evoke threats to organizational autonomy, thereby providing a disincentive to long-term sustainability of collaborative arrangements, as suggested by resource dependence theory (Drees & Heugens, 2013). Interorganizational collaborations are apt to be most beneficial and sustainable when there are relatively equivalent resources being exchanged, so that resource inputs are balanced by providing other types of support that are needed and valued by another organization. However, in the real world, this is seldom the case. More often, organizations have different levels of resources and access to resources, creating resource dependencies that can exacerbate power differentials and potentially limit the sustainability of collaborative efforts. In an environment where resources are inherently limited, nonprofit organizations are especially vulnerable because they tend to provide services to disadvantaged populations that may be unable to produce internal revenues through service fees or membership dues (Ruggiano & Taliaferro, 2012).

Sustainability is likely to be enhanced when the collaborative effort has taken on a life of its own, including developing a separate organizational structure apart from the collaborating organizations, with its own independent funding and its own supportive constituents committed to its survival. Collaborations benefit from being operated relatively autonomously, with their own governance structure, formal memoranda of understanding outlining mutual responsibilities and expectations, and solid communication and decision-making processes (RWJF, 2011). Sustainability is also enhanced when the collaboration has resulted in systemic changes in one or both of the collaborating organizations, whereby the new collaborative venture is considered an integral part of the organization's operations.

Given these various challenges, external incentives may be required for organizations to move out of their traditional silos and cooperate, let alone develop sustainable collaborative relationships. New ventures almost inevitably require additional resources, and collaborative efforts are unlikely to be pursued unless they are perceived to be in the mutual interest of all parties. External incentives might include actual or potential new resources, a fiscal crisis, or other environmental conditions that are perceived to threaten an organization's ability to continue operating as it has in the past. Unfortunately, that also means that when those resource incentives end, it may be more difficult to sustain a collaboration.

The CPFOA initiative provides numerous examples of the potential catalytic effect of economic crises and other external threats (RWJF, 2011). On the one hand, stressful economic conditions encouraged collaboration by providing a way for some communities to utilize existing resources more efficiently and as an incentive for coordinated advocacy efforts designed to benefit everyone. In other communities, however, resource constraints were more likely to result in budget cutbacks, staff reductions, and intensified competition among the organizational partners, threatening the sustainability of the collaborative structures. Challenges are apt to be especially great in collaborations with a relatively weak infrastructure and limited civic engagement, suggesting the importance of developing a strong, inclusive governance approach from the very beginning. As one participant of a CPFOA that ceased operation after the grant period, said: "If we had it to do over again, we would recruit organizations/others with deep pockets, become a 501(c)(3) within the first two implementation years, and hire a staff member to focus on fundraising from the beginning" (RWJF, 2011, p. 27).

Conclusion

Cross-sector collaboration initiatives focus on creating partnerships that enable service delivery organizations to meet the needs of community seniors more effectively and efficiently than they could do individually. Collaborations may focus on system change, on developing new types of programs or services, or on providing existing services more effectively, more efficiently, or to groups of community seniors whose needs are not adequately being met.

11

Community Development Initiatives

Introduction

In this chapter, we describe a number of initiatives that engage older adults as important assets in efforts to make their physical and social environments more aging friendly. While some of the community planning approaches and cross-sector collaborations described in Chapters 9 and 10 have involved older adults in some way, most of these initiatives have been developed by government agencies or community organizations, with older adults playing a secondary role, typically as key informants. In this chapter, we examine initiatives in which older adults play a primary role, including initiatives that have been created, funded, implemented, or governed by older community residents themselves. Many of these initiatives reflect grassroots organizing efforts, accessing underutilized social resources and strengthening community social capital.

Community development initiatives include a variety of approaches for meeting the needs of older residents and promoting aging-friendly communities, ranging from groups of consumers who come together to develop new programs for themselves or other older adults, to organized efforts by groups of citizens to advocate for more aging-friendly policies, programs, or community infrastructure. The primary focus might be on social interaction, service access, social action, or some combination. Some initiatives are entirely freestanding and grassroots, while others are developed and supported by existing service organizations or government agencies. What is critical is that community members themselves are driving these efforts, rather than simply serving as service recipients, participants, or informants, as is typical with community planning efforts and cross-sector collaborations. Because they are consumer led, these initiatives face a number of potential challenges, including engaging all segments of the community, maintaining consumer involvement, and developing sustainable financing and organizational structures.

The Need for Community Development

As we have seen, neighborhood environments increase in importance in later life. As a result of mobility limitations, the loss of employment and other meaningful social roles, and ageist societal norms and values that undermine community participation, older adults spend more time in their homes and neighborhoods than do younger age groups (Forrest & Kearns, 2001); today's elders, moreover, have spent more time in their homes and neighborhoods over the course of their lives compared to previous generations (Phillipson, Bernard, Phillips, & Ogg, 1999). Furthermore, as proposed by the environmental docility hypothesis, individuals with lower levels of cognitive and physical functioning are apt to be more affected by external conditions than are those with higher levels of functioning (Lawton & Simon, 1968).

Unfortunately, the increased salience of neighborhood environments for older adults does not necessarily mean that those environments are well suited to meet their social needs. Environments that are ill designed for normal ageing-related changes may create access barriers that contribute to reduced elder social participation and intergenerational solidarity, potentially resulting in decreased status, decreased participation in decision-making processes, and decreased control over their own lives (Silver & Miller, 2003). Furthermore, as documented by Robert Putnam in his classic work, *Bowling Alone* (Putnam, 2000), recent decades have seen a decline in the sense of community, in the stability of communities, in the amount of contact among neighbors, and in general "neighborliness" in many communities. Although the evidence is somewhat mixed (Phillipson 2007), as we described in Chapter 6, it appears that the importance of neighborhood-based social ties has been steadily declining, while that of nonneighborhood ties has been increasing, especially among individuals who are younger or employed (Guest & Wierzbicki, 1999). For older adults dependent on neighborhood ties, this can promote a sense of social isolation, social exclusion, and ultimately a sense of disempowerment.

Lacking opportunities to utilize and expand their capacities for contributing to the community, and often sensing that those contributions are undervalued, it is no wonder then that many older adults are defined primarily as problems and come to see themselves that way as well. Seeing aging primarily as a "problem" leads to the creation of a variety of supportive programs and services designed to offer assistance to older adults, with resources primarily going toward developing programs and services that are provided by formal organizations and service delivery systems composed of trained professionals and other "experts," known as the "aging enterprise" (Estes, 1993; Wacker & Roberto, 2013). Such efforts frequently overlook the inherent strengths and natural supports that already exist in these communities, including neighbor-to-neighbor links of mutual support, informal support structures, the role of churches and other community entities, and other individual, family, and community resources. Granted, many of these structures have declined, but they have not disappeared, and services provided by formal social service organizations do not necessarily replace them.

This well-intentioned focus on "helping" older adults—and on older adults as needing help—has been termed the *new ageism* (Binstock, 2005; Kalish, 1979). While ageism traditionally sees older adults as a problem undeserving of attention and support, the new ageism sees older adults as deserving of our sympathy and support because of their dependence and helplessness. It is an improvement, granted, but older adults still are seen primarily as a problem and deficient, rather than as full human beings with strengths as well as limitations, who can give as well as receive. Older adults typically are seen primarily as service recipients or resource consumers rather than as contributors to communal well-being and an integral part of any solution.

Aging-friendly community initiatives, on the other hand, take a more preventive approach that focuses on improving community structures to reduce social isolation and social exclusion of older adults. A key focus of many of these initiatives is on identifying and ameliorating deficiencies in physical and social environments and in societal institutions. Furthermore, older adults and other community members are considered to be important contributors to their communities and to these community change processes. With this in mind, many of the aging-friendly initiatives we have described so far engage older community members as key informants or advisors, providing important information about infrastructure problems and barriers to be addressed primarily by community planners, service providers, and other experts. In this chapter, we consider initiatives that take these inclusionary efforts one step further, engaging older adults and other community members themselves as central actors in efforts to promote stronger, more engaged communities.

The types of community development efforts described in this chapter focus on enhancing and better utilizing existing community resources, beginning with the capacities and potential contributions of all community residents, including older adults. Rather than focusing primarily on the problems experienced by communities, these initiatives focus on the assets that communities have. All community members, including the oldest, are seen as resources who have something to contribute to their communities, rather than being seen only as service users or resource consumers. "This new movement is characterized by a belief that significant, sustainable community change can only be brought about by developing and utilizing the social fabric in the targeted communities" (Anderson & Milligan, 2006, p. 21).

Community development efforts such as these work to enhance community aging friendliness by focusing primarily on enhancing the supportive capacity of interest groups and their members, rather than large-scale system change. This asset-based community development (ABCD) approach

(Mathie & Cunningham, 2003) builds on the principles of collective efficacy theory (Sampson, Raudenbush, & Earls, 1997), which emphasizes the role of interpersonal relationships and other community social resources as a basis for constructive change. From this perspective, the most basic and powerful resources in our communities are not its formal institutions, but rather community members themselves and their relationships with one another. These are the bonds of kinship, friendship, and neighborhood, which are the characteristics of *Gemeinschaft*, in the words of German sociologist Ferdinand Tönnies (2001). The interpersonal bonds of Gemeinschaft contrast with the more formal, impersonal network of legal and contractual relations expressed by the term *Gesellschaft*, based not on connection, but on rationality and calculation of personal benefit, that to a great extent has become a hallmark of Western society.

Despite an apparent decline in neighborhood involvement, social relationships continue to have substantial influence, especially in the lives of older adults. Some have argued that "networks, enhanced and multiplied by technology, penetrate our lives so deeply that 'network' has become the central metaphor around which our thinking and our economy are organized" (Kelly, 1999, p. 2). The United States already has among the highest rates of voluntary association membership in the world (Schofer & Fourcade-Gourinchas, 2001), and new forms of intentional social organizations are emerging, in part in response to declines in the stability of traditional family and informal social networks and in their ability to meet the needs of increasing numbers of older community members from diverse communities (Feinberg et al., 2011; Gilbert, 2002; Salamon, 2012; Szinovacz & Davey, 2008). Community-based social networks, in their various forms, have substantial potential for addressing the well-being of their older members, as well as advocating for communitywide approaches to respond to the current and future needs of all older persons (Welzel, Inglehart, & Deutsch, 2005).

Aging-friendly community development initiatives have the potential to foster what has been called the "core economy," the various forms of social assistance typically provided by families, neighbors, and voluntary organizations, which have tremendous value to individuals and society, but for which money is not usually exchanged (Cahn, 2006). John McKnight argued that society is like a four-legged stool, with informal associations of like-minded citizens being the fourth support (McKnight, 2013). Unlike not-for-profit organizations, which usually are formal and hierarchical, associations tend to be informal and horizontal, relying primarily on the experience and knowledge of member citizens and in so doing enhancing citizens' social and political capital. Most such efforts begin as groups of like-minded individuals working collaboratively to advance their common interests and in many cases evolve into formal organizations. In a fundamental way, this represents the basic idea behind civil society and "urban citizenship" (Buffel, Phillipson, & Scharf, 2012).

Older adults themselves are important community resources and need to be included in community development efforts. As noted by W. H. Thomas and Blanchard (2009), among others, older adults share responsibility for helping to create mutually beneficial communities. Engagement in meaningful social roles, furthermore, enables older community members to utilize their experience and wisdom to promote community well-being (Morrow-Howell et al., 2001).

Aging-friendly community development initiatives also need to facilitate older adults' engagement in the change process to ensure that interventions are targeted most effectively to their specific needs and preferences. For this reason, the World Health Organization's (WHO's) Global Network of Age-Friendly Cities and Communities program, described in Chapter 9, includes "promot[ing] elder contributions and social inclusion" as one of its eight key objective areas (WHO, 2007) and suggests that older residents can be involved not only as information sources regarding the aging friendliness of their city but also as critical stakeholders in helping to set priorities, propose solutions for action, and monitor progress. However, among local governments responding to the National Association of Area Agencies on Aging's (n4a's) 2010 survey of cities and towns in the United States, only 30% reported that they actively solicited any kind of input from older community members regarding ways to meet their needs (n4a, 2011), and such efforts typically involve a relatively small number of individuals, who tend to be among those who already are most socially active and civically engaged.

In addition to involving older adults in identifying what they would like to change, aging-friendly community development initiatives have the potential to engage them in helping to facilitate those changes. This can require capacity building to enhance older residents' knowledge and skills, as well as providing the supports necessary to enhance their ability to participate fully (e.g., by identifying other community partners to assist them in their efforts or by accessing other community and outside resources to support their efforts).

Examples of Community Development Initiatives

We now describe a number of aging-friendly community development initiatives, which in various ways strive to access and enhance the potential of older adults and other community members for helping their communities to become better places to live and to age. Initiative goals and program models vary substantially from community to community. Some primarily focus on meeting the needs of current community residents (e.g., program development and service provision), while others focus primarily on fostering system change (e.g., advocacy); many initiatives involve a combination of direct services and system change.

Some initiatives are relatively informal efforts, based on friendship circles and informal social relationships, reflecting the notion of Gemeinschaft (Tönnies, 2001). Other efforts grow into formal organizations, such as retiree associations (e.g., AARP, Age Concern UK); elder advocacy organizations (e.g., Gray Panthers); elder membership and service provision associations (e.g., Villages); mutual assistance organizations (e.g., time banks); and volunteer service provision collectives (e.g., Coming Home Connection).

Community-Driven Program Development and Service Provision

The *Community Ambassadors Program for Seniors* (CAPS) in Fremont, California (http://capseniors.org/), for example, is a unique partnership between the city of Fremont Human Services Department and 12 ethnic and faith-based organizations. CAPS utilizes volunteers from historically underserved ethnic and faith-based communities (Indian, Taiwanese, Muslim, Latino, Sikh, Filipino, and multiethnic Christian) to serve as "ambassadors" between older adults within these communities and the existing aging services network. CAPS integrates program participants through a strength-based model that engages older adults in fostering a communitywide safety net. Developed initially with the help of a $300,000 grant from the Robert Wood Johnson Foundation, the program has been sustained with ongoing support from local government, grants, corporate sponsorship, and individual donations. To date, more than 150 ambassadors have been trained, annually contributing more than 2,000 volunteer hours and serving more than 600 of their aging community members.

This project has generated linking capital, as ambassadors inform community members about the availability of services and inform service agencies about the particular needs and values of their communities, as well as bridging capital, as ambassadors meet with family groups and social networks to foster enhanced intergenerational understanding and support. Further, social integration is enhanced as ambassadors meet with groups of community seniors in their own language and culture where the seniors naturally congregate, thereby promoting bonding capital (Blair, 2010). In addition, the model is being considered for adoption in other cities and serves as the basis for a Senior Peer Advocate (SPA) program to serve the entire county.

Time banking is another approach to creating intentional informal helping networks that include older community members. Time banking "involves the creation of a social network of members who exchange services, with each member committing to both giving and receiving services" (Marks, 2012, p. 1231), using time credits as a medium of exchange (Seyfang, 2003). Time banking is predicated on the idea that every community member has something to offer, and everyone also has something that they need. While time banks include persons of all age groups, they are apt to be especially beneficial for older adults, whose potential contributions to community well-being are frequently underestimated. Many time banks begin with particular groups defined by geography, neighborhood identification, or interest group but grow to be available communitywide. Based on informal helping networks that traditionally have existed within extended families, immigrant populations, religious institutions, and other interest groups, time banks provide opportunities for members to obtain assistance when needed, provide assistance that contributes to other members' well-being, and reinforce a sense of community engagement and identity among members of all ages, thereby potentially contributing to community aging friendliness. Some of the impacts reported by time bank members include increased social connections, increased ability to age in place, and improved quality of life (Visiting Nurse Service of New York [VNSNY], 2009). Related to this is an increased sense of belonging to a community, both as a recipient of support and as a contributor to the well-being of others and to the community as a whole. Of particular note, in one study, 93% of time bank members said that they had interacted with or made friends with individuals of different ages, backgrounds, or cultures than their own (VNSNY, 2009). Some time banks, such as the Community Connections time bank of the VNSNY, include referrals to other community services beyond what is provided by time bank members. Consequently, among Community Connections members, 93% saw the time bank as a place to obtain information about services in the community, and two thirds reported increased ability to access those services. Time banking has been shown to be especially beneficial for Spanish-speaking older adults and those with the lowest incomes (VNSNY, 2009).

Advocacy and System Change

Contra Costa for Every Generation (CCEG) was a countywide community development initiative that engaged more than 200 residents over the age of 50 in efforts "to make our local communities good places to age—supporting our aspirations to stay healthy, live independently and lead full and productive lives" (John Muir/Mt. Diablo Community Health Fund, 2006, p. 31). Participants represented communities throughout the county and were diverse racially, ethnically, by gender, by age, and by employment status. Advocacy efforts were developed by workgroups focused on six different areas of concern identified by older community members: involvement in the community, housing, transportation, health care and wellness, neighborhood quality of life, and support services. A steering committee coordinated workgroup efforts, while also working to raise community awareness regarding aging issues. Among its accomplishments was the development of a Senior Ambassadors program, which helped older adults assume leadership roles on local governmental planning and advisory bodies with responsibility for issues potentially affecting older community residents. CCEG was developed and supported by grants from local and regional community health foundations, as well as from county government, but proved unsustainable when funders grew dissatisfied with the initiative's slow pace of development.

The *Vital Aging Network* (VAN) began as a small group of aging advocates in Minnesota who wanted to find a way to promote "vital aging" through personal development and meaningful and mutually beneficial community involvement opportunities. Founders were convinced that older adults represented an under-utilized resource, and they sought to promote productive roles for all older adults rather than just health and human services for the frail elderly. With support from the University of Minnesota and a number of foundations, VAN has grown into a statewide network "to promote self-determination, civic engagement and per-sonal growth for and with people as they age through education, leadership devel-opment and opportunities to connect" (http://vital-aging-network.org/).

Among VAN's initiatives is a statewide network called Vital Force that helps communities become more aging friendly by engaging older adults in responding to pressing community needs or opportunities. To assist this process, VAN devel-oped the "Vital Communities Toolkit," a Web-based toolkit that helps individu-als and community leaders identify potential civic engagement opportunities that could improve their communities for seniors.

Recognizing the importance of capacity building, VAN developed the Advocacy Leadership in Vital Aging (ALVA) Certificate Program in collaboration with the University of Minnesota's College of Continuing Education. This pro-gram was designed to enhance senior participants' understanding of aging issues, relevant environmental conditions and public policies, and potential strategies for enhancing their aging friendliness, leading to a project designed to enhance per-sonal well-being or community aging friendliness. In 2008, VAN refocused the ALVA program to include persons 50 and older, renaming it Evolve: Re-igniting Self & Community (ERSC). ERSC is an 8-month program designed to help par-ticipants "(re)discover purpose, build your community leadership skills, plan and implement a project that contributes to the common good, and become a part of a high-energy network for exchange of ideas, connections and support" (http://vital-aging-network.org). Among the projects undertaken to date are the follow-ing: creating patio container gardens that are accessible for older people; working with the state of Minnesota to help rewrite state building codes to include univer-sal design; developing a program to help relieve isolation of Hmong elders in the community; advocating for sidewalks, paths, and bikeways needed to encourage physical activity; and designing a t'ai chi class especially for the needs of people 50 and older.

Elders in Action, a volunteer-led, community-based senior advocacy group established in 1968 in Portland, Oregon, has created an Age Friendly Business Certification program, whereby trained older adult volunteers assess the age friendliness of a business in accordance with a set of established age-friendly criteria, including customer service, accessibility, layout, signage, website content and navigation (http://eldersinaction.org/about-age-friendly-businesses). Businesses are then given direct feedback on how they can better respond to the needs of aging consumers, and certified businesses appear in an annual directory that is distributed to over 8,000 seniors in the Portland metropolitan area. Elders in Action has licensed its training and certification process to other nonprofit groups around the country, including senior organizations in at least 12 states.

Combined Models

While most social entities (e.g., membership organizations, professional associations, labor unions, religious organizations, and political parties) exist primarily to serve the utilitarian group interests of their members, they also have the potential to engage in joint actions designed to promote the aging friendliness of their communities.

The *Calgary Elder-Friendly Communities Project* (CEFCP) represents a model of community engagement and aging in place capacity building in culturally diverse urban neighborhoods. While not a U.S. initiative, we include the project here because of its seminal contribution to the development of collaborative aging-friendly initiatives in the United States and elsewhere. Developed by the University of Calgary Faculty of Social Work in collaboration with the Calgary Regional Health Authority, the City of Calgary, Calgary Family Services, Jewish Family Services, and the Calgary Catholic Immigration Society, the project combined elements of cross-sector collaborations and community development. However, unlike typical cross-sector collaborations, the focus of organizational efforts was on supporting capacity development for community older adults, who were integrally involved in every aspect of the initiative.

The CEFCP included the design and implementation of senior-initiated community development projects to address community-identified needs. Older neighborhood residents assumed leadership roles in community change efforts, with support from professional community development workers (Austin et al., 2005). In each neighborhood, seniors themselves selected priority issues, developed a work plan, and initiated action. All programming decisions were made by senior-led groups, which were also responsible for community organizing activities, such as workshops on accessing resources, local conferences, social activities, and environmental improvements. By engaging individuals of diverse ages and ethnicities in community projects, the project helped to enhance community capacity and social capital that could persist long after the project ended (Austin et al., 2005). In addition, specific aging-friendly outcomes included consumer-identified environmental enhancements such as the placement of postal boxes in seniors' complexes and an annual conference that attracts seniors from across Calgary to discuss common concerns.

The *Community Living Campaign* (CLC) began in 2006 to develop effective ways to enhance informal support networks to benefit elders and persons with disabilities in San Francisco. CLC's mission is "transforming lives by building aging- and disability-friendly neighborhoods" (http://www.sfcommunityliving.org/index.html). It does this by "empower[ing] seniors and people with disabilities to come together, organize, and use their many skills and interests to reduce isolation and end economic and other barriers to aging in their own homes and neighborhoods" (http://www.sfcommunityliving.org/index.html). CLC's strategy is "to leverage the power of relationships to improve services and support" (http://www.sfcommunityliving.org/index.html). CLC focuses on three methods of action: individualized support, community networks, and system change.

The CLC promotes individualized support by building social networks comprising small communities of caring friends dedicated to ensuring the right of seniors and people with disabilities to live independently in the community. Unlike traditional social agencies that focus on deficits and needs, these social networks celebrate, draw inspiration from, and organize around the dreams, interests, and gifts of those at its heart. Staff and peer advocates host Connections for Healthy Aging workshops to help participating seniors and people with disabilities to become better prepared and more empowered to advocate for themselves and others. Trained Community Connectors, typically seniors or persons with disabilities, organize neighborhood networks designed to meet needs in areas such as food delivery, home repairs, healthy aging, and social activities. CLC also has helped to develop a time bank for Bay area residents. Finally, CLC is actively involved in advocacy efforts to improve communitywide services and supports for seniors, persons with disabilities, and their care providers. Key issues include improving hospital discharge planning and support, preserving adult day health services, and advocating for greater financial support.

The *Brookline Community Action Network* (BrooklineCAN) is a townwide initiative with dual purposes: (a) to help older residents obtain access to needed services; and (2) to promote greater community livability for people of all ages (http://www.brooklinecan.org/). Membership benefits include information about preferred contractors and service providers, a monthly newsletter, and educational programs. Efforts to promote community livability have included advocating for pedestrian safety, encouraging the town to adopt a Complete Streets policy, monitoring sidewalk conditions in commercial areas after snowstorms, advocating for stronger enforcement of laws requiring property owners to keep sidewalks clear of snow and ice, providing information on the availability of public restrooms, providing an online guide to residential buildings with elevators, assessing the elder friendliness of new parking meters, advocating for improved parking options for providers of in-home care, and advocating for tax relief and improved housing options for low-income older adults. BrooklineCAN also persuaded the Town of Brookline to join WHO's Global Network of Age-Friendly Cities and Communities (described previously in Chapter 9).

The idea for BrooklineCAN originated in a 3-year cross-sector collaboration between older community residents, the town's Council on Aging, and three private nonprofit social service organizations, including Jewish Family and Children's Service, which provided education programs, household help, and peer connections to residents of a neighborhood in North Brookline. BrooklineCAN is entirely member driven, with volunteer committees addressing member recruitment, service referrals, communications, education programs, and livable community advocacy. In addition to annual membership fees of $25, BrooklineCAN receives in-kind human and administrative support from the Brookline Council on Aging and fiscal sponsorship from the Brookline Senior Center.

The *Village model* is a grassroots approach whereby older community residents develop their own local community-based membership associations to provide and receive support, promote healthy aging, and enhance their ability to age in place. In exchange for annual membership dues, Villages typically provide a variety of supportive services (e.g., transportation, grocery shopping, household help) and informal supports (e.g., friendly visits or phone calls from other Village members), organize social activities, and assist members in accessing other needed services from for-profit and not-for-profit community service providers, often at a reduced rate (Scharlach et al., 2012). Consumer engagement is a key feature of these organizations, with older adults typically taking primary responsibility for developing each Village, providing oversight and governance, assisting with day-to-day operations, providing core financing, and providing supportive services to other members (McDonough & Davitt, 2011).

Since the first Village in the Beacon Hill neighborhood of Boston in 2002, the Village model has proliferated rapidly, expanding to more than 140 Villages by 2015, with at least as many currently in development elsewhere in the United States and in other countries, so that some consider Villages to be a "consumer movement." In addition, Villages have formed a peer association, the VtV Network, which offers technical assistance, facilitates resource sharing, and organizes national and regional meetings. The VtV Network is considered to be "the largest and fastest growing of all the age-friendly development networks," according to Grantmakers in Aging (2013, p. 16), a national association of funders supporting aging issues. It should be noted, however, that Villages are not universally available; furthermore, Villages tend to attract members who are white, economically secure, and with relatively low levels of disability, compared with national averages for older adults in the United States (Greenfield et al., 2012).

Based on our review of published and unpublished reports, we have identified seven "core characteristics" of the Village model: grassroots (i.e., developed by consumers); membership driven (i.e., members play key operational roles); self-governing (i.e., independent nonprofit organizations); self-supporting (i.e., financed primarily through dues and donations); service provision (i.e., services provided by staff or volunteers); service coordination (i.e., referrals to vetted discounted service providers); and a holistic approach (i.e., services to meet member needs as well as social activities and engagement opportunities) (Lehning, Scharlach, & Davitt, 2015).

Preliminary evidence from an ongoing study of California Villages suggests a number of benefits of Village membership, including reported improvements with regard to social engagement, service access, and health and well-being, as well as increased ability to age in place (Graham, Scharlach, & Price Wolf, 2014). In this study, nearly 80% of respondents agreed that they knew more people as a result of Village membership, 59% felt more socially connected, about one half reported improved quality of life, and more than three fourths indicated that Village membership enhanced their confidence in their ability to age in place. Village-sponsored social activities, attended by three quarters of Village members, were particularly associated with enhanced social engagement, health and well-being, and service access.

In addition to the benefits received by Village members, more than one third of Villages are involved in direct or indirect efforts to make their overall communities more aging friendly, according to our 2012 national survey of Villages (Scharlach et al., 2014). We found that about one fourth of Villages were working to improve community responsiveness toward older persons through public presentations and advocacy efforts, and one tenth were working to achieve specific physical improvements in the built environment, such as safer crosswalks or sidewalk benches. Furthermore, it seems likely that, by coordinating and activating members' social capital and consolidated purchasing power, Villages might enable members to negotiate for better quality services at a lower cost, potentially yielding improvements in the quality of aging-related goods and services available throughout the entire community. As noted by Irene Hoskins, past president of the International Federation on Aging, "Villages may be ideal conduits to lead efforts towards an age-friendly city".

Community Without Walls (CWW), in Princeton, New Jersey, is a grassroots peer support organization that also includes family members. CWW was started in 1992 by a middle-aged couple with personal experience caring for aging parents, a friend who was a geriatric social worker, and another friend active in community affairs (http://cwwprinceton.org/Who-We-Are.aspx). Members assist one another with social support, information, education, and advocacy, while also taking full responsibility for planning programs, recruiting new members, and submitting required government reports. CWW's 460 members are organized into six chapters, called Houses, each with 50 to 100 members who help one another as needed and create and participate in a variety of small-group social and educational activities. Through its advocacy efforts, CWW also has fostered improvements in local aging services, as well as senior housing, transportation, and health services.

Challenges and Opportunities

A major strength of community development models is their ability to activate and even expand underutilized community human and social capital. In this way, community-based organizations are able to provide through volunteer labor what more formal organizations usually must pay for. However, this strength may also be their greatest limitation, in that community volunteers are apt to lack the expertise and financial resources needed to develop a successful organizational structure. Developing and sustaining consumer-driven initiatives requires expertise with regard to a variety of roles, such as the following: community organizing, resource brokerage, advocacy, group facilitation, consumer education, training, volunteer development, and management and administration (McDonough & Davitt, 2011). Village leaders, for example, have identified the following themes as keys to the long-term sustainability of their organizations: financial stability; adequate human resources; formal operational plans and procedures; interorganizational collaborations; and community recognition and support (Scharlach et al., 2014). There is only so much that a group of citizens can do, and sustainability is apt to require resource inputs of various kinds from external sources. For these reasons, grassroots programs that depend on volunteers are apt to require substantial funding and support from external sources.

In an effort to obtain needed expertise, administrative supports, and other external resources, many consumer-driven initiatives have established formal or informal collaborations designed to capitalize on existing community resources. Senior centers and similar entities, for example, help to foster informal action networks by providing meeting space, office space, computers, telephones, administrative support, and other in-kind resources to older community members. However, reliance on external resources also can result in a reduction in the power and autonomy of the consumer-driven effort, as described by resource dependence theory, evoking the concern that consumer initiatives could be co-opted by more powerful forces.

In responding to the multifaceted needs of older community members, aging-friendly community development initiatives focus on a variety of interconnected issues affecting the health and well-being of individuals, families, organizations, and communities. This typically requires them to cross traditional disciplinary boundaries, making them inherently unstable to the extent that they transcend existing administrative, funding, and program silos. Furthermore, by their very nature, community development initiatives are likely to require change efforts directed at multiple community stakeholders and systems.

Promoting sustainable community change is apt to require skills in a wide variety of interrelated areas: enhancing the ability of individual community members to participate in change efforts (e.g., improving knowledge and skills, promoting physical and psychosocial functioning, enhancing coping strategies, empowerment); strengthening existing social networks (e.g., promoting social engagement, enhancing social support, developing social capital); enhancing organizational and system capacity to meet the needs of older community members (e.g., increasing service availability, accessibility, affordability, and appropriateness); developing more responsive communities (e.g., convening and coordinating planful change efforts); or facilitating social change (e.g., advocating for more aging-friendly social and economic policies, fostering public awareness, promoting more aging-friendly attitudes and beliefs) (Scharlach, 2009). Given the complexity and diversity of the competencies required, community change almost always requires the involvement of various partners, substantial commitment of resources, and a process for enhancing the capacity of leading individuals and organizations.

Consumer initiatives typically begin as what Weber called "charismatic organizations," developed by a small number of visionaries who inspire others to join them in their efforts. Developing more stable organizational structures that can sustain the effort in the absence of those initial charismatic leaders can be a challenge for consumer-driven organizations, as has been found with some Villages (Scharlach et al., 2014). While some organizations may be able to maintain a charismatic authority structure for the long term, transition from charismatic to bureaucratic authority structures may be especially important in organizations that are developed by older adult volunteers, few of whom are likely to be able to sustain high levels of involvement and leadership activity indefinitely. On the other hand, it is possible that authority structures that are more bureaucratic may discourage member engagement, suggesting the importance of finding the right balance between charismatic and bureaucratic authority structures as consumer-driven initiatives evolve over time.

Community initiatives also tend to include limited segments of the population. Participants tend to be identified through active participation in existing organizations (e.g., seniors' clubs, church groups, exercise classes, etc.) or through snowball recruiting through existing social networks. It is therefore possible that these initiatives replicate and exacerbate existing patterns of social isolation and political exclusion. The availability of necessary human and economic resources can be a challenge for communities that already are underresourced. Villages, for example, tend to include members who are younger, less economically insecure, and less likely to reside in communities with low or middle socioeconomic status than the general U.S. population ages 65 or older (Administration on Aging, 2012; Greenfield, Scharlach, Lehning, Davitt, & Graham, 2013).

Conclusion

Aging-friendly community development initiatives appear to have substantial potential for enhancing participants' ability to age in place while also promoting constructive changes in the overall community. Community development initiatives also may enable communities to benefit more fully from the wisdom and untapped energies of their older residents by facilitating opportunities for members to participate in volunteer activities, paid work, and other types of civic engagement. A potential secondary effect of community development initiatives is their ability to enhance a general sense of community identity and identification, as people gain an increased recognition of their commonality with other community members, see how their own well-being is connected to the well-being of the overall community, gain a better understanding of their role in the overall community and begin to see positive results from their constructive efforts to participate in the life of the community (Cottrell, 1976). In doing so, community development initiatives may help to reinvigorate and transform a sense of community to include all members, especially those whose ability to participate is reduced by dint of the aging process, and how it and those affected are perceived. With this in mind, "ensuring and enabling supportive environments" is one of three major priority areas of the International Plan of Action on Ageing (United Nations, 2002).While serious concerns have been raised regarding the sustainability of community development models such as these, initiatives generally have demonstrated surprising staying power. For example, at least 90% of Villages that have been developed are still in operation, although the jury is still out given that the majority of operating Villages are less than 3 years old. Initiatives also vary regarding the extent to which they actively involve older community members, and there has been little research regarding the potential benefits of such initiatives—for the participants, as well as for their communities. Furthermore, community change involving the physical environment is likely to require the involvement of local governments, which are better positioned to enhance the age friendliness of the physical environment through zoning changes, housing incentives, transportation improvements, and other infrastructure enhancements.

PART IV

AGING-FRIENDLY COMMUNITIES—CHALLENGES AND OPPORTUNITIES

12

The Challenges of Making Communities More Aging Friendly

Introduction

Making communities more aging friendly is a promising approach for addressing the needs of older adults, their families, and their communities. First, aging-friendly community initiatives reflect a shift from the traditional residual and selective approaches to improving elder health, well-being, and engagement that provide services to older adults after a problem has already developed. For example, the majority of long-term services and supports in the United States, such as home health or adult day health care, are typically only available to those who demonstrate need, such as a disability or social isolation. Aging-friendly communities, in contrast, are potentially universally available to everyone living in the neighborhood, town, city, or county targeted for change. Furthermore, many of the recommended community changes emphasize prevention rather than the amelioration of problems once they have occurred. Walkable neighborhoods, for example, may increase community residents' physical activity and thereby prevent or delay future disability. As we described in Chapter 7, health and social services that address existing problems are a critical component of aging-friendly communities. In an aging-friendly community, however, these supports are combined with policies, programs, and infrastructure changes that seek to reduce the need for residual interventions.

Second, aging-friendly community efforts highlight a growing recognition that interventions that focus solely on the individual are insufficient. Instead, these initiatives aim to improve person–environment fit by addressing the changing needs of the individual, his or her environment, and interactions between the two. Prior to the development of these initiatives, policies such as the Americans With Disabilities Act signaled the realization that home and community environments can create barriers for individuals with disabilities (Szold, 2002). As we described in Chapter 2, aging-friendly community initiatives extend this recognition by calling for community changes that could address a variety of developmental needs in later life, including not only compensation for potential functional limitations but also continuity, control, connection, contribution, and challenge. Furthermore, these initiatives, to varying degrees, target the social environment, the physical environment, and their interactions (Alley et al., 2007).

Third, aging-friendly community initiatives have the potential to mitigate population segmentation and the "us-versus-them" perspective that tends to dominate discussions about social welfare policies and programs. The AdvantAge Initiative, for example, promotes the idea that aging-friendly environments can benefit people of all ages (Hanson & Emlet, 2006). As noted by Alley and colleagues (2007), aging-friendly community initiatives seek to create "age-based" community changes that primarily benefit older adults, as well as "age-related" changes that also hold the promise of addressing the needs of other residents (p. 13). Clearly, some programs that contribute to aging friendliness, such as senior centers or supports for informal caregivers, will largely assist older adults and their families. Others, however, could have a broader impact. For example, as noted by Kerschner and Hardin (2006), "Providing good transportation for the public does not necessarily result in good transportation for seniors, but improving transportation for seniors will improve transportation for everyone" (p. 5).

Finally, aging-friendly efforts typically view older adults not only as recipients of services but also as key contributors to initiative development and implementation. As we described in Chapters 9, 10, and 11, there is substantial variation in elder involvement between initiatives, but all tend to include older adults in a way both quantitatively and qualitatively different from many other long-term supports and services. In their idealized form, aging-friendly initiatives reflect W. H. Thomas and Blanchard's (2009) concept of "aging in community," in which older adults are considered valued members of their communities and work with other residents to create a place that is healthy for people of all abilities and ages.

While aging-friendly community initiatives incorporate a number of innovative strategies to address the needs and wants of older adults, there are significant challenges to their development, implementation, and evaluation. In this chapter, we critically analyze these challenges. We begin by discussing concerns about the ability of aging-friendly initiatives to address the needs of the entire range of older adults and communities. We then examine the barriers to moving from the development and assessment phases of an initiative to actually bringing about aging-friendly community change. Finally, we note some of the limitations of the scholarly literature, which may impede the proliferation and success of aging-friendly initiatives in an era of evidence-informed policies and programs.

Potential Exclusion

A key component of aging-friendly efforts is the meaningful participation of older adults; indeed, this is often viewed as necessary to ensure the success of local initiatives (Menec et al., 2011). As we described in Chapter 9, for example, community planning models often begin with a comprehensive assessment of older residents and other stakeholders. Even when using an existing framework, such as the World Health Organization's (WHO's) Age-Friendly Cities and Communities program or the Visiting Nurse Service of New York's AdvantAge Initiative, this assessment allows the local initiative to tailor its effort to the unique needs of the community. Cross-sector collaborations, described in Chapter 10, similarly view older adults as valued partners in their efforts to improve existing services and foster a sense of community. Older adults participating in Naturally Occurring Retirement Community Supportive Service Programs (NORC-SSPs), for example, may serve on advisory councils, advocate for local policy changes, or participate in community education campaigns (Bedney & Goldberg, 2009). The community development models we delineated in Chapter 11 offer perhaps the greatest opportunities for elder involvement. For example, most Villages, including the first Village in the Beacon Hill neighborhood of Boston, were formed by a group of older adults who wanted to create supports for each other to remain in their own home (Beacon Hill Village, 2014). Older adults continue to make critical contributions to the administration, provision, and funding of services and supports long after a Village has been launched (McWhinney-Morse, 2009; Poor, Baldwin, & Willet, 2012).

This emphasis on the active participation of older community residents, however, raises several interrelated challenges. First, aging-friendly initiatives may have difficulty soliciting and maintaining older adults' involvement. Community change can be a lengthy process. Communities participating in the WHO program, for example, may spend years conducting a comprehensive community assessment and developing a strategic plan. Similarly, anecdotal reports suggest that Villages take years between the initial idea and actually enrolling and serving members. Older adults' commitment to and enthusiasm for the initiative could potentially fade over time. In addition, the ability of older adults to provide human or financial resources to an initiative may decrease if they experience the declines in health and well-being that become increasingly likely in later life. Research on Villages, for example, suggested this is a major concern among organizational leaders, particularly as newer members may not have the same level of passion for their Village as the founders (Lehning, Davitt, Scharlach, & Greenfield, 2014).

Second, it is unclear whether aging-friendly community initiatives are including the perspectives of older community residents with diverse health and physical capabilities, racial and ethnic backgrounds, financial resources, and levels of social engagement. Aging-friendly initiative leaders have expressed concern about whether less civically minded older adults are participating in community assessments and other initiative activities (Neal et al., 2014). Even initiatives that emphasize the creation of neighborhood social capital and social support networks may be neglecting the needs of the most socially isolated elders. In our research with Villages, for example, many have described member word of mouth as their most effective marketing strategy, potentially contributing to the homogeneity of Village membership (Lehning et al., 2015). If Villages primarily tap existing social networks, they may miss those with small or nonexistent social networks.

Furthermore, identifying policy, programmatic, or infrastructure change priorities that reflect the heterogeneity of older community residents can be a major challenge. The label *older adults*, for example, refers to a population that comprises multiple generations experiencing a variety of life transitions. Those who are in their 60s are likely quite healthy, while those in their 80s are at a higher risk for functional impairments (Federal Interagency Forum on Aging-Related Statistics, 2012) or some form of dementia (Alzheimer's Association, 2014). There are also many differences among older adults with regard to their experience of major role transitions that can occur in later life, including leaving the workforce, providing care to a parent or spouse, becoming a grandparent, or losing a spouse, among others.

A potential major gap in aging-friendly community initiatives is their ability to solicit the participation of older adults from diverse racial and ethnic backgrounds. This is concerning for a number of reasons. Cultural variations regarding expectations and preferences associated with the experience of aging will likely affect the methods and targets for aging-friendly community change. Between now and 2050, the proportion of the older adult population that is White is projected to decrease from 79% to 61%, while the proportion of older adults who are Latino, African American, Asian, or other races or ethnicities is expected to nearly double (Federal Interagency Forum on Aging-Related Statistics, 2012). Without the active participation of all racial and ethnic groups, aging-friendly initiatives may only be relevant for a smaller and smaller segment of community residents.

Because aging-friendly community initiatives are a relatively new type of intervention, little is known about racial and ethnic preferences for aging-friendly changes to social and physical environments. However, previous research has documented differences between African American and White elders in terms of expectations around family members' responsibility for care (Bradley et al., 2002), awareness of available services (Calsyn & Winter, 1999a), and perceptions that formal service providers are responsive to their needs (Scharlach et al., 2006). This suggests there may be important differences in perspectives on aging-friendly communities by race and ethnicity.

Furthermore, minority elders are at a higher risk for poor quality of life in later life, given the persistence of health disparities by race (Schoeni, Martin,

Andreski, & Freedman, 2005). For example, African Americans report poorer self-rated health than Whites (Borrell & Crawford, 2006), particularly at older ages (Kington & Nickens, 2001). African Americans experience a faster decline in physiological functioning and on average have a higher biological age compared to Whites (Levine & Crimmins, 2014). Racial disparities in health and well-being are often due, at least in part, to disparities in education and income (Fuller-Thompson, Nuru-Jeter, Minkler, & Guralnik, 2009; Schoeni et al., 2005), as older African Americans and Hispanics are more likely to live in poverty than Whites or Asians (Federal Interagency Forum on Aging-Related Statistics, 2012).

While some aging-friendly initiatives, notably the AdvantAge Initiative, call attention to the ways income can create significant disparities in later life, it is unclear the extent to which these programs are developing specific action items related to this segment of the older adult population. For example, as noted by Hanson and Emlet (2006), the AdvantAge Initiative does not include livable income as an essential element of an aging-friendly community; furthermore, the WHO Global Age-Friendly Cities and Communities Project's eight key domains do not explicitly include safety and security, which are of particular importance to individuals living in poorer communities. Older adults with financial resources already enjoy a number of advantages, including access to higher quality health care and long-term services and supports (Scharlach, 2012). There is some indication that several aging-friendly community initiatives have targeted better resourced communities. Many Villages, for example, have been developed in communities that are predominantly middle to upper-middle class (Greenfield et al., 2013). Racial and ethnic minorities and those with low incomes, however, also may be more likely to live in underresourced neighborhoods without aging-friendly environments. These neighborhoods may be characterized by problems such as crime, traffic, deteriorating infrastructure, and excessive noise, which in turn may contribute to unhealthy behaviors, such as drinking, smoking, or avoiding outdoor physical activity (Ambrose Gallagher et al., 2010; Echeverria, Diez-Roux, Shea, Borrell, & Jackson, 2008; Hill & Angel, 2005). This indicates a higher need for aging-friendly community changes among the same groups who may be excluded from the development, implementation, and evaluation of such efforts. This exclusion, which may be unintentional, could potentially exacerbate health and well-being inequities in later life (Scharlach, 2012).

Finally, a number of aging-friendly community initiatives, including Villages, the WHO Global Age-Friendly Cities and Communities Project, and the AdvantAge Initiative, explicitly call for community and organizational leaders to adapt their model's general framework to the unique needs and wants of each local community. Our review of existing resources and literature, however, suggests there is little guidance on how to do this. As we discussed in Chapter 4, aging-friendly community initiatives typically have three goals: (a) minimizing physical barriers to aging well, (b) enhancing social engagement, and

(c) optimizing multidimensional health and well-being. There are likely multiple pathways to achieve these goals depending on the resources and assets of the community, as well as such characteristics as population density, weather, and geographic terrain. For example, even though more than two thirds of older adults in this country live in rural or suburban communities (Frey, 2007), too often their needs are not addressed by the aging-friendly community literature (Lui et al., 2009). The relevance of recommended components of an aging-friendly community may vary between communities that are urban, suburban, or rural. For instance, adequate public transportation may be particularly important for older adults living in dense urban areas, while supporting travel by personal automobile may be a high priority in rural areas with few alternative transportation options. The Age-Friendly Rural/Remote Communities project in Canada, for example, emphasizes helping family and friends to provide rides to older adults over providing public transit (Menec et al., 2011).

Community groups also are likely to differ regarding their priorities for aging-friendly improvements. Community characteristics ranked highest by respondents to the AARP Public Policy Institute's national survey of more than 4,500 adults age 50 and older (Harrell, Lynott, Guzman, & Lampkin, 2014), for example, varied substantially in accordance with the needs and interests of particular groups. Older adults with disabilities or with family caregivers, for example, wanted better transportation for people with limitations. They were less interested than those without disabilities in improved parks, pedestrian-friendly streets, or better buses or subways. Yet, these elders seldom are able to attend community town hall meetings or participate in the kinds of focus groups convened by community planners and researchers, which typically recruit members from active senior center participants. Among respondents with the lowest incomes, the top three priorities were increased police presence, transportation services, and increased affordable housing, reflecting the realities of having fewer resources and being more vulnerable, resulting in a greater need for basic services. We also note that increasing police presence consistently was ranked first or second, even though personal safety from crime is seldom included in aging-friendly community models. Not surprisingly, personal safety was found to be more of a concern for nondrivers, people with disabilities, and those with lower incomes. Having more public parks was a priority only for the highest income group, most likely because they have the discretionary time to make use of such amenities.

The desirability of certain aging-friendly community changes may also vary depending on the community. As we discussed in Chapter 5, some community residents (both younger and older) may respond to proposed aging-friendly community changes with NIMBY (not in my backyard) and BANANA (build absolutely nothing anywhere near anything) resistance (Plater-Zyberk & Ball, 2012). Some residents may object to any efforts to develop mixed-use development, high-density housing, or homes that include accessibility features because of privacy concerns, safety considerations, a desire for more space, or lifestyle preferences. Furthermore, some communities and their residents may resist universal standards or checklists for fear of losing their uniqueness.

In our observations, adequately responding to the unique needs of the community and all of its older residents presents a major challenge to the proliferation and success of aging-friendly community initiatives. In Chapter 3, we discussed theories from environmental gerontology, particularly the ecological model of aging (Lawton & Nahemow, 1973), that call attention to the interactions between individuals and their environment. Using the language of Lawton, these frameworks propose that such outcomes as health, well-being, and aging in place reflect the degree of fit between personal "competence" and environmental "press" (Lawton, 1982). Older adults with more health, financial, and social resources can better navigate a variety of environments, while those who are socially isolated, economically vulnerable, or experiencing physical or cognitive limitations require a social or physical infrastructure that is more supportive of their needs. What Lawton recommended at a more microlevel, and what aging-friendly communities are trying to achieve at a more macrolevel, is creating environments that allow older adults to achieve their "zone of maximum performance potential" or their "zone of maximum comfort," in which the environment is neither excessively demanding nor overly supportive. The ecological model of aging highlights that one size does not fit all when making a community more aging friendly. However, local initiatives often need some guidance regarding aging-friendly community change. There is a need to find a balance between identifying universal aging-friendly characteristics versus tailoring everything to the community context. It remains unclear whether any existing aging-friendly community initiatives have been able to achieve this balance to date.

Implementing Community Change

A second major category of challenges involves moving from the assessment-and-planning stage to bringing about meaningful community change. Aging-friendly community initiatives, such as WHO's Global Age-Friendly Cities and Communities Project, have been criticized for being more successful at developing aspirations and plans rather than actual implementation of changes in policies, programs, and infrastructure (Barusch, 2013).

A major barrier to creating more aging-friendly social and physical environments is the lack of support for large-scale change from government agencies and other relatively stable funding sources. Consumer-driven community development models, which tend to emphasize nonmedical services and supports provided by nonprofessionals, often do not qualify for the government contracts and public insurance reimbursement that fund more traditional aging services.

In our research with Villages, many organizational leaders reported that they rely on time-limited grants from local foundations to maintain their operations, which may limit their long-term sustainability. Some of the local physical infrastructure changes typically targeted by community planning models, such as improved roadways and sidewalks or more accessible public transit, require significant funds at a time when state and local governments are already struggling to balance their budgets. As the elderly population increases, furthermore, cities are likely to experience increased demand for government services, causing even more strain on local government budgets (Wolf & Amirkhanyan, 2010).

Grantmakers in Aging has developed a Funder for Age-Friendly Communities initiative to increase financial support for these efforts, but to our knowledge this has led to funding in a very small number of communities. This raises questions regarding whether aging-friendly community initiatives can only thrive in communities that already have the public or private resources to fully support the endeavor (Scharlach, 2012). There is a great deal of heterogeneity in the communities currently working to become more aging friendly. Members of the AARP Network of Age-Friendly Communities, for example, include a variety of cities, towns, and counties, such as San Francisco; Washington, D.C.; Macon-Bibb, Georgia; Highland Park, Michigan; and St. Louis County, Missouri. In communities with fewer resources, it is possible that aging-friendly initiatives will not achieve their goals due to a lack of funding.

In the United States, the federal government has not played much of a leadership role in incentivizing or supporting aging-friendly community initiatives. Federal efforts to date have mostly been in the form of time-limited demonstration programs. The 2002 reauthorization of the Older Americans Act, for example, supported NORC-SSP demonstration projects at 45 sites in 26 states; however, many of these projects ceased operations or retracted substantially when funding ended. Similarly, the 2006 reauthorization of the Older Americans Act, for example, included funding for a Community Innovations for Aging in Place (CIAIP) demonstration program, which provided 3 years of support for 14 communities in the United States to implement local initiatives. Another short-lived program was the U.S. Environmental Protection Agency's (EPA's) Building Healthy Communities for Active Aging National Recognition Program, which gave awards to local communities through partnerships with nongovernmental organizations (e.g., the National Blueprint Office, the Robert Wood Johnson Foundation). In each of these cases, time-limited funding undermined communities' ability to sustain efforts once the program ended.

Area agencies on aging (AAAs), which are mandated by the federal Older Americans Act to address the needs of older residents by developing area plans, offering some direct services (e.g., case management, information and referral), contracting with local service providers, and advocating at the local and state levels, are seriously underfunded and seldom have the economic or political capital to carry out their mission. Most AAAs, furthermore, do not collaborate regularly with other key stakeholders, such as public health departments, local and regional planning agencies, public transit providers, or low-income housing developers. At the national level, furthermore, with a few notable exceptions, there is limited collaboration or coordination among relevant federal departments and offices, including the Administration on Aging, Department of Transportation, Department of Housing and Urban Development, Corporation for National and Community Service, and Centers for Medicare and Medicaid Services, among others, with regard to initiatives, grant programs, or regulations that could contribute to local communities' aging friendliness.

The aging-friendly community movement, furthermore, coincides with a time of relative fiscal austerity. The federal government appears to be prioritizing deficit reduction over the provision of social welfare programs. The federal budget sequestration, for example, which has been in effect since 2013, mandates automatic spending cuts to discretionary programs. State and local governments are still recovering from the Great Recession of 2007–2008. In this time of limited governmental resources, perceptions that making communities more aging-friendly involves everything but the kitchen sink could overwhelm local governments, nonprofits, and other stakeholders attempting to launch and roll out an initiative.

One recommendation to avoid this feeling is to implement changes incrementally. For example, infrastructure modifications to improve older driver safety can be made alongside regular maintenance work. Another recommendation is to prioritize changes that are relatively low cost, such as a city adopting a policy that encourages the incorporation of visitability features in new housing. But, in the absence of government mandates, home developers, architects, and builders ultimately make the decision whether to incorporate universal design principles into new construction based on perceptions about market demand. To date, however, consumers have been slow to embrace housing with obvious accessibility features.

As many existing initiatives acknowledge, particularly those using a cross-sector collaboration approach, making a community more aging friendly requires not only the cooperation but also the active contribution of a variety of stakeholders. Aging-friendly initiatives necessarily involve the participation of individuals and agencies with jurisdiction over a number of areas, including aging services, transportation, public health, city planning, housing, health care, parks and recreation, and civic engagement, among others. Furthermore, aging-friendly initiatives require expertise in a large number of tasks, including management and administration, community organizing, education and training, volunteer development and supervision, advocacy, and brokering.

Interprofessional and interdisciplinary collaboration, however, can be difficult given that many of the relevant actors operate within funding and regulatory silos. Forming and maintaining collaborations across diverse partners require time, energy, dedication, and funding. Participants from different professions and disciplines are likely to have different social constructions of the challenges and opportunities of an aging population. Turf wars may arise when participants perceive that other members of the collaboration are encroaching on their area of expertise. Participants will need to develop a structure for the collaboration, agree on decision-making processes, and select leadership. The collaboration will need staff to provide the critical administrative support that would likely fall through the cracks if left to volunteers. Perhaps the greatest challenge to forming and maintaining these collaborations is finding external funding sources. If collaborations rely on donated time and effort by partner organizations, they run the risk of losing resources if these organizations change priorities, perceive the collaboration's efforts as conflicting with their mission, or experience fiscal difficulties.

As we discussed in Chapter 10, creating aging-friendly communities is the type of large-scale change that requires a *collective impact* approach (Kania & Kramer, 2011). Collective impact is an emerging strategy for addressing the complex social problems that no single organization, sector, or profession is equipped to address single handedly. More traditional approaches to collaboration can address problems that are technical, reflect clearly defined problems, and have agreed-on solutions. Many cross-sector collaborations to create more aging-friendly communities have primarily targeted technical problems, such as the limited availability and effectiveness of services.

The collective impact approach, in contrast, recognizes that complex social problems do not emerge from the activities of a single individual or a social service agency, but rather from the activities of a variety of actors, including businesses, nonprofits, governments, and the general public. Therefore, all of these actors must also participate in developing and implementing solutions. Such an approach may be necessary for initiatives to achieve the larger-scale changes that will truly make a community aging friendly. While there has been little research to date evaluating the effectiveness of this approach, there are successful examples in the areas of public education and environmental conservation (Kania & Kramer, 2011). Financing collective impact, however, remains an issue because few foundations and other funders are willing to provide the necessary resources to facilitate sustained cross-sector collaborations over the long term.

Developing an Evidence Base

A third major category of challenges for aging-friendly community initiatives emerges from the limited research that has focused on these types of interventions. In Chapters 5, 6, and 7, we cited research from a wide range of disciplines providing empirical support for aging-friendly changes that minimize physical barriers, enhance social engagement, and optimize health and well-being. Often, these studies examine just one aspect of the social and physical infrastructure, such as home modifications or falls prevention. To date, the majority of peer-reviewed publications on aging-friendly communities offer a description of the concept as a whole (e.g., Alley et al., 2007) or a case study of one community's efforts (e.g., Hanson & Emlet, 2006). Published reports produced by aging-friendly initiatives are often more focused on the process of developing the initiative and determining priorities rather than documenting individual, family, or community outcomes. Consequently, there is limited evidence regarding the actual effectiveness of current aging-friendly community initiatives, including what does and does not work, on behalf of what goals, and under what conditions.

There are a number of barriers to conducting rigorous evaluations of aging-friendly community initiatives. Because many of these efforts are relatively new and have not moved from the planning to the implementation stage, few existing studies are able to look longitudinally to make causal inferences about the effects of aging-friendly communities over time. Initiatives also may have difficulty measuring and analyzing the wide variety of changes to the social and physical environment involved in making communities more aging friendly. The combination of local variations to the models and the importance of considering the unique context make it difficult to compare communities.

Aging-friendly community initiatives seldom are based on an explicit theory of change or linked to the rich body of conceptual and empirical scholarship regarding community change processes in general (e.g., Weil & Gamble, 1995). Furthermore, as outlined in Chapter 3, while research studies on aging-friendly communities regularly cite theories from environmental gerontology, such as the ecological model of aging and more recently the ecological framework of place, the general consensus among scholars is that these theories offer little guidance for research (Scheidt & Norris-Baker, 2003). There is a need for the development of a conceptual framework that hypothesizes testable transactional relationships between older individuals and their physical and social environments.

There are at present few systematic cross-national empirical evaluations of the aging-friendly approaches that cities have implemented (Beard & Petitot, 2010; Buffel et al., 2014). However, given that many program models (e.g., WHO, NORC-SSP, Villages) vary substantially across implementation sites, there is a need to better understand how program models are actually implemented. For example, less than one fourth of Villages actually reflect the seven "core characteristics" identified by Village movement leaders (Lehning et al., 2015). These variations could reflect efforts to refine a basic program model to fit local conditions, a gap between model developers and community-level implementers, or idiosyncratic predilections of the individuals or organizations that are most engaged in developing each initiative locally.

Finally, there is a general recognition among initiatives that they need to conduct methodologically rigorous evaluations of the processes by which outcomes are achieved. In 2012, WHO started developing a set of indicators and an assessment tool for participating communities to measure their aging friendliness. Based on an extensive review of the literature, consultations with experts, and a pilot study, WHO recently released a draft version of a set of core indicators (WHO Centre for Health Development, 2015). While still a work in progress, this framework includes input indicators (i.e., resources and structures that facilitate aging-friendly change), output indicators (i.e., interventions in the social and physical environment), outcome indicators (i.e., short- and medium-term changes to the social and physical environment), and impact indicators (i.e., population health and well-being). In addition, the framework emphasizes equity across all indicators.

WHO recommends that local communities that adopt these indicators use existing data sources as much as possible. Using existing data is one way to save on evaluation costs, but data reflecting these aging-friendly community characteristics at the community level are limited. Understanding the degree to which the social infrastructure supports health, well-being, and aging in place, for example, is particularly challenging using existing data sources. Many existing initiatives do not have the resources necessary to implement the initiative, much less pay for an evaluation, and it is not clear where initiatives will find the human and financial resources for these assessments. Some cities and towns have devoted significant resources to collecting data from residents and creating publicly available data sets and geographic information system (GIS) maps, while others lack the funding, expertise, or interest for such endeavors. Data collected by many federal agencies (e.g., Bureau of Labor Statistics, Federal Transit Administration) are often available only at the county or metropolitan statistical area (MSA) level, restricting accurate assessment of characteristics at the city or town level. In addition, most existing data provide information primarily on the presence or absence of aging-friendly policies, programs, and infrastructure but do not fully assess the aging friendliness of the community. For example, an older adult may live within walking distance of a bus stop but is unable to use it because there is no bench or protection from the weather, the vehicle is not accessible to those with a disability, or the costs are too high.

Addressing these barriers to conducting methodologically rigorous evaluations of aging-friendly community initiatives is critical to these interventions helping older adults minimize physical barriers to aging well, enhancing social engagement, and optimizing health and well-being. There currently is a dearth of empirical evidence on which to base decisions about which interventions are apt to produce which results and under which conditions. Benchmarks are needed by which a city or town can measure success toward the goal of becoming more aging friendly. Research can offer guidance to initiatives that must make difficult choices about where to focus their human and financial resources, such as what percentage of housing should allow alternative arrangements or be multifamily to ensure that older adults have an adequate number of housing options. Research can also lead to evidence-informed policies and practices to facilitate elder involvement, cross-sector collaboration, and communitywide assessment and planning that take into account the needs of all older residents.

Conclusion

While making communities more aging friendly is a promising approach to improving elder health, well-being, and the ability to age in the community, some of its most innovative features contribute to its greatest challenges. Aging-friendly communities call for significant changes in the social and physical environment, recognizing that the community context influences individuals' ability to age well. Infrastructure changes, however, are likely to require substantial investment of financial and human resources, which may be particularly difficult to obtain given the lack to date of much public funding. Without adequate funding, aging-friendly initiatives may potentially become stuck at the assessment-and-planning phase or only achieve small-scale changes. Questions also remain regarding the ability of aging-friendly initiatives to solicit the meaningful participation of diverse groups of older residents, including those representing different racial and ethnic backgrounds, socioeconomic positions, ages, and sexual orientations and gender identities. Without widespread participation, aging-friendly initiatives may potentially ignore the needs and preferences of particular groups of older adults. Finally, the combination of a variety of communitywide changes, limited implementation, and local variations creates major challenges to developing an adequate evidence base regarding the effectiveness of interventions designed to help communities become more aging friendly.

In the next chapter, we discuss a number of strategies to help communities address these challenges, as well as promising future directions for aging-friendly communities.

13

Conclusion

Aging-Friendly Communities—Present and Future

Introduction

This chapter summarizes the current status of knowledge regarding aging-friendly communities and implications for future directions, addressing where we are now, where we need to go, and how we might get there. We begin by reviewing some of the major themes of this book, including the characteristics that make a community aging friendly and implications for developing effective aging-friendly initiatives. We then present recommendations for public policies and knowledge development that can support efforts to create aging-friendly communities. Finally, we consider the possibility of creating more integrated, inclusive communities for the benefit of all, which will ultimately contribute to the advent of a "society for all ages."

Characteristics of Aging-Friendly Communities
What Makes a Community "Aging Friendly"?

A community can be considered aging friendly if it enables community members to live full and meaningful lives as they age, consistent with aging-related developmental needs and priorities. This definition embodies the concept of livability reflected in the healthy cities movement and other efforts to promote the health and well-being of all community residents. However, aging-friendly communities also embody four other key attributes that differentiate them from general efforts to make communities more livable for everyone: (a) *elder friendly*, in that they focus especially on promoting the well-being of current elderly residents; (b) *developmental*, supporting constructive developmental processes, especially but not exclusively in the latter part of the life cycle; (c) *communal*, promoting constructive community bonds and systems; and (d) *transactional*, promoting dynamic processes of person–environment adaptation over time (Scharlach, in press). Achieving community aging friendliness requires that communities provide adequate opportunities and supports for full community participation regardless of age, as well as supports and opportunities especially geared to the needs and abilities of older community members.

Aging-Friendly Community Components

In this book, we have identified a number of essential components of aging-friendly communities, in three general areas: (a) mobility and accessibility; (b) social engagement; and (c) multidimensional health and well-being.

Mobility and accessibility require the removal of age- and disability-based barriers to getting where one needs to go, as well as necessary supports to do so. Private spaces and relevant public spaces should promote healthy aging, and individuals should be able to move easily and safely from one to the other. As we saw in Chapter 5, communities can support aging-friendly mobility and accessibility by offering a variety of affordable housing options that support residential normalcy and stability; by providing alternative forms of transportation that are comfortable, convenient, and safe; and by promoting land use that reduces automobile dependence and other environmental barriers.

Social engagement includes social bonds (e.g., informal social networks, personal relationships, social support) and social participation (e.g., social activities, meaningful social roles, religious and cultural participation). As noted by Lui and his colleagues, "A supportive context with positive social relations, engagement and inclusion is a core prerequisite for ageing well" (Lui et al., 2009, p. 120). In its *Report to the Nation on Livable Communities*, AARP added that "one defining characteristic of a livable community is the high level of engagement of its residents with one another and with the life of the community itself" (AARP Public Policy Institute, 2005a, p. 20).

Social engagement requires a supportive physical and social infrastructure that provides opportunities for meaningful interpersonal connections, employment and volunteer roles, and social and cultural activities, without restrictions based on age or disability. As discussed in Chapter 6, communities can promote social engagement by offering meaningful social roles for older adults, by encouraging reciprocal social exchanges that foster interdependence rather than inequity and disempowerment, by facilitating access to resources that promote personal well-being and fulfillment, and by including older residents as key partners in all aspects of community life.

Multidimensional health and well-being include physical, psychosocial, cultural, and spiritual well-being (Scharlach & Hoshino, 2012), as well as opportunities for continuity, compensation, control, connection, contribution, and challenge. Promoting health and well-being requires the removal of age- and disability-based barriers to health-related services and opportunities, as well as necessary formal and informal supports. As discussed in Chapter 7, communities can promote elder health and well-being by offering a wide range of affordable and quality health care and social supports that support basic safety and security, personal control, and the ability to delay or avoid undesired relocation. Health promotion and disease management programs also are important components of communitywide efforts to foster health and well-being throughout the life course, thereby ameliorating or delaying a mismatch between personal competence and environment capacity and minimizing or ameliorating the need for more intensive long-term services and supports in later life.

The physical and social infrastructure components required to foster mobility and accessibility, social engagement, and health and well-being are inherently interrelated. For example, a community is simultaneously a physical space (e.g., neighborhood), a social space (e.g., social boundaries and norms), and a set of social bonds (e.g., a sense of community). Furthermore, physical and social components interact and interpenetrate to imbue spaces with meaning, thereby creating a sense of place.

We are also mindful of a number of cross-cutting issues, such as access, disparities, and scope. As we discussed in Chapter 12, ensuring access requires attention to issues such as availability, affordability, physical and social accessibility, appropriateness, and acceptability. Overcoming disparities requires attention to a variety of economic, geographic, linguistic, cultural, and ability factors. Appropriate scope requires aligning aging-friendly community efforts with the needs of particular geographic and social spaces, whether a neighborhood or municipality, urban or rural, a geographic/spatial community or a virtual/consensual community.

Developing Aging-Friendly Initiatives

Goals of Aging-Friendly Initiatives

The goals of aging-friendly initiatives are consistent with the goals that have been identified for U.S. health and long-term care systems in general. In terms of health, the aims of aging-friendly initiatives are consistent with the "triple aim" identified by the Centers for Medicare and Medicaid Services Institute for Healthcare Improvement (Berwick, Nolan, & Whittington, 2008): better outcomes, better care, and better cost control. For aging-friendly initiatives, better outcomes refers to improved quality of life (e.g., health, safety, stability), as well as social integration and community participation. Better care means developing physical infrastructures, social environments, and associated programs and services that are adequate, appropriate, accessible, and affordable and that promote consumer choice and control. Finally, aging-friendly initiatives themselves need to be cost-effective, efficient, and affordable even for communities with fewer available resources.

Like the model system of long-term services and supports (LTSS) proposed by Kaye (2014), aging-friendly initiatives aim to promote "community living over institutionalization, integration over segregation, and full social participation over isolation" (p. 754). A model system, furthermore, "should be equitable across age groups, disability categories, and other individual characteristics, economically sustainable yet generous enough to reasonably meet demand, and targeted broadly" (Kaye, 2014, p. 754). Finally, the system "should be accountable through measurement and reporting of quality and outcomes, including indicators of expenditures, utilization, health status, and consumer quality of life, participation, and satisfaction" (Kaye, 2014, p. 754).

Tasks of Aging-Friendly Initiatives

Helping communities become more aging friendly requires an integrative approach that fosters transformations in physical and social infrastructure and systems through the use of relevant community change principles and processes. Based on findings from our 2009 national survey of community aging initiatives (Lehning, Scharlach, & Price Wolf, 2012) and other evidence, we have seen that successful growth and sustainability require that aging-friendly initiatives attend to the five interrelated issues identified in Chapter 8: commitment, capacity, collaboration, consumer involvement, and comprehensiveness/specificity.

Commitment. Enhancing aging friendliness requires a significant commitment of time, energy, and political capital by community leaders and other key stakeholders. Often, a champion is needed to promote the idea of aging friendliness, convince community leaders that becoming more aging friendly is in their interest, and encourage diverse sectors to work together in new ways in spite of turf issues and funding limitations. One respondent to our 2009 national survey (Lehning et al., 2012, p. 308), for example, noted the importance of "convincing local leaders that there is a need for specialized community services to enhance aging-in-place within neighborhoods as the older adult population continues to increase." When there is strong support from community leaders, as is the case in New York City, Westchester County, Atlanta, and Phoenix, among many others, aging-friendly initiatives tend to grow and prosper. When that support flags, as in Contra Costa County, California, initiatives are more likely to fail.

Capacity. Because they typically exist outside institutionalized funding streams, aging-friendly initiatives tend to be reliant on government demonstration projects or time-limited foundation grants, leaving them especially vulnerable when funding ends, as we saw with participants in the federal Community Innovations for Aging in Place (CIAIP) and Naturally Occurring Retirement Community Supportive Service Program (NORC-SSP) demonstration projects and in the Robert Wood Johnson Foundation's Community Partnerships for Older Adults program. NORC-SSPs in New York State, on the other hand, have been able to survive even without federal funding, largely because of ongoing support from the state of New York and from New York City. Villages and other consumer-driven support networks also may be somewhat less vulnerable to changes in time-limited external support because of the relatively stable core financial support afforded by membership dues.

Collaboration. As suggested by the asset-based community development model described in Chapter 11, communities have extensive existing assets that can serve as the basis for aging-friendly community change. Sustainable community change requires the combined efforts of all major community sectors, including the public sector, the nonprofit sector, civil society, the private sector, and individual consumers.

Local governments have a number of mechanisms by which they can promote aging friendliness, including zoning, planning, public infrastructure, and budget decisions (Rosenthal, 2009). However, collaboration among local governmental departments and agencies (e.g., planning, transportation, health, parks and recreation, public works) is essential and needs to include local area agencies on aging (AAAs). AAAs are uniquely positioned to take a leadership role in fostering aging-friendly community change, based on their mandate under the Older Americans Act to plan and coordinate efforts to meet the needs of local older adults. However, such efforts tend to be hampered by AAAs' lack of resources and political influence in the context of other local needs.

The nonprofit sector includes health care providers, social service providers, and other community organizations that typically were created to meet needs that are not being met in the private marketplace. Community organizations such as these have frequently taken a leadership role in developing aging-friendly community initiatives, such as Age-Friendly NYC, most NORC-SSP programs, and about 20% of Villages. Housing providers also are critical to the success of efforts to promote aging friendliness within geographically defined locations. Local community foundations also have an important role to play in contributing to the development and sustainability of local aging-friendly efforts.

Civil society includes mutual assistance organizations, social clubs, religious institutions, and other organizations developed by and for the benefit of their members, reflecting "the associations in which we conduct our lives and which owe their existence to our needs and initiatives, rather than to the state" (Figueira-McDonough, 2001, p. 108). While sometimes omitted from characterizations of community sectors, civil society is critical to a sense of community and to efforts to create community change.

The private sector also has an important role to play. However, the role of business has been relatively minor in most community initiatives, typically limited to participation in community planning efforts. Age-Friendly New York City, for example, includes local businesses in its Aging Improvement District planning councils, and initiatives in other cities sometimes include representatives from the Chamber of Commerce or other business organizations. Local governments can facilitate greater private-sector involvement in a variety of ways, for example, by offering tax incentives or waiving zoning requirements to encourage private developers to incorporate accessibility features into new housing. And, nonprofit organizations can offer training and technical assistance, as the National Association of Home Builders does through its Certified Aging-in-Place Specialist program. Ultimately, however, the private sector's involvement in helping communities become more aging friendly will be dictated in large part by consumer demand.

Consumer involvement. For many reasons, the role of older adults in creating aging-friendly cities is especially important. While nearly every aging-friendly initiative involves older community members in some way, involvement is most often as key informants (e.g., participating in discussions of the adequacy of various community systems, as in most World Health Organization (WHO) Global Age-Friendly Cities and Communities sites); consumer–development initiatives (e.g., the Village model) are relatively unique in the extent to which they strive to engage older adults in nearly every aspect of initiative functioning, including initiative development, governance, financing, operations, and service provision.

Even when initiatives have focused explicitly on engaging older adults, there has been relatively little attention to which older adults are being included and which voices are not being heard. Furthermore, racial, ethnic and cultural groups are apt to have differing needs and preferences, suggesting the importance of tailoring aging-friendly initiatives to their particular needs. As we saw in Chapter 12, the older adults who are most apt to be involved at the local level and are thereby most likely to shape and benefit from any changes tend to be persons who already have the personal, social, and economic resources to be able to devote time and energy to advocacy efforts. Furthermore, local governments require sufficient economic and political resources to launch aging-friendly planning efforts and participate in national and international initiatives.

Most published reports about aging-friendly community initiatives have described efforts in large urban settings, with relatively little attention to rural settings or suburbs, where the majority of older Americans now live (Lui et al., 2009). Those individuals, groups, and communities less likely to benefit from aging friendly community processes, whether intentionally or unintentionally, are often the same ones that have tended to be excluded from access to other resources and opportunities. For these reasons, the movement to create aging-friendly communities has been critiqued as potentially reinforcing or exacerbating existing social, economic, and political power structures (Gonyea & Hudson, 2015). Making the benefits of aging friendliness available to communities with limited resources requires intentional efforts to supplement community economic and social capacity, whether through an infusion of external resources or through activation of existing social capital by strengthening social networks, fostering civic engagement, and promoting community solidarity.

Comprehensiveness. Despite their avowed goal of communitywide system change, the focus of most aging-friendly community initiatives to date has been relatively limited. While the eight WHO Global Age-Friendly Cities and Communities domains (WHO, 2007) provide an inspiration and sometimes a framework for aging-friendly activities, local initiatives tend to be considerably more pragmatic, often focusing less on system change and more on initiating or expanding specific programs and services. As one illustrative example, of 172 projects proposed to Belgium's Walloon government for funding under its age-friendly program, only 3 even mentioned the WHO framework (Buffel et al., 2014).

Perhaps most comprehensive are initiatives that promote the concept of "age in everything." Age-Friendly New York City, for example, asks public agencies, businesses, cultural organizations, religious institutions, community groups, and individuals to consider policy and practice changes designed to create a city more inclusive of older adults and more sensitive to their needs (http://www.nyam.org/agefriendlynyc/about-us/). The Atlanta Regional Commission, the planning and intergovernmental coordination agency for the 10-county metropolitan area, is aligning all departmental planning and operations toward achieving its goal of creating "Lifelong Communities" (http://www.atlantaregional.com/aging-resources/lifelong-communities). Similarly, older volunteers participating in the Embracing Aging initiative in York County, Pennsylvania, met with York administrators to introduce the concept of an "age in everything" lens, drafted an "age-friendly designation" program for businesses, and created a York County Community Foundation grant-making strategy for funding programs and services that help advance their Embracing Aging goals (http://www.yccf.org/aging.asp).

A comprehensive approach to the community change process also is needed. It seems likely that effective and sustainable community change will require a combination of the three types of community aging initiatives we discussed in Chapters 9, 10, and 11. Such a multifaceted approach might involve an assessment of community needs, development of a coordinated plan based on a theory of change, collaborative involvement of multiple community sectors, as well as active engagement of community residents.

A number of initiatives provide model examples of relatively comprehensive aging-friendly change efforts. The Quebec Age-Friendly Cities Initiative (AFC-QC), for example, involved 700 municipalities in a three-stage participatory community-building process that engaged individuals and local organizations in efforts to transform the quality of life of older adults in their community. The Livable Communities for All Ages Learning Collaborative (LCC) of the National Association of Area Agencies on Aging (n4a) supported local efforts in six communities, which brought together multiple community sectors, including local government leaders, AAAs, citizen groups, and numerous other stakeholders. These initiatives identified community needs and priorities, determined long- and short-term goals and objectives, and developed action plans, which typically were implemented with the assistance of trained self-directed volunteer teams (n4a, 2015). In Larimer County, Colorado, for example, the Partnership for Age Friendly Communities (PAFC) initiated projects designed to enhance mobility options to improve access to key services and quality-of-life opportunities; ensure a sufficient variety of appropriate housing options; improve community attitudes, values, and behaviors toward aging; and raise the profile of aging as a political issue.

Implications for Public Policy

Governments have an important role to play in efforts to help communities become more aging friendly, including creating models, standards, and fiscal incentives for individuals and communities to undertake aging-friendly improvements, as well as enhancing public awareness of such efforts. Most aging-friendly initiatives, however, reflect independent efforts of individual communities, developed with little or no involvement from state or federal governments. Even the two U.S. cities participating in the initial phase of WHO's Global Age-Friendly Cities Project had involvement developed primarily by nongovernmental entities (Portland State University and the New York Academy of Medicine). The absence of centralized government leadership and support is a barrier to widespread dissemination and adoption of aging-friendly policies and programs. To provide adequate incentives and remove administrative barriers that affect efforts to make communities more aging friendly, policy changes are needed at the state and federal levels.

Some states have provided invaluable support for particular aging-friendly initiatives, such as New York State's ongoing funding for NORC-SSP programs (NORC Blueprint, 2011). A number of states also have passed laws requiring inclusion of universal design features in publicly funded construction, and a few have recommended or mandated selected universal design features in new single-family homes or multifamily buildings. In a few notable instances, states have initiated comprehensive planning efforts designed to improve statewide preparedness for societal aging (e.g., Minnesota's Aging 2030, California's Long-Range Strategic Plan on Aging), although actual plan implementation has been extremely limited. Even in Indiana, one of the few states to sustain a statewide aging-friendly effort, progress has been slow. In 2006, Indiana implemented the AdvantAge Initiative needs assessment survey statewide, the first state to do so, with funding from the U.S. Administration on Aging, the Indiana Family and

Social Services Administration Division of Aging, and the Indiana University Center on Aging and Community. In 2007, the state launched a Communities for Life initiative, supporting community planning and development in local neighborhood NORCs. However, it was not until September 2014 that a Lifelong Indiana Coalition was developed to "secure broad, inclusive support for policies, investments and direct services that support more age- and ability-friendly communities" (see http://lifelongindiana.org/about/). Clearly, there is a need for substantially greater involvement of state leaders and policymakers in fostering aging-friendly communities.

Current federal initiatives hold some promise of promoting aging-friendly system change. Aging and Disability Resource Centers, care transition programs, and community care incentives such as Money Follows the Person all have substantial potential to facilitate greater coordination among health and social service providers, thereby improving access to the compensatory supports needed for maximizing multidimensional health and well-being. The Veteran-Directed Home and Community-Based Service Program, along with other consumer-directed initiatives, can enhance consumer control and autonomy in the face of disabilities. Accountable care organizations, evidence-based disease prevention programs, and other features of the Affordable Care Act incentivize health promotion and disease prevention efforts, primarily as a means for reducing higher cost hospital and emergency room use. In addition, a number of current programs, such as the Alzheimer's Disease Supportive Services Program, promote state initiatives designed to create coordinated systems of community-based care that recognize the potential contributions of public, private, and nonprofit entities as well as individuals and their families. Another positive sign is the development of a Partnership for Sustainable Communities, a coordinated effort by the U.S. Department of Housing and Urban Development (HUD), the U.S. Department of Transportation (DOT), and the U.S. Environmental Protection Agency (EPA). This collaboration aims to promote federal programs, policies, and legislative proposals that help communities nationwide improve access to affordable housing, increase transportation options, enhance economic competitiveness, support community revitalization, and enhance the unique characteristics of their communities, while working to align federal policies and funding to promote collaboration, accountability, and effectiveness (http://www.sustainablecommunities. gov/mission/about-us).

Examples from other countries provide instructive models regarding the possible benefits of governmental action. In Belgium, for example, the Walloon regional government provided 60 cities with approximately $50,000 per year for local projects designed to promote aging friendliness. The projects include physical infrastructure adaptations (e.g., improving access to public buildings, installing benches, or developing walking paths); improving social engagement (e.g., increasing senior activities programs and intergenerational activities, developing Internet courses for isolated elders, or including seniors on local consultative councils): and enhancing information access (e.g., creating directories regarding pensions, health, mobility, housing, and cultural activities).

Implications for Research and Knowledge Development

Research and knowledge development have lagged behind program development and implementation, as leaders have focused primarily on promoting the idea of aging friendliness and encouraging local initiatives (Moulaert & Garon, 2015). Further research and knowledge development are needed regarding how aging-friendly community initiatives are developed and implemented, the outcomes they produce, and the relative costs and benefits for various stakeholders.

The evaluation model developed by the WHO Centre for Health Development, described in Chapter 12, provides a useful framework for considering potential research implications regarding the inputs, outputs, outcomes, and impacts needed for effective aging-friendly community change. Assessing inputs requires knowledge about potential enabling factors likely to affect program effectiveness, including the adequacy of existing physical and social contexts, changes considered potentially valuable by older adults and other key stakeholders, and available social, political, and economic resources. In Chapters 4 and 12, we discussed the strengths and limitations of a variety of methods that have been used to assess community needs and capacity, including conducting focus groups or interviews with older adults or persons knowledgeable about their needs (e.g., WHO's Global Age-Friendly Cities); surveying older community members (e.g., AdvantAge Initiative); surveying city planners or other local government employees (e.g., n4a's Maturing of America surveys); or compiling publicly available information, such as census data, police records, real estate records, crime rates, or housing costs (e.g., Best Cities for Successful Ageing). Especially promising are recent efforts to develop Web-based apps that integrate multiple sources of information for use by researchers, planners, as well as consumers and incorporate mapping technology, preference survey results, nationally available quantitative measures, and public policy information (e.g., AARP's Livability Index).

Considerably greater conceptual and empirical development is needed with regard to outputs, the particular strategies a community uses to achieve desired aging-friendly outcomes. With regard to elder mobility, for example, research might examine the relative use of available options such as increasing the availability of public transportation (e.g., fixed-route buses, personalized paratransit services); improving the built environment (e.g., enhanced neighborhood walkability, road design, vehicle customization); providing social supports (e.g., volunteer drivers, companions, personal assistance); or enhancing the functioning of older adults themselves (e.g., strength training, flexibility exercises, sensory aids).

Research efforts might begin by mapping existing initiative sites (e.g., communities participating in the WHO or AARP network) in comparison to similar nonparticipating communities to identify community characteristics associated with model implementation. Particular attention should be given to factors likely to have an impact on initiative success and sustainability, such as community commitment, organizational capacity, stakeholder collaboration, consumer involvement, and comprehensiveness. Also needed is longitudinal research examining the evolution in types of community change processes utilized over time and their potential utility.

In this book, we have identified a variety of potential salutary outcomes and impacts of aging-friendly community efforts, including enhanced well-being of individual elders and other community members; improved communitywide social climate, accessibility, and mobility; and increased service adequacy, availability, accessibility, and affordability. As we have noted, accurately measuring the outcomes of aging-friendly initiatives requires improved instrumentation. A number of recent federal and state efforts have yielded improved measures of individual well-being (e.g., the Measure Applications Partnership, convened by the National Quality Forum; measures of Medicaid home and community-based services (HCBS) quality developed by the Agency for Healthcare Research and Quality; Wisconsin's Personal Experience Outcomes Integrated Interview and Evaluation System). Equivalent attention now needs to be given to developing reliable and valid measures of community-level outcomes (e.g., social capital, walkability, accessibility).

Older adults' ability to age in place has been promoted as the primary objective of aging-friendly initiatives, but it is not entirely clear that aging in place is always most desirable for older adults or their communities. Rather than sweeping generalizations regarding elders' preferences, further research is needed regarding the relative advantages and disadvantages of relocation as opposed to staying in place and of living in age-integrated as opposed to age-segregated environments.

Finally, we need to better understand the value proposition for communities of becoming more aging friendly, including the economic or social benefits to older adults and to the entire community, as well as the direct and indirect costs of producing these outcomes. We also need to better understand the potential secondary impacts of interventions, both positive and negative, for various stakeholders. For example, some interventions designed to improve person–environment fit for older adults (e.g., sheltered bus stops) are likely to be beneficial to other community members as well; however, other improvements may actually have deleterious secondary implications for younger adults or even exacerbate accessibility barriers for some younger people with disabilities (and vice versa). As one example, enhancing mobility for older adults with normal age-related general weakness

and balance limitations can involve providing benches, railings, and other supportive structures, which can sometimes serve as physical barriers that restrict
the movement of younger individuals who use wheelchairs.

Transforming Communities

America's cities and towns are experiencing dramatic demographic and social
changes associated with increasing life expectancies and increasing population
diversity. Yet, fewer than half of older Americans responding to a 2013 survey
conducted by USA Today, the National Council on Aging, and United Healthcare
indicated that their communities were doing enough to prepare for the future
needs of the senior population (National Council on Aging, UnitedHealthcare,
& USA Today, 2013).

Aging-friendly community change is likely to require intentional efforts to
implement the kind of integrated, comprehensive community change processes
described throughout this book. Such efforts can benefit from the extensive social
resources and other assets embodied in our existing communities, including the
talents and skills of older community members themselves. Community development efforts can help to activate the underutilized potential contributions of
older individuals and other existing community groups, thereby promoting elder
empowerment, enhancing community social capital, and strengthening civil
society. As noted by the G8 labor ministers in the charter that emerged from
their 2000 meeting in Turin, Italy: "Older people represent a great reservoir of
resources for our economies and societies" (http://www.g8.utoronto.ca/employ-
ment/labour2000_ageing.htm).

Efforts to promote community aging friendliness are hampered by outdated
physical, service delivery, and support infrastructures based primarily on a set of
assumptions about older adults, their families, and their communities that often
reflect the realities of the post–World War II era, more than 60 years ago. Yet, conditions have changed dramatically since that time, leaving communities woefully
unprepared for 21st century challenges and possibilities. Overcoming the forces
that promote social exclusion of older community members is apt to require fundamental changes in our societal structures, values, and institutions. Ensuring
the basic well-being of all community members, including today's older adults as
well as those who are not yet older, will require transformations in major community institutions (Buffel et al., 2012), including how communities are designed,
built, and paid for.

As historian Andy Achenbaum noted, "A new demographic revolution
demands novel structural responses" (Achenbaum, 2005, p. xi). Recognizing the
inevitability of population aging, communities need to begin to incorporate an
"aging-in-everything" perspective in local policy and programmatic decisions,

as is already being done in a number of cities and towns. Furthermore, while communities can continue to serve as important demonstration sites for developing and testing initiatives responsive to local conditions, true societal aging friendliness will require major changes at the federal level. The Americans With Disabilities Act, for example, holds substantial potential for overcoming access barriers experienced by older adults, especially if the provisions of the act are recast to focus more directly on prominent aging-related conditions rather than primarily focusing on wheelchair access. AAAs could be held accountable for carrying out their mandated role of ensuring the well-being of community seniors, and they should be allocated the necessary resources to carry out that mandate. Other policy changes suggested by Scott Ball and Kathryn Lawler (2014) include national standards for planning and zoning to reduce automobile dependence and promote mixed-use development, vouchers and tax incentives to promote the development of supportive housing, and Medicaid waivers to foster improved coordination between housing and supportive services.

As we have noted, real change in community structures and national policies is difficult, and often hard won, but it also brings opportunities for enhanced community well-being as well as more effective use of available social and economic resources. Aging advocates have a role to play in raising public awareness regarding the potential value of investing individual and communal resources in enhancing the participation and well-being of older community members. Seniors themselves need to be empowered to advocate on their own behalf and on behalf of forthcoming cohorts of older adults. The California Senior Leaders Alliance (http://www.calseniorleaders.org/) is one example of a program that identifies older adults who are making a difference in their indigenous communities, matches them with university students for cross mentoring and cross-generational learning, and then organizes them to advocate for state policies designed to improve conditions for older adults and make communities more aging friendly.

Some community initiatives have grown from a focus on local physical and social environments into national networks focused on major social policy change. The Gray Panthers, for example, began as a small group of recently retired women who wanted to improve the living conditions experienced by other retirees. The effort grew into a national advocacy organization, which was still rooted in a collection of local networks and conveners. While they have championed a variety of political and social causes, a particular focus of their efforts has been system change designed to promote the well-being of older adults through more affordable housing, better health care access, and combatting ageism in all its forms. While frequently national in scope, such efforts also reverberate to local conditions that have an impact on community aging friendliness.

The success of the Gray Panthers mirrors many of the accomplishments of the independent living movement. This grassroots movement began with a handful of individuals with disabilities who advocated for greater physical and attitudinal accessibility in their local environments and led to the Americans With Disabilities Act as well as a national network of Centers for Independent Living charged with providing peer-led support for persons with disabilities and advocating for enhancements in community capacity for meeting the needs of persons with disabilities. Whether the aging-friendly communities movement, promoted nationally by AARP and globally by WHO, can have a similar impact remains to be seen.

Conclusion

Communities throughout the country and throughout the world are embarking on innovative initiatives designed to respond more effectively to the needs of their current aging residents and to prepare for the future impact of an aging society. As we have seen, most of these initiatives are in early stages of development and have not yet fulfilled their full potential to help communities become truly aging friendly. Lessons learned from these early efforts can pave the way for future efforts to ultimately create a multitude of environments that truly are "vital communities" (Achenbaum, 2005), where aging well not only is possible but also perhaps even becomes the norm. Ultimately, community is more than a physical space or even a social environment; community helps us to define who we are and what is possible.

The challenge ahead is not only to promote the well-being of older adults but also to transform the very nature of society, from one in which age determines what is possible to a society in which age is no longer a barrier to full participation. Ultimately, we look to the possibility of creating a society for all ages, where people are more fully integrated into a societal fabric of many textures, many colors, and indeed many ages, all of which are seen as contributing in important and necessary ways to the society as a whole. As described by former United Nations Secretary-General Kofi Annan nearly 20 years ago while introducing the United Nations Year of Older Persons: "A society for all ages is multigenerational. It is not fragmented, with youths, adults and older persons going their separate ways. Rather, it is age-inclusive, with different generations recognizing—and acting upon—their commonality of interest".

By becoming more aging friendly, communities can advance this vision of true age inclusiveness. Working together, this is a future that is within our power to create.

Appendix

RESOURCES FOR CREATING
AGING-FRIENDLY COMMUNITIES

Assessment Tools

AARP. (2014, July). *AARP Community Survey*. Retrieved from http://www.aarp.org/livable-communities/info-2014/aarp-community-survey-questionnaire.html

AARP Public Policy Institute. (2015). *Livability Index*. http://www.aarp.org/ppi/issues/livable-communities/info-2015/livability-index.html

Milken Institute. (n.d.). *Best cities for successful aging* Retrieved from http://successfulaging.milkeninstitute.org/

Stanford Center on Longevity and MetLife Mature Market Institute. (2013, March). *Livable Community Indicators for sustainable aging in place*. Retrieved from https://www.metlife.com/assets/cao/mmi/publications/studies/2013/mmi-livable-communities-study.pdf

United Nations Economic Commission for Europe. (2015, July 9). *Active Ageing Index*. Retrieved from http://www1.unece.org/stat/platform/display/AAI/Active+Ageing+Index+Home

World Health Organization. (2007). *Checklist of essential features of Age-Friendly Cities*. Retrieved from http://www.aarp.org/content/dam/aarp/home-and-family/livable-communities/2013-12/3-age-friendly-cities-checklist.pdf

World Health Organization Centre for Health Development, Kobe, Japan. (2014). *Measuring the age-friendliness of cities: A guide to using core indicators*. Retrieved from http://www.who.int/kobe_centre/ageing/age_friendly_cities/AFC_Indicator_Guide_Pilot_English.pdf

Books

Abbott, P. S., Carman, N., Carman, J., & Scarfo, B. (Eds.). (2009). *Re-creating neighborhoods for successful aging*. Baltimore, MD: Health Professions Press.

Cisneros, H., Dyer-Chamberlain, M., & Hickle, J. (Eds.). (2012). *Independent for life: Homes and neighborhoods for an aging America*. Austin: University of Texas Press.

Golant, S. (2015). *Aging in the right place*. Baltimore, MD: Health Professions Press.

Stafford, P. (2009). *Elderburbia: Aging with a sense of place in America*. Westport, CT: Praeger.

General

AARP Livable Communities initiative: http://www.aarp.org/livable-communities/

Grantmakers in Aging Age-Friendly Communities Initiative: http://www.giaging.org/issues/community-development/

WHO Global Network of Age-Friendly Cities and Communities: http://agefriendlyworld.org/en/

Guides and Toolkits

AARP. (2014). *Evaluating your age-friendly community program: A step-by-step guide.* Prepared for AARP by M. B. Neal & I. Wernher, Portland University Institute on Aging. Retrieved from http://www.aarp.org/content/dam/aarp/livable-communities/documents-2014/NAFC-Conference/AARP%20Network%20of%20Age-Friendly%20Communities%20Evaluation%20Guidebook.pdf

AARP. (n.d.). *AARP Age-Friendly Communities tool kit.* Retrieved from http://www.aarp.org/livable-communities/network-age-friendly-communities/

AARP Public Policy Institute. (2005). *Livable communities: An evaluation guide.* Retrieved from http://www.aarp.org/content/dam/aarp/livable-communities/plan/assessments/livable-communities-an-evaluation-guide-2005-aarp.pdf

Generations United and the MetLife Foundation. (2015). *Creating an Age-Advantaged Community: A toolkit for building intergenerational communities that recognize, engage and support all ages.* Retrieved from http://www.gu.org/Portals/0/documents/Reports/15-report-intergenerational-creating-an-age-advantaged-community-toolkit.pdf

Handler, S. (2014). *A research and evaluation framework for age-friendly cities.* Manchester, England: UK Urban Ageing Consortium.

National Association of Area Agencies on Aging and Partners for Livable Communities. (2007). *Blueprint for Action: Developing a livable community for all ages.* Retrieved from http://n4a.membershipsoftware.org/files/07-116-N4A-Blueprint4ActionWCovers.pdf

Ontario Seniors' Secretariat, Accessability Directorate of Ontario, University of Waterloo, & McMaster University. (2013). *Finding the right fit: Age-friendly community planning.* Retrieved from http://www.seniors.gov.on.ca/en/resources/AFCP_Eng.pdf

Public Health Agency of Canada. (n.d.). *Age-Friendly Communities in Canada: Community implementation guide and toolbox.* Retrieved from http://www.phac-aspc.gc.ca/seniors-aines/publications/public/afc-caa/guide/index-eng.php

U.S. Environmental Protection Agency. (2013). *Building healthy communities for active aging national recognition program.* Retrieved from http://www.epa.gov/aging/bhc/

International Initiatives

Austin, C. D., Des Camp, E., Flux, D., McClelland, R. W., & Sieppert, J. (2005). Community development with older adults in their neighborhoods: The elder friendly communities program. *Families in Society, 86*(3), 401–409.

Dublin Declaration of Age-Friendly Cities and Communities. (2011, September). Retrieved from http://www.emro.who.int/images/stories/elderly/documents/dublin20declaration.pdf

Ireland Age Friendly Cities and Counties Programme: http://agefriendlyireland.ie/

Keefe, J., & Hattie, B. (2007). *Age-friendly cities project, Halifax site.* Retrieved from https://www.novascotia.ca/seniors/pub/2007_AgeFriendlyCitiesReport.pdf

Public Health Agency of Canada, Age-Friendly Communities: http://www.phac-aspc.gc.ca/seniors-aines/afc-caa-eng.php

World Health Organization. (2007). *Global Age-Friendly Cities: A guide.* Retrieved from http://www.who.int/ageing/publications/Global_age_friendly_cities_Guide_English.pdf

Journals and Peer-Reviewed Articles

Alley, D., Liebig, P., Pynoos, J., Banerjee, T., & Choi, I. H. (2007). Creating elder-friendly communities: Preparations for an aging society. *Journal of Gerontological Social Work, 49*(1–2), 1–18.

Brick, Y., & Lowenstein, A. (Eds.). (2011). Ageing in place. *Global Ageing: Issues & Action,* (2) (entire issue).

Green, G. (2013). Age-friendly cities of Europe. *Journal of Urban Health, 90*(Suppl 1), 116–128.

Hudson, R. B. (Ed.). (2015). Making a home in the city: The age-friendly community movement. *Public Policy & Aging Report, 25*(1).

Lehning, A., Chun, Y., & Scharlach, A. (2007). Structural barriers to developing "aging-friendly" communities. *Public Policy & Aging Report, 17*, 15–20.

Lui, C. W., Everingham, J. A., Warburton, J., Cuthill, M., & Bartlett, H. (2009), What makes a community age-friendly: A review of international literature. *Australasian Journal on Ageing, 28*(3), 116–21.

Menec, V. H. (2011). Conceptualizing age-friendly communities. *Canadian Journal on Aging, 30*(3), 479.

O'Hehir, J. (2014). *Age-friendly cities and communities: A literature review.* Adelaide, South Australia: Centre for Work + Life, University of South Australia.

Plouffe, L., & Kalache, A. (2010). Towards global age-friendly cities: Determining urban features that promote active aging. *Journal of Urban Health: Bulletin of the New York Academy of Medicine, 87*(5), 733–739.

Scharlach, A. (Ed.). (2009, Summer). Creating aging-friendly communities. *Generations, 33*(2).

Scharlach, A. (2012). Creating aging-friendly communities in the United States. *Ageing International, 37*, 25–38.

Scharlach, A. E., & Lehning, A. J. (2013). Aging-friendly communities and social inclusion. *Ageing & Society, 33*, 110–136.

Local Initiatives

AARP. (2015, June 25). Member list, AARP Network of Age-Friendly Communities. Retrieved from http://www.aarp.org/livable-communities/network-age-friendly-communities/info-2014/member-list.html

Age-Friendly America Database, Grantmakers in Aging Inventory of Age-Friendly Initiatives: http://www.giaging.org/programs-events/community-agenda/community-agenda-database/

Age Friendly NYC. (2012). *Creating an Age Friendly NYC one neighborhood at a time: A toolkit for establishing an aging improvement district in your community.* Retrieved from http://www.nyam.org/agefriendlynyc/docs/Toolkit_Report_0321-VA-new.pdf

Atlanta Regional Commission. (2014). Lifelong communities: A framework for planning. Retrieved from http://www.atlantaregional.com/aging-resources/lifelong-communities

Center for Home Care Policy and Research, Visiting Nurse Service of New York. (2003, June). *Best practices: Lessons for communities in supporting the health, well-being, and independence of older people.* Retrieved from Visiting Nurse Service of New York website http://www.vnsny.org/advantage/tools/advantage_best.pdf

Clark, K. (2012). Age-friendly Philadelphia: Bringing diverse networks together around aging issues. *Journal of Housing for the Elderly, 26*(1–3), 121.

Hanson, D., & Emlet, C. A. (2006). Assessing a community's elder friendliness: A case example of the AdvantAge initiative. *Family & Community Health, 29*(4), 266–278.

Reports

AARP. (2015). Livable communities. In *AARP policy book: AARP public policies 2015–2016,* Chapter 9. Retrieved from http://policybook.aarp.org/the-policy-book/chapter-9

AARP Public Policy Institute. (2014, April). *What is livable: Community preferences of older adults.* Retrieved from http://www.aarp.org/content/dam/aarp/research/public_policy_institute/liv_com/2014/what-is-livable-report-AARP-ppi-liv-com.pdf

American Planning Association. (2014). *Policy guide: Aging in community.* Retrieved from https://www.planning.org/policy/guides/pdf/agingincommunity.pdf

Feldman, P. H., Oberlink, M. R., Simantov, E., & Gursen, M. D. (2004). *A tale of two older Americas: Community opportunities and challenges: 2003 AdvantAge Initiative National Survey of Adults Aged 65 and Older.* New York, NY: Center for Home Care Policy and Research, Visiting Nurse Service of New York.

Grantmakers in Aging. (2013, April). *Age-friendly communities: An introduction for private and public funders.* Retrieved from http://www.giaging.org/documents/130402_GIA_AFC_ Primer.pdf

Kochera, A., Straight, A. K., & Guterbock, T. M. (2005). *Beyond 50.05: A report to the nation on livable communities: Creating environments for successful aging.* Washington, DC: AARP.

Maturing of America: Getting communities on track for an aging population. National Association of Area Agencies on Aging, 2005: http://n4a.membershipsoftware.org/files/ MOAFinalReport%281%29.pdf

National Association of Area Agencies on Aging. (2015) Making your community livable for all ages: What's working! Retrieved from http://www.n4a.org/files/n4aMakingYourCom-munityLivable1.pdf

National Association of Area Agencies on Aging, MetLife Foundation, International City/ County Management Association, National Association of Counties, National League of Cities, and Partners for Livable Communities. (2011). *Maturing of America II: Communities moving forward for an aging population.* Retrieved from http://n4a.membershipsoftware.org/ files/Maturing_of_Ameria_ll.pdf

REFERENCES

AARP. (2013). *Portland takes age-friendly action*. Retrieved from http://www.aarp.org/livable-communities/Plan/planning/info-2014/action-plan-age-friendly-portland-or.html

AARP. (2015). *AARP Network of Age-Friendly Communities tool kit: The member list*. Retrieved from http://www.aarp.org/livable-communities/network-age-friendly-communities/info-2014/member-list.html

AARP Public Policy Institute. (2000). *Livable communities: An evaluation guide*. Washington, DC: AARP Public Policy Institute.

AARP Public Policy Institute. (2005a). *Beyond 50.05: A report to the nation on livable communities: Creating environments for successful aging*. Retrieved from http://www.aarp.org/research/housing-mobility/indliving/beyond_50_communities.html

AARP Public Policy Institute. (2005b). *Livable communities: An evaluation guide*. Washington, DC: AARP. Retrieved from http://assets.aarp.org/rgcenter/il/d18311_communities.pdf

AARP Public Policy Institute. (2012). *Boomers and the Great Recession*. Retrieved from http://www.aarp.org/content/dam/aarp/research/public_policy_institute/econ_sec/2012/boomers-and-the-great-recession-struggling-to-recover-v2-AARP-ppi-econ-sec.pdf

AARP Public Policy Institute. (2014). *What is livable? Community preferences of older adults*. Washington, DC: AARP Public Policy Institute.

Achenbaum, W. A. (2005). *Older Americans, vital communities: A bold vision for societal aging*. Baltimore, MD: Johns Hopkins University Press.

Adams, K. B., Leibbrandt, S., & Moon, H. (2011). A critical review of the literature on social and leisure activity and wellbeing in later life. *Ageing and Society, 31*(04), 683–712.

Aday, R., Kehoe, G., & Farney, L. (2006). Impact of senior center friendships on aging women who live alone. *Journal of Women & Aging, 18*, 57–73.

Adler, G., & Rottunda, S. (2006). Older adults' perspectives on driving cessation. *Journal of Aging Studies, 20*(3), 227–235.

Administration on Aging, U.S. Department of Health and Human Services. (2012). *A profile of older Americans: 2012*. Retrieved from http://www.aoa.gov/Aging_Statistics/Profile/2012/docs/2012profile.pdf

Alexopoulos, G. S., Bruce, M. L., Hull, J., Sirey, J. A., & Kakuma, T. (1999). Clinical determinants of suicidal ideation and behavior in geriatric depression. *Archives of General Psychiatry, 56*(11), 1048–1053.

Alley, D., Liebig, P., Pynoos, J., Banerjee, T., & Choi, I. H. (2007). Creating elder-friendly communities: Preparations for an aging society. *Journal of Gerontological Social Work, 49*(1–2), 1–18.

Altshuler, N., & Schimmel, J. (2010). *Aging in place: Do Older Americans Act Title III services reach those most likely to enter nursing homes?* Princeton, NJ: Mathematica Policy Research.

Alzheimer's Association. (2014). *2014 Alzheimer's disease facts and figures.* Retrieved from http://www.alz.org/downloads/Facts_Figures_2014.pdf

Ambrose Gallagher, N., Gretebeck, K. A., Robinson, J. C., Torres, E. R., Murphy, S. L., & Martyn, K. K. (2010). Neighborhood factors relevant for walking in older, urban, African American adults. *Journal of Aging and Physical Activity, 18*(1), 99–115.

American Planning Association. (2006). *Policy guide on housing.* Policy adopted by American Planning Association (APA) Board of Directors. Retrieved from http://www.planning.org/policy/guides/pdf/housing.pdf

Andel, R., Hyer, K., & Slack, A. (2007). Risk factors for nursing home placement in older adults with and without dementia. *Journal of Aging and Health, 19*(2), 213–228.

Anderson, A. (2004). *Theory of change as a tool for strategic planning: A report on early experiences.* New York, NY: Aspen Institute Roundtable on Community Change.

Anderson, A., & S. Milligan. (2006). Social capital and community building. K. Fulbright-Anderson & P. Auspos (Eds.), *Community change: Theories, practice and evidence* (pp. 21–60). Washington, DC: Aspen Institute.

Andrew, M. K. (2005). Social capital, health, and care home residence among older adults: A secondary analysis of the Health Survey for England 2000. *European Journal of Ageing, 2*, 137–148.

Aneshensel, C. S., Wight, R. G., Miller-Martinez, D., Botticello, A. L., Karlamangla, A. S., & Seeman, T. G. (2007). Urban neighborhoods and depressive symptoms among older adults. *Journal of Gerontology: Social Sciences, 6B*, S52–S59.

Annear, M., Keeling, S., Wilkinson, T., Cushman, G., Gidlow, B., & Hopkins, H. (2014). Environmental influences on healthy and active ageing: A systematic review. *Aging and Society, 34*(4), 590–622. doi:10.1017/s0144686x1200116x

Antonucci, T. C., & Akiyama, H. (1995). Convoys of social relations: Family and friendships within a life span context. In R. Blieszner & V. Bedford (Eds.), *Handbook of aging and the family* (pp. 355–371). Westport, CT: Greenwood Press.

Antonucci, T. C., Fuhrer, R., & Dartigues, J. (1997). Social relations and depressive symptomatology in a sample of community-dwelling French older adults. *Psychology and Aging, 12*(1), 189.

Archer, P. M. (2012). Healthcare reform act's impact on older Americans. *Chart, 110*(4), 9–13.

Arno, P. S., Levine, C., & Memmott, M. M. (1999). The economic value of informal caregiving. *Health Affairs, 18*(2), 182–188.

Atchley, R. C. (1971). Retirement and leisure participation: Continuity or crisis? *The Gerontologist, 11*(1 Part 1), 13–17.

Atlanta Regional Commission. (2007). *Lifelong communities handbook: Creating opportunities for lifelong living.* Atlanta, GA: Author.

Atlanta Regional Commission. (2009). *Lifelong communities: A regional guide to growth and longevity.* Retrieved from http://www.atlantaregional.com/aging-resources/lifelong-communities/archives

Auspos, P., & Kubisch, A. C. (2004). *Building knowledge about community change: Moving beyond evaluations.* New York, NY: Aspen Institute Roundtable on Community Change.

Austin, C., des Camp, E., Flux, D., McClelland, R., & Sieppert, J. (2005). Community development with older adults in their neighborhoods: The elder friendly communities program. *Families in Society: The Journal of Contemporary Social Services, 86*(3), 401–409.

Aytur, S. A. (2007). Promoting active community environments through land use and transportation planning. *American Journal of Health Promotion, 21*, 397–407.

Baily, L. (2004). *Aging Americans: Stranded without options.* Washington, DC: Surface Transportation Policy Project.

Ball, M. S., & Lawler, K. (2014). Changing practice and policy to move to scale: A framework for age-friendly communities across the United States. *Journal of Aging & Social Policy, 26* (1–2), 19–32.

Baltes, M. M. (1988). The etiology and maintenance of dependency in the elderly: Three phases of operant research. *Behavior Therapy, 19*(3), 301–319.

Baltes, M. M., Maas, I., Wilms, H. U., Borchelt, M., & Little, T. (1999). Everyday competence in old and very old age. In P. Baltes & K. Mayer (Eds.), *The Berlin aging study: Aging from 70 to 100* (pp. 384–402). New York, NY: Cambridge University Press.

Baltes, P. B., & Baltes, M. M. (1990). Psychological perspectives on successful aging: The model of selective optimization with compensation. *Successful Aging: Perspectives from the Behavioral Sciences, 1*, 1–34.

Banaszak-Holl, J., Fendrick, A. M., Foster, N. L., Herzog, A. R., Kabeto, M. U., Kent, D. M., . . . & Langa, K. M. (2004). Predicting nursing home admission: Estimates from a 7-year follow-up of a nationally representative sample of older Americans. *Alzheimer Disease and Associated Disorders, 18*(2), 83–89.

Bandura, A. (1969). *Social foundations of thought and action*. Englewood Cliffs, NJ: Prentice Hall.

Bandura, A. (1982). Self-efficacy mechanism in human agency. *American Psychologist, 37*(2), 122.

Bardo, A. R., Applebaum, R. A., Kunkel, S. R., & Carpio, E. A. (2014). Everyone's talking about it, but does it work? Nursing home diversion and transition. *Journal of Applied Gerontology, 33*(2), 207–226.

Barnes, L. L., Mendes de Leon, C. F., Bienias, J. L., & Evans, D. A. (2004). A longitudinal study of Black-White differences in social resources. *Journals of Gerontology, Social Sciences, 59*(3), S146–S153.

Barron, J. S., Tan, E. J., Yu, Q., Song, M., McGill, S., & Fried, L. P. (2009). Potential for intensive volunteering to promote the health of older adults in fair health. *Journal of Urban Health: Bulletin of the New York Academy of Medicine, 86*(4), 641–653.

Barusch, A. S. (2013). Age-friendly cities: A social work perspective. *Journal of Gerontological Social Work, 56*(6), 465–472.

Bassuk, S. S., Glass, T. A., & Berkman, L. F. (1999). Social disengagement and incident cognitive decline in community-dwelling elderly persons. *Annals of Internal Medicine, 131*, 165–173.

Bayer, A., & Harper, L. (2000). *Fixing to stay: A national survey on housing and home modification issues*. Retrieved from http://assets.aarp.org/rgcenter/il/home_mod.pdf

Beacon Hill Village. (2014). *About Beacon Hill Village*. Retrieved from http://www.beaconhillvillage.org/content.aspx?page_id=0&club_id=332658

Beard, J. R., & Petitot, C. (2010). Ageing and urbanization: Can cities be designed to foster active ageing. *Public Health Reviews, 32*(2), 427–450.

Bedney, B. J., & Goldberg, R. (2009). *Health care cost containment and NORC Supportive Service Programs: An overview and literature review*. Retrieved from http://www.norcs.org/page.aspx?id=198924

Bedney, B. J., Goldberg, R. B., & Josephson, K. (2010). Aging in place in naturally occurring retirement communities: Transforming aging through supportive service programs. *Journal of Housing for the Elderly, 24*, 304–321.

Bedney, B. J., Schimmel, D., Goldberg, R. B., Kotler-Berkowitz, L., & Bursztyn, D. (2007, March). *Rethinking aging in place: Exploring the impact of NORC Supportive Service Programs on older adult participants*. Paper presented at the ASA/NCOA Annual Conference, Chicago.

Berke, E. M., Gottlieb, L. M., Moudon, A. V., & Larson, E. B. (2007). Protective association between neighborhood walkability and depression in older men. *Journal of the American Geriatrics Society, 55*(4), 526–533.

Berke, E. M., Koepsell, T. D., Moudon, A. V., Hoskins, R. E., & Larson, E. B. (2007). Association of the built environment with physical activity and obesity in older persons. *American Journal of Public Health, 97*(3), 486–492. doi:10.2105/AJPH.2006.085837

Berube, A., Singer, A., Wilson, J., & Frey, W. (2006). *Finding exurbia: America's changing landscape at the metropolitan fringe*. Washington, DC: Brookings Institution.

Berwick, D. M., Nolan, T. W., & Whittington, J. (2008). The triple aim: care, health, and cost. *Health Affairs, 27*(3), 759–769.

Beverly Foundation. (2010). *The 5 A's of senior-friendly transportation.* Retrieved from http://beverlyfoundation.org/wp-content/uploads/Fact-Sheet-5-the-5-as.pdf

Bharucha, A. J., Pandav, R., Shen, C., Dodge, H. H., & Ganguli, M. (2004). Predictors of nursing facility admission: A 12-year epidemiological study in the United States. *Journal of the American Geriatrics Society, 52*(3), 434–439.

Binstock, R. H. (2005). Old-age policies, politics, and ageism. *Generations, 29*(3), 73–78.

Birditt, K. S., Jackey, L. M., & Antonucci, T. C. (2009). Longitudinal patterns of negative relationship quality across adulthood. *The Journals of Gerontology Series B: Psychological Sciences and Social Sciences, 64*, 55–64.

Blair, T. R. (2010). *Community ambassadors: A community-driven approach to resource access for elders.* Berkeley: University of California, Berkeley.

Bloomberg, M. R., & Quinn, C. C. (2009). *Age friendly NYC: Enhancing our city's livability for older New Yorkers.* Retrieved from http://www.nyc.gov/html/dfta/downloads/pdf/age_friendly/agefriendlynyc.pdf

Bolda, E. J., Saucier, P., Maddox, G., Wetle, T., & Lowe, J. (2006). Governance and management structures for community partnerships: experiences from the Robert Wood Johnson Foundation's Community Partnerships for Older Adults Program. *The Gerontologist, 46*(3), 391–397.

Bookman, A. (2008). Innovative models of aging in place: Transforming our communities for an aging population. *Community, Work & Family, 11*(4), 419–438.

Booth, M. L., Owen, N., Bauman, A., Clavisi, O., & Leslie, E. (2000). Social-cognitive and perceived environment influence associated with physical activity in older Australians. *Preventive Medicine, 31*, 15–22.

Borglin, G., Jakobsson, U., Edberg, A., & Hallberg, I. R. (2006). Older people in Sweden with various degrees of present quality of life: Their health, social support, everyday activities and sense of coherence. *Health & Social Care in the Community, 14*(2), 136–146.

Borrell, L. N., & Crawford, N. D. (2006). Race, ethnicity, and self-rated health status in the behavioral risk factor surveillance system survey. *Hispanic Journal of Behavioral Sciences, 28*(3), 387–403.

Bortz, W. (2009). Understanding frailty. *The Journals of Gerontology Series A: Biological Sciences and Medical Sciences.* doi:10.1093/gerona/glp162.

Bortz, W. M. (1982). Disuse and aging. *JAMA: Journal of the American Medical Association, 248*(10), 1203–1208.

Bradley, E. H., McGraw, S. A., Curry, L., Buckser, A., King, K. L., Kasl, S. V., & Andersen, R. (2002). Expanding the Andersen model: The role of psychosocial factors in long-term care use. *Health Services Research, 37.5*, 1221–1242. doi:10.1111/1475-6773.01053

Brandtstädter, J., & Rothermund, K. (2002). The life-course dynamics of goal pursuit and goal adjustment: A two-process framework. *Developmental Review, 22*(1), 117–150.

Brenner, L. A., Homaifar, B. Y., & Schultheis, M. T. (2008). Driving, aging, and traumatic brain injury: Integrating findings from the literature. *Rehabilitation Psychology, 53*(1), 18–27.

Browdie, R. (2008). The aging network and long-term care: Shared goals and different histories. *Generations, 32*(3), 77–80.

Brown, C., & Henkin, N. (2014). Building communities for all ages: Lessons learned from an intergenerational community-building initiative. *Journal of Community & Applied Social Psychology, 24*(1), 63–68.

Brown, S. L., Nesse, R. M., Vinokur, A. D., & Smith, D. M. (2003). Providing social support may be more beneficial than receiving it results from a prospective study of mortality. *Psychological Science, 14*(4), 320–327.

Browning, C. R., Cagney, K. A., & Wen, M. (2003). Explaining variation in health status across space and time: Implications for racial and ethnic disparities in self-rated health. *Social Science & Medicine, 57*, 1221–1235.

Bruno, D. (2015, January 13). Seniors take Manhattan. *Politico*. Retrieved from http://www.polit-ico.com/magazine/story/2015/01/senior-living-initiatives-ill-take-manhattan-114227.html#.VT1MHpMjlCA

Bryce, E. (2006, September 15). Golf carts could take to the streets. *Herald Tribune*. Retrieved from http://www.heraldtribune.com/apps/pbcs.dll/article?AID=/20060915/NEWS/609150407

Buffel, T., Phillipson, C., & Scharf, T. (2012). Ageing in urban environments: Developing "age-friendly" cities. *Critical Social Policy, 32*(4), 597–617.

Buffel, T., McGarry, P., Phillipson, C., De Donder, L., Dury, S., De Witte, N., . . . Verté, D. (2014). Developing age-friendly cities: Case studies from Brussels and Manchester and implications for policy and practice. *Journal of Aging & Social Policy, 26*(1–2), 52–72.

Buhr, G. T., Kuchibhatla, M., & Clipp, E. C. (2006). Caregivers' reasons for nursing home placement: Clues for improving discussions with families prior to the transition. *Gerontologist, 46*(1), 52–61.

Burkhardt, J. E. (2000). Limitations of mass transportation and individual vehicle systems for older persons. In M. Pietrucha (Ed.), *Mobility and transportation in the elderly* (pp. 97–123). New York, NY: Springer.

Burkhardt, J. E., McGavock, A. T., Nelson, C. A., & Mitchell, C. G. (2002). *Improving public transit options for older persons* (TRB's Transit Cooperative Research [TCRP] Report 82). Washington, DC: Transportation Research Board.

Burman, L. E., & Johnson, R. W. (2007). *A proposal to finance long-term care services through Medicare with an income tax surcharge*. Washington, DC: Urban Institute.

Burns, V. F., Lavoie, J., & Rose, D. (2012). Revisiting the role of neighborhood change in social exclusion and inclusion of older people. *Journal of Aging Research, 2012*, 1–12. doi:10.1155/2012/148287

Butler, R. N. (1963). The facade of chronological age: An interpretative summary. *American Journal of Psychiatry, 119*(8), 721–728.

Byun, P., Waldorf, B. S., & Esparza, A. X. (2005). Spillovers and local growth controls: An alternative perspective on suburbanization. *Growth and Change, 36*(2), 196–219.

Cabaj, M. (2012, February 8). *The ecology for inter-agency collaboration*. Presentation to AASCF & Services for Children and Families, Edmonton. Retrieved from http://www.aascf.com/pdf/EcologyforInterAgencyCollaborationPPpdf%5B1%5D.pdf

Cagney, K. A., Browning, C. R., & Wen, M. (2005). Racial disparities in self-rated health at older ages: What difference does the neighborhood make? *Journal of Gerontology: Social Sciences, 60B*, S181–S190.

Cahn, E. (2006). *Priceless money: Banking time for changing times*. Washington, DC: Timebanks USA.

Caldera, S. (2012). *Social Security: Who's counting on it?* Washington, DC: AARP Public Policy Institute. Retrieved from http://www.aarp.org/content/dam/aarp/research/public_policy_institute/econ_sec/2012/Social-Security-Whos-Counting-on-It-fs-252-AARP-ppi-econ-sec.pdf

California Budget Project. (2009). *Governor signs budget revisions*. Retrieved from http://www.cbp.org/documents/090727_Governor_Signs_Budget.pdf

Calsyn, R. J., & Winter, J. P. (1999a). Predicting specific service awareness dimensions. *Research on Aging, 21*, 762–780. doi:10.1177/0164027599216003

Calsyn, R. J., & Winter, J. P. (1999b). Who attends senior centers? *Journal of Social Service Research, 26*, 53–69.

Campbell, A. J. (2013). Fall prevention: Single or multiple interventions? Single interventions for fall prevention. *Journal of the American Geriatrics Society, 61*(2), 281–284. doi:10.1111/jgs.12095_2

Campbell, A. J., Borrie, M. J., & Spears, G. F. (1989). Risk factors for falls in a community-based prospective study of people 70 years and older. *Journal of Gerontology, 44*(5), M112–M117.

Cappeliez, P., & Robitaille, A. (2010). Coping mediates the relationships between reminiscence and psychological well-being among older adults. *Aging & Mental Health, 14*, 807–818.

Carey, E. C., Covinsky, K. E., Lui, L., Eng, C., Sands, L. P., & Walter, L. C. (2008). Prediction of mortality in community-living frail elderly people with long-term care needs. *Journal of the American Geriatrics Society, 56*(1), 68–75.

Carlson, B. L., Foster, L., Dale, S. B., & Brown, R. (2007). Effects of cash and counseling on personal care and well-being. *Health Services Research, 42*(1p2), 467–487.

Carp, F. M. (1976). Housing and living environments of older people. In R. Binstock & E. Shanas (Eds.), *Handbook of aging and the social sciences* (pp. 244–271). New York, NY: Van Nostrand Reinhold.

Carp, F. M., & Carp, A. (1984). A complementary/congruence model of well-being or mental health for the community elderly. In I. Altman, M. Lawton, & J. Wohlwill (Eds.), *Elderly people and the environment* (pp. 279–336). New York, NY: Plenum.

Carpiano, R. M. (2007). Neighborhood social capital and adult health: An empirical test of a bourdieu-based model. *Health & Place, 13*(3), 639–655. doi:10.1016/j.healthplace.2006.09.001

Carroll, D. A., & Stater, K. J. (2009). Revenue diversification in nonprofit organizations: Does it lead to financial stability? *Journal of Public Administration Research and Theory, 19*(4), 947–966.

Carstensen, L. L. (1993, January). Motivation for social contact across the life span: A theory of socioemotional selectivity. In *Nebraska symposium on motivation* (Vol. 40, pp. 209–254). Lincoln, NE: University of Nebraska Press.

Carstensen, L. L., Isaacowitz, D. M., & Charles, S. T. (1999). Taking time seriously: A theory of socioemotional selectivity. *American Psychologist, 54*(3), 165.

Cattell, V. (2001). Poor people, poor places, and poor health: The mediating role of social networks and social capital. *Social Science & Medicine, 52*(10), 1501–1516.

Center for Universal Design. (1997). *Environments and products for all people.* Raleigh: North Carolina State University, Center for Universal Design.

Centers for Disease Control and Prevention. (2011). *Healthy aging.* Retrieved from http://www.cdc.gov/chronicdisease/resources/publications/AAG/aging.htm

Centers for Disease Control and Prevention. (2013). *Healthy places terminology.* Retrieved from http://www.cdc.gov/healthyplaces/terminology.htm

Centers for Disease Control and Prevention National Center for Injury Prevention and Control. (2010). *Web-based injury statistics query and reporting system (WISQARS).* Retrieved from http://www.cdc.gov/injury/wisqars/index.html

Cerda, M., Diez Roux, A. V., Tchetgen, E., Gordon-Larsen, P., & Kiefe, C. (2010). The relationship between neighborhood poverty and alcohol use: Estimation by marginal structural models. *Epidemiology, 21*(4), 482–489.

Chapman, N. J., & Howe, D. A. (2001). Accessory apartments: Are they a realistic alternative for ageing in place? *Housing Studies, 16*(5), 637–650.

Charles, K. K., & Sevak, P. (2005). Can family caregiving substitute for nursing home care? *Journal of Health Economics, 24*(6), 1174–1190.

Chaskin, R. J. (1997). Perspectives on neighborhood and community: A review of the literature. *Social Service Review, 71*(4), 521–547.

Chaskin, R. J. (2005). Democracy and bureaucracy in a community planning process. *Journal of Planning Education and Research, 24*, 408–419.

Checkoway, B. (1995). Two types of planning in neighborhoods. In J. Rothman, J. L. Erlich, & J. E. Tropman (Eds.), *Strategies of community intervention* (5th ed., pp. 314–326). Itasca, IL: Peacock.

Chen, L., Rex, C., Sanaiha, Y., Lynch, G., & Gall, C. (2010). Learning induces neurotrophin signaling at hippocampal synapses. *Proceedings of the National Academy of Sciences of the United States of America, 107*, 7030–7035.

Chen, S., Mefford, L., Brown, J., Hsu, M., Clem, R., & Newman, L. (2008). Predictors of American elders' home stay: A secondary data analysis study. *Nursing & Health Sciences, 10*(2), 117–124.

Chen, S. Y., & Fu, Y. C. (2008). Leisure participation and enjoyment among the elderly: Individual characteristics and sociability. *Educational Gerontology, 34,* 871–889.

Choi, M., & Mezuk, B. (2013). Aging without driving: Evidence from the health and retirement study, 1993 to 2008. *Journal of Applied Gerontology, 32*(7), 902–912.

Choi, N. G., & Kimbell, K. (2009). Depression care need among low-income older adults: Views from aging service providers and family caregivers. *Clinical Gerontologist, 32*(1), 60–76.

City of Boston. (2014). *Mayor Menino announces elder friendly business initiative in Mission Hill Main Streets.* Retrieved from http://www.cityofboston.gov/news/Default.aspx?id=2328

City of Fremont. (n.d.). *Community Ambassador Program for Seniors.* Retrieved from http://capseniors.org/

Clark, D. O. (1999). Identifying psychological, physiological, and environmental barriers and facilitators to exercise among older low income adults. *Journal of Clinical Geropsychology, 5*(1), 51–62.

Clark, K. (2014). GenPhilly: A strategy for improving the sustainability of aging in community initiatives. *Journal of Aging & Social Policy, 26*(1), 197–211. doi:10.1080/08959420.2014.854135

Clark, K., & Glicksman, A. (2012). Age-friendly Philadelphia: Bringing diverse networks together around aging issues. *Journal of Housing for the Elderly, 26*(1–3), 121–136. doi:10.10 80/02763893.2012.655662

Clarke, P., & George, L. K. (2005). The role of the built environment in the disablement process. *American Journal of Public Health, 95*(11), 1933–1939. doi:10.2105/AJPH.2004.054494

Cohen, G. D., Perlstein, S., Chapline, J., Kelly, J., Firth, K. M., & Simmens, S. (2006). The impact of professionally conducted cultural programs on the physical health, mental health, and social functioning of older adults. *The Gerontologist, 46,* 726–734.

Cohen-Mansfield, J., Dakheel-Ali, M., & Frank, J. (2010). The impact of a Naturally Occurring Retirement Communities service program in Maryland, USA. *Health Promotion International, 25*(2), 210–220.

Collings, P. (2001). "If you got everything, it's good enough": Perspectives on successful aging in a Canadian Inuit community. *Journal of Cross-Cultural Gerontology, 16*(2), 127–155.

Connell, B., & Sanford, J. (2001). Difficulty, dependence, and housing accessibility for people aging with a disability. *Journal of Architectural and Planning Research, 18*(3), 234–242.

Cornwell, B. (2011). Age trends in daily social contact patterns. *Research on Aging, 33,* 598–631.

Cornwell, B., Laumann, E. O., & Schumm, L. P. (2008). The social connectedness of older adults: A national profile. *American Sociological Review, 73*(2), 185–203.

Corporation for National and Community Service. (2008). *Foster Grandparent Program handbook.* Washington, DC: Author.

Corrigan, P. W. (2006). Impact of consumer-operated services on empowerment and recovery of people with psychiatric disabilities. *Psychiatric Services, 57*(10), 1493–1496.

Cottrell, L. S., Jr. (1976). The competent community. In B. Kaplan, R. Wilson, & A. Leighton (Eds.), *Further explorations in social psychiatry* (pp. 195–209). New York: Basic Books.

County Welfare Directors Association of California. (2003). *In-home supportive services: Past, present, and future.* Sacramento: County Welfare Directors Association of California.

Cramm, J. M., Twisk, J., & Nieboer, A. P. (2014). Self-management abilities and frailty are important for healthy aging among community-dwelling older people: A cross-sectional study. *BMC Geriatrics, 14*(28), 1–5. doi:10.1186/1471-2318-14-28

Crittenden, W. F. (2000). Spinning straw into gold: The tenuous strategy, funding, and financial performance linkage. *Nonprofit and Voluntary Sector Quarterly, 29*(Suppl 1), 164–182.

Crowder, K., & South, S. J. (2011). Spatial and temporal dimensions of neighborhood effects on high school graduation. *Social Science Research, 40*(1), 87–106. doi:10.1016/j.ssresearch.2010.04.013

Cruikshank, M. (2003). *Learning to Be Old: Gender, Culture and Ageing*. Lantham, MD: Rowman & Littlefield.

Curl, A. L., Stowe, J. D., Cooney, T. M., & Proulx, C. M. (2014). Giving up the keys: How driving cessation affects engagement in later life. *Gerontologist, 54*(3), 423–433. doi:10.1093/geront/gnt037

Cvitkovich, Y., & Wister, A. (2003). Bringing in the life course: A modification to Lawton's ecological model of aging. *Hallym International Journal of Aging, 4*, 15–29.

Dagger, R. (2003). Stopping sprawl for the good of all: The case for civic environmentalism. *Journal of Social Philosophy, 34*(1), 28–43.

Daniels, R. S. (1994). Demographic, economic, and political factors related to housing for the elderly. In W. Folts & D. Yeatts (Eds.), *Housing and the aging population: Options for the new century* (pp. 369–390). New York, NY: Routledge.

Dechamps, A., Diolez, P., Thiaudière, E., Tulon, A., Onifade, C., Vuong, T., ... Bourdel-Marchasson, I. (2010). Effects of exercise programs to prevent decline in health-related quality of life in highly deconditioned institutionalized elderly persons: A randomized controlled trial. *Archives of Internal Medicine, 170*(2), 162–169.

de Kam, G. R., Damoiseaux, D. J., Dorland, L., Pijpers, R. A., Biene, M. V., Jansen, E., & Slaets, J. P. (2012). *Kwetsbaar en zelfstandig. Een onderzoek naar de effecten van woonservicegebieden voor ouderen*. Nijmegen, the Netherlands: Institute for Management Research.

Dellinger, A. M., Sehgal, M., Sleet, D. A., & Barrett-Connor, E. (2001). Driving cessation: What older former drivers tell us. *Journal of the American Geriatrics Society, 49*(4), 431–435.

Desmond, S. M., Mahoney, K. J., Simon-Rusinowitz, L., & Shoop, D. M. (2001). Consumer preferences for a consumer-directed cash option versus traditional services. *Marquette Elder's Advisor, 3*(1), 1–22. Retrieved from http://scholarship.law.marquette.edu/cgi/viewcontent.cgi?article=1174&context=elders

De Souza Briggs, X., Mueller, E. J., & Sullivan, M. L. (1997). *From neighborhood to community: Evidence on the social effects of community development*. New York, NY: Community Development Research Center, Graduate School of Management and Urban Policy, New School for Social Research.

Detroit Area Agency on Aging. (2010). *Dying before their time II: The startling truth about senior mortality in the Detroit area and urban Michigan*. Retrieved from http://www.daaa1a.org/DAAA/media/Dying%20Before%20Their%20Time%20II%20-%202012%20Final%20Report.pdf

Diaz Moore, K. (2014). An ecological framework of place: Situating environmental gerontology within a life course perspective. *The International Journal of Aging and Human Development, 79*(3), 183–209.

Diez Roux, A. V. (2001). Investigating neighborhood and area effects on health. *American Journal of Public Health, 91*, 1783–1789.

Diez Roux, A. V. (2004). Estimating neighborhood health effects: The challenges of causal inference in a complex world. *Social Science & Medicine, 58*, 1953–1960.

Doty, P., Mahoney, K. J., Simon-Rusinowitz, L., Sciegaj, M., Selkow, I., & Loughlin, D. M. (2012). How does cash and counseling affect the growth of participant-directed services? *Generations, 36*(1), 28–36.

Drees, J. M., & Heugens, P. P. (2013). Synthesizing and extending resource dependence theory: A meta-analysis. *Journal of Management, 39*(6). doi:0149206312471391

Duay, D. L., & Bryan, V. C. (2006). Senior adults' perceptions of successful aging. *Educational Gerontology, 32*(6), 423–445.

Dunham-Jones, E., & Williamson, J. (2012). Retrofitting suburbs. In H. Cisneros, M. Dyer-Chamberlain, & J. Hickie (Eds.), *Independent for life: Homes and neighborhoods for an aging America* (pp. 179–196). Austin: University of Texas Press.

Dupertuis, L. L., Aldwin, C. M., & Bosse, R. (2001). Does the source of support matter for different health outcomes? Findings from the Normative Aging Study. *Journal of Aging and Health, 13*, 494–510.

Eby, D. W., Molnar, L. J., & Kartje, P. S. (2008). *Maintaining safe mobility in an aging society.* Boca Raton, FL: CRC Press.

Echeverria, S., Diez-Roux, A. V., Shea, S., Borrell, L. N., & Jackson, S. (2008). Associations of neighborhood problems and neighborhood social cohesion with mental health and health behaviors: The multi-ethnic study of atherosclerosis. *Health & Place, 14*(4), 853–865.

Edwards, J. D., Lunsman, M., Perkins, M., Rebok, G. W., & Roth, D. L. (2009). Driving cessation and health trajectories in older adults. *The Journals of Gerontology Series A: Biological Sciences and Medical Sciences, 64*(12), 1290–1295.

Edwards, R. D. (2008). Public transit, obesity, and medical costs: Assessing the magnitudes. *Preventive Medicine, 46*(1), 14–21.

Eheart, B. K., Hopping, D., Power, M. B., Mitchell, E. T., & Racine, D. (2009). Generations of Hope Communities: An intergenerational neighborhood model of support and service. *Children and Youth Services Review, 31*(1), 47–52.

El-Khoury, F., Cassou, B., Charles, M., & Dargent-Molina, P. (2013). The effect of fall prevention exercise programs on fall induced injuries in community dwelling older adults: Systematic review and meta-analysis of randomized controlled trials. *BMJ, 347,* 1–13. doi:10.1136/bmj.f6234

Ellis, C. (2002). The new urbanism: Critiques and rebuttals. *Journal of Urban Design, 7*(3), 261–291.

Enguidanos, S., Pynoos, J., Denton, A., Alexman, S., & Diepenbrock, L. (2010). Comparison of barriers and facilitators in developing NORC programs: A tale of two communities. *Journal of Housing for the Elderly, 24,* 291–303.

Ertel, K., Glymour, M., & Berkman, L. (2009). Social networks and health: A life course perspective integrating observational and experimental evidence. *Journal of Social and Personal Relationships, 26,* 73–92.

Estes, C. L. (1993). The aging enterprise revisited. *The Gerontologist, 33*(3), 292–298.

Etkin, C. D., Prohaska, T. R., Harris, B. A., Latham, N., & Jette, A. (2006). Feasibility of implementing the Strong for Life program in community settings. *The Gerontologist, 46*(2), 284–292.

Evashwick, C., & Holt, T. J. (2000). Integrating long-term care, acute care, and housing: Building success through a continuum of care. *Catholic Health Association of the United States.*

Everard, K. M., Lach, H. W., Fisher, E. B., & Baum, M. C. (2000). Relationship of activity and social support to the functional health of older adults. *The Journals of Gerontology Series B: Psychological Sciences and Social Sciences, 55*(4), S208–S212.

Fairchild, D. G., Hogan, J., Smith, R., Portnow, M., & Bates, D. W. (2002). Survey of primary care physicians and home care clinicians. *Journal of General Internal Medicine, 17*(4), 253–261.

Family Caregiver Alliance. (2012). *Selected caregiver statistics.* Retrieved from https://caregiver.org/selected-caregiver-statistics

Federal Highway Administration. (2001). *Highway design handbook for older drivers and pedestrians.* Retrieved from http://www.fhwa.dot.gov/publications/research/safety/humanfac/01103/

Federal Interagency Forum on Aging-Related Statistics. (2012). *Older Americans 2012: Key indicators of well-being.* Washington, DC: Government Printing Office.

Feinberg, L., Reinhard, S., Houser, A., & Choula, R. (2011). *Valuing the invaluable: 2011 update: The growing contributions and costs of family caregiving.* Retrieved from http://hjweinbergfoundation.net/ficsp/documents/10/Caregivers-Save-the-System-Money-With-Uncompensated-Care.pdf

Feldman, P. H., Oberlink, M. R., Simantov, E., & Gursen, M. D. (2004). *A tale of two older Americas: Community opportunities and challenges: AdvantAge Initiative 2003 national survey of adults aged 65 and older.* New York, NY: Center for Home Care Policy and Research.

Fields, N. L., Anderson, K. A., & Dabelko-Schoeny, H. (2014). The effectiveness of adult day services for older adults: A review of the literature from 2000 to 2011. *Journal of Applied Gerontology: The Official Journal of the Southern Gerontological Society, 33*(2), 130–163. doi:10.1177/0733464812443308

Figueira-McDonough, J. (2001). *Community analysis and praxis: Toward a grounded civil society.* New York, NY: Psychology Press.

Fiori, K. L., Antonucci, T. C., & Cortina, K. S. (2006). Social network typologies and mental health among older adults. *The Journals of Gerontology Series B: Psychological Sciences and Social Sciences, 61*(1), P25–32. doi:61/1/P25

Fiori, K. L., Smith, J., & Antonucci, T. C. (2007). Social network types among older adults: A multidimensional approach. *The Journals of Gerontology Series B: Psychological Sciences and Social Sciences, 62B,* 322–330.

Fischel, W. A. (1978). A property rights approach to municipal zoning. *Land Economics, 54,* 64–81.

Foley, D. J., Heimovitz, H. K., Guralnik, J. M., & Brock, D. B. (2002). Driving life expectancy of persons aged 70 years and older in the united states. *American Journal of Public Health, 92*(8), 1284–1289.

Folts, W. E., & Muir, K. B. (2002). Housing for older adults: New lessons from the past. *Research on Aging, 24*(1), 10–28.

Forrest, R., & Kearns, A. (2001). Social cohesion, social capital and the neighbourhood. *Urban Studies, 38*(12), 2125–2143.

Foster-Fishman, P. G., Fitzgerald, K., Brandell, C., Nowell, B., Chavis, D., & Van Egeren, L. (2006). Mobilizing residents for action: The role of small wins and strategic supports. *American Journal of Community Psychology, 38*(3–4), 143–152.

Fox-Grage, W., & Ujvari, K. (2014). *The Older Americans Act.* Washington, DC: AARP Public Policy Institute.

Frank, L. D. (2000). Land use and transportation interaction: Implications on public health quality and quality of life. *Journal of Planning Education Research, 20,* 6–22.

Frank, L. D., Andersen, M. A., & Schmid, T. L. (2004). Obesity relationships with community design, physical activity, and time spent in cars. *American Journal of Preventive Medicine, 27,* 87–96.

Frank, L. D., Schmid, T. L., Sallis, J. F., Chapman, J., & Saelens, B. E. (2005). Linking objectively measured physical activity with objectively measured urban form: Findings from SMARTRAQ. *American Journal of Preventive Medicine, 28*(2), 117–125.

Fredrickson, B. L., & Carstensen, L. L. (1990). Choosing social partners: how old age and anticipated endings make people more selective. *Psychology and Aging, 5*(3), 335.

Freedman, V. A., Grafova, I. B., Schoeni, R. F., & Rogowski, J. (2008). Neighborhoods and disability in later life. *Social Science & Medicine, 66*(11), 2253–2267. doi:10.1016/j.socscimed.2008.01.013

Freeman, E. E., Gange, S. J., Munoz, B., & West, S. K. (2006). Driving status and risk of entry into long-term care in older adults. *American Journal of Public Health, 96*(7), 1254–1259.

Freund, A. M., & Baltes, P. B. (1999). Selection, optimization, and compensation as strategies of life management: Correction to Freund and Bates (1998). *Psychology and Aging, 14*(4), 700–702.

Freund, A. M., & Baltes, P. B. (2002). Life-management strategies of selection, optimization and compensation: Measurement by self-report and construct validity. *Journal of Personality and Social Psychology, 82*(4), 642.

Freund, B., & Szinovacz, M. (2002). Effects of cognition on driving involvement among the oldest old variations by gender and alternative transportation opportunities. *The Gerontologist, 42*(5), 621–633.

Frey, W. H. (2007). *Mapping the growth of older America: Seniors and boomers in the early 21st century*. Washington, DC: Brookings Institution.

Fried, L. P., Carlson, M., Freedman, M., Frick, K. D., Glass, T. A., Hill, J., . . . Zeger, S. (2004). A social model for health promotion for an aging population: Initial evidence on the Experience Corps model. *Journal of Urban Health, 81*, 64–78.

Fried, L. P., Freedman, M., Endres, T. E., & Wasik, B. (1997). Building communities that promote successful aging. *Western Journal of Medicine, 167*, 216–219.

Fuller-Thompson, E., Nuru-Jeter, A., Minkler, M., & Guralnik, J. M. (2009). Black-White differences in disability among older Americans: Further untangling the role of race and socioeconomic status. *Journal of Aging and Health, 21*, 677–698. doi:10.1177/0898264309338296

G8 Ministers of Labour (2000). G8 Turin Charter: Towards Active Ageing. Retrieved from http://www.g8.utoronto.ca/employment/labour2000_ageing.htm

Gallimore, R., Goldenberg, C. N., & Weisner, T. S. (1993). The social construction and subjective reality of activity settings: Implications for community psychology. *American Journal of Community Psychology, 21*(4), 537–560.

Gaugler, J. E., Duval, S., Anderson, K. A., & Kane, R. L. (2007). Predicting nursing home admission in the U.S.: A meta-analysis. *BMC Geriatrics, 7*(13), 1–14.

Gaugler, J. E., Kane, R. L., Kane, R. A., Clay, T., & Newcomer, R. (2003). Caregiving and institutionalization of cognitively impaired older people: Utilizing dynamic predictors of change. *Gerontologist, 43*(2), 219–229.

Gaugler, J. E., Yu, F., Krichbaum, K., & Wyman, J. F. (2009). Predictors of nursing home admission for persons with dementia. *Medical Care, 47*(2), 191–198. doi:10.1097/MLR.0b013e31818457ce

Genworth Financial. (2011). *Genworth 2011 cost of care survey*. Richmond, VA: Genworth Financial.

Gilbert, N. (2002). *Transformation of the welfare state: The silent surrender of public responsibility*. New York, NY: Oxford University Press.

Gill, T. M., Williams, C. S., Robison, J. T., & Tinetti, M. E. (1999). A population-based study of environmental hazards in the homes of older persons. *American Journal of Public Health, 89*(4), 553–556.

Gillespie, L. D., Robertson, M. C., Gillespie, W. J., Sherrington, C., Gates, S., Clemson, L. M., & Lamb, S. E. (2012). Interventions for preventing falls in older people living in the community. *Cochrane Database Syst Rev, 9*(11), CD007146.

Gitlin, L. N. (2003a). Conducting research on home environments: Lessons learned and new directions. *The Gerontologist, 43*(5), 628–637.

Gitlin, L. N. (2003b). M. Powell Lawton's vision of the role of the environment in aging processes and outcomes: A glance backward to move us forward. In K. Warner-Schaie, H. W. Wahl, H. Mollenkopf, & F. Oswald (Eds.), *Aging independently: Living arrangement and mobility* (pp. 62–76). New York, NY: Springer.

Gitlin, L. N., Corcoran, M., Winter, L., Boyce, A., & Hauck, W. W. (2001). A randomized, controlled trial of a home environmental intervention effect on efficacy and upset in caregivers and on daily function of persons with dementia. *The Gerontologist, 41*(1), 4–14.

Gitlin, L. N., Mann, W., Tomit, M., & Marcus, S. M. (2001). Factors associated with home environmental problems among community-living older people. *Disability & Rehabilitation, 23*(17), 777–787.

Glasgow, N., & Blakely, R. M. (2000). Older nonmetropolitan residents' evaluations of their transportation arrangements. *Journal of Applied Gerontology, 19*(1), 95–116.

Glass, T. A., Mendes de Leon, C. F., Bassuk, S. S., & Berkman, L. F. (2006). Social engagement and depressive symptoms in late life: Longitudinal findings. *Journal of Aging and Health, 18*, 604–628.

Glass, T. A., Mendes de Leon, C., Marottoli, R. A., & Berkman, L. F. (1999). Population based study of social and productive activities as predictors of survival among elderly Americans. *British Medical Journal, 319*, 478–483.

Glicksman, A., Clark, K., Kleban, M. H., Ring, L., & Hoffman, C. (2014). Building an integrated research/policy planning age-friendly agenda. *Journal of Aging & Social Policy, 26*(1–2), 131–146. doi:10.1080/08959420.2014.854142

Golant, S. M. (1992). *Housing America's elderly: Many possibilities/few choices.* Newbury Park, CA: Sage.

Golant, S. M. (2002). Deciding where to live: The emerging residential settlement patterns of retired Americans. *Generations, 26*(2), 66–73.

Golant, S. M. (2003). Conceptualizing time and behavior in environmental gerontology: A pair of old issues deserving new thought. *The Gerontologist, 43*, 638–648.

Golant, S. M. (2006). Supportive housing for frail, low-income older adults: Identifying need and allocating resources. *Generations, 29*(4), 37–43.

Golant, S. M. (2008a). Affordable clustered housing-care: A category of long-term care options for the elderly poor. *Journal of Housing for the Elderly, 22*(1–2), 3–44.

Golant, S. M. (2008b). Commentary: Irrational exuberance for the aging in place of vulnerable low-income older homeowners. *Journal of Aging & Social Policy, 20*(4), 379–397.

Golant, S. M. (2011). The quest for residential normalcy by older adults: Relocation but one pathway. *Journal of Aging Studies, 25*, 193–205.

Golant, S. M. (2012). Out of their residential comfort and mastery zones: Toward a more relevant environmental gerontology. *Journal of Housing for the Elderly, 26*, 26–43.

Golden, J., Conroy, R. M., Bruce, I., Denihan, A., Greene, E., Kirby, M., & Lawlor, B. A. (2009). Loneliness, social support networks, mood and wellbeing in community-dwelling elderly. *International Journal of Geriatric Psychiatry, 24*(7), 694–700.

Gonyea, J. G., & Hudson, R. B. (2015). Emerging models of age-friendly communities: A conceptual framework for understanding inclusion. *Public Policy & Aging Report, 25*(1), 9–14.

Gottlieb, B. H., & Gillespie, A. A. (2008). Volunteerism, health, and civic engagement among older adults. *Canadian Journal on Aging/La Revue canadienne du vieillissement, 27*(04), 399–406.

Graham, C. L., Scharlach, A. E., & Price Wolf, J. P. (2014). The impact of the "village" model on health, well-being, service access, and social engagement of older adults. *Health Education & Behavior, 41*(Suppl 1), 91S–97S.

Green, G. (2012). Age-friendly cities of Europe. *Journal of Urban Health, 90*(1), 116–128. doi:10.1007/s11524-012-9765-8

Greenfield, E. A. (2012). Using ecological frameworks to advance a field of research, practice, and policy on aging-in-place initiatives. *The Gerontologist, 52*(1), 1–12.

Greenfield, E. A. (2013). The longevity of community aging initiatives: A framework for describing NORC programs' sustainability goals and strategies. *Journal of Housing for the Elderly, 27*(1/2), 120–145. doi:10.1080/02763893.2012.754818

Greenfield, E. A. (2015). Support from neighbors and aging in place: Can NORC programs make a difference? *The Gerontologist.* doi:10.1093/geront/gnu162

Greenfield, E. A., & Marks, N. F. (2004). Formal volunteering as a protective factor for older adults' psychological well-being. *Journal of Gerontology: Social Sciences, 59B*, S258–S264.

Greenfield, E. A., Scharlach, A. E., Graham, C. L., Davitt, J. K., & Lehning, A. J. (2012). An overview of programs in the National NORCs Aging in Place Initiative: Results from a 2012 organizational survey. Retrieved from http://agingandcommunity.com/wp-content/uploads/2013/10/Greenfield-et-al.-2013.pdf

Greenfield, E. A., Scharlach, A. E., Lehning, A. J., Davitt, J. K., & Graham, C. L. (2013). A tale of two community initiatives for promoting aging in place: Similarities and differences in the national implementation of NORC programs and villages. *The Gerontologist, 53*, 928–938. doi:10.1093/geront/gnt035

Gross, D. L., Temkin-Greener, H., Kunitz, S., & Mukamel, D. B. (2004). The growing pains of integrated health care for the elderly: Lessons from the expansion of PACE. *Milbank Quarterly*, 82(2), 257–282.

Guest, A. M., & Wierzbicki, S. K. (1999). Social ties at the neighborhood level two decades of GSS evidence. *Urban Affairs Review*, 35(1), 92–111.

Guo, K. L., & Castillo, R. J. (2012). The U.S. long term care system: Development and expansion of naturally occurring retirement communities as an innovative model for aging in place. *Ageing International*, 37(2), 210–227.

Gurland, B. J., Wilder, D. E., Lantigua, R., Stern, Y., Chen, J., Killeffer, E. H., & Mayeux, R. (1999). Rates of dementia in three ethnoracial groups. *International Journal of Geriatric Psychiatry*, 14(6), 481–493.

Hadley, J., Rabin, D., Epstein, A., Stein, S., & Rimes, C. (2000). Posthospitalization home health care use and changes in functional status in a Medicare population. *Medical Care*, 38(5), 494–507.

Halloran, L. (2013). Health promotion and disability prevention in older adults. *Journal for Nurse Practitioners*, 9(8), 546–547. doi:10.1016/j.nurpra.2013.05.023

Handy, S. (2005). Smart growth and the transportation-land use connection: What does the research tell us? *International Regional Science Review*, 28(2), 146–167.

Hank, K. (2011). Societal determinants of productive aging: A multilevel analysis across 11 European countries. *European Sociological Review*, 27(4), 526–541.

Hank, K., & Erlinghagen, M. (2010). Dynamics of volunteering in older Europeans. *The Gerontologist*, 50(2), 170–178.

HanleyBrown, F., Kania, J., & Kramer, M. (2012). Channeling change: Making collective impact work. *Stanford Social Innovation Review*, 20, 1–8.

Hansen, J. C., & Hewitt, M. (2012). PACE provides a sense of belonging for elders. *Generations*, 36(1), 37–43.

Hanson, D., & Emlet, C. A. (2006). Assessing a community's elder friendliness: A case example of the AdvantAge Initiative. *Fmaily & Community Health*, 29(4), 266–278.

Hao, Y. (2008). Productive activities and psychological well-being among older adults. *Journal of Gerontology: Social Science*, 63B (2), S64–S72.

Harewood, R. H., Pound, P., & Ebrahim, S. 2000. Determinants of social engagement in older men. *Psychology, Health and Medicine*, 5, 75–85.

Harrell, R., Lynott, J., Guzman, S., & Lampkin, C. (2014). *What is livable? Community preferences of older adults*. Washington, DC: American Association of Retired Persons Public Policy Institute.

Harrington, C., Carrillo, H., Wellin, V., Miller, N., & LeBlanc, A. (2000). Predicting state Medicaid home and community based waiver participants and expenditures, 1992–1997. *The Gerontologist*, 40(6), 673–686.

Hayashi, N., Ostrom, E., Walker, J., & Yamagishi, T. (1999). Reciprocity, trust, and the sense of control a cross-societal study. *Rationality and Society*, 11(1), 27–46.

Hayutin, A. (2012). Global trends in population aging: Exacerbating social exclusion? [Abstract]. *The Gerontologist*, 52(S1), 457–457.

Healy, T. C., Peng, C., Haynes, M. S., McMahon, E. M., Botler, J. L., & Gross, L. (2008). The feasibility and effectiveness of translating a matter of balance into a volunteer lay leader model. *Journal of Applied Gerontology*, 27(1), 34–51.

Heath, G. W. (2006). The effectiveness of urban design and land use and transport policies and practices to increase physical activity: A systematic review. *Journal of Physical Activity and Health*, 3, 55–76.

Hebert, L. E., Beckett, L. A., Scherr, P. A., & Evans, D. A. (2001). Annual incidence of alzheimer disease in the united states projected to the years 2000 through 2050. *Alzheimer Disease & Associated Disorders*, 15(4), 169–173.

Hebert, L. E., Weuve, J., Scherr, P. A., & Evans, D. A. (2013). Alzheimer disease in the united states (2010–2050) estimated using the 2010 census. *Neurology, 80*(19), 1778–1783. doi:10.1212/WNL.0b013e31828726f5

Heckhausen, J., & Schulz, R. (1995). A life-span theory of control. *Psychological Review, 102*(2), 284.

Hensher, D. A., & Reyes, A. J. (2000). Trip chaining as a barrier to the propensity to use public transport. *Transportation, 27*(4), 341–361.

Herbel, S., Rosenbloom, S., Stutts, J., & Welch, T. (2006). *NCHRP project 9-36, task 50.* Washington, DC: American Association of State Highway and Transportation Officials.

Heron, M., Hoyert, D. L., Murphy, S. L., Xu, J., Kochanek, K. D., & Tejada-Vera, B. (2009). Deaths: Final data for 2006. *National Vital Statistics Reports, 57*(14), 1–134.

Herzog, A. R., Franks, M. M., Markus, H. R., & Holmberg, D. (1998). Activities and well-being in older age: Effects of self-concept and educational attainment. *Psychology and Aging, 13,* 179–185.

Hess, T. M., & Ennis, G. E. (2012). Age differences in the effort and costs associated with cognitive activity. *Journals of Gerontology Series B: Psychological Sciences and Social Sciences, 67,* 447–455.

Hill, T. D., & Angel, R. J. (2005). Neighborhood disorder, psychological distress, and heavy drinking. *Social Science & Medicine 61*(5), 965–975.

Hinterlong, J. (2006). Racial disparities in health among older adults: examining the role of productive engagement. *Health & Social Work, 31,* 275–288.

Hodge, G. (2008). *Geography of aging: Preparing communities for the surge in seniors.* Montreal, Canada: McGill-Queen's University Press.

Hoffman, C., & Schwartz, K. (2008). Eroding access among nonelderly U.S. adults with chronic conditions: Ten years of change. *Health Affairs, 27*(5), w340–w348. doi:10.1377/hlthaff.27.5.w340

Holland, S., Burgess, S., Grogan-Kaylor, A., & Delva, J. (2011). Understanding neighbourhoods, communities and environments: New approaches for social work research. *British Journal of Social Work, 41,* 689–707. doi:10.1093/bjsw/bcq123

Holmes Research. (2007). *Healthy Aging Initiative: An innovative model for strategic grantmaking, 2001—2006 evaluation report.* Retrieved from http://www.johnmuirhealth.com/content/dam/jmh/Documents/Community/HAI_Evaluation.pdf

Holstein, M. B., & Minkler, M. (2003). Self, society, and the "new gerontology." *The Gerontologist, 43*(6), 787–796.

Holt-Lunstad, J., Smith, T. B., & Layton, J. B. (2010). Social relationships and mortality risk: A meta-analytic review. *PLoS Medicine, 7*(7). doi:10.1371/journal.pmed.1000316

House, J. S., Robbins, C., & Metzner, H. L. (1982). The association of social relationships and activities with mortality: Prospective evidence from the Tecumseh Community Health Study. *American Journal of Epidemiology, 116*(1), 123–140.

House, J. S. (2001). Social isolation kills, but how and why? *Psychosomatic Medicine, 63,* 273–274.

Hughes, S. L., Seymour, R. B., Campbell, R. T., Desai, P., Huber, G., & Chang, H. J. (2010). Fit and Strong! Bolstering maintenance of physical activity among older adults with lower-extremity osteoarthritis. *American Journal of Health Behavior, 34*(6), 750.

Hughes, S. L., Seymour, R. B., Campbell, R. T., Huber, G., Pollak, N., Sharma, L., & Desai, P. (2006). Long-term impact of fit and strong on older adults with osteoarthritis. *The Gerontologist, 46*(6), 801–814. doi:46/6/801

Hunt, M. E., & Gunter-Hunt, G. (1986). Naturally occurring retirement communities. *Journal of Housing for the Elderly, 3*(3–4), 3–22.

Huxhold, O., Miche, M., & Schüz, B. (2014). Benefits of having friends in older ages: Differential effects of informal social activities on well-being in middle-aged and older adults. *The Journals of Gerontology Series B: Psychological Sciences and Social Sciences, 69*(3), 366–375.

Inam, A., Levine, J. C., & Werbel, R. (2002). *Developer-planner interaction in transportation and land use sustainability* (MTI Report 01-21). San José, CA: Mineta Transportation Institute, San José State University.

Ingersoll-Dayton, B., Saengtienchai, C., Kespichayawattana, J., & Aungsuroch, Y. (2004). Measuring psychological well-being: Insights from Thai elders. *The Gerontologist, 44*(5), 596–604.

Institute of Medicine. (1986). *Improving the quality of care of nursing homes.* Washington, DC: National Academies Press.

Institute of Medicine. (2008). *Retooling for an aging America: Building the health care workforce.* Washington, DC: National Academies Press.

Ivery, J. M., Akstein-Kahan, D., & Murphy, K. C. (2010). NORC supportive services model implementation and community capacity. *Journal of Gerontological Social Work, 53*(1), 21–42.

Jackson, R. J. (2003). The impact of the built environment on health: An emerging field. *American Journal of Public Health, 93*(9), 1382–1384.

Jacobs, J. (1961). *The death and life of great American cities.* New York: Random House.

Jang, Y., Mortimer, J. A., Haley, W. E., & Borenstein Graves, A. R. (2004). The role of social engagement in life satisfaction: Its significance among older individuals with disease and disability. *Journal of Applied Gerontology, 23*(3), 266–278.

Jette, A. M., Tennstedt, S., & Crawford, S. (1995). How does formal and informal community care affect nursing home use? *The Journals of Gerontology Series B: Psychological Sciences and Social Sciences, 50*(1), S4–S12.

Jirovec, R. L., & Hyduk, C. A. (1998). The type of volunteer experiences and health among older adult volunteers. *Journal of Gerontological Social Work, 30*, 29–42.

Johnson, R., & Schaner, S. (2005). Value of unpaid activities by older Americans tops $160 billion per year. *Perspectives on Productive Aging, 4*, 1–5.

Johnson, R. W. (2008). The strains and drains of long-term care. *Virtual Mentor, 10*(6), 397.

Joint Center for Housing Studies of Harvard University. (2014). *Housing America's older adults: Meeting the needs of an aging population.* Retrieved from http://www.jchs.harvard.edu/research/housing_americas_older_adults

Jovanis, P. P. (2003). Macrointerventions: Roads, transportation systems, traffic calming, and vehicle design. In K. Warner-Schaie, H. W. Wahl, H. Mollenkopf, & F. Oswald (Eds.), *Aging independently: Living arrangement and mobility* (pp. 234–247). New York: Springer.

Kahana, E. (1982). A congruence model of person-environment interaction. In M. Lawton, P. Windley, & T. Byerts (Eds.), *Aging and the environment: Theoretical approaches* (pp. 97–121). New York, NY: Springer.

Kahana, E., & Kahana, B. (1996). Conceptual and empirical advances in understanding aging well through proactive adaptation. In V. L. Bengtson (Ed.), *Adulthood and aging: Research on continuities and discontinuities* (pp. 18–40). New York, NY: Springer.

Kahana, E., Bhatta, T., Lovegreen, L. D., Kahana, B., & Midlarsky, E. (2013). Altruism, helping, and volunteering: Pathways to well-being in late life. *Journal of Aging and Health, 25*(1), 159–187.

Kahana, E., Kelley-Moore, J., & Kahana, B. (2012). Proactive aging: A longitudinal study of stress, resources, agency, and well-being in late life. *Aging & Mental Health, 16*(4), 438–451.

Kahana, E., Midlarsky, E., & Kahana, B. (1987). Beyond dependency, autonomy, and exchange: Prosocial behavior in late-life adaptation. *Social Justice Research, 1*(4), 439–459.

Kalish, R. A. (1979). The new ageism and the failure models: A polemic. *The Gerontologist, 19*(4), 398–402.

Kane, R. A. (2012). Thirty years of home-and community-based services: Getting closer and closer to home. *Generations, 36*(1), 6–13.

Kane, R. L., Homyak, P., Bershadsky, B., & Flood, S. (2006). Variations on a theme called PACE. *The Journals of Gerontology Series A: Biological Sciences and Medical Sciences, 61*(7), 689–693. doi:61/7/689.

Kania, J., & Kramer, M. (2011). Collective impact. *Stanford Social Innovation Review, 9*(1), 36–41.

Kassner, E. (2011). *Home and community-based long-term services and supports for older people.* Washington, DC: AARP Public Policy Institute. Retrieved from http://assets.aarp.org/rgcenter/ppi/ltc/fs222-health.pdf

Kaufman, J. (2014, September 12). Elderly New Yorkers, here for the duration. *New York Times.* Retrieved from http://www.nytimes.com/2014/09/14/realestate/elderly-new-yorkers-here-for-the-duration.html?_r=0

Kaufman, S. (1986). *The aging self.* Madison: University of Wisconsin Press.

Kawachi, I., Kennedy, B. P., Lochner, K., & Prothrow-Stith, D. (1997). Social capital, income inequality, and mortality. *American Journal of Public Health, 87*(9), 1491–1498.

Kaye, H. S. (2014). Toward a model long-term services and supports system: State policy elements. *The Gerontologist,* 54 (5): 754–761. doi:10.1093/geront/gnu013

Kaye, H. S., Harrington, C., & LaPlante, M. P. (2010). Long-term care: Who gets it, who provides it, who pays, and how much? *Health Affairs, 29*(1), 11–21. doi:10.1377/hlthaff.2009.0535

Keefe, B., Geron, S. M., & Enguidanos, S. (2009). Integrating social workers into primary care: Physician and nurse perceptions of roles, benefits, and challenges. *Social Work in Health Care, 48*(6), 579–596.

Kelly, K. (1999). *New rules for the new economy.* New York, NY: Penguin.

Kelsey, J. L., Procter-Gray, E., Hannan, M. T., & Li, W. (2012). Heterogeneity of falls among older adults: Implications for public health prevention. *American Journal of Public Health, 102*(11), 2149–2156. doi:10.2105/AJPH.2012.300677

Kemper, P., Komisar, H. L., & Alecxih, L. (2005). Long-term care over an uncertain future: What can current retirees expect? *Inquiry: A Journal of Medical Care Organization, Provision and Financing, 42*(4), 335–350.

Kendig, H. (2003). Directions in environmental gerontology: A multidisciplinary field. *The Gerontologist, 43*(5), 611–614.

Kendig, H., & Stacey, B. (1997). Driving, cessation of driving, and transport safety issues among older people. *Health Promotion Journal of Australia, 7*(3), 175–179.

Kerschner, H., & Hardin, J. (2006). *Transportation innovations for seniors: A synopsis of findings in rural America.* Retrieved from http://www.ctaa.org/webmodules/webarticles/articlefiles/Senior_Rural_Innovations.pdf

Kim, J., & Cheh, V. (2010). *Effect of CPFOA partnerships on vulnerable adults' ability to age in place: Findings from the Second Community Survey of Older Adults.* Princeton, NJ: Mathematica Policy Research.

King, W. C., Belle, S. H., Brach, J. S., Simkin-Silverman, L. R., Soska, T., & Kriska, A. M. (2005). Objective measures of neighborhood environment and physical activity in older women. *American Journal of Preventive Medicine, 28*(5), 461–469.

Kington, R. S., & Nickens, H. W. (2001). Racial and ethnic differences in health: Recent trends, current patterns, future directions. In N. Smelser, W. Wilson, & F. Mitchell (Eds.), *America becoming: Racial trends and their consequences* (pp. 253–310). Washington, DC: National Academy Press.

Klinenberg, E. (2002). *Heat wave: A social autopsy of disaster in Chicago.* Chicago, IL: University of Chicago Press.

Knight, T., & Ricciardelli, L. A. (2003). Successful aging: perceptions of adults aged between 70 and 101 years. *The International Journal of Aging and Human Development, 56*(3), 223–246.

Kochera, A. (2002). *Accessibility and visitability features in single-family homes: A review of state and local activity.* Retrieved from AARP website http://assets.aarp.org/rgcenter/il/2002_03_homes.pdf

Kochera, A., Straight, A. K., & Guterbock, T. M. (2005). *Beyond 50.05: A report to the nation on livable communities: Creating environments for successful aging.* Washington, DC: AARP.

Koerner, S. S., Kenyon, D. B., & Shirai, Y. (2009). Caregiving for elder relatives: Which caregivers experience personal benefits/gains? *Archives of Gerontology and Geriatrics, 48,* 238–245.

Koffman, D., Raphael, D., & Weiner, R. (2004). *The impact of federal programs on transportation for older adults.* Washington, DC: AARP Public Policy Institute.

Kogan, A. C., Gonzalez, J., Hart, B., Halloran, S., Thomason, B., Levine, M., & Enguidanos, S. (2013). Be well: Results of a nutrition, exercise, and weight management intervention among at-risk older adults. *Journal of Applied Gerontology, 32*(7), 889–901. doi:10.1177/0733464812440043

Komisar, H. L., & Thompson, L. S. (2007). *National spending for long-term care.* Washington, DC: Georgetown University Long-Term Care Financing Project. Retrieved from Http://ltc.Georgetown.edu/pdfs/natspendfeb07.Pdf

Kosma, M. (2014). An expanded framework to determine physical activity and falls risks among diverse older adults. *Research on Aging, 36*(1), 95–114. doi:10.1177/0164027512469215

Kostyniuk, L. P., & Shope, J. T. (2003). Driving and alternatives: Older drivers in Michigan. *Journal of Safety Research, 34*(4), 407–414.

Kramer, J. S., Philliber, S., Brindis, C., Kamin, S., Chadwick, A., Revels, M., . . . Valderrama, T. (2005). Coalition models: Lessons learned from the CDC's community coalition partnership programs for the prevention of teen pregnancy. *Journal of Adolescent Health, 37*(3), S20–S30.

Krause, N. (1997). Received support, anticipated support, social class, and mortality. *Research on Aging, 19,* 387–422.

Krause, N. (2001). Social support. In R. H. Binstock & L. K. George (Eds.), *Handbook of aging and the social sciences* (pp. 272–294). New York: Academic Press.

Krieger, N., Chen, J. T., Waterman, P. D., Rehkopf, D. H., & Subramanian, S. V. (2003). Race/ethnicity, gender, and monitoring socioeconomic gradients in health: A comparison of area-based socioeconomic measures—the public health disparities geocoding project. *American Journal of Public Health, 93,* 1655–1671.

Kubisch, A. C., Auspos, P., Brown, P., Chaskin, R., Fulbright-Anderson, K., & Hamilton, R. (2002). *Voice from the field II: Reflections on comprehensive community change.* Washington, DC: Aspen Institute. Retrieved from http://www.aspeninstitute.org/sites/default/files/content/images/rcc/VoicesfromtheFieldIII.pdf

Kubzansky, L. D., Subramanian, S. V., Kawachi, I., Fay, M. E., Soobader, M., & Berkman, L. (2005). Neighborhood contextual influences on depressive symptoms in the elderly. *American Journal of Epidemiology, 162,* 253–260.

Kumar, S., Calvo, R., Avendano, M., Sivaramakrishnan, K., & Berkman, L. F. (2012). Social support, volunteering and health around the world: Cross-national evidence from 139 countries. *Social Science & Medicine, 74,* 696–706.

LaCroix, A. Z., Guralnik, J. M., Berkman, L. F., Wallace, R. B., & Satterfield, S. (1993). Maintaining mobility in late life. II. smoking, alcohol consumption, physical activity, and body mass index. *American Journal of Epidemiology, 137*(8), 858–869.

Laditka, S. B., Corwin, S. J., Laditka, J. N., Liu, R., Tseng, W., Wu, B., . . . Ivey, S. L. (2009). Attitudes about aging well among a diverse group of older Americans: Implications for promoting cognitive health. *The Gerontologist,49*(S1), S30–S39.

Lakdawalla, D. N., Bhattacharya, J., & Goldman, D. P. (2004). Are the young becoming more disabled? *Health Affairs, 23*(1), 168–176.

Lang, F. R., & Baltes, M. (1997). Being with people and being alone in late life: Costs and benefits for everyday functioning. *International Journal of Behavioral Development, 21,* 729–746.

Lauder, W., Sharkey, S., & Mummery, K. (2004). A community survey of loneliness. *Journal of Advanced Nursing, 46*(1), 88–94.

Lawton, M. P. (1982). Competence, environmental press, and the adaptation of older people. In M. Lawton, P. Windley, & T. Byerts (Eds.), *Aging and the environment: Theoretical approaches* (pp. 33–59). New York, NY: Springer.

Lawton, M. P. (1985). The elderly in context perspectives from environmental psychology and gerontology. *Environment and Behavior, 17*(4), 501–519.

Lawton, M. P. (1998). Environment and aging: Theory revisited. *Contributions to the Study of Aging, 26,* 1–32.

Lawton, M. P. (1999). Environmental taxonomy: Generalizations from research with older adults. In S. L. Friedman & T. D. Wachs (Eds.), *Measuring Environment Across the Life Span: Emerging Methods and Concepts* (pp. 91–124). Washington, DC: American Psychological Association.

Lawton, M. P., Altman, I., & Wohlwill, J. F. (1984). Dimensions of environment-behavior research. In I. Altman, M. Lawton, & J. Wohlwill (Eds.), *Elderly people and the environment* (pp. 1–15). New York, NY: Plenum.

Lawton, M. P., & Nahemow, L. (1973). Ecology and the aging process. In C. Eisdorf & M. Lawton (Eds.), *The psychology of adult development and aging* (pp. 619–670). Washington, DC: American Psychological Association.

Lawton, M. P., & Simon, B. (1968). The ecology of social relationships in housing for the elderly. *The Gerontologist, 8,* 108–115.

Lee, J. S., Zegras, P. C., & Ben-Joseph, E. (2013). Safely active mobility for urban baby boomers: The role of neighborhood design. *Accident Analysis & Prevention, 61,* 153–166. doi:10.1016/j.aap.2013.05.008

Lees, L., Slater, T., & Wyly, E. K. (2007). *Gentrification.* London, UK: Routledge.

Legislative Analyst's Office. (2009). *Considering the state costs and benefits: In-Home Supportive Services program.* Retrieved from http://www.lao.ca.gov/2010/ssrv/ihss/ihss_012110.aspx

Lehning, A., Davitt, J., Scharlach, A., & Greenfield, E. (2014). *Village sustainability and engaging a diverse membership: Key findings from a 2013 national survey.* Retrieved from http://agingand-community.com/wp-content/uploads/2014/03/Villages-Report-2013_FINAL.pdf

Lehning, A., Scharlach, A., & Davitt, J. (2015). Variations on the Village model: An emerging typology of a consumer-driven community-based initiative for older adults. *Journal of Applied Gerontology.* Published online May 5, 2015, doi: 10.1177/0733464815584667

Lehning, A., Scharlach, A., & Price Wolf, J. (2012). An emerging typology of community aging initiatives. *Journal of Community Practice, 20*(3), 293–316.

Levine, M. E., & Crimmins, E. M. (2014). Evidence of accelerated aging among African Americans and its implications for mortality. *Social Science & Medicine, 118,* 27–32.

Leyden, K. M. (2003). Social capital and the built environment: the importance of walkable neighborhoods. *American Journal of Public Health, 93*(9), 1546–1551.

Liebig, P. S., Koenig, T., & Pynoos, J. (2006). Zoning, accessory dwelling units, and family caregiving: Issues, trends, and recommendations. *Journal of Aging & Social Policy, 18*(3–4), 155–172.

Lillyman, S., & Land, L. (2007). Fear of social isolation: Results of a survey of older adults in gloucestershire. *Nursing Older People, 19*(10), 26–28. doi:10.7748/nop2007.12.19.10.26.c8245

Lindberg, B., & MacInnes, G. (2010). *Health care reform provisions affecting older adults and persons with special needs.* Washington, DC: National Academy of Elder Law Attorneys. Retrieved from https://www.naela.org/App_Themes/Public/PDF/Advocacy%20Tab/Health%20Care%20Reform/Health%20Care%20Provisions%20Affecting%20Older%20Americans.pdf

Litwak, E., & Longino, C. F. (1987). Migration patterns among the elderly: A developmental perspective. *The Gerontologist, 27*(3), 266–272.

Liu, S. Y., & Lapane, K. L. (2009). Residential modifications and decline in physical function among community—dwelling older adults. *The Gerontologist, 49*(3), 344–354. doi:10.1093/geront/gnp033

Locher, J. L., Ritchie, C. S., Roth, D. L., Baker, P. S., Bodner, E. V., & Allman, R. M. (2005). Social isolation, support, and capital and nutritional risk in an older sample: Ethnic and gender differences. *Social Science & Medicine, 60*(4), 747–761.

Longino, C. F., Perzynski, A. T., & Stoller, E. P. (2002). Pandora's briefcase: Unpacking the retirement migration decision. *Research on Aging, 24*(1), 29–49.

Lubben, J. E. (1988). Assessing social networks among elderly populations. *Family & Community Health, 11*(3), 42–52.

Lui, C., Everingham, J., Warburton, J., Cuthill, M., & Bartlett, H. (2009). What makes a community age-friendly: A review of international literature. *Australasian Journal on Ageing, 28*(3), 116–121.

Luoh, M. C., & Herzog, A. R. (2002). Individual consequences of volunteer and paid work in old age: Health and mortality. *Journal of Health and Social Behavior, 43*(4), 490–509.

Lynott, J., Taylor, A., Twaddell, H., Haase, J., Nelson, K., Ulmer, J., McCann, B., & Stollof, E. (2009). *Planning complete streets for an aging America.* Washington, DC: AARP Public Policy Institute.

Lyyra, T., & Heikkinen, R. (2006). Perceived social support and mortality in older people. *Journals of Gerontology: Series B: Psychological and Social Sciences, 61*, S147–S152.

Mack, R., Salmoni, A., Viverais-Dressler, G., Porter, E., & Garg, R. (1997). Perceived risks to independent living: The views of older, community-dwelling adults. *The Gerontologist, 37*(6), 729–736.

Maier, H., & Klumb, P. (2005). Social participation and survival at older ages: Is the effect driven by activity content or context? *European Journal of Ageing, 2*, 31–39.

Mair, C., Diez Roux, A. V., & Galea, S. (2008). Are neighborhood characteristics associated with depressive symptoms? A review of evidence. *Journal of Epidemiology & Community Health, 62*, 940–946. doi:10.1136/jech.2007.066605

Maisel, J., Smith, E., & Steinfeld, E. (2008). *Increasing home access: Designing for visitability.* Washington, DC: AARP Public Policy Institute.

Manheimer, R. J. (1998). The promise and politics of older adult education. *Research on Aging, 20*, 391–414.

Manton, K. G., Corder, L., & Stallard, E. (1997). Chronic disability trends in elderly United States populations: 1982–1994. *Proceedings of the National Academy of Sciences, 94*(6), 2593–2598.

Marcum, C. S. (2013). Age differences in daily social activities. *Research on Aging, 35*, 612–640. doi:10.1177/0164027512453468

Marks, M. B. (2012). Time banking service exchange systems: A review of the research and policy and practice implications in support of youth in transition. *Children and Youth Services Review, 34*, 1230–1236.

Marmot, M. G., Bosma, H., Hemingway, H., Brunner, E., & Stansfeld, S. (1997). Contribution of job control and other risk factors to social variations in coronary heart disease incidence. *The Lancet, 350*(9073), 235–239.

Marmot, M. G., Smith, G. D., Stansfeld, S., Patel, C., North, F., Head, J., . . . Smth, G. (1991). Health inequalities among British civil servants: The Whitehall II study. *The Lancet, 337*(8754), 1387–1393. doi:10.1016/0140-6736(91)93068-K

Marottoli, R. A., Mendes de Leon, C. F., Glass, T. A., & Williams, C. S. (1997). Driving cessation and increased depressive symptoms: Prospective evidence from the new haven EPESE. *Journal of the American Geriatrics Society, 45*(2), 202–206.

Martin, L. G., Freedman, V. A., Schoeni, R. F., & Andreski, P. M. (2009). Health and functioning among baby boomers approaching 60. *The Journals of Gerontology Series B: Psychological Sciences and Social Sciences, 64*(3), 369–377. doi:10.1093/geronb/gbn040

Mathie, A., & Cunningham, G. (2003). From clients to citizens: Asset-based community development as a strategy for community-driven development. *Development in Practice, 13*(5), 474–486.

Mathieson, K. M., Kronenfeld, J. J., & Keith, V. M. (2002). Maintaining functional independence in elderly adults the roles of health status and financial resources in predicting home modifications and use of mobility equipment. *The Gerontologist, 42*(1), 24–31.

Matz-Costa, C., Besen, E., James, J. B., & Pitt-Catsouphes, M. (2014). Differential impact of multiple levels of productive activity engagement on psychological well-being in middle and later life. *The Gerontologist, 54*(2), 277–289.

McCallum, J., Simons, L. A., Simons, J., & Friedlander, Y. (2005). Patterns and predictors of nursing home placement over 14 years: Dubbo study of elderly Australians. *Australasian Journal on Ageing, 24*(3), 169–173.

McCann, J. J., Hebert, L. E., Li, Y., Wolinsky, F. D., Gilley, D. W., Aggarwal, N. T., ... Evans, D. A. (2005). Effect of adult day care services on time to nursing home placement in older adults with Alzheimer's disease. *Gerontologist, 45*(6), 754–763.

McCormack, G. R., Giles-Corti, B., & Bulsara, M. (2008). The relationship between destination proximity, destination mix and physical activity behaviors. *Preventive Medicine, 46*(1), 33–40.

McCrae, R. R., & Costa Jr, P. T. (1990). *Personality in adulthood: Emerging lives, enduring dispositions.* New York: Guilford.

McCrea, R., Shyy, T., Western, J., & Stimson, R. J. (2005). Fear of crime in Brisbane individual, social and neighbourhood factors in perspective. *Journal of Sociology, 41*(1), 7–27.

McDonough, K. E., & Davitt, J. K. (2011). It takes a village: Community practice, social work, and aging-in-place. *Journal of Gerontological Social Work, 54*(5), 528–541.

McHugh, K. E., & Mings, R. C. (1996). The circle of migration: Attachment to place in aging. *Annals of the Association of American Geographers, 86,* 530–550.

McKnight, J. (2013). *The four-legged stool.* Dayton, OH: Kettering Foundation.

McLaughlin, S., Connell, C., Heeringa, S., Li, L., & Roberts, J. (2010). Successful aging in the united states: Prevalence estimates from a national sample of older adults. *Journal of Gerontology: Social Sciences, 65B* (2), 216–226.

Mcmahon, S., & Fleury, J. (2012). External validity of physical activity interventions for community-dwelling older adults with fall risk: A quantitative systematic literature review. *Journal of Advanced Nursing, 68*(10), 2140–2154. doi:10.1111/j.1365-2648.2012.05974.x

McPherson, M., Smith-Lovin, L., & Brashears, M. E. (2006). Social isolation is America: Changes in core discussion networks over two decades. *American Sociological Review, 71*(3), 353–375.

McWhinney-Morse, S. (2009). Beacon Hill Village. *Generations, 33*(2), 85–86.

Means, R. (1997). Home, independence and community care: Time for a wider vision? *Policy and Politics, 25,* 409–419. doi:10.1332/030557397782453228

Mendes de Leon, C. F., Glass, T. A., & Berkman, L. F. (2003). Social engagement and disability in a community population of older adults the new haven EPESE. *American Journal of Epidemiology, 157,* 633–642.

Menec, V. H., Means, R., Keating, N., Parkhurst, G., & Eales, J. (2011). Conceptualizing age-friendly communities. *Canadian Journal on Aging, 30*(3), 479–493. doi:10.1017/S0714980811000237

Messeri, P., Silverstein, M., & Litwak, E. (1993). Choosing optimal support groups: A review and reformulation. *Journal of Health and Social Behavior, 34,* 122–137.

MetLife Mature Market Institute. (2008). *The MetLife market survey of adult day services and home care costs.* Retrieved from http://www.metlife.com/assets/cao/mmi/publications/studies/mmi-studies-2008-adshc.pdf

MetLife Mature Market Institute. (2010). *The MetLife report on aging in place: Rethinking solutions to the home care challenge.* Retrieved from https://www.metlife.com/mmi/research/aging-in-place.html#insights

Miller, E. A. (2006). Explaining incremental and non-incremental change: Medicaid nursing facility reimbursement policy, 1980–98. *State Politics & Policy Quarterly, 6*(2), 117–150.

Miller, E. A. (2012). The affordable care act and long-term care: Comprehensive reform or just tinkering around the edges? *Journal of Aging & Social Policy, 24*(2), 101–117. doi:10.1080/08959420.2012.659912

Milne, D. (2012). Olmstead, new freedom, and real choice system change grants: Bringing the disability movement to older adults. *Generations*, 36(1), 44–51.

Minkler, M. (1992). Community organizing among the elderly poor in the United States: A case study. *International Journal of Health Services*, 22, 303–316.

Minkler, M., & Wallerstein, N. (2005). Improving health through community organization and community building–A health education perspective. In M. Minkler (Ed.), *Community organizing and community building for health* (2nd ed., pp. 26–50). New Brunswick, NJ: Rutgers University Press.

Montgomery, R. J. (1999). The family role in the context of long-term care. *Journal of Aging and Health*, 11, 383–416.

Mor, V., Zinn, J., Gozalo, P., Feng, Z., Intrator, O., & Grabowski, D. C. (2007). Prospects for transferring nursing home residents to the community. *Health Affairs*, 26(6), 1762–1771. doi:26/6/1762.

Morrow-Howell, N., Hinterlong, J., Rozario, P. A., & Tang, F. (2003). Effects of volunteering on the well-being of older adults. *Journal of Gerontology: Social Sciences*, 58B, S137–S145.

Morrow-Howell, N., Hinterlong, J., & Sherraden, M. (2001). *Productive aging: Concepts and challenges*. Baltimore, MD: John Hopkins University Press.

Moulaert, T., & Garon, S. (2015). Researchers behind policy development: Comparing "age-friendly cities" models in Quebec and Wallonia. *Journal of Social Work Practice*, 29(1), 23–35.

Mui, A. C. (2002). The program of all-inclusive care for the elderly (PACE) an innovative long-term care model in the united states. *Journal of Aging & Social Policy*, 13(2–3), 53–67.

Musick, M. A., & Wilson, J. (2003). Volunteering and depression: The role of psychological and social resources in different age groups. *Social science & medicine*, 56(2), 259–269.

Nasvadi, G., & Wister, A. (2009). Do restricted driver's licenses lower crash risk among older drivers? A survival analysis of insurance data from british columbia. *The Gerontologist*, 49(4), 474–484. doi:10.1093/geront/gnp039

National Alliance for Caregiving and AARP. (2004). *Caregiving in the U.S.* Retrieved from http://www.caregiving.org/data/04finalreport.pdf

National Alliance for Caregiving and AARP. (2009). *Caregiving in the U.S.: 2009*. Retrieved from http://www.caregiving.org/data/Caregiving_in_the_US_2009_full_report.pdf

National Association of Area Agencies on Aging. (2011). *The maturing of America—Communities moving forward for an aging population*. Washington, DC: Author.

National Association of Home Builders. (2014a). *Certified aging-in-place specialist (CAPS)*. Retrieved from http://www.nahb.org/category.aspx?sectionID=686

National Association of Home Builders. (2014b). *What is universal design?* Retrieved from http://www.nahb.org/generic.aspx?genericContentID=89934

National Council on Aging. (2010a). *Straight talk for seniors on health reform*. Retrieved from http://www.ncoa.org/assets/files/pdf/130812-5-key-facts.pdf

National Council on Aging. (2010b). *Strategic Metrics and Results Tracking (SMART) findings*. Washington, DC: Author.

National Council on Aging, UnitedHealthcare, & USA Today. (2013). *The United States of Aging Survey*. Retrieved from http://www.ncoa.org/assets/files/pdf/united-states-of-aging/2013-survey/USA13-Full-Report.pdf

National Highway Traffic Safety Administration. (2014). *Handbook for designing roadways for the aging population*. Retrieved from http://safety.fhwa.dot.gov/older_users/handbook/aging_driver_handbook_2014_final%20.pdf

Neal, M., DeLaTorre, A., & Carder, P. (2014). Age-friendly Portland: A university-city-community partnership. *Journal of Aging & Social Policy*, 26(1), 88. doi:10.1080/08959420.2014.854651

Neidrick, T. J., Fick, D. M., & Loeb, S. J. (2012). Physical activity promotion in primary care targeting the older adult. *Journal of the American Academy of Nurse Practitioners, 24*(7), 405–416. doi:10.1111/j.1745-7599.2012.00703.x

Nelson\Nygaard Consulting Associates. (2002). *San Francisco Bay area older adults transportation study: Final report.* San Francisco, CA: Author.

Neugarten, B. L., Havighurst, R. J., & Tobin, S. S. (1961). The measurement of life satisfaction. *Journal of Gerontology, 16,* 134–143.

Newcomer, R., & Griffin, C. (2000). Community planning and the elderly. In R. Rubinstein, M. Moss, & M. Kleban (Eds.), *The many dimensions of aging* (pp. 239–252). New York, NY: Springer.

Newman, K. S. (2003). *Different shade of gray: Midlife and beyond in the inner city.* New York, NY: New Press.

New York Academy of Medicine. (2012). *Creating an age-friendly NYC one neighborhood at a time.* New York, NY: New York Academy of Medicine.

Ng, T., & Harrington, C. (2011). *Medicaid home—and community-based service programs: Data update.* Washington, DC: Kaiser Family Foundation.

NORC Blueprint. (2011). *NORC Blueprint: A guide to community action.* Retrieved from http://www.norcblueprint.org/

Norris-Baker, C., & Scheidt, R. J. (1990). Place attachment among older residents of a "ghost town": A transactional approach. *Journal of the Environmental Design Research Association, 21,* 333–342.

Nutbeam, D. (1998). Evaluating health promotion—progress, problems and solutions. *Health Promotion International, 13*(1), 27–44.

Ogden, L. L., Richards, C. L., & Shenson, D. (2012). Clinical preventive services for older adults: The interface between personal health care and public health services. *American Journal of Public Health, 102*(3), 419–425. doi:10.2105/AJPH.2011.300353

Ohmer, M. L. (2008). The relationship between citizen participation and organizational processes and outcomes and the benefits of citizen participation in neighborhood organizations. *Journal of Social Service Research, 34*(4), 41–60.

Okun, M. A., Yeung, E. W., & Brown, S. (2013). Volunteering by older adults and risk of mortality: A meta-analysis. *Psychology and Aging, 28*(2), 564–577.

Oman, D., Thoresen, C., & McMahon, K. (1999). Volunteerism and mortality among older adults: Findings from a national sample. *Journal of Health Psychology, 4,* 301–316.

Ormond, B. A., Black, K. J., Tilly, J., & Thomas, S. (2004). *Supportive services programs in naturally occurring retirement communities.* Washington, DC: US Department of Health and Human Services, Assistant Secretary for Planning and Evaluation, Office of Disability, Aging, and Long-Term Care Policy.

Oswald, F., & Rowles, G. D. (2006). Beyond the relocation trauma in old age: New trends in today's elders' residential decisions. In H. Wahl, C. Tesch-Römer, & A. Hoff (Eds.), *New dynamics in old age: Environmental and societal perspectives* (pp. 127–152). Amityville, NY: Baywood.

Ouwehand, C., de Ridder, D. T., & Bensing, J. M. (2007). A review of successful aging models: Proposing proactive coping as an important additional strategy. *Clinical Psychology Review, 27*(8), 873–884.

Palley, E., & Rozario, P. A. (2007). The application of the Olmsted decision on housing and eldercare. *Journal of Gerontological Social Work, 49*(1–2), 81–96.

Pardasani, M. P., & Thompson, P. (2012). Senior centers: Innovative and emerging models. *Journal of Applied Gerontology, 31,* 52–77.

Parisi, J. M., Kuo, J., Rebok, G. W., Xue, Q. L., Fried, L. P., Gruenewald, T. L., . . . Carlson, M. (2014). Increases in lifestyle activities as a result of Experience Corps participation. *Journal of Urban Health, 92*(1), 1–12.

Parker, L. A., & Betz, D. (1996). *Diverse partners in planning and decision making*. Washington State University, Cooperative Extension. Retrieved from http://extension.usu.edu/files/publications/publication/pub__9215755.pdf

Patterson, A. C., & Veenstra, G. (2010). Loneliness and risk of mortality: A longitudinal investigation in alameda county, California. *Social Science & Medicine, 71*(1), 181–186. doi:10.1016/j.socscimed.2010.03.024

Paul, C., Ayis, S., & Ebrahim, S. (2006). Psychological distress, loneliness and disability in old age. *Psychology, Health & Medicine, 11*(2), 221–232.

Peebles, V., & Kehn, M. (2014). *Innovations in home-and community-based services: Highlights from a review of services available to money follows the person participants*. Retrieved from http://www.medicaid.gov/medicaid-chip-program-information/by-topics/long-term-services-and-supports/downloads/mfp-field-reports-2014.pdf

Perry, T. E., Andersen, T. C., & Kaplan, D. B. (2013). Relocation remembered: Perspectives on senior transitions in the living environment. *The Gerontologist, 54*(1), 75–81.

Peterson, M. J., Giuliani, C., Morey, M. C., Pieper, C. F., Evenson, K. R., Mercer, V., ... Simonsick, E. M. (2009). Physical activity as a preventative factor for frailty: the health, aging, and body composition study. *The Journals of Gerontology Series A: Biological Sciences and Medical Sciences, 64*(1), 61–68.

Pfeffer, J., & Salancik, G. R. (1978). *The external control of organizations: A resource dependence approach*. New York, NY: Harper and Row.

Pham, H. H., Schrag, D., Hargraves, J. L., & Bach, P. B. (2005). Delivery of preventive services to older adults by primary care physicians. *JAMA: Journal of the American Medical Association, 294*(4), 473–481.

Phelan, E. A., Anderson, L. A., Lacroix, A. Z., & Larson, E. B. (2004). Older adults' views of "successful aging"—how do they compare with researchers' definitions? *Journal of the American Geriatrics Society, 52*(2), 211–216.

Philadelphia Corporation for Aging. (2011a). *Laying the foundation for an age-friendly Philadelphia: A progress report*. Retrieved from http://www.pcacares.org/Files/PCA_Age-Friendly_WhitePaper_web.pdf?utm_source=webpage&utm_medium=whitepaper&utm_term=Age-Friendly_Philadelphia&utm_content=web_pdf&utm_campaign=Age-Friendly_Philadelphia

Philadelphia Corporation for Aging. (2011b). *Proposed zoning code and older Philadelphians: An age-friendly Philadelphia report*. Retrieved from http://www.pcacares.org/files/Report_on_Zoning_Code_and_Aging_June_2011_FINAL

Phillipson, C. (2007). The "elected" and the "excluded": Sociological perspectives on the experience of place and community in old age. *Ageing & Society, 27*, 321–342.

Phillipson, C., Bernard, M., Phillips, J., & Ogg, J. (1999). Older people's experiences of community life: Patterns of neighbouring in three urban areas. *The Sociological Review, 47*(4), 715–743.

Phillipson, C., Scharf, T., Kingston, P., & Smith, A. E. (2001). Social exclusion and older people: Exploring the connections. *Education and Ageing, 16*(3), 303–320.

Pinquart, M., & Sorensen, S. (2001). Influences on loneliness in older adults: A meta-analysis. *Basic and Applied Social Psychology, 23*(4), 245–266.

Pinquart, M., & Sörensen, S. (2003). Differences between caregivers and noncaregivers in psychological health and physical health: A meta-analysis. *Psychology and Aging, 18*(2), 250.

Pinquart, M., & Sorensen, S. (2007). Correlates of physical health of informal caregivers: A meta-analysis. *The Journals of Gerontology Series B: Psychological Sciences and Social Sciences, 62*(2), P126–P137. doi:62/2/P126

Plater-Zyberk, E., & Ball, S. (2012). Longevity and urbanism. In H. Cisneros, M. Dyer-Chamberlain, & J. Hickie (Eds.), *Independent for life: Homes and neighborhoods for an aging America* (pp. 197–208). Austin: University of Texas Press.

Plouffe, L. A., & Kalache, A. (2011). Politics, policy and public health: Making communities age friendly: State and municipal initiatives in Canada and other countries. *Gaceta Sanitaria, 25*, 131–137. doi:10.1016/j.gaceta.2011.11.001

Pollak, P. B. (1994). Rethinking zoning to accommodate the elderly in single family housing. *Journal of the American Planning Association, 60*(4), 521–531. doi:10.1080/01944369408975608

Poor, S., Baldwin, C., & Willet, J. (2012). The village movement empowers older adults to stay connected to home and community. *Generations, 36*(1), 112–117.

Potter, G. G., Plassman, B. L., Burke, J. R., Kabeto, M. U., Langa, K. M., Llewellyn, D. J., . . . Steffens, D. C. (2009). Cognitive performance and informant reports in the diagnosis of cognitive impairment and dementia in African Americans and whites. *Alzheimer's & Dementia, 5*(6), 445–453.

Prenda, K. M., & Lachman, M. E. (2001). Planning for the future: A life management strategy for increasing control and life satisfaction in adulthood. *Psychology and Aging, 16*(2), 206.

Price, R. H., & Behrens, T. (2003). Working Pasteur's quadrant: Harnessing science and action for community change. *American Journal of Community Psychology, 31*(3–4), 219–223.

Pruchno, R. (2012). Not your mother's old age: Baby boomers at age 65. *The Gerontologist, 52*(2), 149–152. doi:10.1093/geront/gns038

Pucher, J., Buehler, R., Merom, D., & Bauman, A. (2011). Walking and cycling in the united states, 2011–2009: Evidence from the national household travel surveys. *American Journal of Public Health, 101*(S1), S310–S317.

Pucher, J., & Renne, J. L. (2003). Socioeconomics of urban travel: Evidence from the 2001 NHTS. *Transportation Quarterly, 57*(3), 49–77.

Putnam, R. D. (2000). *Bowling alone: The collapse and revival of American community.* New York, NY: Simon and Schuster.

Pynoos, J., Caraviello, R., & Cicero, C. (2009). Lifelong housing: The anchor in aging-friendly communities. *Generations, 33*(2), 26–32.

Pynoos, J., Liebig, P., Alley, D., & Nishita, C. (2005). Homes of choice: Towards more effective linkages between housing and services. *Journal of Housing for the Elderly, 18*(3–4), 5–49.

Pynoos, J., Nishita, C., Cicero, C., & Caraviello, R. (2008). Aging in place, housing, and the law. *The Elder Law Journal, 16*, 77–105.

Ramirez, L. K. B., Hoehner, C. M., Brownson, R. C., Cook, R., Orleans, C. T., Hollander, M., . . . & Wilkinson, W. (2006). Indicators of activity-friendly communities: an evidence-based consensus process. *American Journal of Preventive Medicine, 31*(6), 515–524.

Rattan, S. I. (2008). Hormesis in aging. *Ageing Research Reviews, 7*(1), 63–78.

Redfoot, D., Feinberg, L., & Houser, A. (2013). The aging of the baby boom and the growing care gap: A look at future declines in the availability of family caregivers. Washington, DC: AARP Public Policy Institute. Retrieved from http://www.aarp.org/content/dam/aarp/research/public_policy_institute/ltc/2013/baby-boom-and-the-growing-care-gap-insight-AARP-ppi-ltc.pdf

Reeder, B., Meyer, E., Lazar, A., Chaudhuri, S., Thompson, H. J., & Demiris, G. (2013). Review: Framing the evidence for health smart homes and home-based consumer health technologies as a public health intervention for independent aging: A systematic review. *International Journal of Medical Informatics, 82*, 565–579. doi:10.1016/j.ijmedinf.2013.03.007

Repp, T. (n.d.). *Planning tomorrow today: Using the "Contra Costa for Every Generation" civic engagement effort as a model for strategic planning.* Retrieved from http://mackcenter.berkeley.edu/assets/files/edp_cases/PAE/TOC-PAE-20.pdf

Retting, R. A., Ferguson, S. A., & McCartt, A. T. (2003). A review of evidence-based traffic engineering measures designed to reduce pedestrian-motor vehicle crashes. *American Journal of Public Health, 93*(9), 1456–1463.

Richardson, W. C., & Allegrante, J. P. (2002). Shaping the future of health through global partnerships. In C. E. Koop, C. E. Pearson, & M. R. Schwarz (Eds.), *Critical Issues in Global Health (pp. 375–83).* San Francisco, CA: Jossey-Bass.

Riggs, J. A. (2003). A family caregiver policy agenda for the twenty-first century. *Generations*, 27(4), 68–73.

Ritter, A. S., Straight, A., & Evans, E. L. (2002). *Understanding senior transportation: Report and analysis of a survey of consumers age 50*. Washington, DC: AARP Public Policy Institute.

Rizzo, V. M., & Rowe, J. M. (2006). Studies of the cost-effectiveness of social work services in aging: A review of the literature. *Research on Social Work Practice, 16*(1), 67–73.

Robert, S. A., & Li, L. W. (2001). Age variation in the relationship between community socio-economic status and adult health. *Research on Aging, 23*(2), 234–259.

Robert Wood Johnson Foundation. (2011). *Program results report—Community Partnerships for Older Adults*. Retrieved from http://www.rwjf.org/content/dam/farm/reports/program_results_reports/2011/rwjf71882

Robert Wood Johnson Foundation. (2013). *Cash and counseling*. Retrieved from http://www.rwjf.org/en/research-publications/find-rwjf-research/2013/06/cash---counseling.html

Roberts, S. G., & Dunbar R. I. (2011). The costs of family and friends: An 18-month longitudinal study of relationship maintenance and decay. *Evolution and Human Behavior, 32*, 186–197.

Robison, J., Shugrue, N., Fortinsky, R. H., & Gruman, C. (2014). Long-term supports and services planning for the future: Implications from a statewide survey of baby boomers and older adults. *Gerontologist, 54*(2), 297–313.

Robison, J., Shugrue, N., Porter, M., Fortinsky, R. H., & Curry, L. A. (2012). Transition from home care to nursing home: Unmet needs in a home—and community-based program for older adults. *Journal of Aging & Social Policy, 24*(3), 251–270. doi:10.1080/08959420.2012.676315

Rodin, J., & Langer, E. (1977). Long-term effects of a control-relevant intervention with the institutionalized aged. *Journal of Personality and Social Psychology, 35*, 897–902.

Rogowski, J. A., Freedman, V. A., & Schoeni, R. F. (2006). *Neighborhoods and the health of the elderly: Challenges using national survey data* (Population Studies Center research report 06-600). Retrieved from http://www.psc.isr.umich.edu/pubs/pdf/rr06-600.pdf

Rolland, Y., van Kan, G. A., & Vellas, B. (2010). Healthy brain aging: role of exercise and physical activity. *Clinics in Geriatric Medicine, 26*(1), 75–87.

Rosenbaum, S., Teitelbaum, J., & Stewart, A. (2002). Olmstead VLC: Implications for Medicaid and other publicly funded health services. *Health Matrix, 12*, 93–138.

Rosenbloom, S. (2004, November). Mobility of the elderly: Good news and bad news. In *Transportation in an aging society: Transportation Research Board conference proceedings 27* (pp. 3–21). Washington, DC: National Research Council.

Rosenbloom, S. (2009). Meeting transportation needs in an aging-friendly community. *Generations, 33*, 33–43.

Rosenbloom, S., & Herbel, S. (2009). The safety and mobility patterns of older women: Do current patterns foretell the future? *Public Works Management & Policy, 13*(4), 338–353.

Rosow, I. (1974). *Socialization to old age*. Oakland: University of California Press.

Rosso, A., Auchincloss, A., & Michael, Y. (2011). The urban built environment and mobility in older adults: A comprehensive review. *Journal of Aging Research, 2011*, 1–10.

Rothman, J. (2007). Multi modes of intervention at the macro level. *Journal of Community Practice, 15*(4), 11–40.

Rowe, J. W., & Kahn, R. L. (1998). *Successful aging: The MacArthur Foundation study*. New York, NY: Pantheon.

Rowles, G. D. (1983). Place and personal identity in old age: Observations from Appalachia. *Journal of Environmental Psychology, 3*, 299–313.

Rozario, P. A., & Palley, E. (2008). When the private sphere goes public: Exploring the issues facing family caregiver organizations in the development of long-term care policies. *Social Work in Public Health, 23*(4), 49–68.

Rudinger, G., Donaghy, K., & Poppelreuter, S. (2004). Societal trends, mobility behaviour and sustainable transport in Europe and North America: The European union network STELLA. *European Journal of Ageing, 1*(1), 95–101.

Rudman, D. L., Friedland, J., Chipman, M., & Sciortino, P. (2006). Holding on and letting go: The perspectives of pre-seniors and seniors on driving self-regulation in later life. *Canadian Journal on Aging/La Revue Canadienne Du Vieillissement, 25*(01), 65–76.

Ruggiano, N., Shtompel, N., Hristidis, V., Roberts, L., Grochowski, J., & Brown, E. L. (2012). Need and potential use of information technology for case manager–physician communication in home care. *Home Health Care Management & Practice, 24,* 292–297. doi:10.1177/1084822312459615

Ruggiano, N., & Taliaferro, J. D. (2012). Resource dependency and agent theories: A framework for exploring nonprofit leaders' resistance to lobbying. *Journal of Policy Practice, 11*(4), 219–235.

Ryff, C. D. (1989). Happiness is everything, or is it? Explorations on the meaning of psychological well-being. *Journal of personality and social psychology, 57*(6), 1069.

Ryff, C. D., & Singer, B. (2009). Understanding healthy aging: Key components and their integration. In V. L. Bengtson, D. Gans, N. M. Putney, & M. Silverstein (Eds.), *Handbook of theories of aging* (2nd ed., pp. 117–144). New York, NY: Springer.

Saelens, B. E., Sallis, J. F., Black, J. B., & Chen, D. (2003). Neighborhood-based differences in physical activity: An environment scale evaluation. *American Journal of Public Health, 93*(9), 1552–1558.

Salamon, L. M. (2012). *The state of nonprofit America.* Washington, DC: Brookings Institution Press.

Sallis, J. F., & Kerr, J. (2006). Physical activity and the built environment. *President's Council on Physical Fitness and Sports Research Digest, 7,* 1–8.

Sambamoorthi, U., & Findley, P. A. (2005). Who are the elderly who never receive influenza immunization? *Preventive Medicine, 40*(4), 469–478. doi:10.1016/j.ypmed.2004.07.017

Sampson, R. J., Raudenbush, S., & Earls, F. (1997). Neighborhoods and violent crime: A multilevel study of collective efficacy. *Science, 277*(5328), 918–924.

Sands, L. P., Xu, H., Thomas, J., III, Paul, S., Craig, B. A., Rosenman, M., Doebbeling, C. C., & Weiner, M. (2012). Volume of home- and community-based services and time to nursing-home placement. *Medicare & Medicaid Research Review, 2*(3), E1–E21.

Sands, L. P., Xu, H., Weiner, M., Rosenman, M. B., Craig, B. A., & Thomas, J., III. (2008). Comparison of resource utilization for Medicaid dementia patients using nursing homes versus home and community based waivers for long-term care. *Medical Care, 46*(4), 449–453. doi:10.1097/MLR.0b013e3181621eae

Sartori, A. C., Wadley, V. G., Clay, O. J., Parisi, J. M., Rebok, G. W., & Crowe, M. (2011). The relationship between cognitive function and life space: The potential role of personal control beliefs. *Psychology and Aging, 27*(2), 364–374. doi:10.1037/a0025212

Satariano, W. A. (1997). The disabilities of aging—looking to the physical environment. *American Journal of Public Health, 87*(3), 331–332.

Satariano, W. A., & McAuley, E. (2003). Promoting physical activity among older adults: From ecology to the individual. *American Journal of Preventive Medicine, 25*(3), 184–192.

Satariano, W. A., Guralnik, J. M., Jackson, R. J., Marottoli, R. A., Phelan, E. A., & Prohaska, T. R. (2012). Mobility and aging: New directions for public health action. *American Journal of Public Health, 102,* 1508–1515.

Satariano, W. A., Scharlach, A. E., & Lindeman, D. (2014). Aging, place, and technology: Toward improving access and wellness in older populations. *Journal of Aging and Health, 26*(8), 1373–1389.

Scharf, T., Phillipson, C., & Kingston, P. (2003). *Older people in deprived neighbourhoods: Social exclusion and quality of life in old age.* Swindon, UK: ESRC Growing Older Programme.

Scharlach, A. E. (2009). Creating aging-friendly communities. *Generations, 33*(2), 5–11.

Scharlach, A. E. (2012). Creating aging-friendly communities in the United States. *Ageing International*, 37(1), 25–38. doi:10.1007/s12126-011-9140-1

Scharlach, A. E. (in press). Age-friendly cities: For whom? By whom? For what purpose? In T. Moulaert & S. Garon (Eds.), *Age-friendly cities in international comparison: Political lessons, scientific avenues, and democratic issues*. New York, NY: Springer.

Scharlach, A. E., Davitt, J. K., Lehning, A. J., Greenfield, E. A., & Graham, C. L. (2014). Does the Village model help to foster age-friendly communities? *Journal of Aging and Social Policy*, 26, 181–196.

Scharlach, A. E., Graham, C., & Lehning, A. (2012). The "village" model: A consumer-driven approach for aging in place. *The Gerontologist*, 52, 418–427.

Scharlach, A. E., & Hoshino, K. (Eds.). (2012). *Healthy Aging in Sociocultural Context*. New York, NY: Routledge.

Scharlach, A. E., Kellam, R., Ong, N., Baskin, A., Goldstein, C., & Fox, P. J. (2006). Cultural attitudes and caregiver service use. *Journal of Gerontological Social Work*, 47, 133–156. doi:10.1300/J083v47n01_09

Scharlach, A. E., & Lehning, A. J. (2013). Ageing-friendly communities and social inclusion in the United States of America. *Ageing and Society*, 33(01), 110–136.

Scheidt, R. J., & Norris-Baker, C. (2003). The general ecological model revisited: Evolution, current status, and continuing challenges. *Annual Review of Gerontology and Geriatrics*, 23, 34–58.

Scheidt, R. J., & Windley, P. G. (2006). Environmental gerontology: Progress in the post-Lawton era. In J. E. Birren & K. W. Schaie (Eds.), *Handbook of the psychology of aging* (6th ed., pp. 105–125). New York, NY: Academic Press.

Schill, M. H. (2005). Regulations and housing development: What we know. *Cityscape*, 8(1), 5–19.

Schilling, J., & Linton, L. S. (2005). The public health roots of zoning: In search of active living's legal genealogy. *American Journal of Preventive Medicine*, 28(2), 96–104.

Schnittker, J. (2007). Look (closely) at all the lonely people: Age and the social psychology of social support. *Journal of Aging and Health*, 19(4), 659–682. doi:19/4/659

Schoenborn, C. A., Vickerie, J. L., & Powell-Griner, E. (2006). Health characteristics of adults 55 years of age and over: United States, 2000–2003. *Advance Data From Vital and Health Statistics*, 370. Retrieved from http://www.cdc.gov/nchs/data/ad/ad370.pdf

Schoeni, R. F., Freedman, V. A., & Wallace, R. B. (2001). Persistent, consistent, widespread, and robust? another look at recent trends in old-age disability. *The Journals of Gerontology Series B: Psychological Sciences and Social Sciences*, 56(4), S206–S218.

Schoeni, R. F., Martin, L. G., Andreski, P. M., & Freedman, V. A. (2005). Persistent and growing socioeconomic disparities in disability among the elderly: 1982–2002. *American Journal of Public Health*, 95, 2065–2070. doi:10.2105/AJPH.2004.048744

Schofer, E., & Fourcade-Gourinchas, M. (2001). The structural contexts of civic engagement: Voluntary association membership in comparative perspective. *American Sociological Review*, 66(6), 806–828.

Schonfelder, S., & Axhausen, K. W. (2003). Activity spaces: Measures of social exclusion? *Transport Policy*, 10, 273–286.

Schore, J., Foster, L., & Phillips, B. (2007). Consumer enrollment and experiences in the Cash and Couseling program. *Health Services Research*, 42(1), 446–466.

Schulz, R. (1976). Effects of control and predictability on the physical and psychological well-being of the institutionalized aged. *Journal of Personality and Social Psychology*, 33(5), 563.

Schulz, R., & Heckhausen, J. (1996). A life span model of successful aging. *American Psychologist*, 51(7), 702.

Schulz, R., Heckhausen, J., & O'Brien, A. T. (1994). Control and the disablement process in the elderly. *Journal of Social Behavior & Personality*, 9(5), 139–152.

Schutzer, K. A., & Graves, B. S. (2004). Barriers and motivations to exercise in older adults. *Preventive Medicine, 39*(5), 1056–1061.

Seddon, D., & Robinson, C. A. (2001). Carers of older people with dementia: assessment and the Carers Act. *Health & Social Care in the Community, 9*(3), 151–158.

Seeman, M., & Lewis, S. (1995). Powerlessness, health and mortality: A longitudinal study of older men and mature women. *Social Science & Medicine,41*(4), 517–525.

Seeman, T. E., Berkman, L. F., Kohout, F., Lacroix, A., Glynn, R., & Blazer, D. (1993). Intercommunity variations in the association between social ties and mortality in the elderly: A comparative analysis of three communities. *Annals of Epidemiology, 3*(4), 325–335.

Seeman, T. E., Kaplan, G. A., Knudsen, L., Cohen, R., & Guralnik, J. (1987). Social network ties and mortality among the elderly in the Alameda county study. *American Journal of Epidemiology, 126*(4), 714–723.

Seyfang, G. (2003). "With a little help from my friends": Evaluating time banks as a tool for community self-help. *Local Economy, 18*(3), 253–257.

Shapiro, A., & Taylor, M. (2002). Effects of a community-based early intervention program on the subjective well-being, institutionalization, and mortality of low-income elders. *The Gerontologist, 42*(3), 334–341.

Shaw, B., Krause, N., Liang, J., & Bennett, J. (2007). Tracking changes in social relations throughout late life. *Journal of Gerontology; Social Sciences, 62B*(2), S90–S99.

Sheehan, N. W., & Guzzardo, M. T. (2008). Resident service coordinators: Roles and challenges in senior housing. *Journal of Housing for the Elderly, 22*(3), 240–262.

Shenson, D., Adams, M., Bolen, J., & Anderson, L. (2011). Routine checkups don't ensure that seniors get preventive services. *The Journal of Family Practice, 60*(1), E1–E10. doi:jfp_6001l

Shortell, S. M., Bennett C. L., & Byck, G. R. (1998). Assessing the impact of continuous quality improvement on clinical practice: What it will take. *Milbank Quarterly, 76* (4), 593–624.

Silver, H., & Miller, S. (2003). Social exclusion. *Indicators-New York, 2*(3), 5–21.

Simonsick, E. M., Lafferty, M. E., Phillips, C. L., Mendes de Leon, C. F., Kasl, S. V., Seeman, T. E., . . . Lemke, J. H. (1993). Risk due to inactivity in physically capable older adults. *American Journal of Public Health, 83*(10), 1443–1450.

Singelenberg, J., Stolarz, H., & McCall, M. E. (2014). Integrated service areas: An innovative approach to housing, services and supports for older persons ageing in place. *Journal of Community & Applied Social Psychology, 24*(1), 69–73.

Singh, G. K., Siahpush, M., & Kogan, M. D. (2010). Neighborhood socioeconomic conditions, built environments, and childhood obesity. *Health Affairs, 29*(3), 503–512.

Sixsmith, A., & Sixsmith, J. (2008). Ageing in place in the United Kingdom. *Ageing International, 32*(3), 219–235. doi:10.1007/s12126-008-9019-y

Smart Growth America. (2014). *National complete streets coalition.* Retrieved from http://www.smartgrowthamerica.org/complete-streets

Smith, R., Lehning, A., & Dunkie, R. (2013). Conceptualizing age-friendly community characteristics in a sample of urban elders: Exploratory factor analysis. *Journal of Gerontological Social Work, 56* (2), 90–111.

Smith, S. K., Rayer, S., & Smith, E. A. (2008). Aging and disability: Implications for the housing industry and housing policy in the United States. *Journal of the American Planning Association, 74*(3), 289–306.

Smith Conway, K., & Houtenville, A. J. (2003). Out with the old, in with the old: A closer look at younger versus older elderly migration. *Social Science Quarterly, 84,* 309–328.

Spillman, B. C., & Pezzin, L. E. (2000). Potential and active family caregivers: Changing networks and the "sandwich generation." *Milbank Quarterly, 78*(3), 347–374.

Stahl, T., Rutten, A., Nutbeam, D., Bauman, A., Kannas, L., Abel, T., . . . van der Zee, J. (2001). The importance of the social environment for physically active lifestyle: Results from an international study. *Social Science & Medicine, 52,* 1–10.

Staplin, L., Harkey, D., Lococo, K., & Tarawneh, M. (1997). *Intersection geometric design and operational guidelines for older drivers and pedestrians: Vol. 1. Final report*. McLean, VA: Federal Highway Administration.

Stearns, S. C., Bernard, S. L., Fasick, S. B., Schwartz, R., Konrad, T. R., Ory, M. G., & DeFriese, G. H. (2000). The economic implications of self-care: The effect of lifestyle, functional adaptations, and medical self-care among a national sample of Medicare beneficiaries. *American Journal of Public Health, 90*(10), 1608–1612.

Steinfeld, E., Levine, D. R., & Shea, S. M. (1998). Home modifications and the fair housing law. *Technology and Disability, 8*(1), 15–35.

Stellefson, M., Chaney, B., Barry, A. E., Chavarria, E., Tennant, B., Walsh-Childers, K., . . . Zagora, J. (2013). Web 2.0 chronic disease self management for older adults: A systematic review. *Journal of Medical Internet Research, 15*(2), 166–179.

Steptoe, A., Hamer, M., & Chida, Y. (2007). The effects of acute psychological stress on circulating inflammatory factors in humans: a review and meta-analysis. *Brain, Behavior, and Immunity, 21*(7), 901–912.

Steptoe, A., Shankar, A., Demakakos, P., & Wardle, J. (2013). Social isolation, loneliness, and all-cause mortality in older men and women. *Proceedings of the National Academy of Sciences of the United States of America, 110*(15) 5797–5801.

Sterns, R., Antenucci, V., Nelson, C., & Glasgow, N. (2003). Public transportation: Options to maintain mobility for life. *Generations, 27*(2), 14–19.

Stevens, B., Lavin, B., & Cheh, V. (2006). *Improving the connectedness of long-term care providers: Cross site report*. Princeton, NJ: Mathematica Policy Research.

Stevens, J. A., Corso, P. S., Finkelstein, E. A., & Miller, T. R. (2006). The costs of fatal and non-fatal falls among older adults. *Injury Prevention, 12*(5), 290–295. doi:12/5/290

Stevens, N. L., & van Tilburg, T. (2000). Stimulating friendship in later life: A strategy for reducing loneliness among older women. *Educational Gerontology, 26*, 15–35.

Stewart, A. (2014). Blooming prairie city council adopts golf carts ordinance. *The Leader*. Retrieved from http://www.southernminn.com/blooming_prairie_leader/news/article_91a35001-e4b8-5b53-83a3-99ca0dfbb684.html

Stoecker, R. R. (2005). Is community informatics good for communities? Questions confronting an emerging field. *The Journal of Community Informatics, 1*(3). Retrieved from http://www.ci-journal.net/index.php/ciej/article/view/183/129

Stokols, D. (1992). Establishing and maintaining healthy environments: Toward a social ecology of health promotion. *American Psychologist, 47*, 6–22.

Stone, R. I., & Reinhard, S. C. (2007). The place of assisted living in long-term care and related service systems. *The Gerontologist, 47*(Suppl 1), 23–32. doi:10.1093/geront/47.Supplement_1.23

Stutts, J. C. (2003). The safety of older drivers: The U.S. perspective. In K. Warner-Schaie, H. W. Wahl, H. Mollenkopf, & F. Oswald (Eds.), *Aging independently: Living arrangement and mobility* (pp. 192–204). New York: Springer Publishing Company.

Suarez-Rubio, M., Lookingbill, T. R., & Elmore, A. J. (2012). Exurban development derived from Landsat from 1986 to 2009 surrounding the District of Columbia, USA. *Remote Sensing of Environment, 124*, 360–370.

Suen, S. L., & Sen, L. (2004). Mobility options for seniors. In *Transportation in an aging society: Transportation Research Board conference proceedings 27* (pp. 97–113). Washington, DC: National Research Council.

Summer, L. (2007). *Medicaid and long-term care*. Washington, DC: Georgetown University Long-Term Care Financing Project. Retrieved from http://ltc.georgetown.edu/pdfs/medicaid2006.pdf

Sundström, G., Johansson, L., & Hassing, L. B. (2002). The shifting balance of long-term care in Sweden. *The Gerontologist, 42*(3), 350–355.

Szanton, S. L., Thorpe, R. J., Boyd, C., Tanner, E. K., Leff, B., Agree, E., . . . Gitlin, L. N. (2011). Community aging in place, advancing better living for elders: A bio-behavioral-environmental intervention to improve function and health-related quality of life in disabled older adults. *Journal of the American Geriatrics Society, 59*(12), 2314–2320. doi:10.1111/j.1532-5415.2011.03698.x

Szinovacz, M. E., & Davey, A. (2008). The division of parent care between spouses. *Ageing and Society, 28*(04), 571–597.

Szold, T. (2002). What difference has the ADA made? *Planning, 68*(4), 10–15.

Szreter, S., & Woolcock, M. (2004). Health by association? Social capital, social theory, and the political economy of public health. *International Journal of Epidemiology, 33*(4), 650–667.

Tabbarah, M., Silverstein, M., & Seeman, T. (2000). A health and demographic profile of non-institutionalized older Americans residing in environments with home modifications. *Journal of Aging and Health, 12*(2), 204–228.

Talley, R. C., & Crews, J. E. (2007). Framing the public health of caregiving. *American Journal of Public Health, 97*(2), 224–228.

Tang, F., & Lee, Y. (2011). Social support networks and expectations for aging in place and moving. *Research on Aging, 33*(4), 444–464.

Task Force on Community Preventive Services. (2002). The effectiveness of interventions to increase physical activity: A systematic review. *American Journal of Preventive Medicine, 22*(4), 73–107.

Tate, R. B., Lah, L., & Cuddy, T. E. (2003). Definition of successful aging by elderly Canadian males: The Manitoba follow-up study. *The Gerontologist, 43*(5), 735–744.

Taylor, B. D., & Tripodes, S. (2001). The effects of driving cessation on the elderly with dementia and their caregivers. *Accident Analysis & Prevention, 33*(4), 519–528.

Tennstedt, S., Howland, J., Lachman, M., Peterson, E., Kasten, L., & Jette, A. (1998). A randomized, controlled trial of a group intervention to reduce fear of falling and associated activity restriction in older adults. *The Journals of Gerontology Series B: Psychological Sciences and Social Sciences, 53*(6), P384–P392.

Terrazas, A. (2009). Older immigrants in the United States. Retrieved from http://globalaging. org/elderrights/us/2009/immigrants.pdf

Thomas, G. S. (2012, August 31). Population extremes: The youngest and oldest places in America. *The Business Journals.* Retrieved from http://www.bizjournals.com/bizjournals/ on-numbers/scott-thomas/2012/08/sumter-county-fla-has-oldest.html

Thomas, K. S. (2014). The relationship between Older Americans Act in-home services and low-care residents in nursing homes. *Journal of Aging & Health, 26*(2), 250–260. doi:10.1177/0898264313513611

Thomas, K. S., & Mor, V. (2013). The relationship between Older Americans Act Title III state expenditures and prevalence of low-care nursing home residents. *Health Services Research, 48*(3), 1215–1226. doi:10.1111/1475-6773.12015

Thomas, W. H., & Blanchard, J. M. (2009). Moving beyond place: Aging in community. *Generations, 33*(2), 12–17.

Thompson, E. E., & Krause, N. (1998). Living alone and neighborhood characteristics as predictors of social support in late life. *The Journals of Gerontology Series B: Psychological Sciences and Social Sciences, 53*(6), S354–S364.

Thorpe, K. E., Ogden, L. L., & Galactionova, K. (2010). Chronic conditions account for rise in Medicare spending from 1987 to 2006. *Health Affairs, 29*(4), 718–724. doi:10.1377/ hlthaff.2009.0474

Tomaka, J., Thompson, S., & Palacios, R. (2006). The relation of social isolation, loneliness, and social support to disease outcomes among the elderly. *Journal of Aging & Health, 18*(3), 359–384.

Tönnies, F. (2001). *Community and civil society.* Cambridge, England: Cambridge University Press.

Torres, S. (2003). A preliminary empirical test of a culturally-relevant theoretical framework for the study of successful aging. *Journal of Cross-Cultural Gerontology, 18*, 79–100.

Torres-Gil, F., & Hofland, B. (2012). Vulnerable populations. In H. Cisneros, M. Dyer-Chamberlain & J. Hickie (Eds.), *Independent for life: Homes and neighborhoods for an aging America* (pp. 221–232). Austin: University of Texas Press.

Troutman, M., Nies, M. A., Small, S., & Bates, A. (2011). The development and testing of an instrument to measure successful aging. *Research in gerontological nursing, 4*(3), 221–232.

Uchino, B. N. (2004). *Social support and physical health: Understanding the health consequences of relationships.* New Haven, CT: Yale University Press.

Uchino, B. N., Holt-Lunstad, J., Uno, D., Campo, R., & Reblin, M. (2007). *The social neuroscience of relationships: An examination of health-relevant pathways.* New York, NY: Guilford Press.

United Nations. (1998). A 'society for all ages' honours traditional leadership role of elders, Secretary-General says, opening international year of older persons. Retrieved from http://www.un.org/press/en/1998/19981001.sgsm6728.html

United Nations. (2002). *International plan of action on ageing. Retrieved from* http://www.un.org/en/events/pastevents/pdfs/Madrid_plan.pdf

U.S. Census Bureau (2001). Geographic mobility: 1999 to 2000: Table 1. Retrieved from http://www.census.gov/hhes/migration/data/cps/p20-538.html

U.S. Census Bureau. (2004). *American Housing Survey for the United States: 2003, Current Housing Reports, Series H150/03.* Washington, DC: U.S. Government Printing Office. Retrieved from http://www.census.gov/prod/2004pubs/H150-03.pdf

U.S. Census Bureau. (2006). *2005 American Community Survey: Tables S1001 and S1002.* Washington, DC: U.S. Government Printing Office.

U.S. Census Bureau. (2010). *The next four decades: The older population in the United States: 2010–2050.* Retrieved from https://www.census.gov/prod/2010pubs/p25-1138.pdf

U.S. Census Bureau (2012). Geographic mobility: 2010-2011: Table 1. Retrieved from http://www.census.gov/hhes/migration/data/cps/cps2011.html

U.S. Census Bureau. (2014). *65+ in the United States: 2010* (Publication P23-212). Washington, DC: U.S. Government Printing Office.

U.S. Department of Health and Human Services. (2004). *The Older Americans Act national family caregiver support program (Title III-E and Title IV-C): Compassion in action.* Retrieved from http://www.aoa.gov/prof/aoaprog/caregiver/careprof/progguidance/resources/FINAL%20NFCSP%20Report%20July22,%202004.pdf

U.S. Department of Housing and Urban Development (HUD). (n.d.). *Service coordinator program.* Retrieved from http://portal.hud.gov/hudportal/HUD?src=/program_offices/housing/mfh/scp/scphome

U.S. Department of Labor. (2012). *Fact sheet #28: The Family and Medical Leave Act.* Retrieved from http://www.dol.gov/whd/regs/compliance/whdfs28.pdf

U.S. Department of Labor, Bureau of Labor Statistics (2014). Occupational employment statistics, 29-1065 Pediatricians, general. Retrieved from http://www.bls.gov/oes/current/oes291065.htm

U.S. Department of Transportation, Federal Highway Administration. (2007). *Accommodating Bicycle and Pedestrian Travel: A Recommended Approach.* Retrieved from http://www.fhwa.dot.gov/environment/bicycle_pedestrian/guidance/design_guidance/design.cfm#d2

U.S. Environmental Protection Agency Aging Initiative. (2011). *Growing smarter, living healthier: A guide to smart growth and active ageing.* Retrieved from http://www.epa.gov/aging/bhc/guide/2009_Aging.pdf

U.S. Government Accountability Office. (2004). *Transportation—disadvantaged seniors: Efforts to enhance senior mobility could benefit from additional guidance and information* (No. GAO-04-971). Washington, DC: U.S. Government Accountability Office.

Valdemarsson, M., Jernryd, E., & Iwarsson, S. (2005). Preferences and frequencies of visits to public facilities in old age—a pilot study in a Swedish town center. *Archives of Gerontology and Geriatrics, 40*(1), 15–28.

Van Cauwenberg, J., Clarys, P., Bourdeaudhuij, I. D., Van Holle, V., Verté, D., De Witte, N., . . . Deforche, B. (2013). Older adults' transportation walking: A cross-sectional study on the cumulative influence of physical environmental factors. *International Journal of Health Geographics, 12*(1), 1–9. doi:10.1186/1476-072X-12-37

van Groenou, M. B., & van Tilburg, T. (2012). Six-year follow-up on volunteering in later life: A cohort comparison in the Netherlands. *European Sociological Review, 28*(1), 1–11.

van Hoof, J., Kort, H. S. M., van Waarde, H., & Blom, M. M. (2010). Environmental interventions and the design of homes for older adults with dementia: An overview. *American Journal of Alzheimer's Disease and Other Dementias, 25*(3), 202–232.

Van Tilburg, T. (1998). Losing and gaining in old age: Changes in personal network size and social support in a four-year longitudinal study. *The Journals of Gerontology Series B: Psychological Sciences and Social Sciences, 53*(6), S313–S323.

Van Willigen, M. (2000). Differential benefits of volunteering across the life course. *Journal of Gerontology: Social Sciences, 55B,* S308–S318.

Verbrugge, L. M., & Jette, A. M. (1994). The disablement process. *Social Science & Medicine, 38,* 1–14.

Victor, C. R., Scambler, S. J., Bowling, A., & Bond, J. (2005). The prevalence of, and risk factors for, loneliness in later life: A survey of older people in Great Britain. *Ageing and Society, 25*(06), 357–375.

Villareal, D. T., Banks, M., Sinacore, D. R., Siener, C., & Klein, S. (2006). Effect of weight loss and exercise on frailty in obese older adults. *Archives of Internal Medicine, 166*(8), 860–866.

Vincent, G. K., & Velkoff, V. A. (2010). *The next four decades: The older population in the United States: 2010 to 2050* (Current Population Reports P25-1138). Retrieved from https://www.census.gov/prod/2010pubs/p25-1138.pdf

Visiting Nurse Service of New York (VNSNY). (2009). *Impact of the TimeBank on its membership.* Retrieved from http://preview.vnsny.org/system/assets/0000/1267/VNSNY_TimeBank_study_results_summary.original.pdf?1273605850

Vladeck, F. (2004). *A good place to grow old: New York's model for NORC supportive service programs.* New York, NY: United Hospital Fund.

Vladeck, F. (2006). Residential-based care: New York's NORC-supportive services program model. In B. Berkman (Ed.), *Handbook of social work in health and aging* (pp. 705–714). New York, NY: Oxford University Press.

Von Faber, M., Bootsma-van der Wiel, A., van Exel, E., Gussekloo, J., Lagaay, A. M., van Dongen, E., . . . Westendorp, R. G. (2001). Successful aging in the oldest old: Who can be characterized as successfully aged? *Archives of Internal Medicine, 161*(22), 2694–2700.

Wachs, M. (2001). *Mobility, travel, and aging in California.* Berkeley, CA: California Policy Research Center.

Wacker, R. R., & Roberto, K. A. (2013). *Community resources for older adults: Programs and services in an era of change.* Thousand Oaks, CA: Sage.

Wahl, H. (2001). Environmental influences on aging and behavior. In J. Birren & W. Schaie (Eds.), *Handbook of the Psychology of Aging* (5th ed., pp. 215–237). San Diego, CA: Academic Press.

Wahl, H. W., & Weisman, G. D. (2003). Environmental gerontology at the beginning of the new millennium: Reflections on its historical, empirical, and theoretical development. *The Gerontologist, 43,* 616–627.

Wahl, H. W., Fange, A., Oswald, F., Gitlin, L. N., & Iwarsson, S. (2009). The home environment and disability-related outcomes in aging individuals: What is the empirical evidence? *The Gerontologist, 49*(3), 355–367. doi:10.1093/geront/gnp056

Waid, M. D. (2012). *Social Security: A brief overview.* Washington, DC: AARP Public Policy Institute. Retrieved from http://www.aarp.org/content/dam/aarp/research/

public_policy_institute/econ_sec/2012/social-security-brief-overview-fs-AARP-ppi-econ-sec.pdf

Wallace, S. P., Padilla-Frausto, D. I., & Smith, S. E. (2010). *Older adults need twice the federal poverty level to make ends meet in California* (Policy Brief 2010-8). Los Angeles, CA: UCLA Center for Health Policy Research.

Wallerstein, N., & Bernstein, E. (1994). Introduction to community empowerment, participatory education, and health. *Health Education Quarterly, 21*(2), 141–148.

Wang, H. X., Karp, A., Winbald, B., & Fratiglioni, L. (2002). Late-life engagement in social and leisure activities is associated with a decreased risk of dementia: A longitudinal study from the Kungsholmen project. *American Journal of Epidemiology, 155*, 1081–1087.

Weil, M., & Gamble, D. (1995). Community practice models. *Encyclopedia of Social Work, 19*, 577–594.

Weil, M., Gamble, D. N., & Ohmer, M. L. (2013). Evolution, models, and the changing context of community practice. In M. Weil, M. Reisch, & M. L. Ohmer (Eds.), *The handbook of community practice* (2nd ed., pp. 167–193). Thousand Oaks, CA: Sage.

Welzel, C., Inglehart, R., & Deutsch, F. (2005). Social capital, voluntary associations and collective action: which aspects of social capital have the greatest "civic" payoff? *Journal of Civil Society, 1*(2), 121–146.

Whittier, S., Scharlach, A., & Dal Santo, T. (2005). Availability of caregiver support services: Implications for implementation of the National Family Caregiver Support Program. *Journal of Aging and Social Policy, 17*(1), 45–62.

Wieckowski, J., & Simmons, J. (2006). Translating evidence-based physical activity interventions for frail elders. *Home Health Care Services Quarterly, 25*(1–2), 75–94.

Wilcox, S., Bopp, M., Oberrecht, L., Kammermann, S. K., & McElmurray, C. T. (2003). Psychosocial and perceived environmental correlates of physical activity in rural and older african american and white women. *The Journals of Gerontology Series B: Psychological Sciences and Social Sciences, 58*(6), P329–P337.

Wiles, J. L., Leibing, A., Guberman, N., Reeve, J., & Allen, R. E. S. (2012). The meaning of "aging in place" to older people. *Gerontologist, 52*(3), 357–366.

Wilmoth, J. M. (2010). Health trajectories among older movers. *Journal of Aging & Health, 22*(7), 862–881. doi:10.1177/0898264310375985

Wilson, J. (2000). Volunteering. *Annual Review of Sociology, 26*, 215–240.

Windhorst, C., Hollinger-Smith, L., & Sassen, B. (2010). The café plus concept: A different model for different times. *Generations, 34*(1), 91–93.

Wiseman, R. F. (1980). Why older people move theoretical issues. *Research on Aging, 2*(2), 141–154.

Wiseman, R. F., & Roseman, C. C. (1979). A typology of elderly migration based on the decision making process. *Economic Geography, 55*, 324–337.

Wolf, D. A., & Amirkhanyan, A. A. (2010). Demographic change and its public sector consequences. *Public Administration Review, 70*(s1), s12-s23.

Woods, B., Aguirre, E., Spector, A., & Orrell, M. (2012). Cognitive stimulation to improve cognitive functioning in people with dementia. *The Cochrane Library, 2*, 1–78.

World Health Organization. (2002). *Active ageing: A policy framework.* Madrid, Spain: Second United Nations World Assembly on Ageing.

World Health Organization. (2007). *Global age-friendly cities: A guide.* Retrieved from http://www.who.int/ageing/publications/Global_age_friendly_cities_Guide_English.pdf

World Health Organization. (2010). *WHO age-friendly environments programme.* Geneva, Switzerland: Author.

World Health Organization. (n.d.-a). *Application form to join the WHO Global Network of Age-Friendly Cities and Communities.* Retrieved from http://www.who.int/ageing/application_form/en/

World Health Organization. (n.d.-b). *The Ottowa Charter for health promotion.* Retrieved from http://www.who.int/healthpromotion/conferences/previous/ottawa/en/

World Health Organization Centre for Health Development. (2015). *Measuring the age-friendliness of cities: A guide to using core indicators.* Retrieved from http://www.who.int/kobe_centre/ageing/age_friendly_cities/AFC_Indicator_Guide_Pilot_English.pdf

Yaffe, K., Barnes, D., Nevitt, M., Lui, L., & Covinsky, K. (2001). A prospective study of physical activity and cognitive decline in elderly women: Women who walk. *Archives of Internal Medicine, 161*(14), 1703–1708.

Yaffe, K., Fox, P., Newcomer, R., Sands, L., Lindquist, K., Dane, K., & Covinsky, K. E. (2002). Patient and caregiver characteristics and nursing home placement in patients with dementia. *JAMA: Journal of the American Medical Association, 287*(16), 2090–2097.

Young, A. F., Russell, A., & Powers, J. R. (2004). The sense of belonging to a neighborhood: Can it be measured and is it related to health and well-being in older women? *Social Science and Medicine, 59,* 2627–2637.

Young, F. W., & Glasgow, N. (1998). Voluntary social participation and health. *Research on Aging, 20,* 339–362.

Zarit, S. (2009). *Aging families and caregiving.* Hoboken, NJ: Wiley.

Zedlewski, S. R., & Schaner, S. G. (2005). *Older adults' engagement should be recognized and encouraged* (Policy Brief: Prospectives on Productive Aging, no. 1). Washington, DC: Urban Institute Retirement Project, 2005.

Zendell, A. L. (2007). Impact of the Olmsted decision five years later: A national perspective for social workers. *Journal of Gerontological Social Work, 49*(1–2), 97–113.

Zonderman, A. B., Ejiogu, N., Norbeck, J., & Evans, M. K. (2014). The influence of health disparities on targeting cancer prevention efforts. *American Journal of Preventive Medicine, 46*(3), S87–S97.

INDEX